The Queen's South Africa Medal To The Royal Navy and Royal Marines

ALSO BY W. H. FEVYER

The George Medal
The Distinguished Service Medal 1914–1920
The Distinguished Service Medal 1939–1946

The Queen's South Africa Medal To The Royal Navy and Royal Marines

Compiled and edited by
W. H. Fevyer & J. W. Wilson

To Pauline and Yvonne

Contents

Introduction

The awards of the Queen's South Africa Medal, 1899 to 1902, to Naval recipients, have always presented difficulties to the researcher and collector, in particular with regard to the entitlement to bars.

Medals sometimes appear with bars to which there is no entitlement, and conversely, with no bars when there is clear entitlement. In most cases where medals with bars, to which there is no entitlement are found, the bars have been added to enhance the medal. Whether this was done by the recipient who believed he was genuinely entitled to them, or by person or persons unknown for monetary gain we will never know. I have seen medals with bars which by their provenance would appear to be as issued, but there is no note of entitlement on the roll. I feel that in some cases additional research could perhaps prove them correct, but, unfortunately, this is beyond the scope of this work.

In some cases the bars were sent many years after the actual medals and were never attached to the medals. Even to this day no-bar medals may be found which are in fact due bars. For example, the medals for H.M.S. Naiad were despatched in 1904 and the bars "Cape Colony" and "South Africa 1901" in 1922. Some recipients would have had the bars fixed to their medal, others would have sewn them to the medal ribbon, but many would have retired since receiving the medal, and during the course of time the bars they received could well have been mislaid.

This volume is based on the original rolls held at the Public Records Office Kew, reference ADM 171.53. The roll has deteriorated badly over the years and is now only available on microfilm. Although the roll has been repaired the general condition is poor. For example, whole corners of some pages have disintegrated, and in the case of H.M.S. *Monarch* batches of names have been lost. Fortunately, by reference to other sources some of these names have been "rediscovered" and are included in the lists that follow.

The original rolls are handwritten and in roughly alphabetic order, with commissioned officers at the beginning of each block. In many cases it is difficult to interpret the manuscript due to the differing styles of writing, particularly as regards the initials. However, by careful studying of the roll over many years, combined with endless checking of information, it is hoped that in this interpretation errors have been kept to an absolute minimum.

The information contained in ADM 171.53 is as follows:–

> Official or Regimental Number; Name; Number of Medal; Rank or Rating; Number on Ship's Books; Bars Awarded; Where Medal Delivered or Sent.

The number of the medal is merely a consecutive numbering of each medal on the roll for each ship. The bars awarded are signified by the entry of a number or numbers as per the following list:

1 Belmont.	10 Defence of Kimberley.*	19 Elandslaagte.*
2 Modder River.	11 Relief of Kimberley.	20 Tugela Heights.
3 Paardeberg.	12 Defence of Mafeking.*	21 Defence of Ladysmith.
4 Driefontein.	13 Relief of Mafeking.*	22 Relief of Ladysmith.
5 Wepener.*	14 Cape Colony.	23 Laing's Nek.
6 Johannesburg.	15 Orange Free State.	24 Natal.
7 Diamond Hill.	16 Transvaal.	25 South Africa 1901.
8 Belfast.	17 Rhodesia.	26 South Africa 1902.
9 Wittebergen.	18 Talana.*	

* Naval recipients were not entitled to these bars.

Normally the medals were sent to the recipient where he was serving when the medals were ready for issue. However other entries do occur such as:

> Returned to Arsenal; Returned to Mint Feb. 1922; Run; Duplicate(s) (with date issued); Discharged Dead; On Passage Only, not Entitled; Medal Presented by H.M. The King;

If a medal was reissued, in some cases the name of the new recipient is noted. Notes are also made of the dates of despatch of medals and bars.

It will be noted that the medal rolls are frequently divided into two periods; the second being for medals earned in the "Extended Period." This period was from 9th March 1901 to 31st May 1902 inclusive. Its purpose was for an additional allowance to be paid to the officers and men who were serving during that time. In these days of high taxation it is worth noting that the Admiralty order says, "This payment is not liable for Income Tax."

I hope that this volume will be of assistance to the many friends I have made in the fields of research and collecting, and perhaps, relieve a little of the burden on that Great Archive, the Public Records Office.

W.H.F. 1983

H.M.S. BARRACOUTA

Period for which entitled:
26th September 1900 to 23rd October 1900 (1st Commission)
24th October 1900 to 8th March 1901 (2nd Commission)

Extended period:
9th March 1901 to 31st May 1902

Bars	*Total*	*Returned*	*Entitled*
3	19	0	19
2	37	1	36
1	1	0	1
0	282	20	262
	339	21	318

Notes:
Note 1 – See Note 1 on roll for H.M.S. Powerful.

Bars: Cape Colony, South Africa 1901, South Africa 1902

Abbs, M.J.	AB	196.330
Baseley, F.R.	Pte	Ch11.117
Bean, R.J.	Ord	191.338
Cardale, H.S.	Lieut	
Dawkins, S.	AB	187.878
Fox, H.E.	PO2	165.514
Harvey, G.	Arm/Mte	341.305
Hearn, G.	Sergt	Ch7.463
Jehan, T.J.	Act/Gunr	
Keigwin, C.T.	Sub Lieut	
Rayner, E.E.	PO1	169.909
Shepherd, H.A.	Q/Sig	179.926
Shuttle, H.T.	Ord	200.188
Stanger, J.H.	Ord	191.410
Taylor, E.	AB	166.832
Wilkinson, W.J.	AB	180.195
Williams, W.	AB	196.261
Wood, E.E.	Pte	Ch7.604

Bars: Cape Colony, South Africa 1901

Craske, G.E.	Pte	Ch10.803
Gloss, O.Y.	PO1	152.864
Law, G.J.	Pte	Ch6.039
Leake, H.C.	Ord	192.652
Maver, R.G.	AB	181.417

Bars: Cape Colony, South Africa 1902

Adams, E.	AB	182.042
1 Beadnell, C.M.	St/Surgn	
Birch, J.P.	Ord	197.184
Bridge, S.	AB	147.318
Coomber, W.L.	PO1	164.555
Crock, T.	AB	158.554
Cronk, H.	AB	168.155
Dear, W.	Ord	191.755
Gould, R.C.	Boy	203.887
Grant, W.	L/Sig	191.115
Groves, A.J.	L/Sig	172.735
Hall, W.	Gunr.	
Hamerton, A.B.	AB	164.862
Hearnah, W.E.	Ord	191.681
Hunter, J.	AB	171.036
Jackson, J.H.	Boy	203.773
Kinnear, G.R.	Boy	204.323
Macdonald, J.	Ord	199.718
McGraw, W.H.	AB	171.910
Mayne, J.W.	AB	170.329
Morrison, J.	Ord	195.817
Nestor, J.	L/S	187.574
Penman, A.V.	Ord	197.130
Penn, O.A.	AB	163.348
Perkins, J.	Ord	204.394
Pimm, G.	PO2	162.413
Post, A.	Boy	208.314
Smith, A.T.	Ord	195.270
Smith, A.W.	AB	187.603
Trim, C.	Boy	203.337

Duplicate Medals:

Grant, W.	L/Sig	191.115
Groves, A.J.	L/Sig	172.735
Hunter, J.	AB	171.036
McGraw, W.H.	AB	171.910

Returned Medal:

Ing, F.	AB	168.172

Bar: Cape Colony

Marsh, W.C.	AB	193.062

No Bar Medals

Airey, W.	Sto	291.832

No Bar Medals *continued*

Aitchison, A.	PO2	188.892
Alcock, H.C.	Lieut	
Allchin, R.	Ch/Sto	133.285
Allen, T.	Sto	283.076
Anderson, T.	Pte	Ch8.742
Anderson, T.N.	AB	180.421
Andrews, J.	Kroo	
Andrews, J.G.	AB	188.802
Asilimani, W.	Dom	
Badger, H.	AB	167.933
Barnett, E.	Pte	Ch7.317
Barrett, C.	Lieut	
Barrows, G.P.	SBStd	145.628
Batten, A.W.	Pte	Ch8.791
Bean, H.	AB	171.689
Bell, C.	Ch/PO	
Bilby, T.	Ch/Sto	129.550
Bill, J.C.	Pte	Ch10.778
Bishop, W.	AB	186.591
Bishop, W.H.	Sto	276.089
Booth, E.	Ch/ERA	132.319
Boreland, H.	Dom	358.174
Bowditch, J.	AB	171.877
Bower, W.	Sto	151.147
Boxall, F.	Sto	281.480
Boy, Jim.	Kroo	
Brading J.	Act/Ch/Arm	160.479
Britten, H.J.	Payr	
Broomhall, H.	Sto	292.954
Brothers, W.	Pte	Ch6.980
Brown, H.	Ord	208.322
Buddle, W.	Sto	284.313
Budge, J.	Blksmth	133.332
Bull, Jim.	Kroo	
Bullen, A.	AB	168.084
Bumstead, E.J.	Sh/Std/Asst	341.416
Burgess, W.G.	Sto	172.816
Burton, W.S.	Pntr	187.346
Busby, A.	Pte	Ch8.259
Busser, W.	PO1	129.071
Butt, A.	Sto	285.749
Callow, S.	PO1	146.344
Cameron, H.	L/Shpwrt	341.049
Carruthers, J.A.S.	Dom	
Carter, W.	Ch/Arm	177.405
Castle, C.	L/Sto	154.772
Catmore, T.J.	Boy	203.781
Challen, H.T.	AB	185.296
Clarke, A.	Dom	358.676
Cleaver, G.	Sto	285.973
Clemens, J.	AB	192.306
Coffee, Ben.	Kroo	
Cole, Alex.	Kroo	
Cole, G.	L/Sto	131.432
Cole, Josh.	Kroo	
Collins, A.J.	Sto	285.978
Coppinger, W.P.	ERA	268.712
Copplestone, J.A.	Sh/Cook	146.767
Cotesworth, H.	Comdr	
Cracknell, W.G.	Sto	286.065
Cragie, W.J.	Ord	196.554
D'Arcy, A.A.	Pte	Ch8.558
Davey, C.	Ord	196.532
Day, T.	Sto	292.498
Dillon, T.P.	AB	173.772
Douce, A.F.	Pte	Ch8.462
Draper, T.	PO1	137.654
Dyer, J.	L/S	174.631
East, T.	Sto	292.949
Edwards, T.	Sig	186.308
Eklles, Toby.	Kroo	
Ellison, A.A.	Lieut	
Eloy, W.J.	Plmbr/Mte	343.381
Farrell, G.	L/Sto	170.115
Farrell, T.	Blksmth	341.058
Fasner, John.	Kroo	
Feasby, G.	Sto	292.469
Fernie, R.	ERA	268.758
Field, A.F.	AB	181.640
Field, W.J.	Sh/Std	141.524
Finch, G.G.	Art/Engr	
Finch, T.H.	Pte	Ch9.590
Findlay, J.	AB	188.115
Finnis, T.	PO2	168.252
Fisher, J.	Pte	Ch8.216
Flow I, Jas.	Kroo	
Flow II, Jim.	Kroo	
Foakes, E.L.A.	Lieut	
Forster, W.A.	Dom	164.564
Fowler, R.W.	ERA	152.469
Frampton, J.	Sto	294.620
Fuller, C.W.	Sto	276.071
Gage, S.	L/Sto	154.816
Gilbert, G.	Dom	354.780
Goddard, F.	ERA	268.960
Golds, T.W.	AB	176.372
Gorham, F.	Sto	285.979
Grant, G.	Payr	
Green, J.	Shpwrt	146.116
Gregory, F.	Sto	294.661
Griffin, G.	Sto	154.065
Groundrill, J.	Act/Ch/Sto	153.815
Hall, A.H.	2/Wrtr	340.613
Hambrook, J.T.	Ord	196.105
Harknett, W.J.	AB	186.277
Harmon, T.	Ord	194.314
Harrigan, J.	PO1	121.139
Harrison, C.B.	Boy	203.776
Hart, J.	Sto	285.975
Harter, J.J.E.K.	Ch/Carp/Mte	116.994
Harvey, A.	Sto	286.659
Harvey, D.	Sto	282.384
Henry, H.	Sto	281.481
Herbert, G.T.	AB	170.758
Holmes, A.	Sto	276.782
Hopton, A.W.	Sto	294.505
Howlett, F.	PO1	125.833
Humphreys, F.	Act/ERA	269.849
Humphries, W.C.	Sig	201.217
Hutchison, D.	AB	185.762
Irvine, T.	Carp/Crew	343.224

Ives, A.A.	Sto	285.974
Jarvis, H.	AB	185.397
Johnson, Tom.	Kroo	
Johnston, A.	L/Sto	135.002
Juleff, N.	Carp/Crew	340.707
Keeble, J.H.	AB	144.117
Kemp, C.	AB	188.367
Kimber, A.	AB	188.637
King, C.B.	Gunr	RMA7.159
Knight, G.	Pte	Ch6.193
Knight, H.	Pte	Ch8.605
Lane, H.	AB	186.043
Little, S.	Cpl	Ch8.219
Lubbock, M.H.	Lieut	
Lynn, E.	Sto	281.491
McDonald, A.	AB	176.535
MacLeod, E.	PO1	158.026
McNaney, J.	AB	169.977
McTavish, C.	AB	178.855
Manning, E.	Ch/PO	123.545
Margetson, C.C.	Pte	Ply9.430
Mather, R.	AB	187.228
Mathews, J.C.	Ch/Wrtr	133.462
Mayne, W.R.	2/Yeo/Sig	167.410
Millis, H.	Sto	186.100
Mitchell, C.W.	Pte	Ch7.975
Moore, W.L.	Act/Engr	
Morris, A.	Sto	154.855
Morris, C.G.	Act/Ch/ERA	156.252
Morrison, B.W.	AB	167.216
Moss, G.	Pte	Ch8.892
Moysey, A.H.	Engr	
Murphy, W.	L/Shpwrt	115.500
Mutimer, H.W.	Sto	174.281
Newman, Jack.	Kroo	
Newson, W.	Ch/Sto	142.269
Offord, A.A.	L/Sto	153.707
Pack, J.	Dom	356.438
Pallett, F.C.	AB	185.256
Pearson, W.	L/Sto	154.059
Peck, G.	AB	149.994
Peirse, R.H.	Capt	
Perry, J.	AB	162.852
Perry, J.W.	Sto	283.913
Peverell, I.	Sto	142.145
Phillimore, F.W.	PO2	169.934
Potton, W.	Sto	278.444
Potts, C.V.	Pntr	342.186
Powell, C.J.W.	Ch/Carp/Mte	147.179
Powell, J.A.	Sto	156.243
Powell, J.H.	Ch/Sto	144.849
Pullen, J.	AB	189.299
Pyall, J.H.	Arm/Mte	340.064
Quance, S.A.	Dom	353.335
Redstall, A.	Pte	Ch8.840
Regis, M.	AB	165.558
Rigo, T.	Dom	141.336
Roberts, Danl.	Kroo	
Robertson, W.	Ord	196.325
Robinson, A.W.	L/S	151.586
Robinson, J.S.	PO2	165.855
Rolfe, E.	PO1	139.785
Rooks, H.	Ord	196.424
Rose, C.E.	Pte	Ch8.300
Rowe, W.	Sto	284.337
Russell, L.O.	AB	190.393
Salisbury, J.	AB	151.091
Sampson, F.E.	AB	171.702
Sanderson, T.	AB	185.486
Saunders, G.T.	Sto	276.121
Shaw, C.B.	Ord	200.315
Shaw, J.	Pte	Ply9.429
Shepherd, S.C.	Sto	153.823
Sheppard, W.	Sto	285.083
Simmonds, W.	AB	180.619
Sloper, W.R.	Ord	204.324
Smail, W.	L/Sto	277.575
Smeaton, H.	AB	140.740
Smith, C.W.	Sto	276.088
Smith, F.	Sto	175.382
Smith, W.	AB	177.819
Souza, C.J. de	Dom	131.027
Stafford, J.W.T.	Sh/Cpl	350.040
Stainthorpe, G.	ERA	268.016
Stanton, E.	AB	185.742
Staples, A.R.	AB	186.744
Stares, J.	Q/Sig	184.322
Steed, A.	2/SBStd	354.180
Strath, A.W.	Sh/Std	139.637
Swindon, G.A.S.	Ord	200.219
Taylor, G.H.	L/S	165.601
Terry, W.J.	Ord	208.316
Thompson, J.	Sto	285.976
Toby, Robert.	Kroo	
Tresadern, W.	AB	188.514
Trevithick, J.F.	Plmbr/Mte	341.083
Tulip, A.E.	L/Sto	172.802
Turner, R.	2/Sh/Cook	167.214
Valentine, H.A.	PO1	170.714
Wakeham, T.	L/Sto	121.132
Walker, Tom.	Kroo	
Wallace, G.	PO1	110.132
Warner, H.J.	L/Sig	178.528
Warren, F.J.	AB	151.800
Warrington, J.	2/Yeo/Sig	168.907
Waters, W.J.	PO2	168.096
Weston, J.	AB	188.769
White, J.	L/S	180.152
White, T.	Sh/Cpl	128.569
White, T.	AB	178.983
Whitear, H.G.	Ord	208.313
Whitehead, A.	Sto	146.929
Whitton, H.W.	AB	174.118
Widowson, J.W.	Sergt	Ch6.416
Wilkinson, H.R.	Act/Ch/Sto	155.204
Wilson, J.	AB	186.261
Wilson, Matthew.	Kroo	
Woodcock, A.C.	Sto	286.682
Wralten, C.	Ord	192.078
Wright, L.J.	Cpl	Ch9.988
Wrigley, E.	PO1	171.900

No Bar Medals *continued*

Duplicate medals:

Andrews, J.G.	AB	188.802
Cragie, W.J.	Ord	196.554
Grant, G.	Payr	
Hopton, A.W.	Sto	294.505
McDonald, A.	AB	176.535
Sampson, F.E.	AB	171.702
Terry, W.J.	Ord	208.316
Whitear, H.G.	Ord	208.313

Returned medals:

Arthur, S.	Sto	294.654
Athey, W.	Pte	Po10.311
Challis, Tom.	Kroo	
Connors, J.	Pte	Ch8.347
Cook, T.	Sto	291.649
Culver, F.	Pte	Ch10.726
Curtis, W.	Pte	Po9.684
Dale, E.E.	Sh/Std/Boy	342.529
Doran, T.V.L.	Boy	204.325
Farmer, G.B.	Musn	357.653
Finn, J.	Sto	294.502
Long, J.	Sto	280.912
Pargeter, H.	AB	166.477
Ratcliff, E.	Sto	165.118
Stone, C.	AB	188.647
Widdicombe, H.	AB	

EXTENDED PERIOD

Bars: Cape Colony, South Africa 1901, South Africa 1902

Hughes, W.H.C.	Lieut	

Bars: South Africa 1901, South Africa 1902

Walker, R.C.	Sig	204.870

Duplicate medal:

Walker, R.C.	Sig.	204.870

No Bar medals

Ash, S.H.B.	Comdr	
Barboya, J.W.L.	L/S	162.245
Bargewell, E.	Ord	204.953
Blake, J.R.	Carp/Mte	341.000
Brandon, J.A.	Q/Sig	199.664
Brook-Smith, L.A.	Act/Sub Lieut	
Case, C.	Act/Ch/PO	135.681
Clarke, T.	AB	174.773
Crayfourd, F.	Boy	206.713
Davies, J.	Sh/Std	152.525
Dow, H.	Dom	359.933
Greaves, W.	Pte	Ply10.339
Haines, H.H.	PO2	174.040
Hiscock, T.G.	Boy	206.602
Horniman, H.	Payr	
Howard, E.	Sto	291.100
Manning, S.W.	Sh/Std/Asst	342.419
Smith, L.W.	Sig	206.760
Smyth, M.	Pte	Ply10.348

Returned medals:

Moreton, D.	Dom	132.805
Palmer, W.R.J.	Ord	205.852
Too Small.	Kroo	
West, W.C.E.	AB	157.858

H.M.S. BARROSA

Period for which entitled:
11th October 1899 to 8th March 1901.

Extended period:
9th March 1901 to 25th March 1901
(No medals awarded for this period.)

Bars	*Total*	*Returned*	*Entitled*
4	17	0	17
3	7	0	7
2	2	1	1
1	34	3	31
0	134	32	102
	194	36	158

Bars: Paardeberg, Driefontein, Cape Colony, Transvaal

Chubb, J.W.A.	AB	178.485
Cox, F.J.	AB	149.335
Davey, A.	AB	172.719
Fergusson, J.A.	Lieut	
Fisher, J.	AB	176.951
Gardiner, W.J.	L/S	176.721
Gunn, M.G.	AB	171.452
Hall, R.F.	PO2	173.353
Higgins, R.W.	PO1	129.232
Leary, M.	AB	168.070
Morrison, A.	AB	155.981
Neil, J.	AB	178.651
Redmond, J.J.	AB	171.916
Rowley, J.H.	L/S	156.799
Thompson, W.J.	AB	175.096
Tuck, J.	Arm/Mte	147.812
Widdicombe, H.A.	AB	176.255

Bars: Paardeberg, Driefontein, Cape Colony

Andrews, H.	PO2	161.765
Butters, J.	PO2	137.522
Cawse, J.	Ord	184.011
Hobday, C.S.	AB	183.291
Roberts, A.E.	PO1	130.408
Welsh, T.D.	AB	170.589
Wood, J.	AB	176.116

Bars: Paardeberg, Cape Colony

Phillips, W.H.	L/Sig	161.819

Returned medal:

Hill, J.	AB	185.614

Bar: Cape Colony

Allard, A.E.	Pte	Ply7.001
Andrews, H.W.E.	Clr/Sergt	Ply2.380
Barry, J.	AB	178.646
Blomefield, T.C.A.	Lieut	
Boundy, W.	AB	185.158
Burden, C.W.	Pte	Po8.890
Burfield, R.	Pte	Ch8.808
Byrne, W.E.	PO2	168.905
Clark, C.F.	PO1	115.343
Collings, J.	L/S	129.299
Dash, T.E.	AB	184.432
Davis, T.	AB	162.870
Ferguson, R.	AB	174.000
Flynn, D.	AB	185.783
Grant, A.E.	AB	186.059
Gray, J.	Pte	Ply7.653
Hannah, W.	Pte	Po6.183
Hayman, R.	Ord	184.430
Hemmings, G.F.	AB	168.112
Holland, J.	AB	185.220
Hoskin, W.C.	AB	182.594
Kemp, T.	Pte	Ply4.724
Knowles, T.	Pte	Ply7.475
Leary, M.	L/S	169.547
Moon, J.F.	Pte	Ply7.608
Peach, J.J.	Cpl	Ply4.793
Price, A.	AB	182.364
Pursell, H.W.	AB	188.513
Routley, J.	Pte	Ply5.399
Salter, F.	AB	185.222
Swift, T.	AB	160.586

Duplicate medals:

Blomefield, T.C.A.	Lieut	
* Hemmings, G.F.	AB	168.112

* Two duplicate medals issued.

Returned medals:

Mitchell, D.	Pte	Ply7.189
Pascoe, A.	AB	176.288
Saunders, H.A.	AB	174.147

No Bar medals

Abres, L.	Dom	

No Bar Medals *continued*

Adams, C.	AB	173.177
Allen, H.A.	Sto	284.089
Allen, S.	2/Sh/Cook	340.268
Allen, W.	AB	140.755
Austin, W.J.	Sto	285.009
Ayres, G.	Sto	280.273
Bebb, L.A.	Payr	
Bowen, J.	Sto	283.062
Bowring, H.	Lieut	
Brewer, S.	Ch/Sto	133.785
Brown, J.	AB	183.303
Burgess, J.G.	PO2	132.932
Carey, W.J.	Ch/Wrtr	131.913
Cartmeel, J.	Sto	278.876
Charlton, A.H.	Pte	Ply7.978
Clatworthy, G.H.	Ch/Arm	133.688
Coleman, B.	L/Sto	127.187
Coles, F.	AB	185.666
Cook, J.H.	AB	182.730
Dandy, Peter.	Dom	
Davies, Tom.	Kroo	
Davis, G.J.	Sto	285.034
Dawson, J.	Engr	
Douglas, H.	Act/Ch/ERA	151.850
Downey, F.	Ch/Sto	126.396
Doyle, B.	Sto	280.063
Eden, T.L.	Sto	186.925
Edwards, G.B.	Ord	195.104
Ellis, R.J.	Pte	Ply6.253
Fernandez, A.C.	Dom	169.757
Fernandez, A.F.	Dom	143.546
Fernandez, P.	Dom	353.103
Fernandez, Q.R.M.	Dom	164.580
Finch, F.	AB	128.191
Fiquiscido, A.C.	Dom	356.017
Fitch, R.A.	St/Surgn	
Fitzgerald, M.J.	Q/Sig	169.179
Freeman, John.	Kroo	
Glanville, W.	ERA	268.032
Gosling, F.	Sto	285.024
Grassam, A.	Sto	169.785
Grey, D.J.	Sto	282.882
Hanning, C.H.	Sh/Std	157.525
Harding, J.	Kroo	
Harris, G.F.C.	AB	178.676
Harrison, S.	Pte	Ch5.242
Haslam, J.J.	Sto	189.927
Higgins, R.W.	PO1	129.232
Hill, F.	Plmbr	340.156
Hill, S.	Act/Art/Engr	
Hiscock, F.	Ord	191.345
Howard, J.	AB	178.781
Hurford, J.	Sto	172.415
Ireland, S.W.	AB	180.838
Johns, M.G.	Sto	183.042
Kelland, W.	Pte	Ply6.918
Kennah, J.	Sto	278.939
Lamble, G.H.	Sto	278.269
Langmead, C.E.	L/Sto	147.064
Last, F.	Ord	199.119
Lee, R.T.H.V.	Gunr	
Liddicoat, F.	Blksmth	133.086
Lloyd, B.	AB	177.349
Lott, A.	AB	185.021
McCarthy, D.	Sto	279.122
Maher, E.	Shpwrt	99.620
Mello, R. de.	Dom	103.085
Murdiff, J.	Sto	153.457
Murphy, P.	AB	184.855
Parkin, H.	PO1	142.353
Parsons, H.	L/Shpwrt	147.228
Patey, W.N.	PO2	142.071
Perry, F.J.	L/Sto	158.831
Peter, Tom.	Kroo	
Potter, T.A.	Carp/Crew	159.530
Raymond, G.	Sto	167.585
Rennie, A.B.	PO1	138.878
Reynolds, E.	Pte	Ply7.770
Richards, T.G.	2/SBStd	136.901
Sawyer, Joe.	Kroo	
Scott, R.	Sto	280.055
Sheppard, J.T.	L/Sig	138.497
Sixsmith, J.	MAA	120.812
Skinner, F.	Ch/PO	110.150
Smith, E.A.	Pntr	343.103
Solomon, King.	Kroo	
Stancombe, J.	Sto	285.010
Steele, H.W.	Q/Sig	170.729
Sullivan, J.	Sto	173.554
Throckmorton, H.J.A.	Lieut	
Tonkin, J.	ERA	286.226
Tummon, C.	Ch/Carp/Mte	109.786
Tunnard, W.F.	Comdr	
Vivian, A.K.	Ch/Sto	132.250
Watkins, F.G.	AB	174.852
Williams, F.C.	Engr	
Williams, J.	AB	121.179
Williams, J.J.	ERA	268.611
Williams, S.	Asst/Musn.	357.442
Windel, H.	Sh/Std	340.661
Wood, J.	L/Sto	148.185

Duplicate medals:

Austin, W.J.	Sto	285.009
Fernandez, P.	Dom	353.103
Freeman, John.	Kroo	
Glanville, W.	ERA	268.032
McCarthy, D.	Sto	279.122
Smith, E.A.	Pntr	343.103
Stancombe, J.	Sto	285.010
Williams, J.J.	ERA	268.611

Returned medals:

Anderson, John.	Kroo	
Andrew, Jack.	Kroo	
Andrews, A.W.	Pte	Po9.653
Bishop, J.	Dom	
Bull, John (I)	Kroo	
Bull, John (II)	Kroo	
Clayton, H.	Ord	201.330
Curtis, W.	Kroo	

Driver, W.	Sto	295.045	Morrison, K.	Sto	149.850
Elvy, C.F.	AB	192.307	O'Leary, J.	Sto	279.104
Etherington, F.R.	Sto	284.689	Rundle, J.A.	Sto	278.302
Fulker, W.	Sto	354.701	Sampson, J.	Kroo	
Gaffney, T.	Pte	Po9.519	Sampson, T.	Kroo	
George, J.	Dom		Saunders, W.	Sto	282.740
Good, S.			Sea Breeze, T.	Kroo	
Henderson, W.	Sto	286.687	Seymour, T.	Kroo	
John, H.M.	Ord	192.187	Smart, J.	Kroo	
McKay, A.	Dom	355.794	Smith, J.	Kroo	
McKean, G.	Gunr	RMA3.817	Taggart, D.	Sto	281.016
Mitchell, J.W.	Pte	Ch8.377	Warren, G.	Kroo	

H.M.S. BEAGLE

Period for which entitled:

Extended period only:
19th July 1901 to 4th November 1901
4th December 1901 to 31st May 1902

Bars	*Total*	*Returned*	*Entitled*
2	17	0	17
1	0	0	0
0	122	12	110
	139	12	127

Bars: Cape Colony, South Africa 1901

Balchin, E.A.	Pte	Po8.871
Cameron, J.E.	Lieut	
Coffin, E.J.	Pte	Po10.122
Cole, L.G.E.	Cpl	Po8.812
Cox, J.T.	PO1	143.921
Cox, J.T.	AB	198.625
Denham, J.E.	Pte	Po10.135
Gallagher, F.	Sergt	Po4.220
Graham, A.G.S.	Pte	Po9.558
Hardy, A.E.	AB	155.516
Hearn, W.C.A.	Pte	Po9.898
Hubbard, W.	Blksmth	341.723
Hunt, W.C.	Gunr	
McDermott, J.	Ord	192.141
Moon, W.	Pte	Po10.111
Smeeth, A.	L/S	105.857
Tolfree, W.T.	Pte	Po6.842

Duplicate medal:

Moon, W.	Pte	Po10.111

No Bar Medals

Ackland, C.E.	Sto	286.181
Addison, H.	Ord	206.603
Arton, W.	Ch/Sto	125.500
Aves, W.F.	Ord	211.998
Ayles, T.F.	AB	182.713
Benham, A.J.	L/Sto	149.822
Bennett, A.H.	2/SBStd	135.321
Berry, G.F.	L/Shpwrt	119.778
Black, J.	Ord	191.034
Bland, H.S.	Sub Lieut	
Bourne, C.W.	Sto	286.519
Bowen, A.G.W.	Surgn	
Bray, J.	Sh/Cpl	136.131
Brown, A.J.	AB	192.780
Brown, H.J.	L/Sto	173.798
Budden, C.	L/Sto	142.947
Bull, G.E.	Ord	201.903
Burden, C.H.	Sto	283.214
Burgess, A.W.	Ord	194.407
Butterfield, J.C.	L/Sig	177.369
Carter, W.J.A.	Payr	
Choat, C.A.	Ch/PO	98.171
Clamp, A.	Sto	283.189
Clarke, A.E.	AB	188.233
Collins, C.J.	Ord	195.413
Cooper, H.W.	Sig	206.797
Cuthbert, F.	Sto	285.210
Dalgleish, J.	2/Sh/Cook	156.604
Dashwood, T.	AB	185.818
Dickie, G.	AB	133.185
Doughty, J.A.	Ord	206.403
Driscoll, J.	AB	190.055
Duffey, J.	L/S	182.638
Elliott, H.V.W.	Comdr	
Erridge, F.F.	Ord	206.398
Francis, C.H.	AB	182.977
Garrett, H.	AB	174.856
Glazier, T.H.	PO1	142.087
Godden, A.F.	AB	151.908
Good, A.E.	ERA	269.500
Green, W.	AB	190.805
Groom, C.B.	Ch/Sto	122.507
Gruchey, S.D.	Ord	207.551
Guy, H.	2/Wrtr.	186.688
Halligan, C.	AB	189.926
Hanes, G.	PO1	151.083
Hayden, W.F.	AB	189.552
Hayne, M.C.	ERA	269.201
Hill, T.	Ord	199.834
Hills, F.F.	Sto	282.981
Hilton, A.P.	Sto	285.672
Hinton, W.	Sto	288.327
Hooper, E.	PO2	139.222
Jacobs, E.	Sail/Mte	118.203
Johnson, W.J.	Ord	195.859
Jones, R.G.	PO1	129.767
Keating, T.	Pte	Po8.178
Keenan, W.J.	Ch/Arm/Mte	107.035
Lee, A.J.	Sto	282.926
Liversidge, E.W.	Engr	
MacAnley, J.	AB	198.280
McCorkell, W.K.	Sto	282.933
Macdonald, G.	Pte	Ply10.434
Marmon. F.W.	Ord	212.008

Marriott, J.P.R.	Lieut	
Milne. C.R.	L/S	167.614
Milne, H.F.	Ord	206.906
Moxey, M.	Sto	276.622
Norris, J.W.	Arm/Mte	168.568
O'Brien, W.	AB	191.954
Ovenden, W.C.	Ord	206.404
Page, W.J.	Ord	205.345
Pankhurst, C.R.D.	Ord	206.399
Paris, W.R.	Q/Sig	191.494
Pierce, W.C.	AB	145.220
Pill, W.	L/Sto	138.148
Pulley, E.	ERA	159.977
Raines, A.	AB	160.819
Redman, W.	Sto	139.251
Reeves, B.	Pte	Po7.079
Richards, E.J.	AB	190.024
Rolfe, A.H.	Ord	212.088
Rose, J.	PO1	121.373
Rowe, R.C.	AB	145.269
Sainsbury, R.H.	Carp/Mte	159.395
Saunder, H.J.	PO2	181.108
Shanton, E.C.	Ord	206.908
Smith, C.A.	Ord	212.003
Smith, C.F.	Ord	212.009
Stevens, W.E.	Ord	206.902
Sutherland, W.A.G.	PO2	137.968
Tanner, W.R.	AB	196.709
Taylor, E.	Sto	283.225
Thomson, J.McD.	ERA	148.609
Tilley, W.G.	Arm/Crew	342.157
Tingley, G.A.	Ord	200.060
Topple, R.	Sto	276.015
Tregillis, P.W.	PO1	162.939
Tubb, A.T.	Sto	283.807
Tutton, W.	Sto	285.673
Veness, C.	Sig	207.601
Vince, G.T.	AB	186.106
Walter, L.	Pte	Po9.029
Walwyn, H.T.	Lieut.	
Weaver, J.	L/Sto	148.576
Webb, H.J.	Po1	117.757
Wells, H.J.	Boy	206.907
White, A.	Ch/Sto	126.506
Wingar, S.H.	AB	199.022
Woods, G.H.	Pntr	343.185

Duplicate medals:

Garrett, H.	AB	174.856
Hanes, G.	PO1	151.083

Returned medals:

Brown, H.	Pte	Po10.028
Coleman, P.	Ord	193.212
Gardner, P.	Sto	288.108
Hughes, J.P.	Dom	358.086
Ibbetson, A.E.	Dom	353.709
Keane, A.	Ord	194.477
MacDonald, J.	PO2	166.833
Peters, Tom.	Dom	
Smith, A.H.	AB	185.829
Snelling, H.V.	Sto	283.422
Winter, L.F.	Act/Sh/Std	175.876
Wright, A.	Ord	212.024

H.M.S. BLANCHE

Period for which entitled:
31st January 1901 to 8th March 1901

Extended period:
9th March 1901 to 19th July 1901
1st December 1901 to 31st May 1902

Bars	*Total*	*Returned*	*Entitled*
2	13	0	13
1	5	0	5
0	198	43	155
	216	43	173

Bars: Cape Colony, South Africa 1901

Bell, G.A.S.	Surgn	
Bennett, W.J.	Pte	Ply9.910
Blake, A.H.	Sergt	Ply4.776
Coates, A.	Pte	Ply9.842
Hands, J.T.	Pte	Ply6.050
Jepson, H.A.	Pte	Ply6.849
Lewis, F.C.	Pte	Ply9.908
Mayle, G.H.	Pte	Ply5.788
Parks, M.T.	Comdr	
Roberts, E.J.	Sh/Std/Boy	342.240
Robinson, S.	Pte	Ply3.566
Score, A.R.	1/Wrtr	148.717
Steele, R.W.	Pte	Ply9.824

Duplicate medal:

Lewis, F.C.	Pte	Ply9.908

Bar: Cape Colony

Brook R.P.A.	Bugler	Ply9.472
Coles, A.	Pte	Ply6.420
Rowland, F.	Pte	Ply9.876
Whiting, A.	Gunr	
Wonnall, T.G.B.	Payr	

No Bar Medals

Aggett, H.	Sto	282.721
Back, A.E.	Sto	294.860
Barlow, T.	Sto	295.450
Barry, M.	PO1	136.707
Bartlett, J.	AB	168.342
Basnett, E.	Dom	358.303
Beesley, W.J.	ERA	159.912
Bell, G.	Kroo	
Bennie, J.	Ord	202.413
Black, J.W.	Q/Sig	191.015
Blackmore, H.J.	Carp/Crew	343.565
Blake, F.M.	AB	178.535
Block, W.	Ord	200.111
Bobe, E.H.	PO2	172.327
Bond, G.	AB	190.314
Brockinan, E.	PO1	93.824
Brook, J.P.	ERA	268.744
Brooks, J.	L/S	193.351
Brosnahan, T.	Ch/PO	114.126
Brown, E.W.	PO1	155.997
Bryant, W.J.	Ord	194.752
Burris, W.	Ord	202.048
Butland, J.S.	Sh/Std	172.617
Cann, H.	AB	151.840
Carey, J.	L/Sto	165.682
Cave, F.J.	Ord	198.931
Chapple, J.W.	Sto	294.858
Chidgey, R.	Sto	289.855
Clark, J.	Pte	Ply6.552
Coffee, T.	Kroo	
Commins, G.	PO2	150.793
Congo, C.	Kroo	
Coombes, W.J.	L/S	155.392
Cottrill, G.	PO1	155.057
Crawford, W.	Boy	202.168
Cridge, J.E.	AB	192.290
Darch, H.S.	2/SBStd	150.397
Dixon, W.	Pntr	341.633
Drew, H.C.	PO2	112.320
Driscoll, D.	Sto	287.256
Easterbrook, S.J.	AB	173.170
Egan, J.	AB	174.142
Egan, V.	Sto	294.613
Fitzgerald, T.	Sto	139.630
Flaherty, P.	Boy	202.312
Fluck, W.H.	AB	171.619
Ford, A.	Ord	201.716
Forse, W.G.	Sto	276.192
Freeman, J.	Kroo	
Garrett, W.J.	L/Sig	184.925
George, Jim.	Dom	
Gill, N.	Dom	357.706
Greenali, J.C.	ERA	269.440
Grimshaw, P.	Boy	201.376
Hapted, E.J.	Plmbr/Mte	
Harris, A.C.	Ord	200.530
Hart, W.J.	Ord	192.261
Harvey, W.	Pte	Ch6.169
Hayman, C.E.	L/Shpwrt	161.701

Hayman, C.T.	Ch/Arm	147.364
Hill, A.	PO1	119.404
Hilton, J.	Ch/Sto	146.789
Hitchcock, R.	Sto	295.230
Hocking, R.C.	Lieut	
Hook, A.E.W.	Lieut	
Howes, H.A.	Ord	201.629
Hutchings, W.T.	L/Sto	176.686
James, J.A.	Carp/Crew/Mt	140.972
Jones, J.H.	Sto	168.717
Jordan, W.	Sto	295.252
Kendall, W.G.	Ord	199.321
Kindgom, F.	L/Sto	154.961
Kirby, M.	Sto	173.352
Lacey, B.	AB	148.475
Lewis, C.	L/S	162.336
Lewis, G.R.	Sto	285.177
Lomax, E.J.	Boy	202.167
Loxton, F.	2/Sh/Cook	168.885
Luscombe, F.	AB	191.074
McCarthy, T.E.	Ord	200.698
Mahoney, M.	Ord	199.055
Mason, J.	Ord	200.152
Masters, T.H.	Shpwrt	343.439
Milam, J.	Sto	155.420
Mitchell, W.E.	AB	102.235
Moon, W.S.	Boy	203.684
Musgrave, J.	Sto	289.530
Nicks, H.	PO2	156.751
Paintin, H.J.	Ord	203.349
Paramore, A.	Ord	198.349
Payne, H.	2/Yeo/Sig	163.507
Payne, P.	Ord	200.675
Pearce, W.W.	Engr	
Piper, W.J.	AB	155.923
Pinkey, J.H.	Ch/Sto	118.653
Plumley, J.H.	Sto	278.972
Poole, E.	AB	179.251
Purnell, J.J.	Sto	284.002
Purser, J.	Kroo	
Redman, S.J.	Bosn	
Rees, T.V.	Sto	
Reynolds, J.	Sh/Cpl	130.437
Richards, W.	L/S	126.883
Robeson, C.W.	Ord	195.198
Savage, S.G.	Sto	169.293
Shepherd, G.R.	L/Sto	135.519
Sierra Leone.	Kroo	
Slade, W.G.	Q/Sig	194.049
Smart, J.	Kroo	
Smith, A.W.	Ord	198.168
Smith, H.	Cpl	Ply3.523
Smith, W.	Sto	159.904
Snell, J.H.	AB	176.352
Spettigue, R.	Ord	200.582
Stevenson, T.	Ord	197.995
Stokes, G.	Pte	Ply7.715
Triplice, A.	Ord	207.890
Waldron, J.	AB	178.687
Walker, J.	Kroo	
Warren, A.G.	Lieut	
Webber, H.C.	Blksmth	165.113
Wells, T.J.	Art/Engr	
Westlake, H.J.	Arm/Mte	164.880
White, D.	AB	171.678
White, J.	Ch/Sto	132.278
Whyham, M.W.	Asst/Payr	
Wiffin, H.H.	Pte	Ch3.442
Will, G.	Sto	278.598
Williams, A.H.	Ord	201.132
Williams, G.	Kroo	
Williams, T.	Kroo	
Woolland, B.	Sto	287.135
Wreford, A.D.	Dom	357.296

Duplicate medals:

Bell, G.	Kroo	
Commins, G.	PO2	150.793
Coombes, W.J.	L/S	155.392
Driscoll, D.	Sto	287.256
Ford, A.	Ord	201.716
Forse, W.G.	Sto	276.192
Hart, W.J.	Ord	192.261
Loxton, F.	2/Sh/Cook	168.885
Westlake, H.J.	Arm/Mte	164.880
Williams, A.H.	Ord	201.132

Returned medals:

Adams, J.F.	Sto	354.581
Armour, T.	AB	174.556
Bishop, T.	Dom	
Blanche, T.	Kroo	
Bonny, J.	Kroo	
Bunce, T.R.	Pte	Ply6.430
Connelly, D.J.	Pte	Ply6.415
Cooper, E.	AB	
Dan, G.A.	Ord	200.187
Dunnicliffe, C.	Pte	Ply9.110
Holt, E.	ERA	269.995
Howells, J.C.	AB	
Lyons, P.	Sto	292.440
McCarthy, M.	AB	130.927
McCreary, P.	Sto	295.427
Marchington, W.	Pte	Ch10.404
Medway, T.	AB	178.269
Merrall, A.	Ord	200.101
Niger, W.	Kroo	
Parsons, W.	Sto	136.215
Pavis, W.	Dom	
Pearson, A.J.	Sto	295.441
Pickup, C.	Ord	357.014
Reffell, Z.	Kroo	
Savage, J.	Kroo	
Scott, G.W.	Dom	356.850
Smith, T.	AB	180.446
Tucker, J.	Sto	277.679
Williams, J.	Kroo	
Williams, R.	Ord	189.363

EXTENDED PERIOD

No Bar Medals

Abbott, A.W.	Lieut	

Extended Period, No Bar Medals *continued*

Andrews, E.	Ord	206.911
Bailey, G.A.	Sto	297.090
Banbury, F.A.F.	Asst/Payr	
Curno, J.N.	Pte	Po3.980
Finch, W.H.	Ord	206.905
Hulbert, G.E.W.	Boy	206.236
Jackson, H.E.	Sub Lieut	
Johnson, M.	Pte	Ply9.561
Kilma, Almas bin.	Seedie	
Mackney, A.E.	Ord	199.604
Milsom, J.	Pte	Po10.338
Mitchell, A.R.	Plmbr/Mte	343.971
Monatt, J.F.	Sh/Cpl	150.085
Pearson, T.J.C.	Pte	Po10.251
Pragnell, W.E.S.	Ord	206.903
Purvis, T.	Sto	279.700
Smartboy, Jack.	Kroo	
Swale, A.G.	Ord	206.912
Turner, C.W.	Ord	
Ward, E.J.	Ord	206.883
Watson, J.K.	Payr	

Returned medals:

Bajor, (1).	Seedie	
Bajor, (2).	Seedie	
Cruz, Sebastian de	Dom	110.497
Halfdollar, Tom.	Kroo	
Kirkpatrick, C.J.	Act/ERA	270.534
Mortimer, W.E.	Ord	206.608
Moussa, Ali bin.	Interpreter	
Peter, Jack.	Kroo	
Punch, W.	Kroo	
Riches, A.E.	Boy	204.721
September, Tom.	Kroo	
Snowball, Tom.	Kroo	
Twoglass, Tom.	Kroo	

H.M.S. DORIS

Period for which entitled:
11th October 1899 to 8th March 1901

Extended period:
9th March 1901 to 15th April 1901

Bars	*Total*	*Returned*	*Entitled*
8	5	0	5
7	34	1	33
6	11	2	9
5	16	0	16
4	70	3	67
3	33	2	31
2	28	0	28
1	186	3*	183
0	421	75	346
	804	86	718

* See Note 5 below.

Notes:
K – Awarded the King's South Africa Medal with two bars as indicated on the DORIS medal roll. and the K.S.A. Medal Roll.
(K) – Awarded the King's South Africa Medal with two bars as indicated on the K.S.A. medal roll but *not* on the DORIS medal roll.
[K] – Awarded the King's South Africa Medal with two bars as indicated on the DORIS medal roll but *not* on the K.S.A. Medal Roll.
Note 1 – Medal presented by H.M. The King.
Note 2 – Bar 'Johannesburg' substituted for bar 'Wepener' in duplicate medal.
Note 3 – Not entitled to bar 'Wepener', but states medal was lost when asked to return it.
Note 4 – Medal presented by H.R.H. The Prince of Wales.
Note 5 – Includes one medal where bar only was returned.
Note 6 – Two entries are made on the medal roll, but only one medal was issued.
Note 7 – Two medals were issued in error; one was returned.

Bars: Belmont, Modder River, Paardeberg, Driefontein, Johannesburg, Diamond Hill, Belfast, Relief of Kimberley

	Cudd, J.W.	L/S	141.209
1	Porter, J.	D.I.G.	
	Sutton, A.T.	Sto	149.160
	Wyatt, R.J.	Sh/Std	341.138

Duplicate medal:

Sutton, A.T.	Sto	149.160

Bars: Belmont, Modder River, Paardeberg, Driefontein, Johannesburg, Diamond Hill, Belfast, South Africa 1901

James, H.J.	L/S	164.765

Bars: Belmont, Modder River, Paardeberg, Driefontein, Johannesburg, Diamond Hill, Belfast

Amos, F.	Pte	Ply7.429
Ashley, T.W.	PO1	140.045
Bowie, A.	AB	189.321
Chapman, C.	Yeo/Sig	184.094
Chapman, E.	Pte	Ply5.700
Chapple, C.	Sto	279.442
Colwill, S.K.	Arm	108.207
Crook, C.	AB	176.028
Francis, W.C.	Sto	281.418
Franklin, E.A.	Pte	Ply7.471
Gray, A.	Pte	Po8.898
Knox, F.A.	Pte	Po8.903
Lobb, G.	AB	142.828
McCarthy, P.	AB	185.987
Maclean, S.	AB	153.302
Medway, R.A.	AB	189.090
Moon, F.	Ch/PO	100.623
Nevin, F.	Sto	285.634
Norris, J.W.	AB	184.367
Paddy, S.J.	AB	189.064
Parritt, E.	PO1	153.971
Pearse, C.E.	PO2	147.128
Perrey, F.W.C.	AB	190.306

Bars: Belmont, Modder River, Paardeberg, Driefontein, Johannesburg, Diamond Hill, Belfast *continued*

Perth, J.P.	AB	191.222
Rolling, H.	AB	126.128
[2] Sandford, D.J.	L/Sto	159.980
Sharp, J.D.	AB	188.655
Skedgell, A.G.	AB	188.766
Smithfield, A.	Arm/Mte	176.526
Steed, G.C.	Pte	Po8.902
Teed, R.	AB	183.999
Walker, P.	Pte	Ply8.151
Wollacott, A.	Sergt	Ply3.951

Duplicate medals:

Moon, F.	Ch/PO	100.623
Sandford, D.J.	L/Sto	159.980

Bars: Belmont, Modder River, Paardeberg, Driefontein, Wepener, Diamond Hill, Belfast

Returned medal:

Evans, S.	Sto	285.615

Bars: Belmont, Modder River, Paaroeberg, Driefontein, Johannesburg, Diamond Hill

Edwards, A.G.	Ord	188.780
Francis, E.J.	Pte	Ply5.439

Bars: Belmont, Modder River, Paardeberg, Driefontein, Diamond Hill, Belfast

Butcher, C.A.	Pte	Ch9.482
Delbridge, J.	AB	132.905
Devine, W.	Pte	Ch6.131
Oliver, J.	AB	193.335
Percival, W.	AB	131.271
Vick, A.G.	Sto	279.840

Returned medals:

Davey, F.C.	AB	152.905
Hayes, J.	AB	185.934

Bars: Belmont, Modder River, Paardeberg, Driefontein, Relief of Kimberley, Transvaal

Lawrence, T.	AB	189.296

Bars: Belmont, Modder River, Paardeberg, Driefontein, Johannesburg

Boyle, Hon. E.S.H.	Lieut	

Bars: Belmont, Modder River, Paardeberg, Driefontein, Relief of Kimberley

Sillem, W.W.	Midn	

Bars: Belmont, Modder River, Paardeberg, Driefontein, Diamond Hill

Dyer, W.T.	AB	189.120
Wardle, T.F.J.L.	Midn	

Bars: Belmont, Modder River, Paardeberg, Driefontein, Transvaal

Coleman, D.J.	AB	193.564
Donoghue, D.	L/S	150.971
[3] Galvin, J.	AB	188.924
Moore, A.	AB	181.143
Penny, W.H.	AB	180.079
Wise, M.W.	AB	152.069

Bars: Belmont, Modder River, Driefontein, Diamond Hill, Belfast

Bowden, F.W.	AB	189.331

Bars: Paardeberg, Driefontein, Diamond Hill, Belfast, Cape Colony

Booth, A.	Pte	Ply8.206

Bars: Paardeberg, Driefontein, Belfast, Relief of Kimberley, Cape Colony

[4] Colquhoun, W.J.	Lieut	

Duplicate medal:

* Colquhoun, W.J.	Lieut	

* This duplicate medal was returned

Bars: Paardeberg, Driefontein, Relief of Kimberley, Cape Colony, Transvaal

Fagioli, F.	AB	184.796

Bars: Paardeberg, Driefontein, Cape Colony, Transvaal, South Africa 1901

Grant, W.L.	Comdr	

Bars: Orange Free State, Transvaal, Tugela Heights, Relief of Ladysmith, Laing's Nek.

Ledgard, W.R.	Midn	

Bars: Belmont, Modder River, Paardeberg, Driefontein

Addy, E.	Pte	Po8.908
Allen, B.C.	Asst/Payr	
[K] Allen, T.	AB	182.639
Baddeley, A.W.	Pte	Po4.207
Bromley, C.J.	AB	181.140
Campbell, G.W.McD.	Lieut	
Down, A.	AB	190.694
Egerton, W.A.	Midn	
Hamlyn, F.	Pte	Ply7.054
Harris, C.A.	AB	185.596
Haskell, W.G.	PO1	150.642
Hinton, F.J.	PO1	176.876
Hockings, J.C.	Arm/Crew	340.189
Hodge, W.J.T.	AB	181.986
Hollis, N.	Pte	Ch8.397
Hook, J.E.	Ord	190.966
Hunking, J.	PO1	146.696
Ireland, W.H.	AB	176.228

McElligott, J.	Q/Sig	180.874
Mather, P.	Pte	Ply6.231
Pearce, E.H.	AB	189.801
Purves, W.	AB	188.596
Rennison, W.J.	AB	182.645
Rhodden, P.J.	Sto	286.692
Rice, E.	L/Cpl	Po4.386
Serat, J.	Pte	Ply7.062
Slamer, A.	AB	181.598

Duplicate medals:

Allen, T.	AB	182.639
Purves, W.	AB	188.596

Returned medals:

Abbott, A. alias A.H. Williams.	AB	170.300
Barton, E.G.	Sto	286.795
Lockett, W.	Sto	172.988

Bars: Belmont, Modder River, Relief of Kimberley, Orange Free State

Oaten, J.	AB	180.841
Roberts, T.	AB	162.454

Bars: Paardeberg, Driefontein, Johannesburg, Cape Colony

Saunders, F.P.	Midn	

Bars: Paardeberg, Driefontein, Cape Colony, Transvaal

Aitken, R.D.	PO1	126.446
Ash, P.H.	AB	189.102
Bailie, S.P.	AB	185.216
Ball, H.	Gunr	
Bartlett, C.	AB	157.842
Burley, A.	AB	189.314
Cannon, J.	Gunr	
Clark, A.G.	L/S	157.103
Clark, F.R.	AB	156.753
Cockram, W.	AB	187.605
Collings, P.	AB	180.045
Edwards, J.T.	PO1	165.821
Evans, E.	AB	179.506
Folley, J.R.	AB	181.436
Francis, H.G.	AB	184.792
Hartnett, J.C.	AB	190.301
Hayes, T.	Sto	290.279
Hooper, A.E.	AB	189.082
Humphrey, R.	AB	188.558
Langmaid, G.H.	Sto	289.757
Larter, E.A.	AB	188.363
Lyle, C.	AB	185.159
McHardy, J.	PO1	138.839
Marshall, A.	Sto	290.048
Meaden, A.S.	AB	188.649
Murphy, B.	PO1	127.010
Phillips, R.J.	AB	159.289
Quarm, W.A.	AB	189.115
Russell, W.H.	AB	180.391
Stabb, G.A.	PO2	126.308
Stanton, T.E.	AB	153.934
Tabb, T.H.	PO1	122.442
Vallence, J.M.	Sto	287.812

Duplicate medals:

Bailie, S.P.	AB	185.216
Francis, H.G.	AB	184.792
Murphy, B.	PO1	127.010

Bars: Driefontein, Johannesburg, Diamond Hill, Cape Colony

Cooper, V.J.	Pte	Ch7.413
Peile, S.P.	Major	

Bars: Driefontein, Diamond Hill, Belfast, Cape Colony

Harding, E.H.	Pte	Ch10.362

Duplicate medal:

Harding, E.H.	Pte	Ch10.362

Bars: Diamond Hill, Belfast, Cape Colony, Orange Free State

Cunningham, A.B.	Midn	

Bars: Belmont, Modder River, Paardeberg

Harris, R.	L/Sto	151.854
O'Brian, W.J.	Bugler	Ply8.458
Selley, G.	AB	188.825

Bars: Belmont, Moddér River, Relief of Kimberley

Robertson, S.	Midn	

Bars: Modder River, Paardeberg, Driefontein

Mourilyan, E.D.	St/Surgn	

Bars: Paardeberg, Driefontein, Relief of Kimberley

Gibbs, W.	Sto	279.670

Duplicate medal:

Gibbs, W.	Sto	279.670

Bars: Paardeberg, Driefontein, Cape Colony

Clements, W.	AB	136.216
Coleman, F.A.	AB	131.500
Edwards, A.J.	2/SBStd	350.304
Elford, R.	AB	189.322
Gilbert, A.	AB	186.053
Jeans, T.T.	Surgn	
Lang, G.H.	Midn	
Menzies, J.	Midn	
Mitchell, F.	AB	127.134
Monroe, R.	AB	189.982
Nugent, R.V.	2/Yeo/Sig	180.065
Palmer, G.	Sto	278.893
Pitman, J.	AB	188.420
Rainier, J.W.	Midn	

Bars: Paardeberg, Driefontein, Cape Colony *continued*

	Sullivan, P.	L/S	164.602
	Thorn, H.C.	AB	187.681
	Wells, L.	Dom	357.083
	White, A.T.J.	PO2	156.471
	Wilson, T.R.	AB	189.127
	Winkles, J.	AB	131.372

Returned medals:

	Friend, C.	AB	188.280
	Williamson, E.	AB	184.777

Bars: Driefontein, Cape Colony, Transvaal

	Hammett, R.W.	L/Sig	161.837

Bars: Belfast, Cape Colony, Orange Free State

	Denison, B.N.	Midn	

Bars: Cape Colony, Orange Free State, Transvaal

	Kennard, M.A.	Fl/Lieut	
K	Whyte, W.M.C.B.	Payr	

Bars: Natal, South Africa 1901, South Africa 1902

	Hall, H.G. King	Capt	

Bars: Belmont, Modder River

	Aldridge, E.H.	Sto	286.523
	Caltell, S.	AB	124.106
	Collicott, J.	Pte	Ply4.116
	Gilpin, F.H.	AB	185.586
	James, E.	Sto	285.042
	Legg, C.	Sto	286.420
	Luscombe, G.N.	Sto	161.194
	Miller, W.H.	Pte	Ply8.236
	Mogridge, W.	ERA	268.392
	Newton, M.G.	Lieut	
	Phillips, W.J.T.	2/SBStd	156.715
	Smith, A.	Pte	Po7.604
	Tummon, J.P.	AB	189.332
	Virgo, W.H.	Cpl	Ply7.976
	Waghorn, W.	Pte	Ch9.153
	Webb, F.G.	AB	188.531

Duplicate medals:

	Gilpin, F.H.	AB	185.586
	James, E.	Sto	285.042
*	Waghorn, W.	Pte	Ch9.153

* This duplicate medal was returned

Bars: Modder River, Paardeberg

	Hough, W.	AB	187.570

Bars: Paardeberg, Cape Colony

	Bailey, W.T.	AB	168.653
	Lecane, T.	AB	190.061
	Mullane, T.	AB	181.569
	Richards, J.N.	L/S	141.255

Bars: Relief of Kimberley, Orange Free State

	Milford, W.	PO1	122.290

Bars: Cape Colony, Orange Free State

	Incton, J.	L/S	182.536
	Lloyd, L.G.R.	Midn	
	Symonds, C.J.	AB	189.172

Bars: Cape Colony, South Africa 1901

	Bull, H.	AB	195.911
	Fitzmaurice, M.S.	Snr/Lieut	
	Rose, B.J.	Sh/Std/Asst	341.602

Duplicate medal:

	Fitzmaurice, M.S.	Snr/Lieut	

Bar: Belmont

	Boyle, J.	Pte	Ply8.034
	Braco, C.D.	Pte	Ply7.997
	Cokayne, F.G.	Pte	Ply7.695
	Coles, A.	Pte	Ply6.349
	Collinson, C.H.	Pte	Po7.793
	Creasey, W.J.	Pte	Ply7.959
	Davis, A.	Pte	Ply8.058
	Doran, F.	Pte	Ply6.820
	Greenfield, J.H.	Col/Sergt	Ply2.901
	Houstoun, J.F.	Midn	
	Huddart, C.A.E.	Midn	
	Jones, H.	AB	140.282
	Jones, T.	Pte	Po7.004
	Jones, W.T.C.	Capt(RMLI)	
	Murphy, J.P.	AB	191.090
	Olver, R.P.	AB	186.042
	Pitters, E.A.	Pte	Po8.385
	Prothero, R.C.	Capt	
	Southwood, J.H.	PO1	151.628
	Stockman, G.C.	AB	189.408
	Tilley, T.J.	AB	188.352
	Tribbeck, W.C.	Pte	Ply7.958

Duplicate medals:

*	Braco, C.D.	Pte	Ply7.997
	Houstoun, J.F.	Midn	
	Stockman, G.C.	AB	189.408

* Two duplicate medals issued.

Returned medals:

5	Jagger, R.	Pte	Ply7.573
	Plumbe, J.H.	Major(RMLI)	

Bar: Cape Colony

	Andrews, H.P.	Ch/Wrtr	90.598
	Angus, W.A.	Sto	292.071
	Arnold, A.J.	AB	192.034
	Ashton, J.	Sto	289.779
	Austin, S.	AB	198.863
K	Barnes, G.H.	Pte	Ch5.072
	Barnett, T.A.	AB	190.713

	Bazley, W.J.	AB	189.320
	Bird, T.C.	L/S	118.613
	Blackley, W.T.	Ch/SBStd	127.423
	Bluett, W.	AB	180.986
	Booker, J.H.	Pte	Po9.787
	Brading, F.W.	AB	193.862
	Bugg, H.	SB/Attn.	350.451
	Bunter, F.	Arm	155.806
	Burke, W.	AB	191.102
	Burt, J.W.	Sto	295.392
	Calder, J.	AB	185.660
	Cameron, R.B.	AB	187.422
	Carroll, G.	PO1	135.737
	Carroll, M.	AB	181.070
	Carter, R.W.	AB	167.781
	Cawse, S.G.	Pte	Po9.807
	Challenger, H.H.C.	L/Carp/Crew	341.635
	Chant, G.W.	Pte	Po6.690
	Chapman, J.W.	AB	188.593
	Chichester, Sir E.	Capt	
	Clatworthy, S.J.	AB	188.782
	Cloke, G.W.	PO1	128.088
	Clutterbuck, N.S.	Lieut(RMLI)	
	Codner, G.	Sh/Cpl	137.915
	Coke, A.L.N.D.	Midn	
	Collins, A.E.	Shpwrt	341.586
	Congreve, P.W.	L/S	181.266
	Coster, G.A.	Pte	Po9.786
	Cox, E.	Ord	194.201
	Cussack, J.M.L.	Clerk	
	Davis, S.J.	Q/Sig	185.694
	Day, J.	AB	195.751
	Dean, C.	Pte	Po4.394
	Dennison, E.A.	AB	188.516
	Dolbear, S.J.	AB	185.219
	Douglas, S.C.	Midn	
(K)	Edge, R.H.	Ch/Wrtr	105.513
	Elliott, W.H.	AB	190.307
	England, H.T.	Midn	
	Evans, S.H.	AB	189.721
	Ferris, J.W.	Ch/PO	110.082
	Foot, W.H.	AB	189.128
	Forey, J.	AB	166.388
	Gatcliff, A.F.	Lieut Col	
(K)	Gilbert, H.W.	Q/Sig	190.549
	Green, J.	Sto	286.086
	Greetham, C.T.	Engr	
	Griffith, C.W.	Asst/Payr	
	Guard, J.	PO1	114.037
(K)	Hadley, T.	Comdr.	
	Hannaford, J.R.	AB	189.174
	Hardinge, J.T.	Comdr	
	Harris, E.J.	AB	190.741
	Harris, Sir R.H.	Rear Admiral	
	Harris, W.J.	AB	189.325
	Harrison, J.R.	AB	195.079
	Harvey, C.R.	Asst/Payr	
	Hawkins, H.	2/Yeo/Sig	154.035
	Higgs, W.	Carp/Crew	342.682
	Hitchcock, W.	Ch/Yeo/Sig	99.170
	Hodder, E.A.	AB	195.766
	Hore, J.H.	AB	185.562
	Horton, C.E.	SBStd	140.871
	Hughes, H.J.	Q/Sig	184.558
	Hughes, W.H.	Clerk	
	Hunt, W.W.	Midn	
	Hurley, W.H.	AB	137.484
	James, B.P.	AB	189.105
	James, F.T.	AB	185.571
	Jameson, R.D.	Surgn	
	Jarman, H.F.	AB	195.297
	Jerrard, J.J.	AB	186.104
	John, A.	Sto	295.081
	Jones, C.	Bosn	
	Jones, C.H.	Midn	
	Jones, F.W.	AB	189.319
	Kelloe, W.A.	AB	188.539
	Kemp. W.	SB/Attn	350.487
	Lake, G.	AB	185.613
	Lake, G.J.	AB	178.437
	Lamb, A.	AB	181.545
[K]	Lingham, A.	Lieut	
	Linney, A.	AB	194.089
	Lloyd, A.	AB	188.791
K	Luscombe, F. St.L.	Capt	
	McCulloch, J.	AB	110.194
	McKersie, H.	AB	195.377
	McNeill, W.G.	Dom	119.997
	Mainprice, E.W.L.	Asst/Payr	
	Mardon, E.	PO2	159.724
K	Martin, J.	Comdr	
	Mason, J.	Sto	291.869
	Molloy, J.	AB	190.060
	Moore, S. St.L.	Midn	
	Morgans, J.	AB	191.202
	Morris, S.J.	AB	180.510
	Mowlam, E.J.	Asst/Engr	
	Norkett, A.J.	Sto	294.543
	Norris, R.	AB	189.326
	Oliver, G.B.	AB	206.133
	Orley, W.R.	AB	188.973
	Peck, A.M.	Lieut	
K	Perry-Ayscough, S.A.	Lieut	
	Philp, J.	AB	155.891
	Pike, T.	L/S	149.384
	Pope, W.G.	Sto	278.262
	Potter, C.J.	Pte	Po6.723
	Povey, W.T.	PO2	174.192
	Price, W.	Pte	Ch2.336
	Reilly, W.	AB	191.091
(K)	Reypert, C.G.	Bosn	
	Rich, W.	AB	185.232
	Ring, W.J.	Sto	290.367
	Ripley, A.J.	AB	187.879
	Roberts, T.	AB	188.711
	Robins, W.	AB	161.923
	Russell, A.A.	Sto	295.496
	Seymour, J.J.	Pte	Po4.976
	Shedditch, G.W.	Bugler	Po8.057
(K)	Shergold, G.	Q/Sig	182.015
[K]	Slater, J.R.	Pte	Ch7.485
	Soutan, W.L.	Pte	Ch8.848

Bars: Cape Colony *continued*

	Spry, E.J.	AB	187.820
	Sterling, D.J.	Pte	Ply5.846
	Stock, H.	AB	198.682
	Stopford, Hon. A.	Lieut	
	Suter, R.N.	Midn	
(K)	Tambling, W.	L/Sto	172.113
	Toomey, J.	AB	168.349
	Trischler, H.J.R.	Midn	
	Turner, J.H.	Pte	Ch6.810
	Vale, W.	AB	202.226
	Van Koughnet, E.B.	Capt	
	Webster, J.	Sto	292.900
	Wedlake, W.	PO1	148.432
	Western, G.	AB	191.109
	Williams, J.C.	PO2	157.133
	Williams, T.J.	AB	189.190
	Woolley, C.E.A.	Secretary	

Duplicate medals:

	Angus, W.A.	Sto	292.071
+	Arnold, A.J.	AB	192.034
	Brading, F.W.	AB	193.862
*	Burt, J.W.	Sto	295.392
	Cameron, R.B.	AB	187.422
	Green, J.	Sto	286.086
	Hadley, T.	Comdr	
	Hodder, E.A.	AB	195.766
	John, A.	Sto	295.081
	Webster, J.	Sto	292.900
	Williams, T.J.	AB	189.190

+ This duplicate medal was returned.
* Two duplicate medals issued.

Returned medal:

Stearn, W.A.	Ord	200.788

Bar: Orange Free State

Wearing, G.H.	Gunr	
Wellaway, W.	AB	140.730

Bar: Natal

	Barnnorth, E.	Sto	139.685
	Brounger, K.	Midn	
	Donaldson, L.A.B.	Lieut	
	Hannant, B.	Pte	Po5.625
(K)	Hebbes, W.	Act/Ch/ERA	152.802
(K)	Lacey, S.J.	Carp	
	Mahoney, W.	Ch/Bosn	
	Marden, J.	Ord	191.685
	Paris, H.G.	Comdr	
(K)	Richardson, J.	Ch/Engr	
	Screech, S.A.	St/Engr	
(K)	Thomas, W.J.	2/Wrtr	158.888
	Wright, H.C.	AB	191.473

Duplicate medal:

Brounger, K.	Midn	

No Bar Medals

Adams, T.	Pte	Ch9.284
Adlam, C.	Pte	Po3.703
Allen, W.	Sto	282.978
Alner, A.A.	Sh/Cpl	127.798
Anderson, Toby.	Kroo	
Appleton, J.	AB	190.753
Asthma, R.	Dom	
Atkinson, I.	Sto	286.822
Avery, W.J.	Ord	193.013
Bagot, C.	Sto	284.001
Baker, A.E.	Sto	173.568
Bannerman, H.	Sto	178.582
Barr, W.T.	Band	341.203
Barrett, S.	L/Sto	155.701
Bartlett, W.H.	Sto	292.512
Barton, W.	Ord	187.976
Baynes, C.	Plmbr/Mte	282.159
Beacham, A.C.	AB	185.058
Beeching, T.E.	Dom	354.691
Bennett, J.W.	AB	171.563
Betteridge, J.	Dom	356.503
Beynon. W.J.	AB	201.889
Bindon, W.H.	L/Sto	160.747
Blair, C.L.	Sail/Mte	107.703
Blewett, A.	PO1	115.384
Blight, C.J.	ERA	268.476
Boden, S.E.	AB	191.240
Bodle, H.G.	Dom	356.502
Bowell, T.G.	SBStd	150.312
Boyce, A.C.	Pte	Po9.163
Boyle, H.L.	Lieut	
Brady, M.	AB	106.025
Brent, T.H.	Band	340.182
Brett, G.E.	AB	187.048
Bripant, G.T.	Q/Sig	184.444
Brown, F.	Pte	Po6.440
Brown, W.	AB	188.536
Brydie, W.C.	Cooper	148.071
Buckett, A.	AB	185.957
Buckley, H.	AB	201.879
Bunker, T.	Sh/Std	88.113
Burgess, B.J.	ERA	269.239
Burrows, F.C.	Pte	Ch8.532
Burton, A.W.	Sto	292.453
Cahill, J.	Sto	164.525
Canniford, C.	AB	140.211
Card, N.	Boy	197.752
Carr, E.G.	PO2	156.382
Carrie, T.	Sig	197.541
Carter, T.G.	Midn	
Cartwright, S.	Sto	290.094
Chaffe, T.	L/Sto	153.091
Chalty, W.	Dom	132.836
Champion, J.P.	L/S	155.570
Chowen, A.	PO1	118.396
Clarke, J.H.	Dom	140.224
Clarke, R.H.	Ord	197.909
Cockran, A.	Pte	Po8.811
Coleman, P.E.	Sto	295.066
Coles, J.J.C.	Carp/Mte	141.558

Collins, W.	Band	178.277
Colmer, W.J.	Carp/Mte	100.846
Colt, H.A.	Midn	
Congdon, W.	AB	188.008
Connor, J.R.	Carp/Mte	155.468
Coombes, F.W.	L/S	157.105
Corneille, W.	Sto	279.292
Couch, J.J.	Sto	280.071
Courtinage, W.	L/Sto	122.021
Cousins, H.J.	Ord	198.021
Coyde, G.H.	L/Sto	148.772
Cramb, E.E.	PO2	156.341
Crang, E.	AB	174.700
Craven, C.W.	Midn	
Crossing, J.	Ch/Sto	112.261
Crostic-Hill, R.	Midn	
Crow, Jim.	Kroo	
Cudd, G.H.	Ord	201.881
Cuer, W.J.	Ch/Wrtr	133.471
Cummings, A.	Sto	289.743
Dart, G.	AB	189.080
Davies, J.	Sto	285.636
Davis, John.	Kroo	
Davis, T.	PO1	124.511
Dawe, W.R.	Sto	281.624
Dawson, G.	Pte	Ply3.193
Dell, F.	AB	185.185
Dennis, P.W.	Sto	285.011
Devereaux, G.	Sto	282.275
Deveson, A.	AB	176.031
Dick, Tom.	Dom	
Dollar (No1), Tom.	Kroo	
Donovan, M.	Sto	279.118
Dowling, E.	Sto	290.049
Draper, D.J.	L/Carp/Crew	165.016
Drayton, A.	L/Sto	131.981
Durham, J.H.	Sto	281.207
Edmunds, F.J.	Q/Sig	191.008
Edwards, W.E.	Sto	292.565
Edwards, W.H.	Art/Engr	
Etridge, F.W.	Band	340.976
Evans, H.	AB	171.020
Evans, J.S.	Sto	282.849
Featherstonehough, C.H.	Pte	Po9.829
Feltham, G.	Sto	290.265
Ferrier, J.	Sto	294.306
Fitzpatrick, P.E.	AB	190.300
Foord, J.	Sto	286.760
Foster, A.E.	AB	185.281
Fountain, F.J.	AB	136.831
Franklin, W.	Band	340.444
Gale, W.P.	Ch/Band	356.551
Gardener, W.J.	L/S	136.898
Garmey, G.	Pte	Po7.805
George, Jim.	Kroo	157.487
George, Tom.	Kroo	
Glasgow, Tom.	Kroo	
Glover, G.	Pntr	340.164
Goddard, W.	Pte	Ch8.051
Golledge, H.	AB	189.207
Gooch, H.W.	AB	181.019
Gorrell, J.T.	Blksmth	144.334
Gough, G.W.	AB	180.737
Grady, J.	AB	185.738
Gray, W.	Pte	Ply3.220
Greenfield, S.J.	Q/Sig	191.449
Greening, H.	L/Sto	133.789
Grinter, E.E.	AB	189.118
Grossmith, A.M.	Boy	198.322
Gunn, A.	Sto	293.142
Hadder, A.	L/Sto	172.094
Hallett, W.	L/Sto	115.068
Hambley, H.	Sto	284.072
Hands, J.	Ch/Sto	146.909
Hann, E.R.	Sergt	Ply3.276
Harding, J.	L/Sto	153.216
Harding, Joe.	Kroo	
Harley, W.J.	Sto	277.472
Harper, Rev. C.J.	Chaplain	
Harrell, T.F.	Ch/Sto	127.761
Hawkins, W.W.	Sto	285.640
Hayman, J.S.	AB	190.302
Haynes, W.T.	Boy	197.585
Henderson, C.	Sto	171.206
Hennessey, W.	Ch/PO	110.995
Hiam, D.	Pte	Ch9.721
Hicks, R.	Act/Ch/Sto	155.695
Higginson, F.	Pte	Ch5.707
Hilhouse, G.	Midn	
Hinds, J.	Pte	Po8.983
Hobbs, H.J.	Q/Sig	185.667
Hobin, C.R.	Pte	Po8.999
Hodge, E.T.	PO1	95.004
Hollands, N.E.	Ch/Sto	133.240
Holme, G.	AB	115.645
Hooker, G.	AB	179.232
Hooper, H.S.	PO1	153.996
Horam, J.	Sto	155.428
Horn, F.W.	Dom	122.076
Howard, J.	Dom	106.992
Howes, H.G.	Asst/Engr	
Hughes, W.F.	Blksmth/Mte	280.152
Hurrell, W.H.	PO1	159.648
Ide, C.J.	AB	162.867
Ingham, J.	Boy	196.827
Ireland, F.H.	AB	189.193
Isaac, W.T.	L/Sig	184.506
James, H.J.	AB	185.183
Jenks, G.	AB	195.767
Johns, H.D.	L/Carp/Crew	341.524
Johnson, S.	Kroo	
Jones, J.	AB	200.378
Jones, R.	3/Wrtr	340.073
Jones, S.P.	ERA	268.738
Jones, W.G.	ERA	268.449
Jordan, A.	Band	356.342
Keeble, G.	AB	195.390
Knight, W.G.	AB	187.912
Lark, S.E.	Fl/Payr	
Larmont, T.	Q/Sig	174.616
Latham, J.H.	AB	156.349
Lavender, E.	Sto	356.123

No Bar Medals *continued*

Lavers, W.A.	L/Sto	148.775
Lawton, A.	AB	155.837
Le Sauteur, W.P.	PO1	177.133
Ledger, G.F.	AB	177.346
Lennard, T.	PO2	159.834
Leonard, H.	Sto	283.156
Leonard, J.	Sto	146.477
Lester, R.E.	L/Shpwrt	341.588
Liddicott, N.J.	Dom	356.144
Liddle, P.	Sto	280.795
Lloyd, H.	Sto	290.040
Lock, H.N.	Blksmth/Mte	342.187
Locke, H.R.	PO2	132.587
Lockyer, S.	AB	187.917
Londoh, E.	Bosn	
Long, G.	AB	187.150
Lowe, F.A.	Q/Sig	135.287
McAnulty, T.	Sto	285.812
McCoy, J.	Sto	277.696
McElhinney, J.	Sto	149.174
McSweeney, J.	PO1	118.813
McThomson, A.	Sto	294.345
Mabey, G.J.	AB	179.986
Madge, W.	Sto	130.733
Mahony, J.	Sto	162.532
Manning, Jim.	Kroo	
Markwood, W.	Sto	171.951
Marshall, J.J.	Sto	285.624
Mathison, A.	Sto	295.497
Matthews, W.H.	L/S	162.312
Mead, B.	Sto	174.207
Middlecote, W.G.	Sto	281.025
Moad, R.	Sto	286.531
Moore, W.H.	L/S	139.097
Morrell, C.	PO1	117.092
Mountain, C.	PO1	112.106
Moxham, A.G.	Sto	286.825
Munford, G.	AB	199.300
Munn, G.A.	Shpwrt	340.648
Murray, T.E.	PO2	163.909
Newmin, E.	Band	340.181
Nichol, H.G.	AB	199.267
Nooman, W.	Sto	283.883
Norris, R.	PO2	156.062
Norrish, W.	Yeo/Sig	131.409
North, W.	Pte	Po9.827
Norton, A.T.	2/Sh/Cook	168.570
Nowry, A.	AB	184.823
Olley, W.	AB	176.879
Orr, J.F.	Sto	295.213
[1] Palmer, C.	AB	159.298
Palmer, J.	Act/Ch/ERA	141.867
Palmer, J.H.	Ch/Sto	120.362
Parker, R.J.	Ord	192.865
Parsons, E.H.	Sto	279.661
Pasco, J.J.	Ch/Arm	119.007
Passmore, G.H.	ERA	268.327
Pearne, R.F.	Act/Ch/ERA	148.806
Peberdy, T.	AB	158.193
Pedler, J.W.	Dom	166.396
Pennell, A.J.	Sto	285.632
Perrin, C.	Ch/Cook	114.655
Peter, Tom. (1)	Kroo	
Peter, Tom. (2)	Kroo	
Polglass, F.	AB	156.343
Pomeroy, W.	Ch/Sto	119.591
Powell, A.E.	PO1	111.891
Price, J. alias J. Rogers.	L/Sto	103.370
Primmer, J.J.	MAA	137.126
Pryal, M.	AB	155.487
Puleston, T.P.	L/Sto	168.450
Purser, Jack.	Kroo	
Putt, W.H.	AB	189.246
Pye, E.	Sto	162.189
Ramsey, T.	Blksmth	134.614
Reed, A.E.	AB	140.488
Reed, J.	Ord	194.735
Rich, C.H.	Sto	281.430
Rich, H.	2/SBStd	150.404
Richards, A.E.	ERA	153.245
Roberts, A.	Sto	292.931
Rodgerson, W.	Sto	354.285
Rose, A.E.	Pte	Po7.859
Rowe, F.	Ord	198.682
Rowe, H.	PO2	138.443
Rowe, R.	AB	189.807
Rundle, J.V.	PO1	123.042
Ryan, C.W.	AB	109.569
Sabben, H.H.	St/Comdr	
Saunders, D.	Act/Ch/ERA	159.885
Savage, Jack.	Kroo	
Saxby, E.	Sto	286.684
Seath, T.W.S.	Asst/Payr	
Seberoy, E.C.P.	2/Cooper	341.822
Senora.	Dom	
Shearing, A.J.	AB	134.678
Shears, J.S.	ERA	268.815
Shepherd, W.	L/Sto	161.722
Silvester, E.W.	Pte	Po8.982
Simpson, T.S.	Sto	282.571
Sleeman, W.	Sto	280.132
Smith, W.	AB	191.089
Snell, T.	Dom	161.740
Sobey, T.	Sto	281.636
Sparrow, A.J.	Band	123.227
Spence, T.	Sergt	Po5.674
Spinks, F.W.	AB	156.844
Spry, A.J.	AB	185.140
Stares, O.	Pte	Po8.891
Steele, E.B.	Sto	279.712
Steggles, A.	Sto	286.033
Stemmert, M.	Dom	
Stevens, W.S.	AB	199.459
Stevenson, J.B.	PO1	124.217
Stewart, P.	PO1	106.810
Stock, S.G.	Ord	191.684
Stockdale, T.J.	Sto	154.476
Stone, W.J.	AB	132.917

Stribling, W.S.	Fl/Engr	
Strickland, F.	Band	179.159
Stuart, D.	Midn	
Styles, E.G.	Clerk	
Sullivan, J.	AB	180.461
Tait, R.	Ord	199.692
Taylor, H.B.	Pte	Po9.804
Thomas, John.	Kroo	
Thompson, A.E.	Ord	199.302
Thompson, J.W.	AB	186.847
Toby, III, Tom.	Kroo	
Todd, H.D.	Sig	191.712
Tombs, C.	Sto	285.622
Tozer, T.	Pte	Ply7.977
Tremaine, A.E.	AB	189.116
Trewolla, J.	L/Carp/Crew	340.307
Truscott, A.E.	AB	198.927
Tulley, O.P.	AB	176.740
Turner, G.	Band	153.925
Tylor, T.J.	Ord	201.877
Vickers, T.	AB	178.784
Vosper, J.W.	Ch/Sto	131.434
Walden, W.E.	Band	340.041
Walker, Tom.	Kroo	
Wall, E.J.	Pte	Ply8.135
Wallis, J.H.	Band	155.110
Walters, R.H.	Lieut	
Warner, W.	Dom	111.422
Webb, S.	AB	182.633
Webster, W.T.	Pte	Ply8.183
Wells, J.	AB	188.653
Welsford, F.W.	Sto	290.042
West, G.E.	Sto	292.575
Whitlock, H.A.	Pte	Po9.148
Whyman, P.	Kroo	
Wiggins, W.	Pte	Po6.479
Williams, J.H.	ERA	141.811
Williams, S.	ERA	268.468
Wilson, Jim.	Kroo	
Wilson, J.W.	Sto	280.084
Woodbury, E.	AB	187.931
Woodcock, W.	Band	341.280
Woodley, W.	Carp	
Woods, W.	L/Sto	111.791
Wright, G.W.	Shpwrt	341.687
Wyatt, W.	Act/MAA	185.555

Duplicate medals:

* Boden, S.E.	AB	191.240
Coombes, F.W.	L/S	157.105
Edwards, W.E.	Sto	292.565
George, Tom.	Kroo	
Hambley, H.	Sto	284.072
* Ireland, F.H.	AB	189.193
Jones, R.	3/Wrtr	340.073
Moad, R.	Sto	286.531
Roberts, A.	Sto	292.931
Seath, T.W.S.	Asst/Payr	
Simpson, T.S.	Sto	282.571
Warner, W.	Dom	111.422

* Two duplicate medals issued.

Returned medals:

Andrew, A.	Q/Sig	154.421
Baker, C.	Kroo	
Belfast.	Kroo	
Bestman, Tom	Kroo	
Bowden, W.	Ord	188.089
Brisco, J.	Pte	
Brown, H.	Pte	Po3.464
Caddle, A.	AB	189.301
Cliffe, D.	Sto	161.954
Conlan, R.	Sto	290.045
Dandy, Jack.	Kroo	
Davis, I	Pte	Ply8.595
Davis, Tom alias Tom True.	Kroo	
Dean, M.	Sto	280.405
Dibben, R.	PO1	156.957
Douglas, R.P.	Ord	181.680
Ely, A.	Sto	290.305
Evans, S.	Messenger	
Forthergill, H.	Sto	286.761
Fowkes, W.	Sig	188.506
Frame, W.	AB	181.341
Fuller, H.L.	Dom	358.616
Gambier, F.G.	AB	162.767
Gay, J.	Ord	
Gibson, A.	PO2	149.375
Gillespie, J.	Sto	282.211
Grant, F.N.	Lieut	
Hellyer, W.J.		
Hodgetts, J.W.	Ord	190.233
Holcroft, B.	Ord	202.961
Hollins, W.T.	Asst/Payr	
Holmaden, S.M.	Midn	
Hopwood, A.H.	AB	127.914
Ings, E.F.	Dom	137.587
Johnson, T.	AB	
Knapp, M.H.	Surgn	
Landers, J.	AB	181.574
McBean, E.	AB	170.406
Moore, Jim.	Kroo	
Mullins, W.T.	Sto	287.941
Munden, F.C.	Sto	292.884
Newton, H.	AB	143.470
Nicholls, J.	Kroo	
O'Bryan, J.	Sto	290.587
O'Connor, M.	Sto	285.368
Palmer, C.	AB	159.298
Parsonage, J.P.	AB	153.949
Perry, J.	AB	162.852
Phillips, M.A.	Ord	198.932
Pullen, W.G.	Sto	286.672
Saunders, F.J.	Lieut	
Sequeira, J.	Dom	359.080
Shannon, S.	Sto	293.144
Sharp, T.P.	Ord	193.598
Simons, J.	Dom	359.079
Smith, E.A.	Pte	Ply7.494

No Bar Medals *Returned medals, continued*

Souza, M. de	Dom	105.181
Spracklin, W.G.	Ord	181.584
Squelch, R.T.	Pte	Ply8.005
Stevens, W.	Pte	Ch4.045
Taylor, A.D.	Dom	356.143
Taylor, J.		
Thomas, T.		
Townsend, A.	Ord	173.669
Wales, Prince of.	Kroo	
Wall, A.J.	Ord	191.744
Wallington, W.	Sto	291.960
Westall, C.W.	Pte	Po8.677
Williams, C.	Dom	357.010
Wilson, A.A.	AB	195.444
Winter, J.B.	AB	168.257
Wolfe, W.A.	PO2	148.136
Wright, G.	Pte	Po9.097

EXTENDED PERIOD
No Bar Medals

Returned medals:

Lee, P.	Sto	290.756
Pedrick, A.	Sto	171.671

H.M.S. DWARF

Period for which entitled:
6th November 1899 to 19th May 1900

Extended period:
3rd May 1901 to 4th November 1901
10th May 1902 to 27th May 1902
28th May 1902 to 31st May 1902 (Recommission).

Bars	Total	Returned	Entitled
0	286	110	176
	286	110	176

No Bar Medals

Anderson, F.	Sto	166.786
Batey, H.	Art/Engr	
Beaglehole, A.W.	L/S	156.779
Bell, A.E.	Pte	Ch10.388
Bibbings, S.G.	AB	185.458
Bowden, J.H.	AB	189.316
Boy, Jim. alias Shuteye.	Kroo	
Bridgeman, A.H.	Sto	288.208
Britt, J.R.	Ord	195.980
Brommell, J.	Pte	Ply9.093
Butland, W.	AB	148.467
Callicott, J.W.	Dom	112.426
Campbell, E.	Kroo	
Carpenter, W.	Sto	290.800
Catts, A.Y.	Gunr	
Chard, W.T.	Carp/Mte	154.342
Clemesha, R.	AB	162.569
Coggins, A.C.	Arm/Mte	152.492
Collacott, T.	AB	142.707
Compton, C.	Sto	291.481
Conlon, P.J.	Sto	291.464
Connell, J.	PO1	130.349
Dart, H.	PO1	130.860
Day, E.W.	Sto	287.300
Driscoll, E.	Ord	197.702
Dunn, D.	Kroo	
Dunnicliffe, C.	Pte	Ply9.110
Endicott, F.W.	L/Sig	183.550
Flaherty, D.	L/Sto	139.618
Foss, W.E.	AB	191.125
Frost, T.R.	AB	180.797
George, Jim.	Kroo	
Glasgow, Tom	Kroo	
Glasgow (2), Tom.	Kroo	
Griffiths, J.H.	Sto	276.938
Hampherson, D.	ERA	269.316
Harmon, A.	Sto	279.279
Harradon, E.	AB	179.176
Harry, T.	Ord	195.245
Hawkins, R.C.	Sub Lieut	
Henderson, W.H.	Sh/Std	161.438
Henry, R.	L/Sto	153.421
Houston, T.	Ord	200.671
Hunt, J.	AB	88.166
Jarvis, A.R.	AB	176.573
King, Ja Ja.	Kroo	
Lane, D.D.	Lieut	
Macaulay, G.	Kroo	
Martin, A.R.	Ch/Wrtr	133.444
Merceika, E.	Blksmth	111.940
Mitchell, J.C.	Sto	153.547
Parnell, W.	AB	189.068
Payton, J.F.	ERA	165.096
Philps, G.A.	Pte	Po8.730
Pocknell, J.	Sto	286.697
Ralph, W.	L/S	147.036
Ranner, P.W.H.	Cpl	Po6.408
Sandy, G.H.	Shpwrt	141.618
Seabreeze, Tom.	Kroo	
Senior, T.	PO2	138.439
Shakespear, H.F.	Lieut	
Sheehan, T.	Sto	278.244
Sills, W.G.	Sto	166.474
Squires, F.J.	Ord	197.035
Stanfield, T.E.	Sh/Cook	149.788
Sutherland, F.C.	Ord	196.137
Toby, Tom alias Benin.	Kroo	
Trybest.	Kroo	
Vosper, G.E.	AB	353.982
Walker, James.	Kroo	
Walters, H.	Pte	Ply2.082
Ward, J.C.	Pte	Ply8.448
Wath, G.E.	AB	156.873
Watson, W.	Q/Sig	178.012
Webber, J.T.	Dom	357.570
Webber, S.C.	Ord	183.706
Weeks, R.	AB	171.705
West, G.	Sto	290.508
Westcott, W.G.	Surgn	
Whale, Black.	Kroo	
Widger, F.	PO1	124.641
Williams, C.J.	PO1	114.863
Williams, C.J.	2/SBStd	350.353
Wright, H.J.	Pte	Ply4.647

No Bar Medals *continued*

Duplicate Medals:

Flaherty, D.	L/Sto	139.618
Griffiths, J.H.	Sto	276.938
Jarvis, A.R.	AB	176.573
Macaulay, G.	Kroo	
Payton, J.F.	ERA	165.096
Ranner, P.W.H.	Cpl	Po6.408

Returned Medals:

Beugeyfield, J.T.	Pte	Ply8.405
Bestman, T.	Kroo	
Bowling, J.	Kroo	
Brewer, W.	Sto	139.611
Bridle, A.	Dom	357.566
Butcher, W.C.	Kroo	
Dell, F.	Ord	185.185
Dicker, G.	Dom	137.045
Doe, Jim alias Jack Foretop.	Kroo	
Down, A.H.	Dom	356.482
Fortune, T.	Kroo	
Fuge, N.	L/Sto	154.897
Goosney, E.	Pte	Ply9.112
Johnson, B.	Kroo	
Johnson, F.	Kroo	
Metzger, W.	Kroo	
Parker, T.G.	Ord	190.394
Roberts, B.	Kroo	
Roberts, J.	Kroo	
Robinson, R.	Kroo	
Sampson No. 2	Kroo	
Sango, Jack alias Jack Newman.	Kroo	
Savey, J.	Kroo	
Savage, Jack.	Kroo	
Smart, J.	Kroo	
Smith, D.F.	Pte	Ply9.087
Stewart, W.J.	ERA	268.631
Sunday, Jack.	Kroo	
Tommy No. 1.	Kroo	
Tommy No. 2.	Kroo	
Tree, Palm.	Kroo	
Williams, Augustine.	Kroo	
Williams, John.	Kroo	

EXTENDED PERIOD

No Bar Medals

Ahern, P.	Boy	209.003
Allison.	Kroo	
Avery, E.J.	ERA	153.328
Bartlett, R.	AB	157.820
Bone, W.J.	AB	166.873
Broom, R.C.	AB	202.441
Broster, P.M.	Sub Lieut	
Bunt, W.H.	Sto	276.520
Callaghan, E.W.	AB	184.610
Carey, J.	L/Sto	171.319
Chubb, T.A.	Ch/Wrtr	123.048
Church, J.J.	AB	178.787
Cobb, H.L.	Ord	202.448
Coleman, P.	L/Sto	145.090
Collins, W.H.S.	Ord	202.313
Cook, A.	2/Sh/Cook	169.770
Coulthard, J.B.	Ord	200.434
Cox, A.E.	Pte	Ply5.697
Denny, G.H.	L/S	171.574
Derrick, C.	Ord	212.120
Dewar, T.H.G.	Carp/Mte	145.701
Didcote, A.E.A.	L/S	138.308
Doe, Jim.'	Kroo	
Driscoll, P.	AB	203.931
Duckhan, C.H.	Sto	288.883
England, W.U.	Lieut/Comdr	
Evans, A.	L/Carp/Crew	341.896
Farmer, E.	Pte	Ply6.748
Flanagan, M.J.	Sto	285.299
Flying Jib.	Dom	
Foley, W.	Boy	209.001
Fookes, H.W.	Gunr.	
Ford, J.	Pte	Ply10.735
Garters, T.W.	Ord	210.545
Gasser, J.H.	PO1	120.067
Getsom, F.	Dom	358.445
Goddard, W.G.	Sh/Std/Asst	341.248
Halley, A.M.L.	Cpl	Ply7.972
Halloran, W.	Boy	209.556
Harrison, T.E.	Pte	Ply10.731
Henry, W.	Sto	286.499
Hinchey, T.R.	Ord	208.550
Hindmarsh, J.	Art/Engr	
Holliday, W.G.	PO1	139.142
Hook, A.W.H.	Pte	Ply6.778
House, W.J.	AB	141.540
Jackson, W.F.	Ord	197.617
Jefferies, W.M.	Sto	176.680
Jones, G.R.	AB	163.812
Jones, L.O.	Boy	208.775
Joyce, J.	AB	166.028
Kelliher, S.G.	L/Sig	196.336
Kemp, A.E.	Ord	203.715
Lambert, W.	Ord	202.783
Lewis, J.	Ord	216.837
Liddell, C.H.	Sto	289.519
Littlejohns, R.	Ord	202.780
Long, H.J.	AB	160.978
Lurring, J.H.	Pte	Ply10.736
McLoughlin, T.	ERA	270.062
Mahoney, D.	Sto	281.733
Mansbridge, A.C.	AB	182.385
Monrovia.	Kroo	
Neil, W.	Sto	298.206
Northcote, W.	AB	201.583
O'Brien, P.	AB	184.584
Parrott, E.E.	Sto	287.214
Penhallurick, E.T.	L/S	176.530
Peters (II), Tom.	Kroo	
Phillips, E.R.	Boy	209.525
Reilly, P.	AB	197.663
Robinson, C.	AB	180.830
Salt Water.	Kroo	
Short, E.	Pte	Ply3.179

Smith, C.	Boy	210.535
Smith, H.W.	AB	176.120
Smith, S.	Sig/Boy	211.437
Smith, S.J.	Sto	132.846
Snell, J.G.	SB/Attn	350.659
Stabb, W.H.	AB	181.166
Stonelake, A.H.	AB	188.264
Thorney, J.W.	Ord	208.597
Trotman, H.E.	Sh/Std	163.473
Twomey, R.	PO1	164.818
Usher, J.	Pte	Ply10.737
Vinnicombe, R.	Ord	210.547
Walters, A.J.	AB	195.860
Wellington, J.	Kroo	
Westlake, A.	Sto	159.898
Whillock, R.	AB	178.261
White, J.	Sub Lieut	
Whitwarm, L.S.	Surgn	

Duplicate medals:

Flanagan, M.J.	Sto	285.299
Ford, J.	Pte	Ply10.735
Kemp, A.E.	Ord	203.715
Long, H.J.	AB	160.978
Smith, H.W.	AB	176.120

Returned medals:

Andrews, A.H.	AB	185.633
Barretts, C.F.	Dom	359.873
Bassett, F.	L/Sto	126.473
Batten, J.	Sto	279.668
Bennatto, J.	Sto	148.889
Boyle, M.	AB	176.786
Bray, J.	PO1	120.309
Buttonshaw, E.G.	Act/Sh/Std	174.031
Capon, R.A.	L/S	160.422
Collett, F.	AB	182.343
Collins, W.	Act/Ch/PO	117.217
Collins, W.H.	PO1	158.555
Creese, J.J.	L/Sto	158.761
Davie, R.	AB	158.511
Davis, J.	Kroo	
Deakin, D.	AB	175.463
Donald, T.	Carp/Mte	156.145
Downs, W.T.J.	Ch/PO	113.810
Dyer, T.H.	Arm/Crew	342.297
Edwards, C.W.	PO1	126.849
Ellis, W.	AB	156.400
Fitzgerald, W.	Sh/Std/Asst	340.421
Fuge, F.	Sto	277.129
Furze, W.J.	PO1	120.802
Garrett, H.C.	AB	193.578
Giles, H.S.J.	Arm/Crew	191.113
Grey, J.	Kroo	
Haffey, A.	AB	160.614
Harper, J.	ERA	268.516
Harris, E.	ERA	268.929
Harvey, J.	Lieut	
Harwood, T.T.	PO1	117.006
Howells, G.	AB	177.593
Hunt, F.G.	PO1	130.998
Irish, H.	L/Sto	153.579
Jay, A.	AB	180.586
Jordan, C.J.B.	PO1	118.789
Kendall, A.H.	AB	176.865
Keogh, D.J.	AB	177.615
Lake, W.T.	AB	151.541
Lewis, W.	AB	194.488
Little, J.A.	L/Sto	144.846
Little, L.P.	Arm/Crew	175.333
Marle, T.T.	Surgn	
Mead, W.H.	Sto	159.049
Miller, F.H.	AB	190.568
Mitchell, E.G.	PO2	165.568
Mitchell, H.J.	AB	195.043
Monday, Tom.	Kroo	
Newman, H.	Carp/Mte	161.271
Paulin, J.	AB	186.890
Perren, B.	PO1	129.879
Philp, R.E.	Arm/Mte	340.027
Price, J.	Carp/Mte	165.912
Robertson, D.M.	Sto	298.241
Richard, Tom.	Kroo	
Russell, W.	Sto	297.864
Samways, H.A.	Ch/PO	117.566
Stancombe, J.	L/Sto	149.856
Staysail, Jack.	Kroo	
Stone, A.	Sto	169.822
Strudwick, F.G.	Sig	197.378
Sullivan, J.H.	AB	191.117
Tack, Tom.	Kroo	
Taylor, J.	Kroo	
Tiller, W.S.	AB	183.058
Vernon, W.G.	Carp/Mte	147.453
Waddon, W.H.	Ch/PO	97.809
Ward, F.R.	ERA	268.026
Webber, S.C.	Sto	188.706
Wellington, J.	Kroo	
Wilkie, W.H.	ERA	163.110
Wilkins, T.H.	AB	166.354
Williams, E.J.	Sto	276.484
Williams, J.	Arm/Crew	153.176
Williams, Tom.	Kroo	
Wood, S.	Sto	276.822

H.M.S. FEARLESS

Period for which entitled:
5th December 1899 to 23rd August 1900

Bars	Total	Returned	Entitled
0	151	6	145
	151	6	145

Notes:
* Recipients presented with medals on 'Ophir'.

No Bar Medals

	Abbott, J.	AB	158.096
	Ahier, A.E.	AB	158.638
	Alexander, H.W.J.	AB	186.066
	Alexander, R.	2/Yeo/Sig	142.929
	Allan, A.E.	Sh/Cook	146.768
	Ansell, C.W.	AB	182.981
	Arnold, J.	Ch/PO	120.670
	Atkins, C.H.	Pte	Po5.950
	Ayling, J.	2/Yeo/Sig	184.885
	Bavage, S.	Sto	283.995
	Bell, A.	Ch/Carp/Mte	132.407
	Bennett, J.	Ch/PO	55.655
	Bentley, G.W.	Ch/Arm	127.975
	Berry, E.J.	Sto	283.960
	Boffa, P.	Dom	157.485
	Brady, C.	Pte	Po7.666
	Breeze, C.E.	Pte	Po8.506
	Brewer, W.J.	Sh/Std	151.080
	Brown, J.W.	PO1	169.397
	Bruford, F.J.	L/Sto	143.652
	Bywater, J.	AB	183.997
	Caines, F.H.	Plmbr/Mte	284.394
	Calleja, G.	Dom	141.345
	Carpenter, H.	L/Sto	163.630
	Carter, A.J.	PO1	120.600
	Chambers, W.T.	AB	161.847
	Clarke, F.R.E.	Lieut	
	Clouston, D.L.	Sto	284.522
	Cole, T.	Sto	282.513
	Collings, J.A.	Pte	Po9.233
	Colwell, A.T.	AB	165.486
	Congdon, R.N.	L/Sto	123.974
	Conway, L.	Pte	Po8.126
	Cooke, J.	Pte	Po8.509
	Cosson, W.	Pte	Po8.505
	Cownden, C.R.	AB	167.495
	Dathan, J.E.	Payr	
	Dauncey, A.K.	AB	168.273
	Davis, H.C.E.	Ch/Sto	142.166
	Daw, A.L.	PO1	127.943
	Denison, H.E.	Sub Lieut	
*	Dingle, A.	AB	182.842
	Dodsworth, T.	Pte	Po4.223
	Doughty, A.E.	Sto	288.354
	Downs, G.	Sto	283.988
	Driscoll, W.	Sto	280.036
	Dudman, F.	AB	175.123
	Dunk, J.	Blksmth	340.390
	Durley, H.	Arm/Mte	175.181
	Earley, E.	L/Sto	152.598
	Edwards, A.J.	AB	186.093
	Fagence, J.	Ch/Sto	133.720
	Fanning, B.	Sto	284.578
	Farey, A.J.	AB	185.869
	Fisher, T.	Pte	Po7.239
	Fisk, P.	Sto	278.738
	Floyd, H.R.P.	Comdr	
	Ford, E.J.	L/Sig	178.220
	Gillespie, J.	Sto	282.211
	Gordon, E.J.	Sto	281.785
	Grace, T.	PO2	150.691
	Groves, J.H.	AB	185.873
	Guncill, T.	Ch/Sto	127.600
	Hall, W.H.	Art/Engr	
	Hardie, G.S.	Sto	280.851
	Harman, H.	Sto	281.787
	Harvey, T.	2/Sig	155.389
	Hatch, R.	Sto	283.661
	Hawkins, G.J.	AB	169.007
	Hayward, S.E.	AB	161.563
	Heilbronn, W.R.	AB	170.019
	Hewitt, J.	2/SBStd	153.170
	Hogg, J.T.	Sto	284.028
*	Holdway, W.	L/Sto	151.709
	Hone, W.W.	AB	182.695
	Howe, W.	AB	185.398
	Howgego, W.	L/Sto	171.966
	Hughes, S.	ERA	131.819
	Irish, E.	Sto	287.765
	James, F.	L/Carp/Crew	341.996
	Jerram, A.J.	Pntr	341.649
	Kemp, A.W.	Pte	Po8.504
	Kennedy, T.W.B.	Snr/Lieut	
	Kirby, W.H.	Pte	Po8.651
	Lacey, F.	AB	170.669
*	Lee, W.R.	AB	183.187
	Leonard, F.J.	AB	184.441
	Lessells, R.	ERA	268.797

	Liebermann, F.J.	AB	162.950
	McCracken, H.	Sto	283.972
	McDonald, C.	ERA	269.154
	Marsh, J.	Sto	282.470
*	Martin, J.F.	Sto	142.963
	Maxey, T.L.	ERA	152.680
	Mears, E.	PO1	119.317
	Meredith, C.	Sto	283.743
	Milligan, P.	L/Sto	177.390
	Milne, J.	Sergt	Po2.618
	Muir, W.	AB	181.942
	Newman, C.	Sto	278.170
	Nutley, J.	AB	163.416
	Ousley, H.N.	Sto	284.121
	Padginton, A.W.	AB	183.616
	Page, W.R.	Sto	278.041
	Paine, J.G.	Pte	Po7.253
	Phillips, C.	Sto	285.645
	Pinhay, O.B.	AB	183.358
	Porter, A.H.	AB	186.495
	Powis, T.H.	Gunr	
	Profitt, J.E.	PO2	159.669
	Purdy, L.	L/S	152.910
	Purnell, F.D.	AB	183.408
	Quin, J.	Sto	287.749
	Reeves, W.H.	AB	151.817
	Reynolds, E.R.	Ch/ERA	119.054
	Robinson, I.R.	Sto	283.985
	Rogers, H.J.	Sto	276.703
	Ross, G.T.	Arm/Mte	340.458
	Sanderson, H.R.	2/Wrtr	168.260
	Scott, J.	PO2	141.463
	Scott, W.	AB	182.675
	Shambrook, J.H.	AB	176.895
	Shenton, J.T.	Lieut	
	Sims, A.J.	Sto	276.502
	Sledge, W.G.S.	L/S	167.259
	Smyth, J.R.	Pte	Po4.785
	Sparks, J.H.	L/S	177.307
	Stannard, A.	AB	159.726
	Steedman, W.	Carp/Crew	283.943
	Stockham, R.J.	Sto	287.864
	Sutton, H.T.	AB	183.209
*	Taylor, E.	L/Sto	153.866
	Taylor, J.	MAA	134.750
	Tipper, E.	Sto	281.190
	Ventura, J.	Dom	146.431
	Wardell, E.W.A.	AB	177.255
	Watts, C.W.	L/Shpwrt	340.932
	Wheatland, A.	PO1	162.290
	White, J.	Pte	Po4.154
	Williams, W.F.	Pte	Po8.503
	Williams, W.R.	Ch/Engr	
	Wilson, G.	St/Surgn	
	Wright, J.	Sh/Cpl	149.647
	Wright, L.	PO1	160.650
	Zahara, V.	Dom	119.724

Duplicate medals:

	Ansell, C.W.	AB	182.981
†	Sutton, H.T.	AB	183.290

† Two duplicate medals issued.

Returned medals:

Ellul, G.	Dom	157.929
Mitchell, J.	Art/Engr	
Muscatt, G.	Dom	167.052
Rawle, M.	PO1	136.189
Slim, H.W.	Ord	185.875
Stirling, A.F.	SBStd	169.727

H.M.S. FORTE

Period for which entitled:
11th October 1899 to 16th August 1900

Extended period:
24th June 1901 to 3rd December 1901
5th April 1902 to 11th May 1902
15th May 1902 to 31st May 1902 (Recommission).

Bars	*Total*	*Returned*	*Entitled*
5	23	0	23
4	4	0	4
3	1	0	1
2	10	1	9
1	128	6	122
0	517	102	415
	683	109	574

Notes:
Note 1 – Medal presented by H.M. The King.
Note 2 – Two entries on the medal roll; only one medal was issued.

Bars: Orange Free State, Transvaal, Tugela Heights, Relief of Ladysmith, Laing's Nek.

Ball, T.W.	Yeo/Sig	185.004
Carpenter, W.	AB	176.202
Coote, A.	AB	162.850
Course, A.T.	L/S	168.987
Dennett, H.J.	AB	180.156
Douglas, J.B.	Sto	281.507
Evans, J.	AB	167.339
Finch, J.	PO1	177.881
Frost, H.J.	Sto	281.543
Holland, E.	Gunr	
Hunt, G.P.E.	Lieut	
1 Jones, E.P.	Capt	
Keep, W.	Sto	281.614
Kelly, J.	SBStd	131.893
McCarthy, W.	AB	165.737
Mason, J.	AB	164.450
Moore, F.	AB	158.514
Morsman, F.	Ord	196.702
Small, W.	PO1	138.198
Tume, W.D.	Pte	Ch6.465
Williams, C.R.	AB	158.210
Williams, N.G.	PO1	132.921
Woolnough, H.J.	AB	152.896

Duplicate medals:

Carpenter, W.	AB	176.202
Douglas, J.B.	Sto	281.507

Bars: Orange Free State, Transvaal, Relief of Ladysmith, Laing's Nek.

Byrne, E.H.	AB	171.048
Steel, J.M.	Sub Lieut	

Bars: Transvaal, Tugela Heights, Relief of Ladysmith, Laing's Nek.

Jarvis, W.B.	AB	182.180
Melvill, F.W.	Lieut	

Bars: Transvaal, Relief of Ladysmith, Laing's Nek.

Hooper, G.	Arm/Crew	342.666

Bars: Tugela Heights, Relief of Ladysmith

Brodest, G.	AB	134.273
Campbell, R.D.	AB	182.897
Grove, C.F.M.	Pte	Ch9.105
Kingston, G.W.	AB	163.864
Lilly F.J.	St/Surgn	
Sharp, W.	AB	173.762
Tunbridge, H.	PO1	164.179

Returned medal:

West, C.W.	PO1	115.157

Bar: Relief of Ladysmith

Bramble, C.	AB	175.975
Hicks, J.	L/Carp/Crew	340.215

Bar: Natal

Allen, J.R.	Sto	288.082
Appleby, M.	Sto	162.723
Austin, H.	AB	164.361
Baker, R.A.	AB	192.873
Barr, J.	Ord	196.337
Barraby, D.	Sto	287.514
Bean, A.C.	Surgn	

Bean, D.S.	L/S	151.647
Bennett, V.A.	Sto	282.051
Bergin, J.C.P.	AB	165.647
Blades, H.W.	AB	196.887
Boveington, P.J.	PO1	126.879
Bushell, A.E.	PO1	156.648
Carter, J.E.	L/Sergt	Ch7.933
Chamberlain, G.	L/S	160.467
Chambers, R.	AB	173.842
Chambers, W.J.	Pte	Ch.9.124
Clark, J.	Sto	289.197
Clarke, H.P.	Sto	288.004
Cleave, E.J.	PO1	107.785
Clifford, E.A.	PO1	148.384
Cobb, G.H.	Ord	200.918
Colegate, W.H.	Pte	Ch8.515
Colman, R.W.	AB	181.538
Coombes, J.H.	AB	179.223
Coppin, E.J.	PO1	156.937
Crane, E.B.	AB	154.359
Crittenden, E.G.	Sto	281.505
Cutting, W.	L/S	179.870
Davidson, G.	Arm/Crew	341.665
Davis, G.	Pte	Ch9.871
Dawes, A.	AB	138.256
Dearman, H.	Pte	Ch9.155
Dods, J.A.R.	Pte	Ch9.148
Drake, P.	L/S	181.630
Duxbury, A.	Ord	195.487
Elsey, H.	AB	182.066
Emery, G.	AB	196.046
Fowler, J.C.	Pte	Ch7.452
Freeman, W.	Sto	284.886
Froude, A.E.	Pte	Ch7.446
Fuller, C.	AB	195.964
Gennings, A.	Pte	Ch9.159
Giggins, S.T.	AB	183.748
Gill, J.P.	PO2	156.224
Godfrey, J.W.	PO2	174.760
Grice, J.	Pte	Ch4.965
Griffiths, A.G.	L/S	163.020
Grundy, T.	Pte	Ch9.094
Hammant, J.	AB	189.166
Hawkins, S.H.	PO1	148.378
Higman, J.E.	Arm	341.080
Hursell, H.J.	Pte	Ch9.119
Jackson, A.	L/Cpl	Ch8.004
Jeacock, H.	AB	145.551
Jewitt, T.	AB	173.846
Jezzard, F.	PO2	170.192
Johnson, P.	Lieut	
Kendrick, W.	AB	174.620
Kennet, L.	Sto	281.583
King, H.	AB	167.541
Lane, A.V.	AB	181.861
Langlands, A.J.	AB	164.788
Lewis, E.	AB	195.445
Lifton, A.H.	Shpwrt	342.645
Littlejohns, J.S.	AB	188.344
Lovett, J.C.	Sto	170.116
McGuigan, S.	AB	199.678
McRorie, H.	AB	193.844
Massy-Dawson, F.E.	Lieut	
Miller, F.C.	AB	178.172
Miller, J.	Sto	282.372
Moss, H.H.	AB	158.339
Nevill, D.	AB	151.116
Newton, A.	Pte	Ch7.083
Niven, D.	AB	181.005
Parker, J.	Sto	284.845
Pearcey, A.	Pte	Ch10.044
Perkes, C.	AB	166.919
Pickering, R.H.	AB	190.357
Pigott, J.	AB	150.924
Pitcher, H.T.	PO2	150.821
Porter, W.	Sto	283.022
Prior, A.	AB	200.217
Rainsbury, A.E.	AB	159.709
Rattle, H.	AB	178.637
Rogan, P.	AB	159.845
Rose, W.	PO2	115.702
Rous, W.	Q/Sig	184.284
Rowland, A.W.	AB	172.556
Ruston, P.	Pte	Ch9.052
Saunders, F.J.	AB	162.285
Saunders, J.G.	AB	190.406
Shakeshaft, S.	Pte	Ch10.062
Shorter, G.	AB	161.616
Sims, R.W.	AB	179.585
Singer, H.H.	AB	151.114
Smith, A.E.	AB	170.673
Smith, A.W.	Bugler	Ch4.821
Smith, J.B.	AB	172.066
Soper, F.A.	Pte	Ch7.471
Soper, F.J.	AB	180.104
Staniland, G.	Pte	Ch4.485
Stevens, W.	Pte	Ch4.045
Swinerd, R.N.	Sergt	Ch2.518
Terry, E.	AB	127.853
Thomson, A.B.	AB	193.987
Thorburn, J.L.	Ord	196.324
Toland, J.	PO2	181.008
Turner, A.	Ord	190.042
Vanson, R.	AB	159.262
Venn, A.E.	PO1	128.562
White, J.L.	Pte	Ch7.798
Whittingham, J.	Sto	164.543
Wilcox, W.J.	Q/Sig	138.523
Wilson, H.J.	Ord	196.019
Wood, G.E.	L/S	184.131
Woodward, A.W.	SB/Attn	350.428
Woolgar, S.	Pte	Ch9.872
Wraight, G.	Sto	283.011

Duplicate medals:

Barr, J.	Ord	196.337
Sims, R.W.	AB	179.585
x Turner, A.	Ord	190.042
Wood, G.E.	L/S	184.131

x Two duplicate medals issued.

Bar: Natal *continued*

Returned medals:

Green, H.	Ord	184.920
Harvey, W.	AB	154.005
Mundie, J. alias Simpson.	Sto	284.847
Payne, E.	AB	189.167
Robertson, G.	Sto	165.416
Tickner, J.H.	Sto	158.784

No Bar Medals

Acock, H.J.	Pntr	340.339
Adams, A.	Ord	196.098
Aitken, J.W.	Sto	290.051
Alabaster, H.	L/Sto	152.735
Allsop, J.J.	Sto	285.123
Apps, W.R.	St/Engr	
Ashmore, F.G.	AB	136.478
Baker, G.W.	Ch/Sto	137.776
Banks, R.	ERA	268.806
Barling, H.W.	Sto	281.047
Barton, J.W.	Sto	169.219
Barton, W.J.	Sto	281.682
Batten, G.A.	Ord	196.387
Beaglehole, J.	Shpwrt	114.872
Begg, W.	Asst/Engr	
Bell, A.D.	Ord	196.386
Boaty, W.	L/Sto	131.154
Bolten, W.	L/Sto	127.620
Brassington, S.	Blksmth	162.001
Brookes, H.	Q/Sig	182.603
Brown, T.F.	Engr	
Calabar, Tom.	Kroo	
Campbell, J.Y.	Boy	196.334
Charles, R.	Asst/Payr	
Chisholm, G.	Sto	288.013
Chitson, A.R.	Plmbr/Mte	341.643
Churchyard, W.	Sto	282.995
Cook, J.	L/Shpwrt	132.437
Coward, A.	Dom	354.179
Cox, A.	Sto	281.549
Daines, H.W.	Q/Sig	190.565
Darcey, J.T.	L/Sto	135.017
Davis, W.	Sto	284.887
Deacon, T.H.W.	Carp	
Dean, W.F.	L/Sto	155.232
Di Costa, C.	Dom	356.160
Downes, G.	ERA	269.211
Eastwood, T.	Sto	288.774
Evans, F.A.	Ord	195.956
Everest, W.H.	Sto	288.871
Fairbrass, A.	Sto	284.885
Fever, J.H.	Sto	151.681
Finden, H.W.	Cooper	140.660
Flatley, J.	Pte	Po7.260
Ford, H.G.	Carp/Mte	162.201
Foulger, C.E.	Pte	Ch9.147
Friday, Jack.	Kroo	
Fright, J.	Ch/ERA	120.405
Gambia, F.W.	AB	162.767
German, A.J.	MAA	114.886
Graves, W.J.	Pte	Po9.132
Green, F.	Sto	277.682
Guscolt, T.J.	Sh/Cpl	160.723
Hanley, T.	Ch/Sto	139.897
Harvey, J.H.	Sail/Mte	162.392
Haynes, F.E.	Q/Sig	147.862
Hodge, S.	Sh/Cook	127.535
Hodge, W.A.	Sto	155.187
Humphrey, H.	Ch/Sto	121.626
Hurst, H.	Sto	288.052
Johncock, J.	Sto	155.256
Johnson, F.	Sto	288.841
Jones, G.	Pte	Po6.815
Knott, J.H.	AB	190.946
Lawrence, W.E.	Dom	357.226
Lether, W.H.	Ord	196.328
Love, H.H.	ERA	269.339
Macleod, M.	Sto	284.227
McNab, J.	L/Sto	133.307
Maddy, A.	Boy	201.782
Marno, F.	Ord	202.996
Martin, C.	Sto	165.880
Martin, J.	Sto	288.721
Mason, J.	Ord	196.093
Mathews, W.T.H.	Act/PO	109.842
Matterface, F.	PO1	145.658
Mead, J.R.	Ord	196.331
Medhurst, R.J.	Cook/Mte	340.947
Mehaffey, S.	Dom	357.325
Mercer, H.	Carp/Crew	342.649
Metters, W.H.	Sto	285.015
Miranda, B.	Dom	354.673
Nankivell, G.T.	L/Sto	159.083
Newman, A.T.	Sto	174.265
Nichols, W.H.	Sto	173.115
Norbury, H.	AB	127.139
Oliver, J.	Gunr	
Page, C.	Ch/Sto	143.023
Palmer, John.	Kroo	
Patterson, H.	Q/Sig	144.627
Pearson, S.H.	Sto	290.224
Phoebe, Tom.	Kroo	
Randall, H.W.	Act/Lieut	
Rearden, T.	L/Sto	153.737
Regelous, F.	AB	162.890
Reid, G.S.	Ord	96.326
Richards, C.	Sto	288.769
Richards, R.M.	Surgn	
Rickett, W.	Sto	289.196
Riley, J.W.	Sig	191.217
Russell, R.A.	Dom	357.089
Ryall, F.	L/Sto	167.209
Sanders, E.H.	Ch/Sto	119.659
Saunders, E.	Ord	198.687
Seabreeze.	Kroo	
Shields, W.M.	Sto	289.221
Simmonds, H.J.	Sto	288.083
Simpkins, H.J.	Dom	357.407
Smith, C.H.	Sto	286.918
Smith, J.E.	Sto	281.575
Snowball.	Kroo	

Sparkes, R.C.	Capt	
Steel, G.S.	Bosn	
Stephens, V.W.	ERA	268.437
Stobbart, J.F.	ERA	157.689
Stubbs, T.P.	Sto	288.788
Sutton, J.J.	Sto	288.808
Taylor, W.	L/Sto	136.235
Thomas, E.	PO1	147.291
Tidnam, T.J.S.	Boy	196.090
Tod, Rev. W.M.	Chaplain	
Townsend, G.W.	Sto	285.487
Trainel, P.	Sto	290.050
Tuck, O.F.	Payr	
Twohig, J.	Sh/Std	141.674
Walkey, G.T.H.	Ord	201.610
Warlow, J.	Ch/Arm	157.067
Watling, E.L.	L/Sto	155.217
Watson, A.	ERA	268.563
Watson, G.R.	Ord	187.586
Watts, J.F.	Ch/ERA	146.176
Wellington, W.A.	Pte	Ch9.189
Wilkinson, W.R.	Boy	196.338
Williams, F.G.	AB	185.382
Winter, W.H.	L/Sto	166.442
Woodland, W.F.	Ch/Sto	119.741

Duplicate medals:

Eastwood, T.	Sto	288.774
Mason, J.	Ord	196.093
Tidnam, T.J.S.	Boy	196.090

Returned medals:

Africa, Jack.	Kroo	
Andrews, Jack	Kroo	
Annett, J.	AB	186.778
Barber, W.	Kroo	
Barrett, T.	Sto	168.726
Bestman, Tom	Kroo	
Curtis, T.	Sto	174.443
Davis, S.H.	Sto	285.527
Eber, D.	Kroo	
Elwis, W.	ERA	160.546
Ford, G.T.	Dom	357.383
Freeman, Tom.	Kroo	
Gilbert, J.	Ord	200.772
Hicks, A.J.W.	Sto	288.750
Hill, J.	Sto	288.849
Hixson, A.W.H.	Sh/Std/Asst	170.044
King, T.	Sto	288.700
King, W.	Interpreter	
Lewis, Jim. alias Hirain.	Kroo	
Lewis, John. alias Tom Thumb.	Kroo	
Marker, B.G.	AB	164.384
Marriott, F.	Band	
May, W.G.	Sto	281.580
Milner, R.N.	Ord	196.419
Month, C. alias August.	Dom	132.830
Moralee, T.	Sto	286.976
Murray, T.	Sto	288.712
Odgers, W.	Dom	355.881
Owen, T.	AB	162.785
Perryman, G.	Sto	282.247
Peters, Tom.	Dom	
Plane, Jack.	Kroo	
Pougher, J.W.	Boy	196.750
Royall, T.	Kroo	
Seager, A.C.	Dom	169.768
Stevens, J.	Carp/Crew	342.643
Sutherland, J.	Sto	287.008
Sweeney, J.	3/Wrtr	182.893
Tartar, Tom.	Kroo	
Tickler, J.	Kroo	
Toby, Jim.	Kroo	
Toby, John.	Kroo	
Toby, Tom I.	Kroo	
Toby, Tom alias Plymouth.	Kroo	
Turner, J.	Sto	281.617

EXTENDED PERIOD

Bars: Cape Colony, South Africa 1902

Bunton, C.L.W.	Surgn	
Kelly, J.D.	Lieut	

No Bar Medals

Acott, H.M.	AB	177.997
Adams, J.	Pte	Ply8.638
Alexander, E.	Ord	207.187
Allan, R.	Pte	Ply7.588
Allen, A.W.	L/S	161.215
Amadi.	Seedie	
Ansell, A.	Sto	296.903
Arthur, J.T.	AB	170.422
Baker, J.W.	Sto	298.171
Baker, R.	Boy	211.809
Ball, T.	Sto	293.811
Barber, A.W.	Act/Lieut	
Barnett, W.H.	Sergt	Ply4.828
Barron, H.	Ord	203.574
Barton, J.	L/S	180.656
Basford, W.C.	Ch/Sto	141.272
Bax, W.L.	Sto	172.863
Baxter, W.S.	Pte	Ch11.181
Beales, A.	Sto	276.723
Bell, C.E.	Sto	297.972
Bennett, L.W.	Ord	206.698
Birch, A.J.	Sto	283.788
Birch, G.W.	Sto	293.879
Bird, T.H.	Ord	206.561
Blackmore, W.H.	Ord	211.766
Bond, E.	L/Sig	190.449
Boucher, E.	Asst/Payr	
Bourner, W.H.	L/Sto	277.078
Bowyer, H.	AB	157.350
Boyle, P.	Ord	199.717
Brigden, W.	Sto	298.163
Broom, A.	Boy	211.826

No Bar Medals *continued*

Brotherstone, A.	AB	165.845
Brown, P.	Sto	293.928
Brown, Tom.	Kroo	
Bryan, C.	Ord	203.566
Buck, C.J.	Sto	290.226
Budgeon, G.	AB	189.226
Burrell, F.	AB	192.688
Butcher, R.C.	Ord	172.699
Butler, E.	Pte	Ply10.679
Cannell, J.J.	AB	186.848
[2] Cantell, J.R.	PO1	137.403
Cartlidge, W.	L/Cpl	Ply10.333
Chapman, H.W.	L/Sto	154.123
Clarke, W.A.	Sto	283.483
Clayton, A.	PO1	173.677
Clover, A.	Pte	Ply10.682
Coaker, T.B.	Boy	211.824
Coggan, W.G.	Ord	212.382
Condron, E.	Sto	295.103
Cooke, W.	AB	141.841
Cornelius, A.	PO1	128.981
Cowey, H.	Pte	Ply10.681
Cross, C.S.	AB	164.892
Cureton, W.	Sto	295.134
Cuthbert, G.	L/Sto	176.834
Darlington, G.	Pte	Ply3.442
Daniels, W.T.G.	AB	181.029
David, T.M.	Asst/Surgn	
Davies, R.P.	ERA	269.652
Davis, Tom.	Kroo	
Davis, T.S.	AB	186.283
Dawson, J.	Sto	286.981
Denbeigh, S.H.	Sig	191.510
Dines, G.W.	Pte	Ply10.647
Domaille, F.M.	Arm/Crew	341.118
Douglas, G.L.	Ord	197.524
Dunkley, A.	Pte	Ply8.654
Earl, T.G.O.	2/Wrtr	354.550
Edser, W.H.	Sto	298.029
Ellis, G.W.	AB	184.149
Ellis, J.	AB	194.312
Etherington, C.J.	Sto	289.583
Eversleigh, F.	Ch/Sto	120.463
Farley, R.J.	Ord	212.447
Felton, F.	L/Sto	284.241
Ffrench, C.	ERA	269.789
Field, W.F.	Sto	297.967
Fleming, F.W.	Ch/Sto	129.504
Fletcher, A.P.	Sto	290.203
Fletcher, W.	ERA	269.521
Foster, E.W.	Pte	Ply6.895
Franklin, E.E.	AB	164.434
Freegard, F.H.	Pte	Ply10.666
Gardiner, D.T.	Boy	206.897
Gardiner, L.V.	AB	174.155
Gascoigne, E.A.	Sto	298.148
Gentry, C.W.	Pte	Ply10.597
Gibbons, A.E.	Sto	289.581
Gissing, R.J.M.	Sto	287.573
Godsmark, W.H.	Bosn	
Goldup, H.	PO1	162.292
Goode, W.E.	AB	190.573
Goodlow, G.	L/Carp/Crew	343.165
Grace, R.E.	PO1	166.744
Gray, W.E.	Dom	354.404
Greenland, A.L.	AB	187.377
Grice, F.	Ord	199.705
Grimwood, J.J.	L/Sto	280.329
Gunton, W.H.	Boy	211.821
Hansom, J.	AB	152.889
Harbour, H.	Cooks/Mte	342.404
Hardy, P.	AB	172.915
Harrison, J.	Sto	298.169
Hartley, C.	Pntr	344.342
Hayes, G.	Sto	174.378
Hayward, J.	Pte	Ply8.366
Headlong, J.	Sto	298.117
Helyer, P.J.	Sub Lieut	
Hilder, W.	L/Sto	136.032
Hogben, T.	PO1	145.294
Hogg, W.	Pte	Ply9.559
Hollingsworth, W.	PO1	164.895
Hollow, H.J.	Cpl	Ch8.636
Holloway, D.R.	Ch/Sto	140.414
Holmes, D.	L/Sto	167.285
Hood, J.	L/S	141.693
Hook, H.C.	AB	169.963
Hornby, G.	AB	173.915
Horne, W.	AB	192.273
Horne, W.C.	AB	160.944
Hoskyns, P.	Capt	
Hughes, W.	AB	152.884
Huxtable, J.	Pte	Ply7.763
Innes, E.H.	Payr	
Ireland, T.B.	Boy	211.825
Jackson, W.	PO2	158.687
Jameson, T.R.	Sto	289.580
Jarvis, G.H.	AB	168.418
Jennings, T.G.	AB	168.658
Jones, T.J.	Ord	198.316
Joyce, J.	Boy	212.044
Judd, W.	Sto	298.030
Juma.	Dom	361.070
Keith, J.	Sto	152.404
Lacey, A.E.	ERA	268.695
Lambert, T.	Pte	Ply5.290
Lawrence, W.	Sto	291.613
Leahy, J.P.	SBStd	150.259
Lee, G.M.	AB	190.273
Leech, J.	Sto	297.460
Lewer, A.J.	Sh/Cook	166.988
Longhurst, C.E.	Ord	205.047
Longmate, R.	AB	185.905
Loraine, G.	AB	195.714
Love, W.A.	Boy	211.793
Luckett, G.	Arm	171.949
McDonald, J.	Q/Sig	194.292
McDonald, R.	AB	197.544
McGhie, H.B.	Asst/Engr	
Mahomet, Juma.	Dom	361.686
Mann, G.A.	PO1	121.693

Marryat, H.D.	Lieut	
Marsh, C.P.	Ord	196.734
Mason, J.	Arm/Crew	342.822
Mayers, J.A.	AB	181.106
Mathers, J.	AB	176.735
Meakin, P.	Sto	298.160
Monroe, H.S.	Lieut	
Moon, A.	Ord	182.553
Moore, A.	AB	185.378
Moore, J.	Sto	298.104
Morris, G.	Pte	Ply8.162
Morris, G.	Sto	277.629
Morris, T.	Sto	293.846
Mould, H.	Sto	289.579
Murray, R.	Pte	Ply10.697
Nokes, H.	Art/Engr	
Noon, G.	Sto	298.162
O'Doherty, J.	Ord	205.544
Old, J.T.	PO1	142.663
Osbourne, G.W.	Pte	Ply7.529
Pacey, C.	Dom	358.509
Paddock, F.	Pte	Ply10.694
Page, F.	Sto	298.123
Page, W.J.	Sto	286.336
Pannell, A.F.	AB	174.730
Parker, W.	Sto	298.120
Patrick, A.J.	AB	190.216
Peck, C.	AB	183.660
Pennill, G.	Act/Ch/Sto	149.569
Perkin, F.H.	Ord	205.672
Perram, W.E.	Bugler	Ply10.491
Pescud, W.	AB	194.465
Pettitt, V.	Sto	286.920
Pither, J.E.	Ch/ERA	160.638
Plowman, G.	Sh/Cpl	136.882
Portbury, S.J.	Gunr	
Postle, G.J.	Ord	203.436
Pretty, R.C.	AB	179.906
Prigg, R.	SB/Attn	350.742
Prowse, A.	Boy	211.497
Prynn, J.	Dom	94.770
Pugsley, C.	Ch/Sto	141.106
Ramsay, G.	St/Engr	
Ransom, J.A.	ERA	269.069
Rice, A.B.	Sto	295.142
Richardson, J.T.	AB	189.380
Riches, C.	L/Sto	278.457
Rickwood, P.H.	ERA	268.514
Robinson, W.H.B.	Ord	195.959
Rodgers, P.	Sto	289.596
Rogers, P.	Sto	289.600
Rose, G.	Sto	293.783
Rowe, S.J.	Sto	298.119
Rowse, W.J.	Pte	Ply10.648
Roy, W.A.	Sto	291.101
Rudge, G.J.	Sto	298.118
Ruskin, B.F.	Ord	211.788
Salamin.	Seedie	
Scarlett, G.J.	Pte	Ply10.675
Scott, J.M.	Sto	286.980
Seacy, G.	Ord	205.473
Sealey, J.R.	Pte	Ply3.544
Sheffield, B.C.	Pte	Ply10.678
Shepherd, L.N.	Q/Sig	192.866
Shaw, L.R.	Sto	286.103
Sidell, A.	L/Sto	279.875
Simcox, G.W.	Blksmth	340.074
Simmindinger, W.	AB	188.747
Simmonds, F.	Sh/Std	171.239
Simmonds, R.E.	AB	183.561
Simpson, A.	L/S	181.971
Sircott, T.	AB	192.910
Smith, H.	AB	184.183
Smith, H.W.H.	Carp/Crew	343.909
Smith, J.	Pte	Ply10.665
Smith, J.	2/Cooper	342.514
Smith, J.E.	Carp	
Smith, W.D.	PO2	184.673
Smouton, C.	AB	193.043
Snell, H.	Bosn	
Snowden, H.	L/Sto	279.881
Souza, C. de.	Dom	128.383
Sparrow, W.	Act/Ch/Arm	173.372
Spurgeon, H.	L/Sto	286.921
Stephens, J.M.	L/S	168.960
Stevens, T.	L/Sto	174.414
Stubbings, R.G.	Boy	211.816
Styles, J.	Sto	292.353
Taylerson, W.D.	Sig/Boy	209.017
Taylor, H.	Act/Gunr	
Temperton, W.	Sto	290.202
Thompson, C.	Pte	Ply8.443
Thompson, F.R.	Boy	211.828
Thompson, G.	Sto	286.987
Thompson, W.E.	Ord	195.331
Thompson, W.J.	AB	181.550
Thornton, O.	Sto	298.155
Throp, T.W.	Ord	205.479
Tock, A.C.	L/S	186.653
Tomlinson, W.	Sto	289.585
Traynor, J.	Sto	278.744
Upcraft, T.H.	Q/Sig	185.160
Urquhart, F.	Yeo/Sig	169.626
Vas, Y.P.	Dom	
Waddington, W.	MAA	113.502
Wallace, W.	PO1	153.983
Wardle, J.W.	Sto	172.234
Watling, T.	Ord	200.113
Watson, H.	Boy	211.507
Way, A.H.	ERA	269.214
Weddick, J.	AB	193.944
Weeks, H.	Pte	Ply10.664
Weight, E.W.	Sto	298.156
Welch, H.F.	AB	182.768
Wells, J.C.	Sto	298.168
Wells, W.C.	Sto	289.821
Wentworth, E.	Ch/ERA	127.887
Whittaker, J.R.	ERA	268.148
Whitwood, A.	Ord	191.734
Wickens, C.	Act/Ch/Sto	122.766
Worth, W.C.	Plmbr/Mte	341.531
Wortley, F.J.	Sig/Boy	209.608

No Bar Medals *continued*

Wright, H.W.	Act/Lieut	
Wright, G.J.	Sto	295.522
Young, J.	Kroo	360.013
Young, W.H.	AB	182.579

Duplicate medals:

Ansell, A.	Sto	296.903
Baker, J.W.	Sto	298.171
Burrell, F.	AB	192.688
Clover, A.	Pte	Ply10.682
David, T.M.	Asst/Surgn	
Dawson, J.	Sto	286.981
Gunton, W.H.	Boy	211.821
Mann, G.A.	PO1	121.693
* Mayers, J.A.	AB	181.106
Parker, W.	Sto	298.120
Richardson, J.T.	AB	189.380
Rogers, P.	Sto	289.600
Sidell, A.	L/Sto	279.875
Snowden, H.	L/Sto	279.881
Watling, T.	Ord	200.113
Whitwood, A.	Ord	191.734

* Two duplicate medals issued.

Returned medals:

Amari, A. bin.	Dom	
Barry, J.	Sto	282.117
Boning, G.	Sto	298.164
Briglin, G.	Shpwrt	341.535
Brine, S.	Sto	287.055
Brown, A.E.	AB	186.770
Callaghan, W.	Sto	279.113
Clark, A.	Ord	195.378
Cocker, Tom.	Dom	
Colquhon, T.	Carp/Mte	341.187
Daines, W.A.	Dom	358.961
Daynes, W.J.	L/Sto	161.970
De Souza, C.	Dom	128.383
Eaton, G.A.	PO2	157.979
Forster, T.M.	Ord	205.021
Forte, Ali.	Seedie	
Foulger, J.C.	Sto	292.579
Harding, F.H.	Pte	Ply8.484
Harnisi, M, bin.	Seedie	
Hunt, E.	AB	190.111
Juma, Juno.	Dom	
Kennar, T.	PO2	171.801
Mahomet.	Dom	361.686
Maidment, W.R.	Sto	293.098
Mark, T.	Pte	Ply10.707
Markland, A.	Ord	206.992
Maroff.	Seedie	
Marshall, C.	Shpwrt	169.265
Massey, H.	Pte	Ply3.757
May, W.E.	AB	182.353
Mazaire.	Seedie	
Mesurra.	Interpreter	
Mirazi, K.	Seedie	
Norcott, W.	Sto	281.492
Olney, S.F.	Boy	212.390
Petch, C.F.	Payr	
Peterson, P.	Dom	
Porter, J.	Dom	359.018
Proctor, H.	L/S	155.365
Rose, T.D.	Ord	203.567
Sambo, J.	Dom	359.908
Sambo, Jack	Kroo	
Sayai.	Seedie	
Shuan.	Seedie	
Sierra Leone, Tom.	Kroo	
Smartlad Jack.	Dom	359.340
Smith, J.	Carp	
Sparrow, W.	Act/Ch/Arm	173.372
Stewart, C.H.	Sto	297.371
Stewart, J.	Carp/Crew	344.276
Stocker, C.	Sail/Mte	179.616
Taylor, H.	Gunr	
Thompson, G.	PO1	136.970
Wesley, John.	Dom	
Whiting, A.E.	AB	202.770
Woladi.	Seedie	
Young, D.	L/S	167.471

H.M.S. GIBRALTAR

Period for which entitled:

Extended period only:
13th April 1901 to 28th December 1901
4th February 1902 to 31st May 1902.

Bars	*Total*	*Returned*	*Entitled*
1	4	0	4
0	669	52	617
	673	52	621

Bar: Cape Colony

Bouverie, C.W.P.	Lieut	
Hatcher, J.O.	Lieut	
Hudson, W.J.V.	Comdr	
Lewis, R.H.	Pte	Ch10.297

No Bar Medals

Abbinett, T.J.	Sto	279.600
Adams, C.W.	Ord	200.414
Adams, J.W.	Sto	277.258
Adams, W.	L/Sto	131.949
Adams, W.F.	Ord	195.243
Addington, C.J.	Ord	205.213
Adlam, J.W.	AB	183.376
Aikman, R.	Sto	286.850
Allan, W.	AB	177.128
Allen, A.J.	Boy	210.058
Allen, F.H.	ERA	269.976
Allen, G.L.	Gunr	RMA7.510
Allen, J.W.	Ord	206.900
Allison, J.L.W.	Lieut	
Ames, M.F.	PO1	127.808
Anderson, J.	Kroo	
Arscott, H.H.	Band	164.629
Aspey, W.T.	Dom	359.574
Austin, J.	Sto	276.992
Aylmore, W.P.	AB	195.640
Badcock, W.A.	PO1	151.384
Bailey, A.	Carp/Mte	131.761
Bailey, A.	Pte	Po10.569
Baillie, S.	ERA	269.170
Banks, F.	Sig/Boy	208.065
Banyard, J.H.	Cpl	Po10.228
Barber, F.W.	L/S	171.736
Barker, C.R.	ERA	269.557
Barnard, W.F.	Act/Ch/Sto	133.722
Barnes, W.T.	Carp/Crew	341.031
Barrett, A.	L/Sto	276.619
Bartlett, W.C.	Cook/Mte	167.309
Basketter, W.	Bosn	
Bastable, W.H.	L/Sto	144.786
Bearman, F.	Ch/Arm	124.823
Beattie, R.T.	L/S	175.103
Beecham, A.R.	Act/Bombdr	RMA5.645
Bennett, G.	Sto	297.094
Bentley, W.	Q/Sig	159.181
Berry, T.J.	Gunr	RMA2.153
Bingham, H.	PO1	132.070
Biss, J.	AB	181.541
Blackman, A.	Pte	Po10.571
Blackman, W.	Ord	200.391
Blackmore, P.L.	ERA	269.899
Blunt, A.	Ord	200.058
Booker, G.L.	Sto	295.851
Boswell, G.W.	AB	182.956
Botcherby, R.	Sto	133.013
Bottle Beer.	Kroo	
Bourne, G.	AB	185.101
Bow, A.J.	Sto	173.011
Bowen, T.E.	AB	183.151
Bowie, R.T.	St/Surgn.	
Bradley, A.	AB	189.630
Brehant, H.J.	Ord	205.359
Brent, E.C.	Midn	
Brewer, J.J.	Midn	
Brighton, F.J.	Act/Bombdr	RMA7.585
Brinton, A.J.	Sto	276.869
Bromley, R.W.	Sub Lieut	
Brooks, S.	AB	187.065
Brooks, W.	Sto	295.839
Brooman, S.S.	PO1	152.268
Brough, J.	Act/Bombdr	RMA3.587
Brown, E.	Band	164.621
Brown, G.	Pte	Po9.077
Brown, H.A.	Clerk	
Brown, J.R.	Boy	209.671
Brown, W.	Sto	277.200
Brown, W.G.	Act/Ch/Sto	154.578
Bruce, R.	AB	177.643
Bryan, W.H.	Boy	205.168
Buckingham, H.E.	Ch/Yeo/Sig	145.903
Buckland, R.Q.	Ord	204.778
Bull, E.A.	Sto	290.527
Burch, G.T.	Act/Bosn	
Burnett, R.	Sto	276.820
Burns, W.	PO1	125.146
Burt, J.C.	Act/Carp	

No Bar Medals *continued*

Burton, G.	Ord	203.201
Bussey, B.	Ch/PO	130.577
Butcher, C.	Ord	194.271
Butcher, W.	Boy	206.785
Butler, A.	Sto	286.435
Button, A.	PO1	117.100
Cadogan, F.C.	Midn	
Caffyn, A.E.	Cook/Mte	341.734
Caldwell, W.	AB	191.937
Calton, J.	Gunr	RMA6.036
Cameron, A.	Cpl	RMA8.288
Campbell, D.	AB	177.504
Carney, J.	Sto	277.255
Carter, F.J.	AB	114.159
Carter, T.E.	AB	195.915
Casey, P.	Sto	174.374
Chambers, H.H.	PO1	118.783
Chapman, J.H.	AB	147.000
Chubb, W.G.H.	Gunr	RMA7.701
Clark, C.J.	Pntr	340.253
Clark, T.W.	Ord	199.961
Clarke, A.	Ord	200.938
Clarke, A.W.	PO2	168.915
Clayden, A.W.	Ord	204.977
Cleeve, J.	Sto	287.671
Clinton-Baker, L.	Comdr	
Coaster, J.G.	Pte	Ply9.188
Codrington, W.J.	Surgn	
Coker, J.	Kroo	
Coles, H.	Sto	285.997
Coles, W.J.	Bugler	RMA5.590
Collett, H.	Cpl	RMA6.328
Collins, J.	Ord	199.840
Collis, W.G.	PO1	123.712
Compton, R.	Cpl	Po6.360
Connor, T.	Band	341.878
Cook, A.G.	Pte	Po9.502
Cook, F.	AB	199.535
Cook, J.T.	Gunr	RMA7.232
Cook, M.W.	Ord	205.173
Cook, W.H.	Ord	204.971
Cooper, G.S.	PO1	136.294
Cooper, R.L.	AB	128.553
Cooper, S.F.	Ord	202.133
Cooper, W.H.	Boy	205.186
Coponet, J.A.	Ord	203.978
Copplestone, O.N.	ERA	172.808
Corbridge, W.E.	Blksmth/Mte	342.595
Cotton, A.H.	Boy	215.180
Counsell, A.H.	Sto	295.807
Counsell, G.	Sto	295.829
Cozens, T.R.	Ch/PO	126.325
Crawford, G.	Ch/Sto	119.781
Crees, C.R.	ERA	268.062
Cribbs, J.	AB	136.467
Croker, F.	Sto	148.015
Cromie, J.	Sto	297.290
Crook, A.	AB	176.503
Crotty, B.	AB	189.486
Crout, G.R.	Pte	Ply3.901
Cryan, T.	Ord	206.706
Cunningham, J.H.D.	Midn	
Cunningham, T.	AB	195.135
Curtis, A.W.	Sto	295.834
Curtis, C.A.	AB	195.181
Cutting, G.	2/Wrtr	340.610
Dale, G.H.	Ch/Sto	117.979
Dance, A.R.	Gunr	RMA8.292
Daniels, G.H.	Boy	205.172
Davidson, J.	Sto	280.286
Davies, C.F.	Gunr	RMA7.652
Davies, E.	AB	191.203
Davis, A.G.	L/S	170.026
Davis, S.	Ch/Sto	133.804
Daw, J.H.	Sh/Std	94.434
Day, E.W.G.	Pte	Po6.628
Day, J.R.	Pte	Po8.067
Dayman, W.H.	Band/Cpl	113.554
Dennis, J.A.	AB	181.090
Dick, J.D.	Lieut	
Dodridge, W.R.	St/Payr	
Dominy, W.C.S.	Ord	204.709
Domvile, A.C.W.	Mid	
Donnellan, B.	Ch/ERA	117.000
Donoghue, E.	Ord	197.355
Donaldson, R.J.	Boy	204.936
Draper, W.	Ord	209.361
Duffett, A.E.	Ord	206.916
Duffett, F.	Sh/Std/Asst	342.194
Duguid, A.	Gunr	
Dumbleton, W.A.	Ord	209.152
Duncan, J.H.	ERA	269.301
Dunn, J.	Ord	199.619
Dunstall, W.E.	Sto	295.857
Dyer, A.	Ord	202.487
Dymond, J.	Pte	Ply10.349
Eagle, T.C.W.	Sto	277.011
Eddy, A.H.	Ch/ERA	120.173
Ellcoat, G.	Sto	284.490
Ellender, G.W.	Ord	205.225
Ellicock, A.E.	Sig	204.844
Elliott, W.	Gunr	
Elsey, R.	AB	201.907
Ely, J.	Boy	208.276
Evans, C.W.	Ord	196.291
Evans, S.R.	Sig	203.545
Exall, S.	Ord	199.904
Fairbairn, B.W.M.	Lieut	
Fairborn.	Kroo	
Fairbrass, J.W.	Boy	208.238
Farmer, W.A.	Sto	289.440
Farrance, G.W.	L/Sto	281.894
Farthing, R.C.	Boy	206.791
Faulkner, G.	AB	129.303
Ferrett, A.H.	Sig	202.702
Field, A.	AB	134.872
Field, H.C.D.	Lieut	
Finson, T.	PO1	173.108
Fisher, F.C.	Asst/Engr	
Fisher, W.	Sto	280.206
Flannigan, P.N.	Art/Engr	

Flecknor, A.	Gunr	RMA7.689
Flynn, J.	AB	191.176
Folland, S.J.	Boy	206.915
Ford, F.	Boy	206.165
Foster, E.W.J.	Band	341.304
Fozard, C.	Sh/Cpl	146.880
Frampton, A.	PO1	123.821
Frampton, P.J.	Boy	210.057
Fraser, R.M.	Mid	
Freeman, No. 1.	Kroo	
Freeman, E.	L/Sergt	Ch10.121
Freemantle, R.	Arm	168.565
French, J.H.	Gunr	RMA7.573
Frost, J.A.	Ord	199.947
Fry, A.	Gunr	RMA7.512
Fryer, E.A.	L/Sto	133.738
Fryson, D.W.	Ord	205.154
Gaines, J.A.	AB	198.623
Gale, F.A.	Band	341.748
Gardner, W.F.	Pntr	131.746
Gardyne, E.B.	Mid	
Garwood, H.S.	Engr	
Gaskell, A.	Ord	205.504
Gent, A.W.	Sto	295.847
Gentry, A.E.	Ord	199.975
George, E.E.	Sto	287.891
Gibson, E.R.	Sto	162.309
Gibson, J.	Sto	276.662
Gilhooley, F.	Sto	276.366
Gillard, E.	AB	189.485
Gillett, W.A.	Gunr	RMA7.244
Gillies, W.C.	Fl/Payr	
Glanville, E.	Sh/Cpl	141.864
Glossop, P.A.	Dom	359.302
Glue, A.	Pte	Po10.138
Godfrey, F.	Sto	295.832
Godman, L.	AB	199.252
Goff, S.E.	Ord	206.919
Gollop, A.J.	Ord	215.330
Goodenough, W.E.	2/Cooper	342.811
Goss, G.	AB	188.489
Gout, W.	SB/Attn	350.672
Grant, C.H.	PO1	116.429
Grant, F.J.	Dom	355.489
Gray, H.	Dom	355.949
Gray, W.L.	Ord	199.871
Grayston, E.	Ord	205.449
Green, R.	Boy	205.590
Greenfield, G.	Sto	295.859
Gregory, J.	Ch/Sto	131.851
Griffin, A.	Pte	Po8.392
Griffin, A.E.	Sergt	RMA3.841
Groves, S.C.	L/Sto	165.177
Guile, H.	AB	163.842
Gulliver, J.E.	Boy	205.011
Hailey, G.	Dom	357.546
Hall, E.E.	PO1	123.219
Hall, H.	Ord	206.727
Hallman, A.F.	L/S	178.024
Halloran, M.	AB	194.548
Halls, E.	Blksmth	165.863

Hammond, J.S.	Ord	199.600
Hammond, W.J.	Sto	280.457
Hancock, C.E.	L/Sto	157.238
Hankin, A.J.	Carp/Mte	142.172
Harding, C.W.	Sto	173.002
Hardy, J.T.	AB	195.031
Harris, H.W.	Band	341.613
Harris, V.T.	AB	197.989
Harrison, G.	L/S	149.996
Harrison, H.	Boy	206.743
Hartley, Rev. F.C.	Chaplain & Naval Instr.	
Hartley, W.F.	Ord	205.227
Harvey, J.R.	Mid	
Harwood, H.J.	Boy	204.985
Hayman, F.	AB	176.086
Haynes, W.	Dom	359.204
Hayward, A.E.	Sto	295.853
Hayward, J.	Ord	205.187
Hayward, W.	Sto	286.186
Hazlegrove, G.W.M.	Ord	210.063
Healy, M.	PO1	110.865
Heath, T.	Boy	210.056
Henbrey, W.F.	Ord	199.653
Hendley, T.	Gunr	RMA7.688
Hewish, P.	Ord	206.724
Higgs, P.L.	Pte	Po10.542
Hillier, L.C.	Ord	195.386
Hobbs, H.L.	Ord	204.381
Hodder, W.T.	Ord	200.054
Hodge, D.S.	Band/Cpl	116.559
Homes, H.J.T.	Ord	181.761
Holmes, T.J.	Sto	295.845
Homer, S.	Sto	295.840
Hood, C.T.S.	Ord	205.764
Hook, C.	Sto	297.271
Horwood, J.H.	Sto	295.858
Hounsell, G.	Dom	357.582
House, W.	AB	188.080
Howard, A.	Ord	204.701
Howe, W.D.	Ord	200.064
Hunt, G.	Ord	203.330
Huntley, H.	AB	148.124
Hutson, G.E.	Carp/Mte	141.327
Jackson, E.	AB	198.356
James, C.	AB	186.108
James, J.	Arm	343.947
Jane, H.G.	L/Sig	171.141
Janvrin, R.B.	Mid	
Jarvis, H.	Ord	192.736
Jefferies, G.H.	Sto	295.844
Jefferys, W.	Arm/Crew	167.643
Jelley, W.C.	Ord	195.165
Jenkin, J.	Carp/Mte	153.856
Jew, F.R.	L/S	181.751
Johnson, F.J.	Sto	290.013
Johnson, H.C.	Asst/Engr	
Johnson, W.	AB	198.355
Johnston, W.J.	AB	187.075
Jones, A.E.	Pte	Ply9.467
Jones, E.	Sig	201.967

No Bar Medals *continued*

Jones, W.C.	Ord	194.809
Kelly, P.	Sto	286.882
Kerr, A.	ERA	269.478
Kerr, D.F.	Pte	Po10.057
King, F.G.	Sto	173.814
King, M.	Ch/Sto	121.348
King, W.G.	AB	169.086
Kingman, L.C.F.	AB	190.045
Kitchen, D.	AB	187.242
Knight, A.G.	L/Sea	176.968
Knight, F.J.	Sto	342.354
Knight, G.W.	AB	186.704
Knight, H.E.	PO2	176.903
Lainsbury, W.	Ord	206.601
Lanes, A.	Sto	293.356
Lapidge, W.	PO1	152.955
Lawrence, E.	Ord	199.891
Lawrence, R.W.	AB	177.115
Leadbetter, A.	Ord	199.645
Lee, E.	Sto	171.260
Lee, F.	AB	193.040
Lenty, F.C.	AB	200.416
Lewis, C.La P.	Lieut	
Lewis, H.	Sto	295.919
Lewis, Tom.	Kroo	
Leyden, R.H.	Dom	171.406
Liddle, W.	Gunr	RMA4.319
Lingard, C.	L/Sto	173.800
Linington, J.R.	MAA	112.303
Little, J.F.	Ord	206.777
Littlefield, B.	L/S	177.736
Lloyd, T.	Band	114.842
Lock, H.H.	AB	195.196
Lovett, H.W.	Sto	295.831
Lowman, C.H.	Dom	355.443
Lowman, W.V.	Dom	356.292
Luckham, A.	Ord	205.584
Lyons, W.J.	Pte	Po10.477
McCarthy, C.	Pte	Po10.596
McConnell, T.	PO1	161.525
McCrudden, W.	AB	188.125
McLoughlin, E.	Gunr	RMA8.041
Maconochie, H.	Bombdr	RMA6.880
Macpherson, F.	PO1	171.818
Mace, F.	Gunr	RMA7.300
Mace, W.E.J.	Gunr	RMA8.331
Macklin, S.	Dom	355.813
Madell, C.P.	AB	172.012
Main, G.A.M.	Band	342.280
Major, C.F.	Gunr	RMA8.252
Manning, J.H.	Boy	208.248
Mansell, A.	Dom	356.966
Manser, F.	Blksmth/Mte	342.340
Mansfield, F.	L/S	163.414
Marr, G.D.	L/Sto	280.770
Marshall, A.E.	Ord	206.740
Marshall, P.G.	AB	182.040
Marter, J.	Pte	Po10.554
Martin, F.S.	L/S	176.859
Martin, W.H.	Arm/Mte	342.428
Maunders, F.J.	Sto	295.855
Maxwell, H.G.	Boy	208.875
May, E.F.	Dom	356.022
May, F.F.	Asst/Engr	
Mayston, H.F.G.	Clerk	
Meade, F.H.	Ord	204.886
Meredith, G.F.	Boy	205.732
Merry, C.C.	Asst/Clerk	
Moore, A.W.	Rear Admiral	
Morgan, H.G.	ERA	269.550
Morris, O.	Sergt	Po5.740
Mortimer, W.T.D.	Ord	205.678
Moth, A.E.	AB	201.912
Murphy, S.G.	Pte	Po6.559
Murray, D.	Gunr	RMA7.255
Myers, F.	PO2	162.780
Nelmes, C.	Sto	295.841
Newberry, H.	Ch/PO	130.955
Newell, S.R.	Ord	210.061
Newham, J.	Gunr	RMA8.429
Newland, J.W.	Gunr	
Norton, L.	Sto	284.100
Nunn, A.J.	2/Yeo/Sig	166.228
O'Brien, A.L.	Mid	
O'Keefe, S.T.	AB	149.605
O'Leary, J.	Sh/Cpl	137.116
O'Neil, J.	PO2	177.543
Offer, T.	L/Sto	143.033
Ogburn, J.E.	Art/Engr	
Oldfield, S.	Sto	295.391
Osman, P.C.	AB	176.476
Paffett, W.	Ch/Sto	119.881
Page, R.J.	PO2	182.380
Page, W.A.	Sto	286.871
Palmer, G.W.	AB	182.298
Palmer, G.W.	Ord	206.917
Parish, E.	Gunr	RMA8.137
Parker, A.	Band	340.141
Parkin, W.H.J.	PO1	180.199
Passmore, P.	Boy/Wrtr	344.716
Pauls, T.	Ord	205.845
Pavey, F.J.	Ch/Cook	128.277
Payne, A.H.	Sto	170.778
Payne, W.G.	Ord	210.021
Peacock, H.	PO1	136.381
Peacock, J.W.	Gunr	RMA8.267
Pearce, C.	Pte	Ply10.460
Pearce, W.E.	Cooper	157.073
Pearce, W.J.	Sto	288.641
Pearson, T.H.	Pte	Po7.472
Peate, W.C.	Ord	205.510
Pemberton, J.F.	Yeo/Sig	163.787
Penfound, H.	Bosn	
Pennells, P.W.	Ord	204.757
Pennill, J.	Sto	280.450
Percival, W.H.	Sto	276.700
Perry, W.A.	Sto	286.811
Peters, L.C.	Major	
Petley, F.T.	Ord	205.223
Philbrick, A.	Dom	134.085
Pike, W.	Sto	281.278

Pilbeam, H.C.	AB	198.435
Pilcher, W.E.	Ord	196.370
Pinninger, C.J.	L/Sea	188.358
Pirie, W.	Pte	Po10.540
Pitman, W.	Sto	295.916
Pitt, W.	Ord	201.906
Plumley, F.	Sto	285.648
Podger, C.S.	Gunr	RMA8.343
Pointer, H.	Pte	Po10.553
Ponton, L.H.	AB	197.988
Poole, M.H.	Sto	295.827
Pope, C.R.	Shpwrt	340.161
Powers, G.	Ord	191.999
Pratt, A.J.	Gunr	RMA8.305
Prowse, W.F.	Ch/SBStd	121.000
Pullen, P.C.	Sig	202.570
Purnell, M.T.	Sto	287.756
Putnam, A.W.G.	SB/Attn	350.598
Quinn, J.M.	Pte	Po7.052
Raby, H.	L/Sto	161.285
Race, G.	AB	174.790
Rae, G.	PO1	139.979
Randall, H.C.	Ord	204.956
Reeds, G.H.	L/Sto	168.877
Rees, O.	Surgn	
Reeves, W.H.	L/Carp/Crew	341.024
Remnant, H.	Ord	195.227
Reynolds, J.	Ord	205.797
Robbins, H.G.	Ord	191.262
Roberts, H.	AB	171.528
Roberts, H.E.	Boy	206.604
Robinson, C.H.F.	Sh/Std/Asst	341.536
Robinson, W.M.M.	Midn	
Rogers, G.	Dom	354.514
Rogers, H.	Ord	201.894
Romia, W.H.C.	Pte	Ply7.904
Ropeyarn, Jack I.	Kroo	
Ropeyarn, Jack II.	Kroo	
Ross, J.P.	ERA	268.263
Round, J.	Sto	286.860
Rowe, T.	Sto	287.878
Rowse, B.A.J.	Ord	202.827
Rowse, J.H.	Carp/Mte	142.939
Russell, H.	Asst/Payr	
Salmon, A.	Band	113.192
Salmond, H.J.	Gunr	RMA6.752
Sanderson, A.G.	Ord	206.605
Satcher, L.	Band	341.354
Scotcher, A.	Sto	288.478
Scott, G.	L/Sto	276.821
Seaman, J.H.	Gunr	RMA5.653
Sears, W.A.	Q/Sig	202.667
Selwood, F.	AB	163.395
Shapland, W.J.	Sto	295.843
Sherred, A.J.	Ord	201.899
Shipp, W.	Sto	295.852
Short, E.	Ord	205.580
Short, E.H.	Yeo/Sig	149.654
Shortland, F.C.	Sail/Mte	138.020
Shute, F.C.	Sto	156.699
Simmonds, A.	Q/Sig	179.054
Simpson, T.	ERA	277.556
Simson, A.F.	Lieut (RMA)	
Sinclair, J.Mc.B	PO1	132.937
Slade, G.H.	Ord	206.899
Slydel, H.J.	PO2	173.859
Smith, A.J.	Sto	276.042
Smith, D.	Gunr	RMA7.479
Smith, E.H.	Ord	206.904
Smith, G.F.	AB	158.582
Smith, H.	Pte	Po10.121
Smith, J.	AB	197.496
Smith, J.B.	MAA	133.369
Smith, P.	Ord	206.918
Smith, W.	Band	115.464
Smith, W.	Sto	284.726
Smith, W.A.E.	Ord	200.448
Smith, W.P.	Dom	359.303
Soffe, H.W.	SB/Attn	350.457
Sopp, M.	Sto	285.873
Spencer, H.	AB	192.825
Spicer, G.	Sto	294.467
Spinks, R.	Boy	210.249
Spring, A.	Sto	295.830
Squibb, W.	AB	201.773
Squibb, W.F.	Ord	205.286
Stack, A.E.	Asst/Payr	
Stafford, J.	Ord	195.155
Stafford, T.R.	Carp	
Staines, G.	L/S	96.631
Stamp, T.	Sig	191.430
Stanley, C.	Pte	Po10.752
Starks, W.H.	Ord	205.583
Stevens, H.R.	Ord	195.209
Stevenson, E.	Lieut	
Stock, S.N.	L/Sto	145.434
Stone, B.J.	Sto	295.848
Stone, H.	Pte	Po10.530
Strugnell, J.J.G.	ERA	177.161
Stubbs, A.E.	Ord	206.756
Stuckberry, W.	PO2	152.969
Sturgess, F.C.	AB	179.964
Styles, J.	Pte	Po10.523
Stynes, J.W.	Pte	Ch11.858
Sutherland, R.	2/Yeo/Sig	167.616
Sweeney, A.E.	Band	121.379
Sweetingham, A.E.	AB	180.207
Symes, F.	Sto	286.261
Symmans, H.E.	AB	187.072
Talbot, H.F.G.	Lieut	
Taylor, C.	Sto	286.581
Taylor, E.	Sto	295.861
Taylor, E.S.	Ord	199.983
Taylor, F.	Sto	290.987
Taylor, J.	AB	153.952
Taylor, W.	Ord	198.118
Taylor, W.C.	Band	341.659
Taylor, W.J.	AB	181.107
Tester, J.A.	Act/Ch/Sto	160.006
Thomas, A.	Sto	295.825
Thomas, B.A.	Boy	210.381
Thorne, F.G.	Ord	209.732

No Bar Medals *continued*

Tiller, H.	L/Sto	131.635
Timmins, J.	AB	186.271
Tipper, W.J.	L/Sig	151.969
Titford, G.	AB	187.433
Tod, T.O.	AB	152.856
Tonkin, R.P.	PO2	183.341
Townsend, F.	Pte	Po7.665
Triggs, W.	Boy	205.020
Trinder, H.W.	Ord	194.099
Turnbull, H.P.	Surgn	
Tutton, J.H.	Sto	157.098
Underhill, E.V.	Lieut	
Vanner, G.H.	Q/Sig	167.237
Venables, G.	Q/Sig	203.160
Vernier, J.B.	Dom	359.206
Vigott, F.J.	Sto	289.768
Vining, H.P.	St/Engr	
Wainwright, C.S.	Pte	Po9.960
Walker, J.	Pte	Po7.971
Wallis, J.	L/S	178.634
Walsh, J.	Ord	205.302
Walters, J.S.	Dom	355.814
Wanstall, R.L.	PO2	165.316
Ware, C.M.	Clerk	
Waterman, J.W.	AB	184.913
Watkins, S.A.	L/S	175.974
Welch, J.	L/Carp/Crew	165.021
West, A.D.	Ord	205.001
Wheatley, J.W.	Yeo/Sig	119.268
White, F.J.	PO1	135.444
White, H.L.	Ord	195.037
Whitelock, H.	Carp/Crew	201.853
Whittern, W.	Pte	Po9.372
Willey, W.H.	Sto	295.860
Williams, G.	Sto	285.880
Williams, P.	Sto	289.765
Williamson, C.R.	Sto	286.854
Willis, F.G.	AB	171.170
Willisson, W.W.	Sto	277.008
Wills, W.J.	Sto	295.915
Wilmot, F.E.	Midn	
Wilson, E.W.	Sto	280.270
Winter, J.	Gunr	RMA5.549
Winzer, W.	Sto	295.837
Wiseman, H.J.	Cpl	Po10.474
Wood, C.J.	Midn	
Wood, G.	Sh/Cpl	150.109
Woollands, H.	Plmbr	341.291
Wrixton, H.	Ord	193.755
Yarram, C.	PO1	138.741
Young, E.W.	Ord	205.711
Young, G.	Ord	204.986

Duplicate medals:

Allen, F.H.	ERA	269.976
Aspey, W.T.	Dom	359.574
Bartlett, W.C.	Cook/Mte	167.309
Bowen, T.E.	AB	183.151
Cadogan, F.C.	Midn	
Codrington, W.J.	Surgn	
Dominy, W.C.S.	Ord	204.709
Domvile, A.C.W.	Midn	
Farthing, R.C.	Boy	206.791
Fraser, R.M.	Midn	
Gibson, J.	Sto	276.662
Guile, H.	AB	163.842
Hutson, G.E.	Carp/Mte	141.327
Johnson, W.	AB	198.355
Jones, A.E.	Pte	Ply9.467
Knight, H.E.	PO2	176.903
Myers, F.	PO2	162.780
Page, R.J.	PO2	182.380
Randall, H.C.	Ord	204.956
Rees, O.	Surgn	
Scott, G.	L/Sto	276.821
Smith, A.J.	Sto	276.042
Smith, P.	Ord	206.918
Stafford, T.R.	Carp	
Stamp, T.	Sig	191.430
Symmans, H.E.	AB	187.072
Taylor, F.	Sto	290.987
Triggs, W.	Boy	205.020
Wainwright, C.S.	Pte	Po9.960
White, H.L.	Ord	195.037
Wrixton, H.	Ord	193.755

Returned medals:

Abrams, G.	Dom	356.356
Blackford, B.W.	Ord	179.135
Bowen, A.	Sto	280.226
Brette, P.	Dom	359.948
Brown, J.T.	AB	194.446
Budgeon, J.H.	Clerk	
Davenport, W.	Ch/Band	104.770
Davies, J.	Sto	154.537
Davis, T.	Kroo	
Denny, A.E.	Sto	282.956
Desmond, M.	Sto	287.257
Ellis, G.	Sto	282.545
Emerson, W.	Sto	290.395
Farmer, E.	Q/Sig	198.406
Farrell, R.G.H.	Band	341.881
Fearnley, A.C.	Ord	203.807
Francis, Jack.	Kroo	
Fulford, E.C.	AB	205.659
Gately, P.P.	Ord	200.117
Gibbs, E.	Ord	201.144
Gilbert, J.	Ord	200.772
Gillender, A.	Ord	197.625
Glass, W.	Bugler	Po9.729
Goodeve, W.	Sh/Cpl	150.103
Grace, E.	Ord	198.014
Hands, T.H.	Gunr	RMA8.396
Handy, A.	Ord	202.489
Hewetson, W.	Comdr	
Johnson, L.	Kroo	
King, W.	Boy	210.255
Leach, A.W.	Ord	205.593
Leighton, W.D.	AB	183.885
Moody, F.	Dom	357.838
Moody, J.	Dom	164.101

Noble, P.G.L.	Pte	Ply8.969
O'Keefe, W.	Sto	160.382
Packham, J.	Pte	Po9.498
Peters, A.J.	Dom	357.645
Pilgrim, C.	Sto	202.955
Pollard, J.	Ord	202.471
Samisi,	Kroo	
Simpo, John.	Kroo	
Stephens, W.V.	Boy	215.299
Stonham, H.	Dom	359.300
Thorne, C.W.	AB	186.708
Tubb, H.	Dom	67.427
Ward, C.	Sto	282.959
Waters, W.G.	Sto	282.241
West, A.G.	Sto	210.238
Wright, T.S.	Sto	288.989
Young, G.W.	Sto	282.952
Zahra, V.	Dom	119.724

H.M.S. MAGICIENNE

Period for which entitled:
11th October 1899 to 6th November 1900.

Bars	*Total*	*Returned*	*Entitled*
1	6	0	6
0	250	20	230
	256	20	236

Notes:
Note 1 – Medal roll states, "Medal engraved for H.M.S. Doris."
Note 2 – Medal roll states, "King's South Africa Medal awarded."
Note 3 – Also noted on Medal Roll as "Toms."
Note 4 – Duplicate medal was returned to Mint.

Bar: Cape Colony

Churcher, A.S.	AB	179.311
Taylor, W.	AB	179.871
Wornast, C.	AB	184.111

Bar: Natal

Bench, G.E.	St/Engr	
Fisher, W.B.	Capt	
Harper, J.E.T.	Lieut	

No Bar Medals

Allen, G.	Dom	354.860
Andrews, Joe.	Kroo	
Appleton, A.	Ch/Sto	147.201
Augwin, S.	Sto	287.186
Avery, S.	Ch/Sto	133.118
Babb, H.	PO2	127.140
1 Barnby, H.M.	Asst/Payr	
Barrick, A.J.	AB	159.674
Baser, F.	Sto	354.264
Binding, G.R.	Sto	278.605
Bishop, W.H.G.	AB	189.161
Blake, F.	AB	162.470
Blank, W.	ERA	268.654
Boon, F.	ERA	173.586
Bowering, A.	AB	180.787
Bradley, E.	AB	191.146
Bradley, F.	Sh/Cpl	350.075
Bransfield, W.	Sto	285.691
Brown, H.J.	PO1	126.951
Buckley, M.	L/Sto	115.272
Bull, W.	Kroo	
Burke, J.	Yeo/Sig	138.847
Bye, R.	L/Sto	123.908
Cain, R.E.	AB	165.817
Callaghan, J.	AB	177.007
Candy, H.	AB	164.613
Catt, G.	AB	179.154
Channing, A.	AB	155.007
Charlick, H.	PO1	127.836
Chichester, I.F.	Lieut	
Clarke, F.	Sto	281.012
Clemas, W.	Sto	355.226
Clisham, J.	Sto	285.614
Coffey, J.	Sto	285.305
Collins, W.S.L.	Ch/ERA	153.083
Connolly, J.	Sto	285.690
Conway, J.	Sto	290.291
Cook, W.J.	Q/Sig	111.469
Cottis, H.	AB	188.077
Counter, W.	Sto	174.252
Cousins, A.	Pntr	124.918
Crocker, W.H.	L/Sto	129.372
Cullis, J.	AB	117.577
Curnow, J.A.	Dom	122.161
Curtis, W.W.C.	Ch/Sto	114.248
Davies, D.	Pte	Ply2.094
Davis, Jim.	Kroo	
Dawe, Jim.	Kroo	
Dawe, S.H.	Q/Sig	185.605
Dillon, P.	Sto	153.455
Dixon, G.	Pte	Ply5.170
Dolan, J.	Sto	154.173
Donovan, P.	Sto	285.683
Dore, J.K.	Sto	285.609
Dreaper, G.A.	St/Surgn	
Drowley, T.B.	AB	166.345
Dunderdale, J.	Shpwrt	341.587
Durant, S.	Pte	Ply8.243
Eddey, F.	AB	163.283
Edwards, T.	Dom	356.945
Egan, P.	L/Sto	149.196
Ellam, R.	AB	128.989
Ellis, W.C.	Blksmth	120.755
Emery, J.F.	Dom	357.379
Endicott, W.	AB	179.683
Erridge, A.J.	Cpl	Ch7.310
Eussof.	Interpreter	
Faulkner, T.	Sto	285.694
Flaherty, P.	Sto	153.152

Flynn, S.L.	Sto	280.372
Foster, J.	Pte	Ply4.641
Frost, C.	PO1	133.531
Fuller, R.	Pte	Ply8.228
Gately, T.	L/Sto	167.899
George, Jim.	Kroo	
Gibby, R.T.	AB	172.678
Gillam, C.W.	Pte	Po9.731
Gillard, G.W.	Sto	278.204
Gordon, J.	Pte	Ply8.241
Gough, G.J.	Sto	158.883
Grant-Dalton, J.F.	Lieut	
Greenhill, A.C.	Q/Sig	191.355
Greenway, F.	Sto	280.155
Gritton, J.T.	AB	118.495
Grosvenor, F.H.	Sto	276.716
Halfyard, C.W.	Arm	153.000
Hambly, A.	Lieut	
Hanghins, A.J.	Carp/Crew	341.475
Hanks, J.	AB	160.182
Hannant, S.	L/S	160.620
Harris, C.A.	AB	166.867
Harris, J.H.	Ch/Carp/Mte	132.427
Harris, R.J.	AB	188.838
Harry, E.J.	Plmbr/Mte	342.630
Hart, D.	AB	148.468
Hatch, R.	L/Sto	280.124
Hatherall, G.E.	Pte	Ply7.105
Hayes, J.	Sto	280.666
Herbert, W.G.	Sto	280.765
Heron, T.	ERA	268.397
Hicks, W.C.	Sto	280.963
Higgins, T.H.	AB	189.159
Hill, T.	AB	160.233
Hingston, E.	AB	188.867
Hodges, C.	Sto	285.616
Hogan, J.	Sh/Cook	140.554
Horn, C.	AB	155.947
Hoskin, H.	Sto	119.376
Hudson, J.A.	Asst/Engr	
Hunt, C.	AB	178.431
Hunt, G.	Sto	279.247
Hutchings, J.	Pte	Ply8.232
James, F.	AB	162.830
James, W.J.	PO1	103.728
Jane, W.W.	Ch/Sto	133.106
Jarvis, J.	Sto	353.992
Jenkins, T.	Dom	357.380
Jones, W.C.	AB	159.301
Jordan, T.	Sto	281.372
Kain, W.E.	L/Sto	129.662
Kavanagh, J.	Sto	155.777
Keegan, R.	L/S	152.203
Kift, S.	Sto	285.600
King, J.H.	Ch/Wrtr	133.448
Kitto, W.J.	Gunr	
Labbett, J.	L/Sto	278.856
Lang, W.	AB	174.543
Larrett, A.	AB	179.429
Lawson, J.	Sto	278.957
Leigh, R.T.	Cooper	169.348
Lewis, A.J.	AB	162.888
Lewis, J.W.	PO1	134.978
Lewis, T.	Kroo	
Light, A.	AB	188.850
Littlejohns, W.	Sto	281.936
Lloyd, W.	AB	185.052
Lolley, J.L.	AB	166.277
Long, S.D.	Sh/Std	149.122
Longstreth, F.	AB	174.802
Lower, C.E.	Carp/Crew	341.459
Luce, W.H.	2/SBStd	150.399
[2] Luke, F.R.	Payr	
Lukey, W.	PO2	138.264
Lyne, J.	AB	187.308
Lynott, D.	Sto	285.692
McCarthy, W.	ERA	268.936
McConnell, J.	Sto	285.592
McDermott, J.	Sto	283.038
McDonald, M.	Cpl	Ch9.355
McGrory, J.	Sto	281.027
McKenna, P.	Sto	279.314
Marker, B.G.	AB	164.384
Marriot, S.J.	Pte	Ply8.227
Masterman, G.W.	Pte	Ply7.418
Mereweather, W.	Sto	170.646
Miller, J.S.	Pte	Ply8.242
Morgan, J.	Ch/PO	103.743
Moyse, E.A.	Sh/Std/Asst	341.516
Nadin, C.	Pte	Ply8.229
Nancollas, W.H.	Art/Engr	
Napper, F.	Sto	280.947
Newcombe, S.	Sto	284.757
Newton, G.E.	AB	155.070
Norman, G.	Sergt	Ply3.912
Northcott, E.E.	PO2	138.983
Nott, C.	Dom	355.539
Nugent, M.	Sto	278.282
Nute, D.C.	Ch/ERA	153.082
Olley, W.A.	AB	178.821
Pardew, A.	PO2	150.664
Pawley, J.T.	Sto	279.644
Pearce, R.H.	Engr	
Pearson, J.	L/Sto	166.780
Penrose, S.	AB	155.990
Perring, H.J.	L/Sto	152.090
Peters, W.B.	PO1	149.351
Pocock, W.H.	Pte	Ply3.303
Pope, W.W.	Q/Sig	162.324
Powell, E.	AB	187.965
Power, J.	Sto	281.360
Prynn, R.B.	AB	188.054
Quaine, M.J.	AB	133.825
Quigley, G.	Sto	279.394
Roberts, E.	Sto	280.703
Roberts, J.	Kroo	
Robertson, R.	Sto	289.728
Robinson, C.D.	Sto	191.193
Rolling, S.	L/Shpwrt	153.883
Rose, T.P.	Sto	146.934
Rowbotham, W.	AB	159.679
Saldanha, J.C.	Dom	

No Bar Medals *continued*

Sammels, W.	Ch/Sto	118.655
Sarsfield, M.	AB	163.777
Savill, H.J.	Lieut	
Scott, J.A.	ERA	155.707
Shea, M.	Sto	285.689
Shepherd, J.T.	Sto	278.949
Shirley, R.A.	AB	188.697
Smith, G.W.	Q/Sig	160.651
Smith, H.	PO1	146.571
Smith, J.	AB	164.757
Spear, C.E.	AB	189.162
Stanton, T.	AB	162.418
Stephens, J.	Arm/Mte	340.232
Syred, A.	Pte	Ply8.222
Tatlock, E.T.	AB	157.038
Thomas, R.	AB	101.713
Torpedo, S.	Kroo	
[3] Tours, F.C.	AB	184.566
Tracey, A.	Sto	285.195
Tucker, P.	AB	180.905
Tutton, G.J.	Sto	285.595
Vines, A.W.	Pte	Ply6.255
Walker, R.H.	AB	163.294
Walsh, T.	Dom	355.614
Waters, R.	Sto	280.966
Watkins, S.	L/Sto	174.360
Watson, J.	Ch/Arm	118.810
Watts, J.E.	ERA	142.258
Webb, W.	ERA	268.540
Wharton, J.	AB	157.568
White, J.	Sto	278.527
Williams, C.J.	Sto	279.567
Williamson, J.E.	L/Sto	136.417
Winchester, T.	Ch/Sto	120.375
Wonnacott, H.J.	PO1	159.228
Wood, W.A.	Ord	188.927
Wood, W.J.	Blksmth	153.270
Woodley, R.	Sto	283.312
Yabsley, N.	Sto	280.394

Duplicate medals:

Babb, H.	PO2	127.140
Dawe, S.H.	Q/Sig	185.605
Endicott, W.	AB	179.683
Gateley, T.	L/Sto	167.899
Gillam, C.W.	Pte	Po9.731
Harris, R.J.	AB	188.838
Larrett, A.	AB	179.429
Lynott, D.	Sto	285.692
Moyse, E.A.	Sh/Std/Asst	341.516
Pawley, J.T.	Sto	279.644
[4] Tatlock, E.T.	AB	157.038
White, J.	Sto	278.527

Returned medals:

Bull, Jim	Kroo	
Crow, Jim.	Kroo	
Dark, Jim.	Kroo	
Fleming, Jim alias Tom Porter	Kroo	
Fleming, P.	AB	134.481
George (2), Jim alias Tom Cocoa.	Kroo	
Jim	Interpreter	
Jordan, P.	Sto	153.172
Keating, M.	Sto	290.786
Lewis, Bestman.	Kroo	
Marchman, C.	Sto	
Niwan, Tom.	Kroo	
Parnell, S.	Kroo	
Peterson, H.R.	Sto	284.290
Purser, W.	Kroo	
Salt, Tom.	Kroo	
Savage, Jack.	Kroo	
Seamen, Jim.	Kroo	
Simmonds, A.E.	Sto	285.618
Tillard, P.T.	Capt	

H.M.S. MAGPIE

Period for which entitled:
12th November 1900 to 8th March 1901

Extended period:
9th March 1901 to 21st June 1901
27th October 1901 to 12th May 1902.

Bars	*Total*	*Returned*	*Entitled*
2	1	0	1
1	13	0	13
0	81	6	75
	95	6	89

Bars: Cape Colony, South Africa 1902

Brailey, E.G.	Pte	Ply6.017

Bar: Cape Colony

Bobbett, H.C.	AB	202.193
Boobier, J.E.B.	AB	150.674
Couling, G.H.R.	AB	190.693
Currey, T.H.	AB	197.405
Driscoll, C.	AB	193.914
Dungey, W.	AB	111.751
Dyas, C.	Ord	196.133
Evans, W.M.	AB	163.002
Gidley, F.S.	Gunr	
Kenyon, R. de G.	Sub Lieut	
Rowe, T.	L/S	181.702
Smith, J.W.	PO1	115.395
Whitehouse, S.	AB	162.325

Duplicate medal:

Smith, J.W.	PO1	115.395

No Bar Medals

Aitey, Tom.	Dom	
Atkinson, J.W.	ERA	269.355
Bevan, E.C.	Sto	290.392
Bloomfield, E.	Pte	Ply5.483
Blumson, G.J.	AB	195.204
Brewer, F.	ERA	165.099
Brown, J.	Ch/Sto	142.427
Bryan, J.	Pte	Ply6.157
Butler, J.	Sto	292.371
Canning, G.	L/S	114.078
Clarke, W.	L/S	141.070
Cole, Jim.	Kroo	
Connolly, M.	Sto	283.840
Crew, Jim.	Kroo	
Cridlin, W.E.	Dom	357.568
Davis, W.	PO2	130.216
Downing, G.W.	L/Sig	160.251
Edgcombe, R.	AB	157.208
Freeman, Tom.	Kroo	
Frost, G.	AB	139.126
Ham, A.J.	AB	112.335
Hanna, J.A.P.	AB	181.951
Herd, W.J.	AB	192.304
Jackson, L.	Art/Engr	
Jumbo, Tom.	Kroo	
Kahoon, C.H.	2/SBStd	350.384
Laird, J.K.	Lieut	
Langman, A.	Arm/Mte	340.188
Lavis, R.	Sto	280.696
Lewis, John.	Kroo	
McCarthy, T.	Sto	279.566
McClure, R.	L/Sto	117.458
McKee, A.	AB	197.520
Macey, J.W.T.	Carp/Mte	98.327
Maker, T.J.	AB	133.662
Noah, Jim.	Kroo	
Pain, A.	2/Wrtr	160.361
Parrack, F.J.	Ch/Sto	162.181
Peter, Tom.	Kroo	
Radmore, J.F.	PO1	134.973
Rice, A.A.	AB	194.829
Richards, Bob.	Dom	
Richards, R.A.	Sub Lieut	
Richards, W.G.M.	AB	190.146
Rogers, C.	L/Sto	127.283
Rowe, E.	Pte	Ply4.713
Shannon, W.G.	Ch/Sto	127.536
Smith, J.	Sto	290.825
Southwood, W.	AB	172.974
Stevens, W.F.	Pte	Po8.818
Stone, F.T.	AB	196.403
Sweeney, P.	Pte	Ply4.288
Thomas, A.W.	Ch/ERA	141.075
Tree, Tom.	Kroo	
Trist, A.D.	AB	167.516
Tucker, R.M.	PO1	123.163
Underwood, J.G.	AB	152.913
Vanstone, F.W.	Sh/Std	138.113
Vickers, J.	AB	135.659
Wall, T.	Pte	Ply4.599
Welch, E.W.	Dom	357.777
Whiteside, H.C.	Surgn	
Winkworth, H.	2/Sh/Cook	176.650
Worsley, W.G.	AB	196.122

No Bar Medals *continued*

Duplicate medals:

* Atkinson, J.W.	ERA	269.355
McCarthy, T.	Sto	279.566
Smith, J.	Sto	290.825

* Two duplicate medals issued.

Returned medals:

Carroll, W.E.	Pte	Ply6.085
Crowley, J.	AB	140.718
Harris, H.	Pte	Ply5.152
Morris, R.G.	Pte	
Smith, J.	Pte	Ply8.578

EXTENDED PERIOD
No Bar Medals

Adams, W.R.	AB	186.609
Ball, C.	Ord	206.909
Broom, F.W.	Pte	Ply10.407
Courtney, V.	Boy	206.898
Donovan, G.P.	Q/Sig	169.953
Hollier, W.J.	Sig	206.304
Hunter, J.	ERA	269.272
Luby, F.W.	Boy	206.768
McMullen, P.	Pte	Ply9.648
Mathews, R.J.	Pte	Ply4.288
Topliss, A.	Boy	205.792

Duplicate medals:

Adams, W.R.	AB	186.609

Returned medal:

Penha, J.B.	Dom	359.868

H.M.S. MONARCH

Period for which entitled:
11th October 1899 to 8th March 1901

Extended period:
9th March 1901 to 31st May 1902.

This medal roll has been damaged resulting in some loss to nearly 17% of the entries.

It has been possible by reference to other sources to recover some of these lost details and where appropriate these have been included. Missing detail is indicated in the roll by the use of brackets, but the spaces inside the brackets are not intended to indicate the exact amount of missing detail. Where the first letter of the surname is known, an entry will be found at the end of that letter's section of the listing.

Bars	*Total*	*Returned*	*Entitled*
8	17	0	17
7	39	0	39
6	52	2	50
5	18	0	18
4	20	2	18
3	33	2	31
2	40	3	37
1	63	5	58
0	969	157	812
Unknown	11	–	11
	1262	171	1091

* Medal presented on Ophir.
\+ Medal presented on Juno.

Note 1 – A duplicate medal was also issued and this, too, was returned.
Note 2 – Also noted on the roll as Gallienne.
Note 3 – This medal was returned but later restored to the recipient's family.
Note 4 – Same man as Constable, A., (Ch11.063); this medal was returned.
Note 5 – Medal roll states, "No medal – Employed on staff of Army and received Gratuity from War Office, presumably he also received the medal."
Note 6 – Although unclear from the roll, this medal may have been restored to the recipient in 1940.
Note 7 – Two medals issued in error; this one was returned.
Note 8 – One of these medals may be to Milham, F.J., A.B., 184.664 whose medal for H.M.S. Partridge was returned, "Received medal for service in Monarch."

Bars: Belmont, Modder River, Paardeberg, Driefontein, Johannesburg, Diamond Hill, Belfast, Relief of Kimberley

Barfoot, W.C.	AB	178.218
Davis, W.A.	PO2	168.141
Fisher, W.S.	AB	170.190
Frater, J.T.	AB	184.665
Fuller, E.F.	PO1	102.649
Gilroy, J.T.	AB	184.646
Grimani, F.	AB	154.420
Green, J.C.	AB	176.356
Hayden, T.	AB	187.911
Holley, W.	L/S	183.520
Knudsen, H.G.	L/S	179.337
Lawrence, E.J.	Ord	185.018
Lowe, E.E.	Gunr	
Mayne, A.H.	AB	157.162
Smith, F.C.	L/S	154.346
Smith, G.F.	AB	163.387
Woodward, L.	L/S	144.115

Duplicate medal:

Green, J.C.	AB	176.356

Bars: Belmont, Modder River, Paardeberg, Driefontein, Johannesburg, Diamond Hill, Belfast

Adams, A.	Pte	Po7.232
Arthur, R.T.	Gunr	RMA5.712
Blades, W.B.	AB	184.295
Breame, R.J.	Pte	Ch9.122
Broadbent, A.B.	Act/Bombdr	RMA4.663
Bull, W.	Pte	Ch10.083

Bars: Belmont, Modder River, Paardeberg, Driefontein, Johannesburg, Diamond Hill, Belfast *continued*

Burgess, S.	Gunr	RMA1.366
Burroughs, E.	L/Sergt	RMA4.281
Collins, A.	Pte	Ch6.637
Duffield, A.	Bugler	Po8.673
Earle, E.	Gunr	RMA5.639
Freeman, H.	Pte	Ch8.588
Harrison, J.	Pte	Ply8.072
Hepton, J.	Sto	278.585
Johnson, H.	Gunr	RMA6.209
Jago, W.J.	PO1	127.684
Keeler, J.G.	AB	178.372
Knox, D.F.G.	Gunr	RMA4.339
Lorden, J.	Pte	Ch9.331
McCullock C.W.G.	Pte	Ch8.758
McFaul, J.J.	Pte	Ch10.061
Marchant, A.E.	Major(RMLI)	
* Norris, J.	Gunr	RMA4.367
Parry, J.	Gunr	RMA3.647
Polley, E.A.	Pte	Ch10.134
Porter, W.H.	Pte	Ch8.590
Read, R.T.	L/S	179.330
Rochford, J.	AB	137.245
Sanderson, W.	Pte	Ch7.785
Silsby, J.	Ord	188.548
Stanford, W.A.	AB	148.089
Stevens, D.	Gunr	RMA5.915
Thomas, G.	Gunr	RMA5.026
Tims, J.	L/Cpl	Ch7.033
Trayfoot, A.E.	Act/Bombdr	RMA5.565

Duplicate medal:

Read, R.T.	L/S	179.330

Bars: Belmont, Modder River, Paardeberg, Driefontein, Johannesburg, Diamond Hill, Relief of Kimberley

Hutchinson, A.E.	AB	167.800

Duplicate medal:

Hutchinson, A.E.	AB	167.800

Bars: Belmont, Modder River, Paardeberg, Driefontein, Johannesburg, Belfast, Relief of Kimberley

Ellis, A.	AB	154.018

Bars: Paardeberg, Driefontein, Johannesburg, Diamond Hill, Belfast, Relief of Kimberley, Cape Colony

Gray, E.J.	L/S	172.658
Penny, H.H.	AB	177.309

Duplicate medal:

Gray, E.J.	L/S	172.658

Bars: Belmont, Modder River, Paardeberg, Driefontein, Johannesburg, Diamond Hill

Ashard, E.G.	Gunr	RMA5.666
Compton, R.W.	Pte	Ch4.872
Hippisley, G.A.	Gunr	RMA6.425

Bars: Paardeberg, Driefontein, Johannesburg, Diamond Hill, Belfast, Cape Colony

Adams, D.	Pte	Po7.578
Allen, F.E.	Pte	Ch4.799
Angell, J.	Pte	Ply8.577
Avery, T.G.	AB	184.669
Baker, H.J.	AB	165.484
Barrett, F.H.	PO1	104.373
Barry, J.	AB	170.533
Boyd, R.	Col/Sergt	RMA2.543
Brien, J.	Ch/PO	109.292
Browning, W.C.	PO1	136.960
Burr, H.N.	AB	179.558
Cass, A.T.	Pte	Ch9.711
Clements, A.	Pte	Po9.140
Donovan, J.	AB	149.109
Driscoll, J.	Ord	165.565
French, A.H.	Lieut(RMLI)	
Harris, C.	Pte	Ply9.287
Jackson, A.	Gunr	RMA7.161
Jackson, W.	Col/Sergt	Ch3.410
James, A.E.A.	L/S	167.819
Johnson, J.	Gunr	RMA3.053
Keilans, F.	Pte	Ply8.633
McGreny, T.B.	AB	185.760
Marshman, E.A.	Gunr	RMA4.568
Miller, S.T.	AB	178.612
Newman, E.J.K.	Lieut	
Olding, T.H.	AB	176.958
Osborne, J.J.	L/S	128.712
Painter, W.	Pte	Ply8.591
Paull, E.	Pte	Po9.138
Phillips, F.W.	Cpl	Po9.548
Robinson, G.	PO2	161.784
Rogers, W.H.C.	Gunr	RMA7.158
Russell, J.	Pte	Po9.541
Scadden, W.G.	AB	170.601
Searle, A.G.	Pte	Ch9.748
Sings, J.	AB	189.104
Smith, M.W.	AB	155.897
Snell, F.	AB	160.321
Stevens, G.E.	Gunr	RMA7.039
Tinmouth, F.	AB	161.885
Tuck, F.	Pte	Po9.408
Wathes, P.O.C.	Pte	Po9.665
Waugh, H.L.	AB	151.974
Webber, J.	Pte	Ply8.763
Wheeler, G.	Sergt	Ply8.647
Williams, A.	Pte	Ply9.280

Duplicate medal:

x Sings, J.	AB	189.104

x Two duplicate medals issued.

Returned medals:

Kennday, J.	Sto	277.029
Kennedy, P.	AB	172.670

Bars: Belmont, Modder River, Paardeberg, Driefontein, Relief of Kimberley

	Dean, F.W.	Snr/Lieut	
	Harvey, E.A.	AB	169.446
*	Read, W.G.	AB	182.574
	Strike, R.W.	PO2	131.295
	West, E.	L/S	166.595
	Wilson, J.W.	AB	134.686

Duplicate medals:

Read, W.G.	AB	182.574
West, E.	L/S	166.595

Bars: Paardeberg, Driefontein, Johannesburg, Diamond Hill, Cape Colony

Carter, S.L.	Pte	Ch10.411
Comben, R.C.T.	AB	183.418
Davidson, J.	Gunr	RMA7.169
Goodyear, W.	Pte	Ch9.734
Perkins, W.	Act/Bombdr	RMA7.436
Smith, R.	2/Yeo/Sig	160.188
Tunnicliffe, P.	PO1	157.437
Turner, J.	Pte	Ply8.770
York, J.	Pte	Ch6.509

Bars: Johannesburg, Diamond Hill, Belfast, Wittebergen, Cape Colony

Carter, A.	Sergt	RMA2.966

Bars: Johannesburg, Diamond Hill, Belfast, Cape Colony, Orange Free State

Back, E.C.P.	Lieut	
Wilson, L.O.	Lieut(RMLI)	

Bars: Belmont, Modder River, Paardeberg, Driefontein

	Brown, W.J.	Gunr	RMA3.283
	Davies, H.C.	AB	181.010
	Deyes, M.P.	AB	185.895
	Ditch, C.	Act/Cpl	Ply5.796
	Easterbrook, E.	Sto	276.955
	Farmborough, J.	AB	182.489
	Fido, T.	AB	143.807
	Hawkings, A.	Pte	Po8.868
*	Herring, C.R.	Gunr	RMA4.540
	Holloway, W.	Gunr	RMA4.520
	Howard, J.H.	Gunr	RMA3.893
	Morcambe, W.	Gunr	RMA5.361
	Poole, H.	AB	187.985
	Read, J.	Gunr	RMA5.715
	Smith, A.	Gunr	RMA5.679

Duplicate medals:

	Deyes, M.P.	AB	185.895
x	Easterbrook, E.	Sto	276.955

x Two duplicate medals issued.

Bars: Paardeberg, Driefontein, Johannesburg, Cape Colony

De Horsey, S.V.Y.	Comdr	

Returned medal:

Stokes, W.P.	Pte	Ply8.675

Bars: Driefontein, Diamond Hill, Belfast, Cape Colony

Returned medal:

Harding, E.H.	Pte	Ch10.362

Bars: Johannesburg, Diamond Hill, Belfast, Cape Colony

Phillips, F.	2/SBStd	350.290

Bars: Transvaal, Tugela Heights, Relief of Ladysmith, Laing's Nek

Hemsley, A.E.	AB	171.602

Bars: Paardeberg, Driefontein, Cape Colony

	Abinett, W.G.	AB	187.530
*	Amos, J.E.	Gunr	RMA4.197
+	Barwell, W.	Pte	Po9.471
	Beggs, J.	Dom	357.116
	Channon, J.	Pte	Ply8.520
	Coew, W.J.	Sergt	RMA4.896
	Cullimore, H.	Sergt	RMA2.772
	Curtis, J.F.	AB	164.045
	Daniels, W.	Pte	Po9.139
	Ford, A.T.	L/S	130.211
	Gardner, J.	Gunr	RMA6.003
	Henley, W.H.	AB	187.598
	Izzard, H.	Pte	Ch9.084
	Jeanes, W.	Gunr	RMA4.271
	Mackintosh, R.S.	Pte	Ply8.514
	Mason, A.P.	Pte	Ch5.929
	Mason, J.E.	Pte	Ch10.364
	Moore, G.	Pte	Ch9.687
	Morgan, R.H.	Capt(RMLI)	
	Morris, E.	AB	150.767
	Oliver, G.W.	Pte	Po7.593
	Poe, W.S.	Lieut(RMA)	
	Richardson, J.H.	Sto	276.784
	Sebon, D.	Pte	Ply8.252
	Semmens, J.	PO2	159.698
	Skipp, A.	AB	175.049
	Smeed, T.E.	Pte	Po8.514
	Stevenson, W.H.	Pte	Ch10.342
	Whitehead, J.	Sto	281.040
	Wiles, G.	Gunr	RMA4.051
	Winning, F.	Gunr	RMA7.171

Duplicate medal:

Morris, E.	AB	150.767

Returned medal:

Edwards, H.J.	2/SBStd	250.304

Bars: Johannesburg, Diamond Hill, Cape Colony

Returned medal:

Walker, G.A.R.	Pte	Ch9.467

Bars: Belmont, Modder River

Allchin, G.	Gunr	RMA3.736
Brinkhurst, E.	Pte	Ch8.623
Brown, C.F.	Gunr	RMA5.052
Bussey, R.	Pte	Ch8.313
Dean, G.J.	AB	147.885
Dean, H.	Act/Cpl	Ch7.365
Dyson, G.H.	Col/Sergt	RMA1.478
Edgson, W.H.	Sergt	Ch2.774
Farrant, C.	Pte	Po8.883
Gosling, A.E.C.	Gunr	RMA4.948
Keeler, G.W.	Sto	282.365
Kemp, E.	Pte	Ch4.981
Leach, D.	Sergt	Ch4.216
Lyne, A.E.	Cpl	Ch8.222
McShane, G.	AB	167.019
Martin, E.	Gunr	RMA6.111
Miller, J.B.	L/S	144.557
Rooke, G.L.	Pte	Ch5.208
Spencer, W.F.	Gunr	RMA5.866
Stubbs, H.C.	Gunr	RMA5.329
Thompson, B.	Ord	188.486
Vass, A.	Pte	Ch8.303

Bars: Paardeberg, Cape Colony

Porter, T.E.	Bugler	Po8.895
Roche, F.C.	AB	156.220

Returned medals:

Doyle, F.	AB	184.651
[1] Robinson, F.	Pte	Ply8.628

Bars: Belfast, Cape Colony

Bull, T.A.	Cpl	Ch7.481

Bars: Cape Colony, Orange Free State

Duncan, H, McR,	AB	188.644
Goy, A.	Ord	201.313
Jones, H.	Comdr	
Martin, J.W.	Pte	Ch9.479
P( ), R.	AB	(.)
R( ), G.	AB	(.)

Bars: Cape Colony, South Africa 1901

Lugg, R.J.	Ord	196.691

Bars: Cape Colony, South Africa 1902

Beith, R.D.	Capt(RMLI)	

Bars: Tugela Heights, Relief of Ladysmith

Dacey, J.	AB	139.228
Derbyshire, A.	AB	136.339
Elston, H.	Ord	190.595
Hoare, G.	AB	163.393

Returned medal:

Clements, G.	AB	187.642

Bar: Belmont

Austin, S.	Ord	187.211
Bennett, A.	Gunr	RMA4.408
Clark, W.	Gunr	RMA4.068
Cotton, H.	Pte	Po6.872
Cunnington, G.R.	Gunr	RMA3.444
Foster, A.	Gunr	RMA5.942
Gill, G.	Sergt	RMA4.335
Hurst, H.T.	AB	188.362
Johnson, W.G.	Pte	Po8.884
Morcambe, W.	Gunr	RMA5.335
Pape, B.H.	Gunr	RMA3.889
Radford, F.H.	Pte	Ply7.470
Rigsby, F.T.	Pte	Ply5.157
Senior, G.	Capt(RMA)	
Simons, J.	Pte	Ch9.995
Steele, J.T.	Pte	Po8.886

Bar: Cape Colony

Beamish, W.F.	Ord	197.814
Brickwood, F.R.S.G.	Ch/Wrtr	155.668
Bruce, R.D.B.	Capt	
Brunt, E.F.	AB	170.412
Collins, E.J.	Pte	Ply8.481
Constable, A.	Pte	Ch11.063
Cudmore, A.	AB	130.272
Culley, A.	AB	110.137
Doncaster, W.	Ord	
Dowling, R.W.	2/SBStd	350.352
Elliott, F.	Gunr	
Ellis, W.M.	AB	139.533
Foulkes, P.	Ord	201.329
Gill, C.	AB	185.154
Grant, S.	SBStd	131.257
[2] Gullicane, H.	2/SBStd	350.388
Howell, E.	Pte	Po8.802
Hughes, W.H.	Gunr	RMA6.512
Johnson, F.I.M.	Ch/Gunr	
Layland, W.	AB	201.326
Lillywhite, G.	2/SBStd	(0.476)
Loram, W.C.	PO1	148.227
Lucas, W.H.	2/SBStd	351.254
McCougherty, D.	AB	176.815
Moat, E.T.	AB	169.955
Morris, W.F.	AB	190.498
Nye, H.W.	AB	187.378
Payne, T.G.	Ord	197.277
Pleasance, P.	AB	180.349
Reed, S.G.	Ord	193.627
Rickard, S.	Ord	199.089
Roberts, E.N.	AB	180.862
Skippen, D.	AB	(. 3)
Smith, T.	Sto	165.431
Stopford, J.	Pte	Ch8.693

Stupple, H.J.	SBStd	140.877
Todd, J.	Gunr	RMA2.770
Tubb, S.	Ord	(1.588)
Westaway, W.H.	AB	159.094
Wood, A.H.	Pte	Ch9.799
Woodhead, G.W.	AB	175.800

Duplicate medal:

Foulkes, P.	Ord	201.329
Lucas, W.H.	2/SBStd	351.254

Returned medals:

Adams, R.W.Q.	AB	176.960
Finch, S.W.	Clerk	
McNully, J.	Ord	201.587
Tretheway, A.	AB	(. 61)

Bar: Natal

Higgins, C.	Gunr	

Returned medal:

Edwards, W.	PO2	117.357

No Bar Medals

Addison, G.E.	AB	184.037
Ahern, J.	AB	191.188
Aherne, D.	PO2	134.963
Ahrens, W.	SB/Attn	350.442
Aldington, W.H.	Pte	Ch9.837
Alexander, A.	Pte	Ply8.697
Alexander, E.	Sto	280.596
Allan, G.	L/Sergt	Ply8.766
Allison, F.	Ord	188.541
Anderson, W.	Ord	201.319
Andrews, A.	Sig	184.421
Andrews, A.	SBStd	350.264
Anscombe, W.J.	Ord	193.555
Appleby, W.	L/Sto	284.788
Armstrong, J.	Ord	198.589
Ashby, E.E.	Boy	197.871
Ashdown, G.A.	Ord	197.559
Aslett, J.	AB	185.338
Assell, W.	Pntr	341.323
Atkins, F.G.	Plmbr	143.967
Avent, E.	L/S	144.269
Avery, E.J.	AB	187.652
Bailey, R.	Dom	(57.543)
Baird, C.R.	AB	185.778
Baldwin, W.E.	Sto	280.608
Bales, W.N.	Pte	Ch10.405
Barker, C.	Asst/Engr	
Barker, R.G.	Pte	Po1.977
Barnard, W.H.	Sto	287.572
Barnes, C.	Ord	197.807
Barrow, T.P.	Act/Ch/ERA	145.535
Bartholomew, A.	Sh/Cpl	350.082
Basquill, J.	Sto	277.928
Bassett, F.H.	L/Cpl	Ch7.283
Batchelor, A.J.	Sto	281.609
Batters, G.T.	L/Sto	144.753
Bayly, C.H.	Capt	
Beal, H.	Sto	285.941
Beaney, A.E.	AB	182.377
Beard, H.C.	PO2	159.127
Beazley, W.	Ord	190.480
Beazley, W.H.	Ord	202.995
Bell, R.	AB	186.903
Bennett, F.	Ch/ERA	141.869
Best, O.G.	AB	184.344
Bestman, T.	Kroo	
Bilton, W.L.	Sto	293.156
Blackmore, V.E.	Pte	Po9.155
Blake, F.	L/Cpl	Po5.311
Blanchard, W.C.	Ord	178.219
Blewett, C.	Pte	Ch6.721
Blockley, J.A.	PO1	132.052
Blundell, G.H.	Blksmth/Mte	287.883
Boaden, W.J.	L/Sto	133.810
Bone, H.G.	Pte	Ch9.356
Boorman, F.	AB	157.161
Borras, J.	Sto	168.878
Boulton, E.A.	Pte	Po9.830
Boulton, T.	Sto	282.897
Bowden, R.	Bosn	
Bracegirdle, J.	Pte	Ply6.225
Bray, R.W.	Ord	196.994
Brian, J.	L/Sto	153.438
Brice, S.J.	3/Wrtr	340.061
Bridgehouse, J.	Dom	355.137
Brislow, S.G.	Ord	200.251
Brook, V.A.	Asst/Engr	
Brooks, W.R.	L/S	122.369
Brown, A.	Act/Engr	
Brown, J.	Kroo	
Browne, D.	Carp/Crew	342.318
Bryce, L.	PO1	129.227
Buck, F.P.	Pte	Ch5.557
Buckley, J.	Sto	171.299
Budd, W.T.	Ord	188.540
Bunn, F.G.	Gunr	RMA5.082
Burbidge, H.G.	Col/Sergt	Po2.061
Burge, C.H.	Sto	174.444
Burkett, W.	ERA	156.251
Burnett, J.W.	ERA	268.364
Burnham, W.J.	Arm/Crew	340.968
Burt, W.	L/Sto	147.525
Buttons, J.	Ord	188.786
Campbell, H.W.	Ord	199.103
Campbelton, J. W.	L/Sto	151.234
Canfield, F.A.	AB	188.581
Carlson, E.J.	Ord	185.917
Carter, J.	AB	192.302
Cathery, H.G.	Sto	279.398
Chamberlin, J.	Ord	203.594
Chambers, F.	Gunr	RMA7.286
Chandler, J.R.B.	Sto	278.635
Chick, J.H.	Pte	Ch10.410
Clark, E.C.	Sh/Cpl	132.079
Clark, J.	Pte	Po5.200
Clarke, S.	L/Sto	128.943
Cleugh, J.	L/Sto	152.353

No Bar Medals *continued*

Clowe, G.H.	Ord	203.620
Cluett, E.A.	Cook/Mte	160.563
Clydesdale, W.	AB	181.945
Coad, W.H.L.	Ch/Sto	119.377
Cockram, W.H.	AB	201.905
Coe, R.	Ord	184.596
Coffee, T.	Hd/Kroo	
Coffee, T.	Kroo	
Coffey, P.	Pte	Ply8.764
Cogger, R.W.	Carp	
Colban, E.L.	L/Sergt	RMA5.341
Cole, A.	Blksmth	341.893
Collier, J.N.	Sto	292.408
Collings, G.	AB	191.143
Collins, J.	AB	172.669
Collins, S.P.	Ord	197.718
Collins, T.	Ord	201.306
Collins, T.E.	PO1	125.533
Collis, H.D.	AB	194.376
Colquhoun, T.	L/Shpwrt	341.187
Cook, C.H.	Ch/Cook	145.761
Cook, W.	AB	116.401
Coombs, A.G.	2/Yeo/Sig	155.986
Cooper, A.	Bugler	Ch10.416
Cooper, H.W.	Ord	203.619
Cordeirs, C.F.	Dom	353.608
Cork, G.	Sto	156.241
Cornwall, J.	Dom	355.386
Coupland, E.	Gunr	RMA4.360
Court, S.W.	Sto	293.172
[3] Cowdery, A.	Pte	Po9.594
Cowling, F.W.	Ord	195.316
Cox, C.A.	AB	194.734
Cox, J.	Pte	Po6.882
Cox, W.G.	AB	194.578
Crabb, J.H.	Sto	167.702
Crancher, R.A.	Ord	184.423
Crawley, W.	Ord	202.963
Creed, J.	3/Wrtr	341.217
Crisp, F.J.	AB	132.528
Cronin, T.	Pte	Ch5.283
Crook, W.	AB	160.424
Crouch, W.G.	SB/Attn	350.481
Crow II, J.	Kroo	
Crowhurst, W.	Ch/Sto	104.949
Cullen, W.J.	Cpl	Po2.171
Cunningham, S.	Ord	189.302
Curchin, W.	Sto	276.119
Curteis, F.J.	Sto	287.487
Curtis, S.	2/Cooper	124.207
Curtis, W.H.	Ch/Arm	145.921
Cuthbert, F.	Ord	184.391
Dance, J.J.	Sto	285.427
Danniels, T.L.	Bosn	
Dart, J.	Sto	284.303
Dart, T.	AB	180.483
Davey, B.J.	Sto	286.826
Davidson, A.M.S.	Ord	185.747
Davies II, J.	Kroo	
Davis, F.	Pte	Po9.828
Davis, F.A.	PO2	148.391
Davis, F.C.	AB	197.730
Davis, M.H.	AB	188.415
Dawson, F.J.	Boy	197.433
Day, W.	SB/Attn	108.688
Deadman, J.	AB	145.293
Delamare, W.S.	AB	
Denny, R.M.	AB	185.880
Dicker, E.	PO2	137.200
Dickson, J.	Kroo	
Diment, S.G.	L/Sto	133.737
Doidge, W.H.	Ord	197.515
Dollar II, T.	Kroo	
Donovan, C.H.	AB	149.945
Douglas, A.C.	Dom	358.943
Dowle, C.J.	Sto	285.381
Dowrich, F.G.	Sto	285.022
Drummy, J.	Ord	197.658
Duke, B.W.	Dom	119.826
Dundas, C.H.	Comdr	
Dunlop, R.J.	Sail	123.789
Eade, J.	AB	176.064
Eade, N.W.	MAA	97.888
Earlis, J.	Ord	197.714
Eastwood, A.G.H.	L/Cpl	Po8.913
Edwards, A.	AB	152.953
Egypt, T.	Kroo	
Ekers, A.	AB	160.208
Elbrow, G.	Fl/Engr	
Elliott, E.A.	Sto	287.433
Elliott, W.D.	AB	139.831
English, J.	AB	187.613
Evans, J.D.	Sto	282.467
Evans, W.	Cook/Mte	340.628
Everest, W.	Gunr	RMA2.697
Evershed, F.C.A.	L/Cpl	Po9.376
Excell, G.H.	Pte	Ply8.584
Faraday, J.	Pte	Ch8.989
Fare, A.J.	Sto	279.460
Farley, J.C.	AB	185.882
Farmer, H.E.	Blksmth	128.915
Farrant, T.	Ord	201.885
Farthing, C.V.	AB	177.271
Fernandes, A.	Dom	356.018
Ferrier, A.M.	Ord	199.050
Filmer, M.	PO1	133.957
Finch, W.A.C.	AB	182.798
Flack, A.T.	Cpl	Ch7.624
Fleming, R.	Gunr	
Flood, J.	PO1	124.627
Flood, T.	Sto	288.817
Foote, T.C.	Gunr	RMA5.884
Ford, F.W.	Gunr	RMA5.777
Ford, G.	Pte	Po9.596
Fortescue, Hon. S.J.	Comdr	
Foster, G.	Sto	286.829
Fowkes, G.	Sto	279.176
Fowler, W.H.	Ch/ERA	113.483
Fowles, E.	PO2	149.599
Frame, W.	Carp/Mte	132.442
Fraser, R.	Gunr	RMA5.265

Freed, H.T.	Pte	Ply8.730
Freeman, J.	Sto	283.126
Freeman II, T.	Kroo	
French, J.	Ord	196.371
French, W.G.	Sto	154.133
Fretwell, G.	AB	181.654
Frieze, W.H.	Sto	279.141
Frost, A.G.	Ch/Sto	141.030
Fullarton, J.	ERA	268.347
Fuller, H.L.	Pte	Po6.595
Gale, J.S.	Ord	186.094
Ganey, J.	Ord	194.866
Gardner, E.J.	Ord	201.331
Gardner, J.	Fl/Engr	
Garlinge, J.E.	Sto	287.471
Gausden, N.F.	L/Sto	160.737
Gay, J.	Carp/Mte	96.436
Gibbons, H.	Ord	188.345
Gibson, F.G.	Ord	201.328
Gilbert, J.A.	L/Sto	120.385
Giles, C.H.	PO2	145.615
Giles, H.R.	Bosn	
Gittings, F.	Surgn	
Glanville, H.	Blksmth/Mte	340.221
Glasgow, P.	Kroo	
Goddard, J.H.	Sto	182.994
Goodard, C.E.	ERA	268.991
Goodwin, H.A.	Ord	189.490
Gore, J.	L/Sto	170.864
Gossop, A.	Ord	177.664
Gould, H.	L/Sto	148.874
Gould, S.J.	Sto	155.970
Grace, M.J.	Sto	285.757
Grasgo, T.	Kroo	
Greagory, E.T.	Ord	180.118
Green, H.	Cook/Mte	169.904
Green, T.W.	Bosn	
Green, W.	Carp/Mte	153.884
Griffiths, P.M.	SS/Asst	174.478
Grindell, J.	AB	177.696
Gritton, J.H.	Arm/Mte	128.254
Guard, T.	Fl/Payr	
Gudgeon, A.	Plmbr	167.795
Hainen, W.	Ch/Sto	141.364
Haines, G.A.	Gunr	RMA4.246
Hair, D.R.	Pte	Ply8.266
Haley, E.	L/S	168.947
Halfyard, R.	PO2	117.748
Hall, D.	AB	185.228
Hall, T.	Ord	196.755
Hallam, G.	Ord	187.565
Hallett, H.J.	Ord	201.637
Hammond, W.J.	Sto	288.720
Handsford, W.H.	Ord	199.289
Harding, W.G.	Act/Ch/ERA	158.816
Hardy, J.	PO1	106.235
Harmer, A.	Ord	184.678
Harriman, T.	L/Sto	(.013)
Harrison, A.	Sto	(6.825)
Harrison, C.W.	L/Sto	167.816
Harrison, J.	Sto	(6.028)
Harrison, S.	L/Sto	(0.171)
Harvey, A.	Sto	(.451)
Harvey, W.	Sh/Cpl	125.756
Hatcher, W.	Ch/Sto	140.658
Hathway, R.C.	AB	128.120
Hawkes, G.	Ord	194.054
Hawkins, W.	Ch/Cook	(.298)
Hawkins, W.L.	Gunr	RMA4.511
Hayes, G.W.	Ch/PO	102.558
Head, W.H.	Pte	Ply8.760
Hearn, J.	Ord	187.657
Hearn, P.J.	Sto	288.852
Hearson, T.	Ord	185.324
Heath, J.H.	PO1	110.222
Henderson, C.F.	Snr/Lieut	
Hennessy, J.	Sto	(0.858)
Herrington, A.	Ord	189.540
Hicks, A.E.T.	L/S	160.831
Hill, C.	Sto	170.502
Hill, J.	Sto	(5.016)
Hindle, A.J.H.	PO1	152.141
Hinson, A.E.	AB	(. 38)
Hire, A.H.	Capt(RMA)	
Hiscock, T.	PO2	104.228
Hoath, G.F.	PO1	143.578
Hobbins, W.S.	Bugler	Ch8.720
Hobbs, A.	ERA	268.086
Hodge, T.	Ord	188.340
Hogben, W.	AB	185.298
Holford, A.F.	Sto	(2.960)
Hollamby, A.	AB	155.568
Holley, F.W.	Sh/Cpl	350.026
Hollingshead, F.	Sto	(92.846)
Holloway, H.C.	SB/Attn	(.432)
Holmes, R.W.	Sto	279.863
Hood, G.W.	Sto	(.777)
Horrell, T.S.	PO1	138.674
House, G.R.	AB	184.336
Howells, A.J.	L/S	124.028
Howard, A.	PO1	124.391
Hoy, W.	Sto	279.018
Hubbard, E.H.	Pte	Ply7.855
Hull, H.A.	Sto	(94.193)
Humphrey, E.J.	Sergt	Ch4.668
Hunt, H.	AB	184.590
Hunt, W.	AB	183.413
Huntley, W.T.	Sto	(2.784)
Hyslop, W.	AB	174.651
H(ist), A.	Pte	(.)
H( ), H.C.	Pte	Ch7.540
H(es), T.J.	Pte	(.)
Ingram, A.H.L.	PO2	144.594
Irvin, E.T.	Sto	293.174
Isaacson, S.	( )	RMA4.738
Jackson, A.T.	Act/Bombdr	RMA7.455
Jackson, W.G.	AB	181.593
James, A.	Sto	354.275
James, G.	Sto	279.195
Jameson, J, McR.	Ord	189.289
Jarvis, H.E.	AB	157.029
Jeeves, E.	Pte	Ch9.123

No Bar Medals *continued*

Jefferson, C.W.	Carp	
Jennings, A.G.	L/S	146.109
Jennings, S.	Gunr	RMA7.442
Jewell, C.	PO1	122.474
Jewell, W.G.	Sergt	Ply3.460
Jib, Flying No 1.	Kroo	
Jobson, W.E.	PO2	136.847
Johnson, A.S.	Q/Sig	188.858
Johnson, G.	Kroo	
Johnson, G.B.	Ch/Sto	154.786
Johnson, T.J.	AB	182.442
Jones, A.	L/Sto	155.490
Jones, E.	Sto	277.624
Jones, G.	Pte	Ply8.273
Jones, J.H.	Lieut	
Jones, N.	Sh/Cpl	146.597
Jones, W.	Ch/Bosn	
Jones, W.R.	Bugler	RMA5.865
Jordan, T.	Ord	198.068
Joyner, A.E.C.	Pte	Ch10.469
Judd, W.E.	AB	188.022
Judge, G.C.	AB	186.349
J( ), A.	( )	(.)
J(on), W.	Ord	(.)
Keating, J.	Ord	200.936
Kelleher, W.F.	L/Sto	142.245
Kennedy, W.	Gunr	RMA5.206
Kent, B.	AB	(. 70)
Keohane, D.	AB	203.385
Keohane, M.	PO2	(. 7)
Key, H.N.	Sub Lieut	
Key, W.H.	Sto	(.)
Kidd, H.	Gunr	RMA4.410
Kidney, J.E.	AB	(. 71)
Kieley, M.	Ch/Sto	(.)
King, E.	Sto	281.599
Kingdom, E.H.	Carp/Mte	(.)
Kinsley, R.	L/Sto	156.652
Kissack, T.	AB	(. 51)
Kitson, (.L.)	L/Sto	(. 68)
Knight, W.H.	Ord	196.085
K( ), H.	Pte	(.)
K(g), H.T.	Pntr	(.)
K(ne), J.	Sto	(. 58)
K( ), P.A.	Cook/Mte	(.)
K( ), ( ).	L/S	(.)
K( ), ( ).	L/S	(.)
K( ), R.	Sail/Crew	(.)
Lamb, R.G.	Pte	(9.464)
Lamble, F.J.	Bosn	
Lancaster, J.	AB	(1.025)
Lander, W.	Arm/Mte	(1.310)
Lane, E.	AB	185.303
Lawrence, A.H.	L/Sto	(. 93)
Lawrence, B.H.	Sig	190.969
Lawrence, F.	Sto	280.899
Lawrence, F.W.	PO1	109.153
Laws, A.J.	ERA	164.183
Laycock, J.	Sto	(5.518)
Layzell, E.	Shpwrt	341.321
Lee, W.C.	MAA	55.704
Lendon, S.	Sto	279.624
Lewis, H.V.	Sto	(3.267)
Lichfield, S.O.	2/Sig	182.044
Lilly, A.H.	PO1	134.707
Littlefield, H.E.	Ord	(03.618)
Lloyd, G.	MAA	(. 54)
Lloyd, J.	Sto	281.080
Lockey, C.F.	AB	188.821
Lowe, J.R.	AB	170.757
Lowton, W.	Ord	(0.083)
Ludgate, R.W.	AB	(3.728)
Lyne, J.P.	Arm/Crew	340.799
McCarthy, D.	Ord	(.876)
McCarthy, J.	AB	155.983
McCulloch, C.W.N.	Lieut	
McDonald, E.	Sto	146.931
McDowall, A.	ERA	268.308
McGettigan, P.	AB	203.036
McGibbon, J.	AB	(3.684)
McGregor, C.	Sto	284.902
McIntosh, J.	Sto	278.634
Mackay, H.	Gunr	(RMA .)
McKay, L.	PO1	(. 23)
McKean, G.	Gunr	RMA3.817
McLure, H.J.	Gunr	(RMA . 5)
Macready, J.	PO2	135.260
McWilliams, S.	AB	185.544
Magee, G.	AB	188.832
Males, A.	Pte	Ch5.197
Manester, H.E.	PO2	142.788
Marchant, S.F.	Ch/Gunr	
Marguer, T.M.	L/Carp/Crew	342.455
Marks, J.	L/Sto	144.378
Marmon, C.J.E.	AB	(.659)
Marshall, J.	Sto	286.193
Martin, G.B.	AB	(. 5)
Martin, L.A.	Gunr	RMA4.302
Maskell, W.T.	Pte	Po5.805
Mason, E.	AB	174.565
Meaden, G.T.	Sh/Std	109.628
Medhurst, J.F.	Ch/ERA	145.720
Medhurst, J.F.C.	2/SBStd	(.379)
Miles, A.E.	Pte	(.)
Miles, R.	Ord	188.799
Millard, C.H.	PO1	125.847
Miller, G.T.	AB	172.542
Milton, H.B.	Ch/Wrtr	136.253
Milton, W.E.	PO1	81.699
Mitchell, E.C.	Sto	282.066
Mitchell, G.	2/Wrtr	340.081
Mitchell, J.	Sto	280.702
Monk, C.	Ord	(4.602)
Moore, A.H.	Ord	(3.622)
Morgan, A.E.	AB	194.266
Morris, C.J.	Sh/Cpl	132.910
Morrison, H.	PO1	120.655
Mortimer, E.	2/Sig	(3.446)
Mortimer, W.H.	Pte	(. 2)
Moul, T.H.	Ord	184.529
Mullen, J.	Ord	(.680)

Murray, G.W.	Sto	285.293
M( ), B.	Sto	(.)
M(o), D.	Bugler	(.)
M(chant), (J. .)	ERA	(.)
M( ), T.	Pte	(.)
Nance, S.	AB	185.134
Neville, D.	L/S	139.522
Newman, A.H.	Ch/Wrtr	133.466
Newman, F.	Dom	356.023
Newman, T.	Kroo	
Newnham, W.	Act/Gunr	
Newson, W.J.	Gunr	RMA7.492
Nichols, R.H.	Ch/Carp/Mte	85.908
Norris, R.	ERA	149.732
O'Brien, J.	AB	(.612)
O'Brien, J.	L/S	(.)
O'Brien, T.	Sail/Mte	(.)
Oakett, J.	Pte	(8.736)
Oliver, J.E.	AB	(. 15)
Olver, C.H.	L/Sto	(.)
Orford, M.C.	Sto	(.058)
Osborne, A.J.	AB	(.568)
Osborne, A.K.	Arm	(3.255)
Osmond, W.	Ord	(.)
Outen, W.	Arm	(3.239)
Packham, S.	L/Sto	114.455
Paice, J.	Pte	Po5.065
Palser, H.G.	Pte	Ch9.150
Parrot, E.R.	Act/Bosn	
Parsonage, F.H.	Ord	190.934
Parsons, R.E.	1/Wrtr	(.)
Patterson, A.	Sto	(. 3)
Pattison, R.	Act/ERA	268.858
Patton, W.	AB	188.359
Pay, W.	L/Sto	146.317
Payne, A.J.	Lieut	
Payne, E.H.	Ord	(. 3)
Payne, F.G.	Ord	(. 10)
Payne, S.T.	PO1	130.197
Peachey, H.E.	AB	176.273
Pearce, H.	Ord	190.484
Pengelly, S.A.	Ord	203.992
Penman, E.E.	L/S	166.908
Pepper, T.	Kroo	
Percy, A.	Ch/Sto	125.603
Peters, E.	Sto	284.774
Pethick, E.E.	Engr	
Petley, W.E.	Act/Bombdr	(RMA .391)
Phillips, N.E.	AB	197.605
Phillips, S.	PO1	109.993
Phillips, W.H.	AB	188.836
Piper, J.J.	Sto	280.991
Pippin, G.H.	Ch/Sto	(.)
Pitman, T.	PO1	125.636
Place, J.S.	Asst/Payr	
Pomeroy, R.	L/Sto	113.408
Poole, G.H.	Ord	193.511
Poorfellow, T.	Kroo	
Pope, H.E.	ERA	151.239
Price, E.G.	Sto	282.704
Price, G.W.	AB	(.)

Prince, S.G.	Pntr	(.026)
Prout, S.	Ch/Sto	(.)
Prowse, W.	Ch/Sto	(.)
Pryke, F.A.	AB	(. 30)
P(ell), C.C.D.E.	Ord	(.)
P( ), C.E.M.	Sto	(.)
P( ), W.H.	Ord	(.)
* Raikes, G.L.	Lieut(RMA)	
Ramsay, J.	Gunr	RMA2.761
Rashley, A.W.	Sh/Std	135.477
Read, W.J.	Sh/Cpl	115.686
Redclift, E.	AB	198.679
Redfearn, S.	AB	(156. 6)
Redford, H.	Sto	(. 55)
Reed, R.W.	Ord	203.632
Reynolds, C.G.	Ord	197.232
Richards, A.	Ord	187.610
Richards, A.E.	Pte	(. 14)
Richards, J.	Sto	277.910
Richardson, F.C.	Ord	187.575
Riddiford, W.	PO1	(. 77)
* Ridgway, F.	Gunr	RMA4.260
Roach, E.	Arm	(.991)
Roberts, B.	Kroo	
Roberts, F.	St/Comdr	
Roberts, J.	Kroo	
Roberts, J.E.	AB	184.315
Roberts, R.E.	Gunr	RMA7.297
Robinson, A.J.	L/Sto	162.729
Robinson, E.	Pte	(.320)
Rogers, D.	Gunr	(RMA .361)
Rolland, J.	Ord	185.739
Rose, A.	Sto	(. 11)
Rowlands, F.	Arm/Crew	(.981)
Russell, B.A.	AB	196.616
Russell, G.E.	Lieut(RMA)	
R(ason), A.W.	AB	(.)
R(ok), G.	AB	(.)
R( ), J.R.	AB	(.)
R( ), J.R.	Ord	(.)
R(ding), T.	Ord	(.)
Saddleton, H.	Blksmth	166.403
Sampson, J.	Kroo	
Saunders, A.C.	Pte	Ply8.439
Savage, Jack.	Kroo	
Savey, J.	Kroo	
Scahill, J.	Ord	(. 2)
Scamell, A.	Ord	(.)
Scarrott, C.	L/Sto	114.619
Scawn, J.T.	L/Sto	130.100
Scott, F.	Pte	(.)
Sewell, E.W.	L/Carp/Crew	(.)
S(e wick), C.C.	Gunr	(RMA . 13)
Share, C.J.	Ord	(.)
Shave, W.G.	Ord	(7.872)
Shaw, J.E.	PO1	135.374
Shaw, L.	Sto	286.975
Shemmings, F.O.	Ch/Sto	127.342
Shepherd, G.	L/Shpwrt	165.927
Sherrington, D.	Dom	353.564
S(h), ( ).	AB	(.)

No Bar Medals *continued*

Silke, S.	Pte	Po3.350
Sillick, J.H.	Ch/ERA	114.237
Simler, A.J.	L/Sto	147.488
Simpson, T.	Sto	285.806
Sinnott, P.J.	Sh/Cpl	350.098
Skiller, L.	Ord	(. 9)
Smale, H.	Dom	114.425
Smith, C.	Ch/PO	(.)
Smith, C.W.	Pte	Ply8.552
Smith, F.	Act/Gunr	
Smith, F.A.	Ord	(.)
Smith, G.	PO1	146.649
Smith, H.S.	Pte	Po8.752
Smith, I.	Sto	277.976
Smith, J.	L/Sto	161.711
Smith, J.A.	Pte	Ch8.180
Smith, J.H.	Sto	118.438
Smith, P.	Ord	188.365
Smith, T.P.	Ord	(. 7)
Snell, J.	Pte	Ply8.412
Snook, F.O.	AB	156.197
Sole, A.	Sto	(2 0.920)
Spackman, J.	Pte	(5.759)
Speight, R.	Col/Sergt	RMA2.451
Stafford, D.	AB	(. 67)
Stanford, L.C.	AB	161.488
Starmer, C.	Ord	(.)
Stearn, W.	Gunr	(RMA . 36)
Stein, P.	Cooper	111.574
Stevens, I.	Sto	175.405
Stevens, W.H.	PO1	(. 74)
Stockwell, W.G.	PO2	(. 3)
Stone, W.H.	Ord	(.)
Street, G.	Sto	280.910
Stroud, J.S.	Ord	(.)
Stuttaford, F.R.	Ch/Engr	
Sutton, H.	Bosn	
Swan, J.	Sto	149.899
Sykens, L.W.	PO1	124.140
Sykens, J.F.	AB	(.808)
S( ), A.	AB	(.)
S(tt), J.	Pte	(.)
S(pson), J.M.	PO2	(.)
S(s), J.W.	AB	(.)
S( ), R.	Pte	(.)
Tapp, J.	Pte	(8.199)
Tarrant, W.	AB	123.285
Tatler, G.W.	PO2	(. 1)
Taylor, A.J.	AB	(83.967)
Taylor, H.F.	AB	183.515
Taylor, J.	L/Sto	(. 3)
Taylor, M.	Sto	(.)
Tebbenham, S.J.	PO1	124.677
Tether, N.	Pte	(.)
Thompson, A.R.	Arm	340.547
Thornback, J.	Ch/Bosn	
Tick, C.	Ord	(.)
Tiller, E.J.	AB	(. 10)
Tillett, J.A.	AB	178.194
Tink, W.	Sto	(.464)
Toby, E.	Kroo	
Tom, J.	Kroo	
Tomlins, E.J.	Sto	293.188
Toms, W.C.	PO1	126.156
Tonkin, C.S.	Ord	(. 26)
Town, E.J.	Ord	(. 92)
Townsend, A.E.	Ord	(.620)
Tribe, T.W.	Ch/PO	(. 0)
Trimble, G.	L/Sto	112.184
Trott, J.	2/SBStd	(.312)
Truscott, T.R.	AB	187.840
Tuck, H.	Ord	(.382)
Turner, T.	L/Sto	(.296)
* Tye, A.C.	Pte	Ch4.569
Tyrrell, S.B.	Ord	185.300
T( ), T.	Sto	(.)
T(r), F.E.	Pte	(.)
T( ), H.	Pte	(.)
T( ), T.J.	Act/Bombdr	(RMA .)
Underhill, G.	Cpl	Ply8.394
Varney, F.J.	Pte	Ply8.874
Vaughan, J.A.	Engr	
Veale, W.J.	L/Sto	144.730
Vernon, A.A.	Sto	174.454
Vines, A.J.	Sto	279.841
Wainwright, R.E.	Sergt	Po6.151
Wakeham, J.	L/Sto	165.092
Wales, Prince of.	Kroo	
Walke, P.J.	Sto	279.267
Walker, A.J.	Sto	186.156
Walker, C.	Pte	Ch8.497
Wallace, J.E.	SB/Attn	342.016
Walters, E.J.	AB	182.279
Walton, W.H.	Gunr	RMA2.095
Wand, T.E.	Pte	Ch8.521
Ward, A.	AB	202.960
Ward, C.	ERA	162.004
Ward, F.W.	Sto	123.330
Warren, E.W.	L/Sto	137.575
Watkins, R.J.	2/SBStd	350.298
Way, R.C.	Yeo/Sig	124.922
Webber, A.L.	PO1	159.676
Wedge, W.	Sto	154.122
West, A.	AB	134.909
West, A.H.	AB	184.695
West, F.W.	Sto	174.434
Whale, T.	Kroo	
Wheeler, P.V.	AB	197.221
Whelan, J.H.	St/Surgn	
Whicher, J.C.N.	St/Surgn	
White, A.	Act/Ch/Arm	168.649
White, H.T.	Sto	284.305
White, J.W.	Pte	Ply8.626
White, W.	AB	176.754
White, W.A.	L/Cpl	Ch6.780
Whittaker, J.	AB	194.228
Whittle, J.	PO1	140.242
Whyard, W.	ERA	149.733
Wild, H.E.	AB	181.904
Williams, A.E.	Sto	285.239
Williams, J.	PO1	146.963

Wills, G.W.	PO1	112.170
Wills, J.	Ord	201.662
Wilson, A.E.	AB	182.205
Wilson, A.G.	Sto	286.262
Wilson, J.G.B.	Ord	199.265
Windle, A.E.	Sto	291.906
Wood, J.	Gunr	
Wood, R.H.	AB	145.919
Woolley, H.	Pte	Ply8.179
Worden, T.	Cook/Mte	341.499
Worrall, P.H.	Pte	Ch10.406
Wright, R.	Ord	188.797
Yates, E.A.	AB	178.356
York, J.	PO1	123.375
Young, W.	PO1	115.530
Young, W.B.	AB	183.749

Duplicate medals:

Barnard, W.H.	Sto	287.572
Blanchard, W.C.	Ord	178.219
Buckley, J.	Sto	171.299
Dance, J.J.	Sto	285.427
Drummy, J.	Ord	197.658
Farthing, C.V.	AB	177.271
Gardner, E.J.	Ord	201.331
Hall, D.	AB	185.228
Harrison, A.	Sto	(6.825)
Hawkins, W.L.	Gunr	RMA4.511
Johnson, T.J.	AB	182.442
x McCarthy, D.	Ord	(.876)
Miles, R.	Ord	188.799
Newson, W.J.	Gunr	RMA7.492
P( ), W.H.	Ord	(.)
Scamell, A.	Ord	(.)
Simler, A.J.	L/Sto	147.488
Wallace, J.E.	SB/Attn	342.016

Returned medals:

Ashworth, W.H.	Pte	Po8.905
Bannerman, J.	Ord	201.307
Barlow, A.R.	AB	181.900
Bate, R.T.	Surgn	
Bates, J.H.	PO1	149.228
Bawden, A.	AB	156.833
Billiards, G.	Sto	163.539
Bluff, J.	Kroo	
Brine, W.G.	Dom	121.229
Brown, J.	Kroo	
Cain, W.	Pte	Ch8.365
Clark, A.J.S.	AB	183.721
Clunie, H.E.	AB	171.773
Collins, C.T.	Dom	358.352
4 Constable, A.A.	Pte	Po9.160
Cook, H.M.	Ord	198.123
Cooper, W.	Asst/Payr	
Coster, G.	Sto	174.425
Court, F.	AB	180.704
5 Cowan, W.H.	Lieut	
Cowell, R.	Ord	198.074
Currey, T.H.	Ord	199.404
Curtis, H.	Pte	Ch9.705
Davidge, E.J.	AB	159.544
Davis, J.	Kroo	
De Souza, G.	Dom	93.722
Dickens, C.	Kroo	
Duncan, J.	AB	204.251
Dwyer, M.	Sto	279.384
Eade, A.	L/Sto	171.970
Edwards, F.	Sto	280.376
Fordham, H.W.	Ord	193.691
Fremes, E.J.	AB	197.438
Fuller, W.	Ord	187.155
Garwood, G.	Dom	355.389
George, J.	Kroo	
Gibbons, M.	Ord	201.865
Grant, W.	Shpwrt	343.336
Green, W.G.	Ord	195.794
Griffiths, W.	ERA	269.039
Harding, E.H.	Pte	Ch10.362
Hardy, J.	Kroo	
Hickman, R.	Dom	(53.617)
Hill, F.	Ord	183.460
Hill, W.	Sto	(.408)
Hingston, R.W.	Art/Engr	
Hodgson, T.R.	Ord	203.608
Holder, J.	Dom	358.209
Hunt, H.	Sto	158.769
Husk, J.C.	AB	177.943
H(ter), H.E.	AB	(.)
H( ), W.	AB	(.)
Jahn, H.N.	Ord	192.187
Johnson, J.	Sh/Cpl	350.139
Jones, J.H.	AB	165.724
Jones, J.T.	AB	183.422
K( ), ( ).	Ord	(.)
Leach, A.J.J.	Pte	(10.370)
Lewis, A.E.	Sto	(.)
McCann, C.	Shpwrt	342.653
May, P.	Kroo	
Milne, R.	L/Sto	276.117
Mitchell, W.J.	Pte	Ply5.988
Mulkearn, M.	Sto	(. 86)
M( ), W.E.	AB	(.)
Neaves, J.H.	AB	178.772
New, L.G.H.	Ord	188.499
Nicholson, H.	Ord	185.753
Nirey, G.W.	Sto	293.075
Norris, H.	Sto	278.337
Norris, W.F.	AB	190.498
Peter, T. No. 4.	Kroo	
Pinn, T.	Sto	139.864
Pitt, J.	Ord	203.612
Pochin, I.W.	Lieut	
Polley, W.	Ord	(.)
6 P( ), G.	AB	(.)
Reynolds, W.J.	Arm/Crew	(.914)
Riley, J.	AB	(.324)
Robbins, J.A.	Lieut	
Robinson, J.	Sto	(. 50)
Rose, A.J.	Pte	(5.522)
Ryan, W.	ERA	162.123
Sainsbury, C.W.	Shpwrt	342.674

Returned medals continued

[7] Shaw, J.E.	PO1	135.374
Short, W.G.	Sto	285.238
Smith, J.J.	Gunr	
Smith, T.	Kroo	
Spendelow, H.	AB	159.352
Spicer, H.	Sto	181.228
Spicer, J.G.	Yeo/Sig	(.)
Stephens, A.F.	Lieut	
Stephens, T.	PO2	114.718
Strangroom, G.	AB	124.794
Sweeney, M.	AB	(. 1)
Taggart, S.A.	SS/Asst	(4.007)
Taylor, W.	Dom	354.706
Thorpe, A.	AB	(83.270)
Trezise, E.A.	Ord	(8.934)
Vaughan, L.W.G.	Ord	194.531
Wakeham, W.R.	AB	147.131
Walker, T.	Dom	
Walker, T. No. 1	Kroo	
Walker II, T.	Kroo	
Ward, W.C.M.	Ord	197.225
Watkins, H.	PO1	142.564
Welch, J.	Sto	172.269
Wheeler, G.	AB	184.679
Whitbourne, A.	PO1	128.820
White, R.	Pte	
Wilkin, H.D.	Lieut Comdr	
Williams, I.	Kroo	
Williams, S.	Dom	164.439
Witchell, E.F.	Ord	203.023
Woolley, C.P.	AB	136.402

Medals with unknown bar entitlement

The following medals, whose entries on the medal roll have been lost through damage, may or may not have been entitled to bars. Only the first letter of the surname and the number of the medal are known for certain. (See Note 8)

First letter of surname	*Medal No.*	*Total*
L	3029	1
M	3056, 3057, 3092, 3093, 3128, 3129	6
P	3182	1
R	3282	1
S	3310, 3384	2
		11

EXTENDED PERIOD
No Bar Medals

Blomely, W.W.	Sto	126.079
Briggs, C.	Sto	281.487
Brisley, W.T.	Sto	285.133
Brooker, W.	Sto	288.408
Brooks, E.H.	2/Yeo/Sig	156.395
Brunt, G.F.	AB	167.994
Bull, John	Kroo	
Burnside, J.	Gunr	RMA8.910
Cann, J.	Sto	297.087
Capell, A.E.	AB	178.402
Carroll, C.H.	Asst/Payr	
Carroll, J.W.	Sto	290.741
Claxton, J.T.	Sto	280.898
Coughlan, M.	AB	182.650
Cowling, F.	AB	144.229
Cox, F.	Sto	283.024
Cox, G.J.	Sto	277.601
Craig, H.J.	ERA	163.483
Cross, H.J.	Sergt	Ply5.246
Daley, J.	AB	180.469
Davison, T.	ERA	269.080
Daykin, W.	AB	189.398
Deighton, C.H.	Ch/Gunr	
Dorrington, H.T.	Sh/Cpl	151.895
Dunean, J.H.	Sto	288.821
Farrell, H.	L/Sto	279.710
Fletcher, J.H.	AB	138.864
Foot, C.R. de C.	Comdr	
Friend, D.E.H.	Gunr	RMA5.024
Gent, C.	Sto	278.812
Gobby, G.W.	Gunr	RMA4.622
Green, W.J.	Gunr	RMA5.337
Grimshaw, W.	Sto	276.634
Gustard, D.D.	Sto	284.794
Guy, J.	Arm/Mte	173.289
Harkins, W.A.	Ord	209.156
Hayes, J.	Sto	291.664
Hemsley, E.	Sto	288.752
Hopper, S.	Ord	203.194
Hook, W.A.	Ch/ERA	174.458
Horne, C.D.M.	Payr	
Horne, W.J.	Ch/Gunr	
Howe, A.R.	Ord	206.051
Hughes, A.	Pte	Ply3.600
Jago, F.A.	3/Wrtr	341.513
James, C.	AB	182.023
Jones, W.S.	Pte	Ch7.751
Jude, H.N.	Pte	Ply9.743
Keech, F.W.	AB	196.255
Kemp, W.G.	Act/Bombdr	RMA8.596
Knight, J.T.	MAA	135.865
Lavers, W.	AB	179.619
Lovelady, J.	L/Sto	163.652

Lyne, T.J.S.	Gunr	
Lyons, G.J.	Sto	283.619
McCarthy, R.C.	Sh/Std	139.849
McCormick, R.S.S.	Ord	189.373
McKiernin, E.H.	Gunr	RMA5.633
Marsh, W.	Gunr	RMA7.380
Morris, C.S.	Sto	297.235
Nelder, H.	Gunr	RMA8.809
Nisbet, A.R.	Sto	297.084
Partridge, A.E.	Gunr	RMA3.272
Phillips, G.A.	ERA	269.429
Pitts, J.M.	AB	200.163
Poole, G.R.	Capt(RMA)	
Porter, J.	Gunr	RMA3.871
Powell, F.	Ord	216.807
Riley, W.	Sto	297.082
Roberts, H.G.W.	AB	180.582
Roberts, W.J.	ERA	269.012
Rose, B.H.	ERA	268.993
Rowland, G.	SB/Attn	350.564
Seymour, T.W.	Sto	277.169
Spratt, H.W.	Gunr	RMA3.876
Stack, P.	AB	184.088
Standfield, H.	PO1	128.889
Stephens, R.M.T.	Lieut	
Sullivan, J.P.	Gunr	RMA3.071
Talbot, W.J.	Gunr	
Toby, Tom alias Monkey Brand.	Kroo	
Truman, W.J.	SB/Attn	350.525
Unwin, E.	Lieut	
Upton, A.	Sto	288.069
Urell, V.	Carp	
Watkins, W.J.	Gunr	RMA8.830
Webb, J.	Gunr	RMA4.521
Webber, S.B.	AB	181.770
Welbourn, J.	Gunr	RMA5.428
Whearty, J.	Sto	297.080
Wilson, C.A.	ERA	269.097
Winter, A.	Act/Bosn	

Duplicate medal:

Harkins, W.A.	Ord	209.156

Returned medals:

Adey, H.	Yeo/Sig	162.695
Baker, E.F.	AB	188.819
Baker, F.	PO2	165.077
Baker, H.	Pte	Ply7.105
Bartlett, W.H.	Sto	292.512
Brown, G.	SB/Attn	350.708
Brown, W.	ERA	268.689
Chapman, A.G.	Dom	360.331
Cross, T.D.	Ord	208.269
Downs, P.M.	AB	188.532
Fetherstone, R.	Cpl	Po9.608
Fielder, J.A.T.	Asst/Engr	
Gahan, F.J.	Pte	Ply9.959
Galvin, D.	Pte	Ch10.190
Ghent, F.	AB	162.776
Girvin, J.	Ord	208.549
Harris, F.A.	AB	191.597
Higgins, A.	Pte	Po3.548
Jefferies, P.G.	Gunr	RMA4.576
Johnson, P.	Kroo	
Johnson, T.	Kroo	
King, G.	Sh/Cpl	163.491
Lees, F.	Sto	297.086
Lefevre, J.	Kroo	
Long, W.T. alias Ford, G.	Ord	195.740
Lumsden, G.W.	Sh/Std	118.803
Mahony, O.R.	AB	180.896
Patterson, J.	AB	192.293
Peters, I.	Dom	
Purser, W.	Kroo	
Quartermain, T.	SB/Attn	350.541
Richards, P.G.	AB	118.409
Robertson, W.J.	L/Carp/Crew	175.409
Rowsell, E.W.	Ord	200.953
Sharman, A.E.	Sig	187.641
Silver, H.A.	Sto	293.999
Taylor, F.J.	Ch/ERA	145.529
Tossell, H.F.	AB	191.231
Whitmore, H.	L/Sergt	Ch7.661
Williams, J.	Kroo	
Willis, A.	Kroo	
Wright, F.W.	PO1	166.515

H.M.S. NAIAD

Period for which entitled:

Extended period only:
27th April 1901 to 30th November 1901

Bars	*Total*	*Returned*	*Entitled*
2	120	3	117
1	0	0	0
0	154	21	133
	274	24	250

Notes:
Note 1 – Medal roll indicates that bars only are duplicates.
Note 2 – Original medal found so duplicate medal returned to Mint in June 1927. The duplicate had attached to it, 2 x Diamond Hill, 2 x Driefontein, 1 x Cape Colony, 1 x Johannesberg, 1 x Paardeberg and 1 x Belmont bars.

Bars: Cape Colony, South Africa 1901

Ansell, F.C.	PO2	153.531
Ball, C.C.	AB	180.281
Ballard, H.J.	L/Sto	146.248
Barry, W.M.	PO1	157.657
Bethell, Hon. A.E.	Capt	
Bird, A.	Pte	Po10.432
Blondel, W.H.	Ord	195.639
Booth, G.	Gunr	
Bowden, W.	St/Surgn	
Boyd, C.E.	Asst/Clerk	
Bryant, G.	AB	193.086
Butcher, G.	PO1	121.734
Carey, E.S.	Lieut	
Chudley, T.	Sto	293.568
Coley, P.A.	Sto	285.662
Coombes, W.C.	L/Sergt	Po7.336
Cottingham, A.	AB	175.514
Cottrell, C.J.	AB	186.367
Cox, J.	Ord	175.523
Creife, E.	AB	187.055
Dilley, W.	Cpl	Po5.691
Dillon, W.	Pte	Po7.181
Dowell, W.	PO1	146.095
Eagles, J.	Pte	Po10.042
Eddowes, G.	Ord	197.480
Ellis, N.G.	Pte	Po9.869
Ellsbury, O.	Sto	295.036
Elsdon, W.S.	Ord	205.093
Farwell, J.C.	AB	163.117
Ferguson, W.	Ord	200.510
Fermor, F.J.	Sto	290.072
Field, R.A.	Ch/Sto	125.313
Fraser, P.A.	Boy	206.634
Freeland, H.W.	AB	166.370
Garrard, F.J.	L/S	173.072
Gidley, R.G.	PO2	171.686
Godfrey, B.R.	Ord	205.308
Goldring, H.	AB	173.524
Goldsmith, G.E.	AB	180.238
Gosling, C.E.	Sto	295.949
Gray, C.E.	AB	181.647
Greenan, J.	Pte	Po6.887
Hall, F.J.	AB	190.726
Halloran, H.	AB	150.964
Hawkins, G.	L/Sig	192.467
Hayes, M.	L/S	178.991
Helbreu, W.J.	AB	187.046
Hoad, P.	Ord	196.597
Honeysett, A.E.	AB	175.572
Hooper, A.	Ord	205.448
Hopping, F.W.	PO1	146.558
Howlett, F.R.	Sto	283.746
Hurley, J.	Sto	284.721
Johnson, T.J.	Ord	200.584
Kibblewhite, H.	L/S	185.302
Lee, S.H.	PO2	166.374
Leonard, F.C.	Payr	
Leonard, G.	Pte	Po10.149
Lovick, A.E.	Pte	Po10.499
McCarthy, T.	Pte	Po9.965
Maguire, C.	Sto	295.945
Maguire, J.	Yeo/Sig	158.613
Marchant, G.	AB	176.384
Massey, W.S.	Ord	209.737
Matlock, J.H.	Ord	189.768
Mead, W.E.	Sto	284.432
Middleton, H.J.	Sub Lieut	
Miles, C.J.	Pte	Po10.591
Milet, J.	PO2	161.423
Mills, A.E.	Pte	Po9.042
Mitchell, W.R.	Ord	206.296
Moore, F.	Pte	Po4.891
Moulton, W.	AB	150.769
Parsons, B.E.	AB	176.462
Pearce, H.J.	Arm/Mte	341.978
Perry, G.W.	AB	180.015

Petherick, T.	Pte	Po5.307
Phillips, A.F.J.	Q/Sig	188.010
Pink, R.	Sto	296.072
Porter, H.T.R.	Bugler	Po5.547
Pout, P.J.	Ord	206.679
Prentice, J.A.	Ord	206.732
Price, A.	AB	188.740
Rawlings, J.	Ord	199.020
Reed, A.J.	AB	185.674
Rees, J.	AB	190.423
Revell, G.T.	AB	170.315
Riley, F.	L/Sto	149.818
Robinson, F.	Ch/Sto	121.205
Rogers, A.	Pte	Po10.521
Sargeant, E.F.	Ord	196.867
Saunders, J.	Boy	206.792
Scott, H.C.	AB	176.886
Shee, R.J.	Lieut	
Shepherd, B.	AB	181.696
Simpson, A.	Pte	Po9.881
Sinnock, J.G.	Sto	286.702
Slaymaker, W.T.	Pte	Po10.490
Smith, C.	PO1	127.800
Smith, F.	Sto	294.528
Smith, G.	Ord	198.513
Smith, J.	Sto	296.073
Smith, P.E.	Cpl	Po10.227
Tanner, W.	Sto	285.992
Tayson, E.H.	AB	188.755
Tee, G.F.	AB	158.518
Trust, J.G.	L/Sto	131.618
Turner, C.	Sto	296.067
Unwin, W.	AB	165.585
White, H.	PO1	126.255
Whiting, V.J.	AB	193.168
Whitton, T.	Sto	296.075
Wiles, O.A.	PO2	160.121
Wilkins, J.S.	Sig	206.606
Williams, F.	AB	151.901
Wilson, A.	Sto	296.068
Wybrow, T.J.	Pte	Po9.917

Duplicate medals:

Honeysett, A.E.	AB	175.572
Mead, W.E.	Sto	284.432
Smith, J.	Sto	296.073
Whitting, V.J.	AB	193.168

Returned medals:

Ashford, S.	Pte	Ply8.673
Baston, G.W.	AB	179.985
Selwes, A.W.	AB	144.585

No Bar Medals

Archard, A.G.	Asst/Engr	
Archer, A.	ERA	169.331
Arnold, T.W.	Ch/Sto	131.932
Bailey, C.	Sto	173.778
Bankhead, R.	ERA	269.284
Barnes, F.	Pntr	170.465
Barrett, F.	L/Sto	154.724
Barrett, W.C.	Ord	206.319
Bartlett, G.J.	Blksmth	340.320
Batstone, H.J.	Sto	286.015
Bennett, F.	Sto	296.071
Bennett, F.A.	Ord	197.204
Bennett, W.	Ord	189.871
Billett, C.	AB	166.327
Binstead, W.T.	L/S	146.902
Blackman, D.	AB	188.641
Blythe, B.	Sto	175.871
Bowey, J.	Ord	206.848
Braginton, W.	Carp/Crew	343.609
Brain, H.W.	Sto	284.127
Brewer, J.B.	ERA	158.345
Brown, A.	Sto	153.807
Brown, A.	Sto	284.376
Brown, G.	Sto	153.567
Brown, J.	Ch/Sto	113.403
Bryant, W.E.	L/Sto	148.971
Budgeon, W.	Sto	296.070
Bush, W.J.	Sto	284.410
Butters, F.W.	L/Carp/Crew	343.187
Canfield, B.	Sh/Cpl	137.902
Chilton, G.	Sto	290.006
Chiverton, H.T.	Sh/Cook	148.708
Coles, F.A.	Carp/Mte	138.367
Cooney, F.	Carp/Crew	343.471
Cope, H.	AB	158.313
Coughtrey, F.J.	AB	164.611
Cregan, J.	Sto	287.949
Curd, S.	Ord	206.692
Davis, G.C.	Ch/Sto	125.498
Dolan, C.	Sto	171.240
Dowland, E.H.	ERA	269.019
Dunning, J.	Ord	205.736
England, C.	Ord	199.487
Evans, J.	Dom	129.655
Evans, W.H.	Carp	
Field, E.E.	Sh/Std/Boy	342.393
Flucker, D.	Sto	296.076
George, E.	SBStd	350.291
Gilbert, J.	Sig	200.502
Gill, H.	L/Sto	146.311
Gough, H.	Sto	170.085
Grant, W.J.	Sto	290.035
Hammond, C.W.	L/Sto	166.965
Harris, W.	Sto	296.069
Hart, C.T.	PO1	133.541
Hay, C.B.	Pte	Po7.346
Hayes, E.J.	Sig/Boy	205.208
Hayes, J.	Sto	285.355
Hayward, C.	Carp/Crew	343.566
Head, A.J.	Sto	295.826
Hill, E.H.	AB	194.169
Hooper, F.C.	Sub Lieut	
Howe, W.F.	ERA	269.912
Huntbatch, T.H.	Boy	206.228
Hunter, A.	Sto	172.146
Hurden, W.	Sto	286.434
Keeping, T.J.H.H.	Sh/Std	140.283

No Bar Medals *continued*

Kelley, P.	Boy	205.230
Kirkland, J.	Sto	277.793
Larnder, J.	Boy	205.029
Lethby, J.	L/Sto	138.382
Lewis, A.C.	PO1	137.896
Lindsay, G.L.	L/Sto	176.607
Liversidge, J.G.	Ch/Engr	
Long, T.	Sto	296.066
McDermot, G.	Sto	296.064
Manton, R.C.	Sig	203.191
Marshall, R.	L/Sto	276.063
Martin, E.W.	Arm/Mte	167.589
Martin, G.W.	Sto	142.493
Masey, A.J.	PO1	149.651
Maxwell, J.L.	Ch/ERA	158.066
Miller, W.F.	Sto	295.758
Mills, A.	Sto	296.063
Mills, G.	Sto	284.397
Morgan, H.	2/Cooper	340.528
Munro, A.	Dom	354.738
Norman, A.E.	L/S	172.455
Owen, W.J.	Ord	198.545
Park, A.	ERA	269.123
Pitney, F.	Sto	144.769
Portelli, P.	Dom	161.157
Pratt, H.J.	AB	173.045
Reynolds, H.	Sto	291.978
Richmond, E.W.	Ord	204.369
Roberts, C.T.	Sto	276.274
Rogers, J.A.	L/Sto	163.638
Rottenbury, A.	Plmbr/Mte	341.445
Shenele, W.J.	2/Yeo/Sig	157.423
Simpson, R.	Sto	285.652
Smith, E.F.	Ch/ERA	166.941
Smith, W.	Sto	286.831
Souhanny, J.C.	Gunr	
Spencer, A.E.	Ord	197.457
Spurgiss, W.A.	Boy	206.615
Stagus, J.	Dom	358.562
Staples, G.	Sto	167.104
Stolborg, W.	Boy	206.636
Teuma, G.	Dom	356.340
Thomas, G.	Sto	290.984
Tiller, W.	Sto	296.078
Tonge, C.M.	Act/Gunr	
Torrance, W.S.	Asst/Engr	
Turnbull, W.	Sto	290.245
Utting, A.J.	Dom	359.297
Venns, G.	Ch/Sto	112.527
Vinall, G.T.	Sto	157.094
Wade, A.	ERA	268.910
Waller, W.	Cook/Mte	354.283
Ward, G.	AB	170.668
Watson, J.	Sto	286.751
West, A.	Dom	177.050
White, W.J.	Sto	161.327
Wilkie, J.B.	2/Wrtr	172.397
Williams, A.E.	Sto	284.732
Williams, H.R.M.	Lieut	
Wills, W.H.	Ch/Arm	124.880
Wilson, H.	Sto	282.550
Wilson, J.	Carp/Mte	135.161
Woolgar, C.H.	L/S	171.118
Wright, E.	Ord	202.569
Wright, S.	Sto	295.929
Young, F.	Boy	206.811

Duplicate medals:

Dolan, C.	Sto	171.240
2 Norman, A.E.	L/S	172.455
Park, A.	ERA	269.123
Waller, W.	Cook/Mte	354.283
Ward, G.	AB	170.668

Returned medals:

Abbey, F.	Pte	Po9.870
Bailey, W.	Dom	358.990
Coffin, W.	Sto	286.009
Coombes, J.	Sto	159.997
Cooper, P.B.A.	Lieut	
Crawley, J.A.	Boy	206.635
Eades, W.E.	Bosn	
Field, T.W.	Boy	204.546
Flynn, J.T.	Sto	277.326
French, T.J.	Sig	198.669
Humphrey, F.	Dom	175.605
Knight, S.J.	AB	186.713
Lambert, A.	Sto	295.920
Midlake, P.H.	Sto	284.373
Shaw, W.	Pte	Po10.485
Shergold, J.H.	Dom	357.421
Spence, T.	Sergt	Po5.674
Sprake, G.H.	Dom	358.436
Wagstaff, J.	L/Sig	194.702
Westbrook, A.	Sto	355.511
Willard, H.	Sto	295.943

H.M.S. NIOBE

Period for which entitled:
25th November 1899 to 23rd August 1900

Bars	Total	Returned	Entitled
2	1	0	1
1	140	11	129
0	614	84	530
	755	95	660

Notes:
* Recipient presented with medal on 'Ophir'.
† Recipient presented with medal on 'St. George'.
[1] Recipient's full name is C.M.C. Crichton-Maitland.
[2] Two medals were issued in error; one was returned.
[3] Two medals were issued but both were returned.

Bars: Cape Colony, South Africa 1902

	Hocking, F.J.	Ord	191.407

Bar: Cape Colony

	Abel, G.	Sergt	Ply3.892
	Alley, S.W.	Pte	Ply8.130
	Ayrton, C.J.	Pte	Ply7.820
	Backler, G.F.	Pte	Ply8.172
	Bacon, F.E.	Pte	Ply5.280
	Baker, A.J.	L/Cpl	Ply5.638
	Bishop, A.	Ord	190.195
	Bishop, F.A.	AB	159.207
†	Blackler, E.R.	PO1	138.978
	Boland, J.	Ord	194.218
	Bray, J.	Pte	Ply8.149
	Brooks, E.M.	Pte	Ply9.079
	Brown, F.	Pte	Ply9.084
	Brown, F.F.R.	Ord	191.566
†	Bunker, S.	AB	174.718
	Burbridge, W.	AB	153.993
	Burgoyne, F.F.	Ord	192.333
	Cannon, A.H.E.	AB	127.851
	Cash, P.	Ord	184.904
	Chamberlain, J.	L/Sergt	Ply3.859
	Clark, J.	AB	161.919
	Cload, J.H.	Ord	197.081
	Cogan, J.	Pte	Ply5.353
	Collins, E.E.	Ch/PO	104.098
	Connolly, E.	Pte	Ply4.286
	Cook, R.	Pte	Ply8.483
	Coombes, G.	Sergt	Ply2.895
	Croole, R.	AB	155.972
	Davenport, R.C.	Midn	
	Day, C.W.	Pte	Ply7.921
	Denning, G.F.	AB	168.110
	Dixon, A.	Midn	
	Ellicombe, J.	Pte	Ply5.414
	Ellis, A.H.	Pte	Po9.103
	Ellis, J.	Pte	Ply6.997
	Evans, J.	Pte	Ply6.898
	Field, W.	Pte	Ply7.886
	Fisher-Hall, A.W.	Midn	
	Fudge, E.	Sergt	Ply3.763
	Fullen, J.	Pte	Ply8.473
	Furzeman, G.H.	AB	162.876
	Gearing, E.W.G.	AB	167.485
	Gordon, R.J.	Ord	196.199
*	Gosling, J.S.	AB	158.692
	Green, A.E.	Pte	Ply6.766
	Hales, J.	Pte	Ply9.080
	Hamer, S.	L/Cpl	Ply7.768
	Harry, A.	L/S	168.336
	Hearn, C.L.G.	Pte	Ply4.546
	Holden, A.P.	Midn	
	Horn, J.	AB	189.101
	Hudson, J.H.	AB	181.444
	Johnstone, M.	Pte	Ply7.673
	Jones, H.W.	SBStd	137.524
	Justice, J.H.	Pte	Ch1.780
	Kemp, F.	AB	158.321
	Kennedy, W.G.A.	Lieut	
	Kiely, M.	Ord	188.696
	Kunhardt, H.R.	Midn	
	Lane, T.	Ord	195.028
	Law, W.	Pte	Ply6.267
	Legg, L.S.	Act/Bosn	
	Little, M.J.	Pte	Ply8.810
	Loddey, W.	Ord	188.203
	Lucas, G.	AB	178.656
	Lundy, J.W.	AB	155.633
	McDonald, D.	Pte	Ply9.079
	MacFarlan, R.J.	Midn	
	McLaughlin, J.	Pte	Ply7.819
	McLeod, W.H.	AB	172.750
*[1]	Maitland, C.M.C.	Lieut	
	Mills, G.	Pte	Ply6.123
	Moody, A.J.	Pte	Ply6.833
	Murphy, W.	Pte	Ply5.833
	Murren, D.	Ord	187.455

Bar: Cape Colony *continued*

* Musk, W.	2/Yeo/Sig	161.890
Nutt, T.J.	Pte	Ply7.191
Osborne, F.G.	L/Cpl	Ply8.352
Osmond, H.	Pte	Ply6.836
Opie, J.W.	L/S	150.828
Palmer, W.H.	Cpl	Ply4.457
Parker, W.G.	Bugler	Ch11.990
Peacock, A.J.	Pte	Ply7.877
Pepperell, W.G.	AB	163.293
Petch, G.E.J.	Lieut	
Philp, R.E.	Arm/Mte	340.027
Pidgeon, A.J.	Ord	188.779
Pillar, W.J.	PO2	139.636
Pomeroy, C.H.	AB	162.873
Pope, W.H.	Pte	Ply7.806
Rayner, A.	Pte	Ply6.831
Redman, C.S.	Ord	187.465
Richards, P.	Ord	187.172
Ridout, A.E.	L/S	162.827
Robinson, A.	Pte	Ply8.370
Royston, J.	L/S	155.006
Rutherford, G.	Pte	Ply9.180
Sampson, J.	Pte	Ply5.482
Saunders, E.P.	AB	173.949
Screen, E.J.	AB	166.580
Short, A.W.	Q/Sig	190.165
Small, W.J.	Ord	189.288
Smith, J.	AB	114.113
Soper, J.W.	Ord	192.267
Squires, A.E.	L/S	155.274
Staddon, L.	AB	157.955
* Stockley, H.H.F.	Lieut(RMLI)	
Stone, C.	AB	168.171
Stuart, W.	AB	153.947
Sullivan, J.	AB	169.545
Sussex, F.	Pte	Ply9.059
Thomas, E.	AB	153.537
Thomas, J.	AB	183.041
Tierney, T.	Pte	Ply6.536
Trebilcock, B.	Ord	196.810
Trevett, G.C.	Pte	Ply7.840
Tupman, J.A.	Capt(RMLI)	
Wakeham, R.	Pte	Ply7.915
Wall, F.	Pte	Ply9.081
Weiler, C.A.	Pte	Ply6.297
Wight, L.	Pte	Ply8.378
Williamson, W.	Pte	Ply4.473
Wills, S.E.	L/S	165.530
Wills, T.	Pte	Ply8.521
Wilson, H.	Pte	Ply9.091
* Winsloe, A.L.	Capt	
Wood, W.	Pte	Ply3.265
Wright, B.	Bugler	Ply8.848

Duplicate medals:

Burgoyne, F.F.	Ord	192.333
Clark, J.	AB	161.919
x Lane, T.	Ord	195.028
McDonald, D.	Pte	Ply9.079
MacFarlan, R.J.	Midn	
Screen, E.J.	AB	166.580
Soper, J.W.	Ord	192.267

x Two duplicate medals issued.

Returned medals:

Carroll, J.	Ord	193.255
Caulfield, O.	Pte	Ply7.999
Chrichlow, T.H.	Pte	Ply9.088
Crawley, W.A.	Pte	Ply8.475
Daly, P.	Ord	185.785
Hagger, A.A.	Dom	357.539
Nicholas, W.J.	Ord	194.909
Reeves, H.	Pte	Ply5.929
Smith, F.W.	Pte	Ply9.094
Thomson, A.	Pte	Ply7.791
Whiting, A.	Act/Gunr	

Bar: Rhodesia

Atkinson, P.W.J.	Lieut	

No Bar Medals

Ahern, J.	Ord	194.184
Albert, G.H.	AB	106.798
Alevin, W.	Ch/PO	104.616
Allen, H.	Boy Wrtr	341.699
Allen, P.	PO1	136.830
Andrew, C.T.	Ord	193.645
Andrews, A.H.	Ord	185.633
Andrews, S.G.	Clerk	
Armstrong, J.	Sto	287.108
Ash, T.D.	Yeo/Sig	124.245
Auton, J.J.	Pte	Ply3.122
Axworthy, W.H.	Sto	287.353
Back, F.	Pte	Ply4.226
Badcock, E.	Sig	189.192
Bailey, W.H.	L/S	142.686
Baker, H.	Cpl	Ply4.938
* Banbury, W.	Carp	
Bancroft, J.	AB	136.992
Barham, J.	Ord	204.495
Barrett, P.C.	Ord	197.088
Bartlett, G.H.	Sto	283.679
Beard, G.A.	Ord	194.425
Beculoh, J.	Carp/Crew	341.359
Beggs, H.	Sto	287.289
Bell, R.E.	Blksmth/Mte	340.099
Bell, W.J.	Boy	197.427
Best, W.	Pte	Ply2.636
Beul, T.A.	Dom	355.257
Beull, T.	Sto	144.914
Bevan, F.	Ord	195.974
Bicknell, H.	Ord	199.283
Bidgood, W.	Ch/Sto	139.616
Blackmore, J.S.	Arm	132.024
Bligh, W.	Ord	197.369
Bluett, J.	L/Sto	148.870
Boorman, W.J.	Sto	278.595
Borthwick, E.R.	Chaplain	
Bovey, A.	Ord	198.154

Bowles, W.R.	Sh/Std/Asst	340.482
Boyd, R.C.	PO2	131.331
Bradley, C.	St/Surgn	
Bray, E.	Sto	287.352
Bray, W.J.	Ord	191.406
Brennan, J.	Ord	195.799
Brickenden, F.G.	Midn	
Brickwood, R.	Ord	197.375
Brindley, J.	ERA	132.289
Brock, T.C.	Pntr	340.917
Brocklesby, J.P.	Ord	194.510
Brooks, A.J.	Dom	355.853
Broom, J.	Boy	197.404
Broughton, E.	Asst/ERA	269.737
Brown, J.T.	Pte	Ply7.217
Brown, T.	Sto	168.213
Bryan, A.	Dom	131.079
Bryant, S.	Boy	197.445
* Bryer, S.M.G.	Engr	
Buchanan, M.	Sto	291.508
Budgeon, S.G.	Dom	356.415
Bulley, P.	AB	172.682
Burke, D.	Ord	185.936
Burke, T.	Ord	188.884
Burns, W.R.	Ord	191.373
Burt, B.	L/Sto	144.389
Butland, T.J.	AB	193.117
Butler, B.	L/Sto	172.343
Butler, T.	Bandn	353.835
Cain, E.E.	AB	157.122
Callaghan, E.	Ord	197.686
Callard, H.R.	PO2	174.689
Callaway, E.R.	ERA	161.717
Canavan, J.	Ord	187.825
Candeland, A.	Pte	Ply7.644
Carn, G.	Sto	290.136
Carnell, J.A.	L/Sto	152.659
Carroll, J.H.	2/Yeo/Sig	167.228
Cattermole, W.H.	Ord	192.245
Cecil, W.H.	Ord	186.051
Chaddock, W.E.	Pte	Ply2.342
Chapman, J.	Carp/Mte	155.424
Chapman, W.G.	AB	181.442
Chappell, H.	AB	157.835
Chard, W.H.J.	L/Sto	174.393
Cheriton, J.	PO1	120.003
Clark, C.M.	Act/ERA	269.563
Clark, S.	Sto	170.644
Clements, F.	Sto	288.233
Clench, W.H.	SB/Attn	350.480
* Coak, G.	PO1	114.036
Coghlan, P.	Ord	198.702
Cole, W.C.	Sto	287.312
Coleman, J.J.	Sto	280.573
Coles, F.	Pte	Ply4.835
Coles, G.R.	Pte	Ply4.444
Collier, J.	PO2	145.276
Collins, J.	Ord	198.986
Colomb, P.H.	Lieut	
Colwill, D.	Shpwrt	133.777
Colwill, T.	Ord	193.444
Combstock, T.H.	L/S	139.206
Cook, J.T.	Sto	290.876
Cooksley, F.	AB	134.594
Cornick, J.	L/Sto	89.460
Couhig, J.	Ord	198.063
Crabb, F.	Sto	290.951
Craig, J.W.	Surgn	
Crapp, S.	PO1	123.177
Creedon, C.	Sto	291.785
Cribbons, S.	Sto	169.975
Culnan, J.	Sto	288.020
Culverwell, J.	Boy	197.917
Cummings, T.P.	Ord	200.153
Currah, W.F.	Ch/ERA	141.016
Curtis, R.	Boy	197.367
Daley, J.	AB	180.469
Daly, J.	Sto	290.943
Dan, G.A.	Ord	200.187
Dark, A.	Sto	291.482
Dart, T.	Ch/Sto	110.928
Davenport, W.	Band	104.770
Davey, H.	ERA	169.276
Davey, J.S.	Ord	193.129
Davies, A.	Sto	284.284
Davies, G.	Sto	287.360
Davies, S.E.	Sig/Boy	196.936
Davis, A.	Boy	197.409
Delaney, J.	Sto	291.511
Denley, R.	Sh/Cpl	350.156
Derham, P.	Ord	193.137
Diggle, E.G.	Act/Lieut	
Divett, R.	Midn	
Dodd, R.H.	Sto	156.125
Dodge, W.J.	Ord	183.984
Doherty, H.	Sto	287.380
Doherty, J.	Sto	287.377
Dole, H.E.	Ord	197.791
Donovan, D.	PO1	150.620
Donovan, J.	Ord	195.892
Douglas, R.	Act/ERA	269.632
Drake, H.A.	Blksmth/Mte	341.803
Drake-Brockman, C.E.F.	Capt(RMLI)	
Drew, J.	L/Sto	147.257
Driscoll, D.	AB	140.122
Driscoll, J.	Ord	196.176
Drown, J.H.	AB	192.311
Duggan, J.	Sto	287.792
Duggan, M.	Ord	197.687
Duggan, W.	Sto	165.728
Dunn, F.	AB	180.750
Dykins, C.A.	Sto	285.058
Dymond, E.G.	ERA	269.171
Easton, J.	Sto	153.079
Edgecumbe, A.	Sto	278.945
Edgington, A.W.	Ord	181.273
Edwards, C.H.	PO1	126.849
Edwards, W.H.	PO2	143.441
Ellis, W.	AB	156.400
Etheridge, E.	Sto	291.539
Evans, C.H.	Boy	197.366
Evans, J.J.	PO1	81.094

No Bar Medals *continued*

Everett, F.	Pte	Ply9.086		Hawkins, S.L.	Ord	192.258
Every, F.G.	Sto	168.465		Hawton, W.	Carp/Mte	142.241
Fairley, C.S.	Sto	283.043		Hayes, T.	PO1	59.831
Fallon, J.	Ord	194.219		Hayward, E.J.	AB	173.719
Farrant, W.J.	L/S	259.142		Heath, A.	Sto	283.666
Fenton, A.R.T.	L/S	160.982		Hellier, T.	PO1	152.890
Filer, J.	ERA	268.603		Herbert, F.G.	Dom	356.259
Finton, T.	Ord	191.780		Hewer, J.	Pte	Ply5.012
Fitzsimons, J.	Sto	283.682		Hewitt, H.	Ord	188.504
Flinn, G.	Cooper	340.042		Higgins, W.H.	Sto	291.476
Floyd, C.H.	Sto	287.322		Hill, E.H.	Dom	357.538
Flynn, J.	Ord	185.937		Hill, H.	Ch/Arm	128.658
Foley, E.	Sto	287.297		Hill, H.	Ord	192.398
Foley, M.	Sto	138.865		Hill, J.	Band	167.055
Foot, R.G.	Ord	193.536		Hill, W.	Sto	283.557
Forbes, R.	Sto	287.325		Hillier, A.	Ord	199.328
Ford, C.	Sto	148.779		Hinds, A.G.	Sig/Boy	196.556
Frewin, J.	L/Sto	157.448		Hiscox, W.	Sto	287.375
Fry, F.J.	Ch/Sto	130.754		Hitchings, W.A.	Sto	287.365
Fudge, F.A.	Sto	276.943		Hoare, S.	L/S	143.798
Fuge, A.H.	Ord	196.809		Hodge, J.	Boy	197.374
Fuller, H.	Band	124.339	*	Hogan, A.J.	AB	180.318
Furey, M.	Sto	288.125		Hogan, J.	Ord	194.182
Furze, W.J.	PO1	120.802		Hooper, J.	Ord	184.398
Garner, W.	Pte	Ply8.014		Hooper, S.	Dom	357.025
Gaskins, T.	Ord	198.296		Horn, J.J.	Sto	108.525
German, J.L.H.	St/Payr			Hows, A.W.S.	PO2	139.536
Gilbert, B.J.	Sig	196.039		Hughes, W.	Sto	277.765
Glanville, J.	ERA	269.246		Hunt, F.G.	PO1	138.998
Glover, J.T.	Ord	196.079		Hunt, S.	Ch/PO	81.092
Glynn, E.G.	Sto	165.676		Hurley, G.	Sto	290.844
Godolphin, S.	SBStd	82.508	*	Hutchings, F.	Pte	Ply5.808
Gollop, H.	Band	173.308		Irish, H.	L/Sto	153.579
Grant, J.	Act/ERA	269.631		Jackson, G.A.	Boy	197.406
Graves-Burton, R.H.	Lieut			James, J.	Ord	198.265
Gray, E.T.	Ord	189.812		Jarvis, H.	Sto	283.658
Greenhalgh, F.	Sig	196.913		Jenkins, G.C.	Ord	199.347
Griffin, E.	Ch/Sto	144.736		Johns, A.J.	St/Engr	
Gritton, J.	AB	168.253		Johns, H.	L/Sto	149.216
Gruzlien, F.W.	L/Shpwrt	158.835		Johns, M.T.	Ch/Sto	110.917
Haddy, F.J.H.	Ord	185.995		Johnstone, D.	Sto	283.996
Hagram, T.W.	Boy	194.143		Jones, A.E.	ERA	268.193
Halfyard, J.	Boy	197.367		Jones, H.J.	Sto	148.968
Hall, A.W.	Boy	197.435		Jones, J.	Ord	200.673
Hall, J.	Sh/Cook	141.918		Jones, R.	Sto	290.824
Hall, W.	Sto	146.726		Jones, T.	Pte	Po3.043
Hamblin, F.W.	Asst/Engr			Jones, W.	AB	104.013
Hamlyn, E.G.	Sto	159.927		Jugo, J.	Cooks/Mte	354.596
Hamlyn, H.P.	Ord	199.348		Jury, R.R.	Asst/Engr	
Hancock, A.	Pte	Ply8.845		Keast, F.	Sto	287.311
Hancock, W.	Sto	283.837		Keefe, D.	PO1	102.094
Hannaford, E.H.	Ord	200.166		Kelland, A.H.	Ord	195.717
Hannaford, W.	L/S	163.217		Kennedy, H.	Sto	287.328
Hardwick, J.	Ord	180.589		Kennedy, J.	Sto	283.066
Harbinson, R.	Band	155.110		Kennedy, M.	Sto	281.242
Harris, M.	2/Cooper	342.008		Kennedy, M.	Sto	284.101
Harris, W.J.	Ord	191.320		Keohane, P.	Ord	196.680
Harvey, H.E.	Midn			Kidney, W.	L/Sto	168.670
Hawker, R.	Ord	197.439		Kirwin, J.J.	Asst/Engr	
Hawkes, J.H.R.	Ord	194.083		Kitto, C.H.	L/S	153.484
			*	Knight, D.J.	PO1	130.376

Knight, J.	Sto	130.081
Knight, R.	Boy	197.384
Lacey, G.	Ord	188.521
Lancey, J.H.	Ord	192.924
Lane, R.W.	Sto	287.369
Langford, H.	Sig	190.510
Langley, G.	Dom	76.632
Lavers, S.G.	Sto	284.282
Lean, C.	L/Carp/Crew	340.103
Leary, C.	PO1	158.134
Leary, J.	Ord	186.484
Leary, M.	AB	159.099
Lecky, A.M.	Midn	
Lee, M.	Ord	197.659
Legg, R.J.	AB	164.939
Leonard, E.	Ord	198.365
Lester, A.E.	Asst/Engr	
Lewis, John.	Kroo	
Locke, B.J.	Sig/Boy	196.767
Lovekin, R.	AB	156.818
Lowden, H.	L/Sto	152.113
Lowe, L.	Band	177.529
Luckham, W.F.	Sto	276.956
Lush, V.	Cook/Mte	355.522
Luxon, W.C.	Sto	281.450
Lyons, J.	Ord	199.342
McCarthy, T.	Band	127.653
McCausland, D.	Ord	186.889
McClean, J.	Sto	291.782
McCleverty, T.	Sto	291.778
* McCormack, C.	MAA	109.665
McDaid, J.	Sto	287.302
MacDonald, A.	L/Carp/Crew	340.720
McLellon, D.	Ch/ERA	130.336
McNamara, A.	Sto	283.851
Maben, J.E.	Sail	147.533
Mahoney, J.	AB	102.934
Mahoney, J.	Ord	196.189
Maloney, J.	Ord	183.689
Man, J.	Lieut	
Manweiler, C.	Sto	288.175
Marden, J.H.	PO1	118.606
Marks, C.S.	ERA	153.122
Martin, E.J.	L/S	176.984
Masterson, J.	Boy	197.880
Matthews, F.A.	Ord	197.358
Matthews, J.	Ch/Sto	126.474
Meneaud, J.	Sto	355.017
Merrett, S.J.	Act/Gunr	
Miller, G.	Midn	
Miller, J.	Sto	177.397
Miller, L.S.	L/Sig	147.633
* Millington, J.	Pte	Ply6.742
Mitchell, T.J.	Ord	190.256
Mitchell, W.A.	Ord	189.085
Mitchelmore, W.	L/Sto	147.513
Moroney, D.	Sto	285.351
Morris, W.C.	Pte	Ply9.097
Morse, W.H.	PO1	128.084
Moxhay, C.	Ord	193.248
Moyse, A.G.	PO1	145.548

Mudge, F.	PO1	108.571
Mullany, W.	Boy	198.064
Munday, J.D.	Sto	148.871
Murley, A.G.	Boy	197.919
Mullen, G.G.	Sto	287.364
Mullen, J.T.	Sto	287.366
Mutter, H.J.	Ord	188.079
Mutton, W.H.	L/Sto	147.526
Mynard, W.J.	PO1	132.994
Neve, M.W.	Ord	190.576
Newberry, J.	Boy	197.337
Newcombe, F.E.	Sto	281.407
Nile, W.	Sto	287.376
Norris, W.	Ord	192.515
Northcott, A.	Gunr	
Norton, T.A.	Ord	192.653
Nott, W.J.	L/Sto	145.803
O'Neill, J.	Sto	291.495
O'Sullivan, D.	PO2	142.550
Olden, W.	Ch/Sto	110.912
Oliver, H.F.	Lieut	
Olver, A.	Dom	355.855
Orr, A.	Sto	287.371
Partridge, W.	Sh/Cpl	120.903
Pasker, R.S.J.	AB	100.848
Penney, R.J.	PO2	136.904
Perks, S.G.	Dom	357.646
Perry, F.	Sto	285.033
Phillipant, J.H.	Blksmth	146.287
Pitcavin, J.E.	Asst/Clerk	
Poignand, C.A.	Midn	
Pollard, F.J.	Ord	188.512
Pollard, J.	Sto	284.285
Ponting, G.	Band	163.423
Popplestone, A.	L/Sto	148.925
Porter, V.R.	Midn	
Powell, A.	Sto	288.225
Powers, M.J.	Sto	280.126
Preston, F.	L/Shpwrt	163.087
Prew, H.	Act/ERA	296.634
Price, G.	Sto	287.316
Prichard, H.T.	Sub Lieut	
Prudence, W.G.	Ord	194.746
Pryn, R.H.	L/Sto	153.157
Puckey, G.B.	Ord	198.615
Pughs, W.	Ord	192.415
Pyburne, M.	Ord	198.990
Quick, R.	Sto	287.343
Radford, J.	Sh/Cpl	150.071
Raffill, G.	Ord	183.636
Rawlings, W.	Ord	183.451
Ray, F.	Band/Cpl	121.491
Reeves, J.H.	PO2	160.690
Regan, M.	L/Sto	153.456
Reid, H.R.	Ord	186.483
Reid, J.	Boy	197.855
Reinhardt, J.	Sto	283.686
Reynolds, W.	Sto	147.475
Richards, A.	Ord	185.010
Richards, G.S.	Boy	197.429
Richardson, C.D.	Sub Lieut	

No Bar Medals *continued*

	Richardson, R.C.	Midn	
	Roberts, C.B.	Asst/Payr	
	Roberts, C.J.	L/Sto	173.592
	Roberts, G.	PO2	138.512
	Robins, W.G.	Ch/ERA	111.211
	Robinson, J.	Ord	197.377
	Roche, M.	Boy	198.066
	Rogers, A.H.	Sh/Std/Boy	341.837
	Rooke, C.	Sto	276.508
	Rose, C.	Ord	187.982
	Rosevere, W.H.	Asst/Engr	
	Rowe, E.	L/Sto	137.543
	Rowley, E.C.	Ord	198.630
	Ruse, B.S.	Sh/Std/Boy	342.178
	Russell, W.H.J.	Sto	291.457
	Russell, W.J.	L/Shpwrt	147.242
	Ryder, E.C.	Dom	353.374
	Sammells, H.	AB	123.622
	Saunders, E.H.	Fl/Surgn	
	Saunders, J.	L/Sto	130.737
	Scarborough, W.J.	Sto	284.316
	Scoble, G.H.	Ord	200.181
	Seale, C.S.	Sig	197.756
	Sedgman, W.	Ord	193.195
	Sennett, J.	ERA	268.026
	Setters, A.W.	Sto	284.293
	Shapcott, W.	Ord	186.241
	Shapter, C.	Pte	Ply7.594
	Sheppard, D.	Ord	196.176
	Sheppard, G.	Ord	197.911
	Sheriden, C.	AB	113.848
	Shiels, H.F.	Sto	287.798
	Shilbeck, A.H.	Pte	Ply9.068
	Short, T.	Sto	287.235
	Simmons, W.G.J.	Sto	101.740
	Simpson, J.W.	Act/ERA	269.565
	Sims, G.H.	Ord	193.579
	Smale, W.	Pte	Ply5.802
	Smith, C.	Sto	92.593
	Smith, H.G.	Dom	356.790
	Smith, R.	Sto	276.790
	Smith, R.E.	Ch/Sto	115.280
	Smith, W.J.	Ord	198.869
	Solomon, T.J.	PO2	136.190
	Southwood, T.G.	Bosn	
	Speare, W.	Blksmth/Mte	341.591
	Spreat, E.E.	Band	340.505
	Springs, W.L.	PO2	151.978
	Squance, E.	Sto	289.537
	Squires, E.	Sto	291.455
	Staddon, E.J.	AB	187.535
	Stedman, J.A.	Sto	291.463
	Steer, H.	Ord	199.004
	Steer, W.	Ord	188.451
	Stephens, J.A.	PO1	136.704
	Stephens, W.	Sto	290.935
	Stickler, E.	L/Sto	154.935
*	Stone, R.J.	PO1	124.598
	Stoneham, A.	Sto	155.491
	Storey, W.J.	Ch/ERA	136.440

	Stratford, C.	ERA	269.248
	Stratton, E.	Band	117.022
	Strudwick, F.	Boy	197.378
	Stuart, E.H.	AB	115.385
*	Stumbles, G.E.	AB	163.303
	Sullivan, C.	AB	167.561
	Sullivan, J.	Ord	195.265
	Sullivan, M.J.	Shpwrt	342.324
	Sullivan, T.	Ord	198.088
	Sweeney, J.	Sto	290.961
	Sweeting, W.F.	Sto	284.991
	Tarbet, G.McV.	Act/ERA	269.681
	Taylor, F.	Ord	194.511
†	Terry, F.G.	Midn	
	Thomas, D.	Ord	197.451
	Thomas, H.	Ord	188.002
	Thornton, W.C.	Carp/Crew	147.248
	Thoyts, R.E.	Midn	
	Tilling, J.	Pte	Ply9.083
	Timms, W.	Ord	193.185
	Tolcher, C.	Boy	197.372
*	Toms, E.	PO1	133.659
	Tooze, A.	Sto	151.769
	Tremere, W.R.	Boy	197.883
	Trenwith, C.M.	AB	180.974
	Trist, W.	Sto	287.313
	Trout, F.E.	Ord	192.292
	Veale, C.S.	Arm	145.066
	Veale, T.C.	Ord	192.853
	Veale, W.H.	Sto	152.119
	Venn, J.	Sto	284.768
	Vickery, W.	Ord	174.707
	Wade, L.E.	Dom	355.574
†	Walker, B.C.	Midn	
	Walsh, J.	Ord	198.999
	Walsh, M.N.	Sto	290.977
	Walsh, W.	Q/Sig	116.502
	Walters, G.S.	Sig/Boy	196.993
	Warden, R.	Plmbr	115.497
	Warren, H.	Ord	191.374
	Wearne, J.	Ord	193.193
	Webb, D.	Pte	Ply4.052
	Webber, G.	Sto	283.665
	Wellington, W.I.	Sh/Cpl	133.532
*	Wemyss, R.E.	Comdr	
	Wesley, A.	Q/Sig	173.078
	West, C.A.	Sto	285.037
	West, W.	Sto	283.111
	Weymouth, W.	Sto	290.856
	Wheatcroft, C.T.	Dom	356.851
	White, E.	Ord	186.006
	White, S.G.	3/Wrtr	340.597
	Whiting, A.	Sto	163.822
	Whittle, J.	Sto	290.939
	Williams, A.	Sto	284.585
	Williams, E.J.	Ord	195.246
	Williams, G.A.	PO2	126.640
	Wilton, L.R.	Ch/Sto	144.759
	Winter, R.	Arm/Mte	151.416
	Woodman, R.	L/S	143.443
	Woolfe, F.	AB	154.007

* Wreford, F.A.	PO1	112.186
Wreford, J.	PO1	118.542
Wright, W.E.H.	Dom	161.264
Wyatt, J.E.	Ord	197.459
Young, C.W.	AB	148.253
Young, H.	Ord	195.877

Duplicate medals:

Andrews, A.H.	Ord	185.633
Bluett, J.	L/Sto	148.870
Brickwood, R.	Ord	197.375
Combstock, T.H.	L/S	139.206
Davies, A.	Sto	284.284
Davies, G.	Sto	287.360
Hannaford, E.H.	Ord	200.166
Hooper, J.	Ord	184.398
Lee, M.	Ord	197.659
Luxon, W.C.	Sto	281.450
McClean, J.	Sto	291.782
Meneaud, J.	Sto	355.017
Nile, W.	Sto	287.376
Orr, A.	Sto	287.371
Poignand, C.A.	Midn	
Scarborough, W.J.	Sto	284.316
Sedgman, W.	Ord	193.195
Terry, F.G.	Midn	
Thomas, H.	Ord	188.002
Tremere, W.R.	Boy	197.883

Returned medals:

Abbott, J.T.	Ord	195.303
Alleyne, W.J.	Ord	200.161
Ashover, A.	AB	168.050
Bailey, J.	Dom	144.476
[2] Barrett, P.C.	Ord	197.088
Bell, C.	Kroo	
Block, W.	Ord	200.111
Boy, Jim.	Kroo	
Brown, J.	Boy ,	197.442
Bryant, W.J.	Ord	194.752
Burke, J.	Band	340.979
Byrne, J.J.	Ord	199.679
Dart, G.	AB	142.737
Davison, G.	Dom	356.543
Devonald, J.	Sto	282.110
Dockerty, T.	AB	135.690
Dowdle, W.E.	Dom	357.066
Doyle, E.	Sto	287.367
[3] Evans, J.E.	AB	150.681
Finnegan, D.	Ord	198.706
Fitzgerald, T.	Sto	287.338
Fuge, A.H.	Ord	196.809
Fullard, C.	Ord	190.158
Galloway, J.	AB	145.171
Gillham, A.	Sig	195.805
Glasgow, Tom.	Kroo	
Harper, E.	Pte	Ply2.792
Harris, J.	Ord	189.309
Hart, W.J.	Ord	192.261
Hawke, R.	Sto	287.335
Hendy, C.G.	Arm/Crew	177.035
Jackson, S.	Ord	194.220
Jennings, H.N.	Pte	Ply9.089
Johns, E.	Kroo	
Jones, G.B.	Q/Sig	167.497
Jukes, H.E.G.S.	Midn	
Kehoe, L.	Sto	287.304
Kendall, W.G.	Ord	199.321
Lewis, Tom.	Kroo	
McCarthy, T.C.	Ord	200.698
Markham, T.	Ord	198.087
Mason, J.	Ord	200.152
Merrall, A.	Ord	200.101
Meyrick, F.C.	N/Cadet	
Middleton, D.	Sto	290.880
Monaghan, M.	Sto	285.349
Morgan, J.	Kroo	
Morrison, R.	Ord	196.453
Neale, S.	Sto	287.349
Neill, J.	Sto	291.561
Newman, Tom.	Kroo	
O'Keefe, M.	Ord	191.172
Parsemore, A.	Ord	198.349
Paterson, J.C.S.	Midn	
Patterson, J.	Ord	192.293
Payne, P.	Ord	200.675
Phelps, W.H.	AB	179.725
Phillips, J.	Sto	290.937
Phillips, P.	Sto	284.342
Pickup, C.	Ord	367.014
Purnell, A.E.	Sto	291.483
Randells, J.	Ord	188.294
Raymond, H.	Ord	191.800
Real, S.	PO2	83.480
Regan, D.	Sto	287.793
Regan, P.	Sto	290.964
Richards, T.	Sto	284.082
Roberts, John.	Kroo	
Robeson, C.W.	Ord	195.198
Rowland, A.C.	AB	152.887
Sampson, John.	Kroo	
Sancto, R.	Ord	197.391
Seabreeze.	Kroo	
Smith, J.A.	Ins/Mach	
Snowball, Tom.	Kroo	
Spaller, F.	Dom	358.159
Sullivan, P.	Ord	198.364
Tabb, W.J.	Ord	197.092
Vanstone, J.	Ord	190.159
Warner, D.	Boy	197.348
Wayling, H.J.	Act/Bosn	
Webb, A.J.	Sto	287.174
Webber, J.	Boy	197.061
Yabsley, W.H.	Sh/Cpl	131.179

H.M.S. PARTRIDGE

Period for which entitled:
11th October 1899 to 8th March 1901.

Extended period:
9th March 1901 to 2nd January 1902
5th April 1902 to 13th May 1902
14th May 1902 to 31st May 1902 (Recommission).

Bars	*Total*	*Returned*	*Entitled*
2	4	1	3
1	8	0	8
0	162	12	150
	174	13	161

Notes:
* Medal presented on Ophir.

Bars: Cape Colony, South Africa 1901

Boyd, J.	Boy	196.540
Leatham, G.L.T.	Lieut	

Bar: Cape Colony

Andrews, J.	Pte	Ch10.089
Ashmore, G.	AB	136.972
Hall, J.	AB	137.504

Bar: Rhodesia

Baker, F.G.	Asst/Engr	
Bridgman, Hon. R.O.B.	Sub Lieut	
Fryer, H.E.	Surgn	
Hayward, C.J.	Gunr	
Hunt, A.T.	Lieut	

No Bar Medals

Allchin, F.	L/Sto	152.403
Aucliffe, S.	Pte	Ch1.796
Baker, W.R.	L/S	166.050
Bannerman, J.	Ord	201.307
Bee, W.	Kroo	
Britton, J.	AB	174.150
Brooks, R.T.	L/Sergt	Ch7.146
Brown, P.	Sto	276.321
Brown, W.	Kroo	
Cage, H.	Pte	Ch10.036
Callan, J.C.	L/S	168.214
Calver, F.S.	AB	165.612
Charlton, C.	Sto	282.008
Clark, W.	Pte	Ch3.093
Clayton, H.	Ord	201.380
Clegg, R.B.	AB	166.861
Cobb, P.L.	Boy	196.537
* Collins, A.D.	Shpwrt	341.209
Colyer, J.W.	Dom	357.381
Cooper, J.E.	SB/Attn	354.091
Correa, M.	Dom	356.785
Couts, F.M.	Dom	353.692
Cunnington, G.	Boy	196.364
Drake, F.H.	Arm/Mte	341.093
Drake, H.W.	Sto	282.080
Everyday, J.	Kroo	
Eyvell, C.	ERA	268.768
Fairweather, W.	AB	156.110
Farmer, E.C.	ERA	268.199
Farndell, H.	Sh/Cook	129.739
Feldon, S.	PO2	178.093
Gale, H.	ERA	265.650
Goodway, R.	PO2	158.094
Gore, S.	L/Sto	139.900
Hasker, W.	Sto	169.305
Hill, W.	L/Carp/Crew	342.268
Holmes, A.E.	Sto	154.791
Howard, J.	Sto	279.172
Jacob, T.	Kroo	
James, O.H.	Boy	196.355
Jeffery, A.	Ord	196.092
Keogh, J.P.	Ord	192.137
Knight, G.C.	L/Sto	169.228
Lawless, J.	PO1	161.795
Lyons, E.	Sto	282.670
McGuinness, J.	AB	173.666
Maison, W.	Ch/Sto	132.257
Manly, A.W.	Sig	195.020
Matthews, G.	Sto	
Miller, H.	AB	191.589
Moore, D.	Kroo	
Moore, W.	Kroo	
Moreton, D.	Dom	132.805
Mundy, C.W.	Sh/Std	158.038
Nelson, E.	Kroo	
Newton, W.	Sto	168.728
Orpin, G.	Ch/Sto	132.359
Osborne, H.G.	AB	155.847
Patterson, W.G.	AB	171.037

Penney, G.J.	Carp/Mte	170.159
Phillips, W.	AB	164.794
Pinder, W.	AB	166.539
Reed, P.	Dom	354.930
Sali.	Dom	
Scott, F.B.	Sub Lieut	
Slatter, T.	Ord	184.751
Small, Too	Kroo	
Smith, W.	PO1	132.667
Smith, W.R.	Pte	Ch9.568
Snook, S.	2/Wrtr	139.598
Souza, C.A. de	Dom	157.258
Stone, S.	PO2	165.572
Tait, B.	Pte	Ch8.218
Taylor, G.	Ch/Sto	121.271
Walters, F.	AB	192.074
White, A.P.	Q/Sig	176.051
Whitehill, J.	AB	159.626
Williams, J.	Dom	357.647
Wilson, A.J.	Pte	Ch6.618
Young, J.W.	AB	150.667
Young, T.E.	PO1	165.489
Youngs, C.J.	AB	145.170

Duplicate medals:

Slatter, T.	Ord	184.751
Souza, C.A. de	Dom	157.258
Small, Too	Kroo	
Whitehill, J.	AB	159.626

Returned medals:

Beckwith, W.W.	Sig	196.686
Botting, G.H.	Pte	
Delaney, C.	AB	144.167
Lobo, D.M.	Dom	357.209
Townsend, J.W.E.	Lieut	

EXTENDED PERIOD

Bars: Cape Colony, South Africa 1901

Jones, J.J.J.	Sig	202.525

Returned medal:

Thomas, C.H.	AB	192.616

No Bar Medals

Adams, A.	Sto	292.919
Armon, V.S.	Arm/Mte	171.621
Barnes, W.	AB	168.377
Blades, T.	PO2	185.727
Bockett, F.	Pte	Ply9.775
Boddington, C.	Pte	Ply10.708
Burke, J.	Sto	276.476
Clarke, J.	L/Sto	279.038
Clay, J.	Ch/Wrtr	133.197
Collins, A.	L/S	185.357
Corderoy, G.A.	AB	178.339
Curnow, M.	ERA	269.848
Currie, E.	AB	179.789
Davey, E.	AB	178.062
Davies, C.	SB/Attn	350.753
Denny, T.	AB	187.251
Dunn, G.	AB	185.473
Evans, A.F.	Sig	197.359
Friend, R.G.	AB	195.661
Garland, J.	Pte	Ply10.716
Griffin, H.J.	Q/Sig	191.711
Hadley, W.C.	L/S	185.359
Harrison, S.	L/Sig	170.404
Hassam, D.	L/Sto	149.762
Hoar, A.G.	Act/Sh/Std	340.245
King, H.J.	Ch/Sto	132.316
King, S.	Pte	Ply9.968
Lorking, E.	Boy	213.510
Lovelace, J.	Boy	211.819
McAuliffe, D.P.	PO1	159.341
McElvie, T.	Pte	Ply4.433
McLeod, W.W.	ERA	154.153
March, G.	Pte	Ply10.715
Maxted, T.	ERA	269.655
Mitchell, T.S.	Sto	162.107
Mondey, P.	Sto	290.412
Morries, C.	Boy	212.223
Nicholson, H.	AB	185.753
Nickalls, E.	L/Sto	277.386
Parmenter, C.H.	Boy	206.789
Pengelly, S.J.	Pte	Ply5.960
Price, W.F.	Pte	Ply6.723
Read, E.J.	AB	181.606
Reyne, C.V.	Sub Lieut	
Roberts, A.S.	Cpl	Ply8.649
Robinson, A.R.	PO1	140.693
Russell, G.	AB	172.693
Scott, W.	Sub Lieut	
Shepherd, D.H.	PO1	181.256
Sibley, E.J.	AB	181.899
Slim, A.	AB	192.671
Speer, M.J.	Art/Engr	
Stobo, J.	AB	187.811
Stringer, W.A.E.	Sto	286.298
Tedder, A.V.	PO2	185.373
Turner, H.H.	Boy	212.023
Upton, F.	Sh/Cook	163.925
Waite, J.	Sto	297.703
Walton, W.G.	Boy	211.838
Whitworth, J.	Sto	297.556
Williams, J.	AB	170.281
Williams, J.T.	Gunr	
Wood, J.	Ch/Sto	143.523
Wood, W.C.	AB	195.654
Worden, G.T.	PO1	152.957
Wright, W.J.	AB	185.388
Wyatt, F.	AB	194.987
Young, A.E.	Act/Ch/Sto	163.559

Duplicate medals:

Price, W.F.	Pte	Ply6.723
Reyne, C.V.	Sub Lieut	
Robinson, A.R.	PO1	140.693
Slim, A.	AB	192.671
Stobo, J.	AB	187.811
Waite, J.	Sto	297.703

Extended Period, No Bar Medals

Duplicate medals, continued

Whitworth, J.	Sto	297.556

Returned medals:

D'Cruza, A.	Dom	360.468
Kendrick, L.A.	L/Carp/Crew	344.349
Lambert, T.	Pte	Ply5.290
Milham, F.J.	AB	184.664
Souza, F. de	Dom	167.030
Whelan, J.	Surgn	
Ward, W.	Boy	211.848

H.M.S. PEARL

Period for which entitled:

Extended period only:
17th April 1902 to 31st May 1902.

Bars	*Total*	*Returned*	*Entitled*
2	16	2	14
1	0	0	0
0	214	25	189
	230	27	203

Bars: Cape Colony, South Africa 1902

Bear, F.J.	AB	177.351
Bonstow, W.	AB	160.246
Bowden, G.W.	AB	191.625
Clark, C.	L/S	159.156
Collings, H.W.	AB	197.138
Couper, W.	AB	178.746
Hurley, D.	AB	197.862
Hynes, J.	AB	166.525
Jones, W.R.	AB	195.244
Perring, J.R.	PO2	161.012
Ritchie, R.	AB	174.519
Shepherd, H.	AB	156.884
Stonelake, E.	AB	179.561
Thom, J.H.	Lieut	

Duplicate medal:

Hynes, J.	AB	166.525

Returned medals:

Brewer, A.	AB	201.286
Timms, W.	AB	193.185

No Bar Medals

Andrews, H.G.	Ch/Engr	
Ashe, E.P.	Capt	
Baglin, F.W.	Sto	170.880
Baker, W.	AB	179.263
Balkham, F.J.	L/S	186.971
Becks, W.R.	Ord	205.873
Beer, T.H.	Cpl	Ply7.956
Bennett, F.A.W.	Carp/Crew	344.302
Betty, A.H.	Sto	296.852
Bickle, C.S.C.	Dom	358.967
Bond, G.	Sto	292.301
Bowden, R.	Sh/Cpl	138.110
Bradley, J.	Dom	85.251
Broad, P.	Ord	206.824
Brown, J.	Gunr	
Brown, Jacob.	Kroo	
Caldwell, A.	Pte	Ply9.379
Callaghan, A.	AB	172.647
Callaghan, E.	L/S	147.674
Carbin, H.	Ord	206.144
Card, W.A.G.	Sto	357.327
Carr, G.	ERA	268.228
Carroll, B.	Ord	211.626
Cavanagh, T.	AB	115.648
Chambers, J.	St/Surgn	
Christie, J.	Sto	278.341
Clarke, G.J.	AB	124.320
Clatworthy, J.	Sto	297.089
Clayton, A.E.	Pte	Ply9.898
Cleary, J.	Cooper	341.710
Clode, H.J.	Ord	206.173
Cole, J.	Kroo	
Collins, D.	Sto	177.014
Corban, J.	Ord	211.616
Cornthwaite, J.	Sto	277.396
Cotter, W.J.	Ord	211.617
Cousins, G.W.	Pte	Ply7.742
Couzens, D.	L/Sto	150.731
Coward, H.	Pte	Ply9.804
Coyne, J.	AB	187.539
Crockett, W.	Sto	297.096
Crowther, E.	Sh/Std/Asst	343.787
Culverwell, T.	Ord	206.587
Cundy, T.E.	Sto	277.398
Cunningham, H.	Ord	213.839
Dalling, A.V.	Ord	206.180
Daly, P.	Sto	292.304
Daunt, A.	Sto	297.254
Davis, T.	Ord	206.160
Davis, T.H.	Sto	297.239
Diffell, J.	Pte	Ply8.548
Dillon, D.	Sto	175.822
Dixon, W.	L/Sto	163.050
Driscoll, C.	PO1	164.272
Driscoll, J.M.	Ord	211.630
Driver, H.	ERA	268.817
Dunn, R.G.	AB	155.920
Ellery, W.R.	AB	183.570
Everett, W.V.	Ord	205.677
Findley, E.F.	Ord	205.704
Fish, J.	ERA	269.233
Ford, J.F.	Sto	291.543
Foster, A.S.	2/SBStd	350.289
Freeman, C.	Kroo	
Frost, C.W.T.	Sto	289.526

No Bar Medals *continued*

Garvey, M.	PO2	174.866
Gillham, A.	Ord	195.805
Gillham, F.W.	Sto	287.179
Ginger, Tom	Kroo	
Goodman, C.W.	Ord	206.196
Goodwin, F.J.	Pte	Ply9.610
Green, J.	Ch/Sto	129.246
Greenshields, P.	Sto	278.958
Greet, J.D.	Ch/PO	116.566
Gush, A.W.	Lieut	
Hallowes, G.S.	Sub Lieut	
Halstead, E.	Pte	Ply9.896
Hancock, W.H.	Sto	174.218
Harry, E.J.	Arm/Mte	341.355
Head, T.A.	Sh/Cook	156.623
Herbert, F.T.F.	PO2	167.371
Hicks, A.J.A.	Sto	171.309
Hicks, E.T.	AB	184.162
Hill, W.P.	ERA	269.350
Hillier, W.H.I.	Pte	Ply8.033
Hird, J.H.	PO1	106.935
Hobson, G.T.	Sto	297.091
Hollands, F.I.	Sto	290.141
Hudson, A.E.	Lieut	
Humphries, E.	Ord	205.876
Hurley, D.	Sto	278.243
Hutchins, H.	Ch/ERA	140.984
Isaac, E.J.	Ord	206.178
Jeffery, R.J.	Sto	283.057
Johnson, F.	PO1	140.500
Jones, H.A.	Ord	205.837
Jones, W.	Sto	288.253
Jowett, E.	Pte	Ply4.965
Keane, J.	AB	173.998
Kearney, J.	Sto	148.877
Kessell, J.T.	Dom	84.172
Kite, W.B.	Ord	206.143
Knight, F.L.	Ord	206.140
Lamerton, W.	PO1	147.602
Lane, W.C.	Sto	291.531
Leach, J.H.	Q/Sig	191.003
Leahy, W.	Sto	297.252
Leary, T.	AB	165.759
Lemon, W.A.T.	AB	186.290
Lewis, S.	Kroo	
Light, C.F.	Pte	Ply9.807
Luckes, W.A.C.	Sto	279.839
Luckham, C.M.	Payr	
McCarthy, W.	Ord	203.138
McGrath, D.	Sto	283.874
McInnes, A.	AB	177.342
McLaughlin, C.	Plmbr/Mte	344.307
McLaughlin, H.	Sto	276.251
McMillan, J.	Pte	Ply9.061
McNought, J.	Sto	290.386
Main, T.	L/Sto	287.191
Melville, C.	Pte	Ply9.778
Moore, B.	Sto	297.078
Morrison, P.	AB	172.987
Morton, P.	AB	189.053
Mounce, J.	L/Sto	151.855
Moyle, J.	L/Sto	144.721
Munday, J.	Ch/Sto	130.046
Nash, F.J.	Dom	354.470
Neill, W.	Sto	277.746
Nimrod, T.	Kroo	
O'Keeffe, W.	Art/Engr	
Oliver, G.B.	2/Yeo/Sig	197.436
Osborne, W.	Pte	Ply9.673
Palmer, A.H.	Sto	280.208
Palmer, J.E.	Pte	Ply9.826
Pascoe, C.H.	Shpwrt	342.635
Pascoe, J.A.	PO2	137.255
Passmore, W.P.	Pntr	343.094
Pengelly, E.J.	Act/ERA	270.453
Pepperell, W.H.	L/Sto	135.712
Pinches, J.	AB	180.736
Pinnock, A.J.	L/Sig	164.409
Portch, E.	Ord	207.353
Potter, C.	Sergt	Ply6.487
Preece, E.W.	ERA	269.567
Puckey, T.	AB	188.434
Rattenbury, R.	Q/Sig	121.909
Raymond, F.	Ord	208.070
Raymond, F.W.	AB	157.784
Rickard, H.	ERA	149.145
Roberts, John.	Kroo	
Robinson, A.	AB	194.683
Selbey, J.	Pte	Ply3.000
Sheehan, W.	AB	171.345
Shepherd, W.G.	Ord	206.164
Slater, F.	AB	177.295
Smith, A.C.	Carp	
Smith, J.E.	Pte	Ply6.696
Sneyd, C.A.	Pte	Ply9.979
Sowden, E.J.	AB	161.016
Starks, C.H.	Sh/Std	136.719
Sullivan, J.	Carp/Crew	342.386
Sullivan, J.T.	Sto	143.124
Sullivan, T.	Sto	276.314
Sullivan, T.	Sto	292.131
Thayer, H.A.	Sto	292.299
Thorne, G.E.	Dom	169.367
Tinson, J.	Ord	206.171
Trunks, P.	L/Sto	165.228
Turner, H.E.	Q/Sig	175.030
Vincent, T.	PO1	122.936
Vosper, F.W.	AB	200.681
Walsh, P.	Sto	292.327
Walters, H.	AB	114.906
Walters, W.	L/Sto	279.564
Warren, H.J.	Dom	144.920
Warren, W.R.	Arm/Crew	343.003
Weids, L.R.	Ord	206.147
Westlake, H.	Ch/Sto	145.476
Whyte, A.	Pte	Ply9.844
Wilkins, A.	Sto	297.237
Williams, A.	Sto	297.093
Williams, J.	Kroo	
Williams, J.H.	AB	161.472
Wilmott, G.	Dom	359.459

Winfield, W.H.	Bugler	Ply9.351
Wingell, W.	Pte	Ply9.788
Withycombe, W.	Sto	278.260

Duplicate medals:

Callaghan, A.	AB	172.647
Crockett, W.	Sto	297.096
Hancock, W.H.	Sto	174.218
Harry, E.J.	Arm/Mte	341.355
Herbert, F.T.F.	PO2	167.371
Hollands, F.I.	Sto	290.141
Humphries, E.	Ord	205.876
Jones, W.	Sto	288.253
McCarthy, W.	Ord	203.138
McLaughlin, H.	Sto	276.251
Raymond, F.	Ord	208.070
Slater, F.	AB	177.295
Smith, J.E.	Pte	Ply6.696
Walters, W.	L/Sto	279.564
Whyte, A.	Pte	Ply9.844
* Wilmott, G.	Dom	359.459

* Two duplicate medals issued.

Returned medals:

Bell, R.E.	Blksmth	340.099
Davies, G.A.	AB	185.212
Davis, Tom.	Kroo	
Freeman, J.	Kroo	
Harris, R.	Sto	151.854
Harry, A.E.	PO1	168.006
Hedges, A.E.	Dom	212.152
Hocking, F.J.	AB	191.407
Hughes, R.H.W.	Act/Lieut	
Hunter, T.	Dom	359.799
Kennard, H.	AB	192.882
Lavers, W.A.	L/Sto	148.775
Lean, S.J.	Carp/Mte	151.872
Lester, T.	Sto	290.957
Monrovia, J.	Kroo	
Neve, M.W.J.	AB	190.576
Preston, F.C.	Carp/Mte	163.087
Robbins, W.G.	L/S	182.145
Scotland, M.	Kroo	
Smith, R.G.	PO1	125.099
Stephen, W.	Sto	290.935
Tucker, T.	Kroo	
Watkins, S.	L/Sto	174.360
Williams, A.E.	AB	196.572
Wright, S.J.	Ch/Arm	147.263

H.M.S. PELORUS

Period for which entitled:
8th December 1899 to 26th June 1900

Bars	*Total*	*Returned*	*Entitled*
2	1	0	1
1	13	0	13
0	235	20	215
	249	20	229

Notes:
[1] Medal presented by H.R.H. The Prince of Wales in Tasmania.
[2] This officer subsequently received a medal for service in the S.A.C.; the Naval medal was therefore returned to the Arsenal.
* Two ratings are shown on the roll; the lower of the two is shown here.

Bars: Cape Colony, South Africa 1901

Furlong, H.	AB	180.871

Bar: Natal

* Dimond, J.F.	PO2	160.189
Dyble, E.	AB	150.853
Farley, J.S.	AB	166.152
Heesem, W.R.	AB	169.154
Herbert, H.N.A.	PO2	158.045
Holman, W.D.	AB	161.746
* Jones, W.G.	AB	117.113
* Lewis, J.	L/Sig	162.466
* Martin, T.H.	AB	124.014
Mitchell, E.G.	AB	165.568
Murray, J.H.	AB	147.764
Sweeney, E.	AB	178.745
Whiteley, J.	Q/Sig	189.732

Duplicate medal:

Murray, J.H.	AB	147.764

No Bar Medals

* Algar, H.	2/SBStd	147.093
* Ashton, G.A.	ERA	268.935
Astbury, P.	AB	178.532
Bailey, W.A.	AB	187.218
Baker, N.	Ord	189.606
Bareham, C.	Ord	195.843
* Barnes, G.C.B.	Pte	Ply9.040
Barry, J.	Sto	282.117
Barry, J.	Sto	290.963
Bates, W.	Sh/Cook	156.523
Batten, J.	Sto	279.663
Beer, J.	Sto	288.557
* Bennett, G.E.	Dom	101.823
Bennett, H.J.	ERA	269.426
Bent, L.	Dom	357.716
Benyon, W.E.	ERA	269.542
Blagdon, R.	L/Sto	148.881
Blake, N.J.	L/Sto	144.744
* Bowden, J.W.	L/S	150.816
Bowen, J.	Sto	288.558
Briggs, E.	Dom	355.879
Brock, J.H.	Arm/Mte	165.338
Brown, W.	Pte	Ply9.044
Brown, W.H.	Dom	357.447
* Burn, G.H.	Boy/Wrtr	341.625
Cain, F.	AB	169.153
Callaghan, W.	Sto	279.112
Carey, A.W.	Ord	189.605
Carwardine, T.	Dom	357.446
[1] Castle, W.	Lieut	
Checketts, W.	Sto	284.295
Church, F.A.	PO1	128.509
Clark, G.	Ch/PO	115.207
Cloherty, J.	Sto	287.263
* Clough, G.	Sto	165.379
Clyesdale, J.	Sto	277.085
Cockerham, C.	L/Sto	280.113
Cole, A.	Ord	195.330
Cole, G.H.	AB	134.202
Cole, J.S.	ERA	171.295
Cook, J.S.	Sto	278.270
Coombe, W.H.	Ord	192.852
Cornish, W.A.	Ord	194.917
* Critchley, A.	Sto	280.962
Cudmore, R.	AB	159.137
Curtis, J.	AB	162.846
Daniels, J.	Boy	195.332
Daniels, J.W.	Sto	287.161
Davidson, D.	Pte	Ply8.391
Davies, R.	AB	186.004
* Davis, C.W.	L/Sto	174.332
Davis, J.	Sto	99.788
De la Motte, E.	L/S	157.151
Dear, E.J.	Pte	Ply8.465
Downing, E.	Yeo/Sig	134.980
Drake, F.R.H.	Act/Asst/Payr	
Edwards, E.H.	Lieut	
Ellens, C.	AB	139.816
Emdin, A.R.	Ch/Engr	

	Eveleigh, W.	AB	156.356
	Farrow, H.C.	Pte	Ch10.640
	Ferraro, E.C.	L/Sto	149.209
	Fitzgerald, J.	Ord	197.666
	Fletcher, F.W.	Ord	193.577
	Foott, G.H.	St/Surgn	
	Francis, J.	Blksmth	128.929
	Gardiner, M.	AB	157.529
	Gell, R.J.	Sto	287.152
	Giddy, W.H.	AB	137.518
	Gidley, A.J.	Sto	288.561
	Gilbert, R.J.	AB	181.771
	Gilhooley, P.	Pte	Ply5.519
	Gilray, J.	Sto	290.859
	Gloyne, F.	Sto	355.599
	Gosling, J.	Sto	288.555
	Grandfield, W.	AB	121.749
	Greep, F.W.	Sto	281.626
	Greenman, A.	Ord	191.432
	Grimsdale, H.	AB	165.589
	Harmes, R.	Ord	189.981
	Harris, E.J.	Ord	201.029
	Harrison, T.	ERA	269.354
	Hartnell, J.A.	Sto	285.727
	Hendry, C.	Sh/Cpl	96.406
	Hickey, J.	Sto	284.589
	Higgins, W.H.	Sto	153.277
	Hixson, A.G.	Pte	Ply8.314
*	Hoblin, A.	Dom	131.701
	Hodges, T.	ERA	268.705
	Hopkinson, F.	AB	136.834
	Hughes, J.C.S.	Lieut	
	Hulbert, H.C.B.	Capt	
*	Hunt, A.H.	AB	166.057
	Hunt, J.M.	Sto	291.474
	Isaacs, R.	Sig	191.670
	Jackson, W.T.	Bugler	Ply8.478
	Jarvis, G.	Sto	283.690
	Johns, W.T.	AB	160.978
	Kellaway, C.	Sto	287.170
	Kennedy, D.	Sergt	Ply3.040
	Killan, G.H.	AB	179.438
	King, S.A.	Sh/Std	167.097
*	Kneale, J.	2/Cooper	341.211
	Knight, C.J.	AB	153.485
	Lacey, G.F.	Gunr	
	Lamble, J.	Sto	291.530
	Lanfear, F.	Ord	198.290
	Larkin, J.L.	Ord	195.351
	Lean, S.J.	Carp/Mte	151.872
	Lester, T.	Sto	290.957
	Light, J.	Ch/Sto	112.065
	Lowry, O.C.	Ord	201.580
	Luckes, S.	Sto	167.684
	McClure, W.	Ord	196.177
	McGrath, J.	Sto	282.852
*	McGrory, C.	L/Sto	278.919
	Mackinson, W.A.	Ord	191.420
	Mahoney, J.	Sto	277.717
	Mallett, H.	Ch/Sto	130.057
	Manning, J.	Sig	193.956
	Marlton, H.C.	ERA	268.371
	Martin, J.	Ord	201.596
	Maskell, W.	Dom	357.160
	Millman, E.	Ch/ERA	128.931
	Mills, F.H.	ERA	268.095
	Mills, S.	AB	161.111
	Mitchell, C.	Pte	Ply9.045
*	Mitchell, R.	Sto	155.796
	Moore, S.	Ch/Sto	128.612
	Morgan, G.	Sub Lieut	
	Morley, A.J.	Carp	
	Morrissey, D.	Sto	290.978
	Mudge, C.D.	Ord	201.588
	Mudge, W.	Sto	284.764
	Murphy, D.	AB	158.976
	Nettley, A.	AB	161.946
	Nichols, P.	Sto	287.151
	Norton, W.	Sto	287.225
*	O'Dowda, A.F.	Boy	195.680
	Olford, R.B.	PO1	120.539
	Owens, J.	Sto	287.155
	Owens, O.	Sto	291.549
	Pankhurst, T.W.	L/S	167.546
*	Parker, G.R.	Ord	195.437
	Parnell, J.T.	L/S	155.802
	Patham., G.	PO1	130.251
	Payne, J.	PO1	118.844
	Penellum, W.	Ord	194.080
	Petch, C.F.	Payr	
	Pine, G.	PO2	143.463
	Pomeroy, W.	Arm/Mte	340.205
	Popperwell, A.	PO2	156.377
	Potham, W.E.	Plmbr/Mte	341.799
	Price, A.	Sto	280.134
	Pritchard, T.	Shpwrt	341.637
*	Proctor, W.T.	L/Shpwrt	154.976
	Pulham, W.	Sergt	Ply4.369
	Raddon, G.H.	Sto	291.461
*	Rail, A.E.	ERA	268.901
	Read, S.J.	Pte	Ply7.394
	Revato, T.	Carp/Crew	342.014
	Rex, H.J.	Ord	191.579
	Richards, W.H.	Sto	133.523
	Rickard, W.J.	PO1	166.206
	Robertson, D.S.	Pte	Ply7.106
	Rowe, A.E.	Pte	Ply4.715
	Rowe, T.	Sto	290.827
	Roycroft, R.	Sto	287.154
*	Score, G.S.	Sh/Std/Boy	341.549
	Scrivens, C.	Sto	278.601
	Seymour, F.	2/Yeo/Sig	187.866
	Shimmell, A.	Ord	198.983
*	Sincock, S.	Ord	183.889
	Skedgel, G.	Sto	287.153
	Smith, R.G.	PO1	125.099
	Southcott, E.	Ord	190.561
	Stone, J.	Ord	191.429
	Syms, W.J.	L/Sto	147.253
	Tanner, T.J.K.	Ord	195.707
	Taylor, A.W.	Pte	Ply8.978
	Tiller, H.	AB	179.657

No Bar Medals *continued*

	Tilling, J.H.	Carp/Crew	341.796
	Townsend, A.A.	Pte	Ply9.049
	Tozer, E.	AB	188.384
	Tredennick, W.D.	Sto	284.778
	Tribble, S.	AB	189.660
	Vaughan, F.C.	Sub Lieut	
	Vickery, C.	Act/Ch/Sto	152.754
	Vigus, T.H.	Sto	284.318
*	Wagstaff, J.E.	Sig	194.702
*	Walton, G.J.	Ord	195.311
*	Ward, F.J.	Boy	195.356
	Ware, S.J.	Ord	190.123
	Warren, W.	AB	160.985
	Watts, F.G.	Sto	287.169
	Westcott, T.H.	Sto	167.060
	Whatcott, A.R.	Ord	195.352
	Wheeler, T.E.	Sto	139.104
	Whether, G.	Sto	285.722
	Whetty, H.	Ord	191.257
	Whyte, P.	Sto	279.095
	Williams, A.	Ord	184.754
	Williams, A.E.	Ord	196.572
*	Williams, S.J.	Sto	143.878
	Wills, A.A.	Sto	288.556
	Wills, W.H.	Sto	285.718
	Witt, F.W.	AB	138.177
	Wood, F.	Ord	191.422
	Wood, R.H.	Ch/ERA	156.134
	Wood, T.	PO1	104.552
	Woolcombe, L.C.S.	Lieut	
	Woolley, H.	Sto	279.511
	Wright, J.	AB	136.730
	Wright, S.J.	Ch/Arm	147.362
	Young, J.T.	Sto	282.657

Duplicate Medals:

	Bailey, W.A.	AB	187.218
	Baker, N.	Ord	189.606
x	Benyon, W.E.	ERA	269.542
	Cain, F.	AB	169.153
	Coe, W.H.	Ord	192.852
	Daniels, J.	Boy	195.332
	Fitzgerald, J.	Ord	197.666
	Hickey, J.	Sto	284.589
	Hughes, J.C.S.	Lieut	
	Marlton, H.C.	ERA	268.371

x Two duplicate medals issued.

Returned medals:

*	Carey, J.	L/Sto	165.682
	Connolly, J.J.	Sto	
	Connor, J.	Pte	Ply9.047
	Dixon, W.	Pntr	341.633
	Edmonds, G.H.	Dom	356.368
	Fitzgerald, P	Ord	196.190
2	Ford, H.L.U.	Asst/Engr	
	Hanlon, P.	Sto	284.286
	Harvey, E.D.	Ord	191.699
	Healey, J.	AB	150.923
	Hocking, H.W.	Sto	282.876
	Howlings, J.	Pte	Ply6.855
	Kendrick, W.	Sto	149.568
	Kennard, J.	Sto	280.689
	Lewis, H.G.	Sto	158.202
	Lovett, W.	Sto	170.116
	Murphy, M.	Sto	283.092
	Nicholson, J.B.	Asst/Engr	
	O'Brian, P.	Pte	Ply8.984
	Purl, W.	Ord	194.919

H.M.S. PHILOMEL

Period for which entitled:
11th October 1899 to 8th March 1901

Extended period:
9th March 1901 to 1st June 1901
14th September 1901 to 23rd January 1902

Bars	*Total*	*Returned*	*Entitled*
6	2	1	1
5	24	0	24
4	3	0	3
3	4	1	3
2	18	1	17
1	37	7	30
0	181	29	152
	269	39	230

Notes:
* Medal presented by HM The King.

Bars: Paardeberg, Driefontein, Johannesburg, Diamond Hill, Belfast, Cape Colony

*	Bearcroft, J.E.	Capt	

Returned medal:

*	Newton, H.	AB	143.470

Bars: Johannesburg, Diamond Hill, Belfast, Orange Free State, Natal

*	Penny, W.B.	Payr	

Bars: Orange Free State, Transvaal, Tugela Heights, Relief of Ladysmith, Laing's Nek

*	Brookes, J.H.	AB	174.915
*	Burne, C.R.N.	Lieut	
	Davis, G.J.	AB	191.397
	Elliott, J.	AB	183.296
	Forsey, A.	Arm/Mte	340.545
	Franklin, W.H.	PO2	162.393
	Frennett, J.J.	PO1	151.611
	Furze, E.R.	AB	179.182
*	Goddard, A.	Carp/Crew	340.870
*	Gordon, J.H.	AB	183.446
	Haisom, H.J.J.	PO1	104.622
	Halsey, A.	Lieut	
	Hollins, W.T.	Asst/Payr	
*	Hughes, J.E.	AB	161.112
*	Jane, R.W.	AB	147.123
*	Keys, W.	AB	126.194
	Mayne, W.R.	L/S	159.157
*	Payne, G.W.	AB	155.301
	Sargent, T.	PO2	166.132
*	Thompson, P.	Pte	Ply6.337
	Walsh, W.J.	AB	169.042
*	Waring, E.	Yeo/Sig	150.792
*	Weatherhead, J.	PO1	127.747

Duplicate medals:

Brookes, J.H.	AB	174.915
Jane, R.W.	AB	147.123
Walsh, W.J.	AB	169.042

Bars: Transvaal, Tugela Heights, Relief of Ladysmith, Laing's Nek

*	Clutterbuck, F.A.	Sub Lieut	
	Reed, W.C.	L/S	160.218
	Tope, B.J.	L/S	138.708

Bars: Orange Free State, Transvaal, Laing's Nek

*	Bate, T.E.	AB	181.326
	Edwards, J.	AB	188.273
*	Jane, S.	AB	183.152

Bars: Transvaal, Tugela Heights, Relief of Ladysmith

Returned medal:

Martin, G.E.	Arm/Crew	341.134

Bars: Cape Colony, South Africa 1901

Hayslip, A.E.	Sergt	Ply3.531

Bars: Transvaal, Laing's Nek

Muns, A.	AB	188.658

Bars: Tugela Heights, Relief of Ladysmith

Belcher, R.	AB	143.810
Cashman, P.	PO1	159.862
Collacott, A.E.	PO2	164.753
Cross, F.	AB	183.958

Bars: Tugela Heights, Relief of Ladysmith *continued*

Finnecey, H.J.	AB	185.489
Gilbert, A.	Pte	Ply6.355
Hoare, E.H.J.	AB	159.330
Langtry, R.	AB	177.825
Lavis, C.H.	AB	134.125
Mason, F.A.	AB	117.578
Parkinson, J.	AB	171.640
Payne, W.	PO1	113.108
* Stanton, T.	AB	161.630
* Stevens, S.C.	AB	180.960
Wilkes, F.	AB	166.872

Returned medals:

Nickells, A.G.	AB	189.379

Bar: Paardeberg

Brock, W.J.	PO1	124.780

Bar: Natal

* Bailey, C.	AB	183.654
Bassett, W.	AB	156.465
* Bell, J.T.	AB	194.883
* Bennett, E.	AB	183.634
* Borland, J.	Ord	195.585
Brook, W.E.W.	AB	158.926
* Buckingham, G.	Q/Sig	186.246
* Burris, H.	Q/Sig	189.484
* Butler, J.	AB	189.346
* Collings, F.	AB	124.789
* Cosier, J.R.	AB	178.831
* Flood, M.	L/Sto	153.418
Goad, F.T.	PO2	171.515
* Griffiths, W.R.	Gunr	
Jackman, J.	PO2	176.131
James, J.E.	Sto	288.617
Johns, J.F.	AB	181.439
* Johns, R.H.	Ord	192.940
Loader, H.E.	AB	192.494
Miller, T.	Ch/Arm	144.580
* O'Brien, J.M.	AB	169.602
O'D'Grainey, P.	AB	165.513
Radley, W.G.	Cpl	Ply6.521
Reeves, R.	Sto	149.163
* Robinson, F.	AB	167.888
Semmens, E.	PO1	121.278
Skillern, G.	Sto	288.216
* Trevaskis, J.	Sto	287.344
Woods, A.F.	L/Sig	176.047

Returned medals:

Cousins, T.	AB	143.500
Elliott, H.	St/Surgn	
O'Shea, P.	L/Sto	163.083
Rawle, H.	Act/Ch/PO	136.189
Roberts, J.	PO1	150.871
Shepherd, G.E.	AB	183.106
Withers, A.L.	Act/Asst/Payr	

No Bar Medals

Abdullah (No 1).	Seedie	
Airey, W.	Dom	354.313
Ali.	Seedie	
Andres, H.	Dom	159.811
Annett, W.J.	Pte	Ply4.774
Arthur, E.H.	Dom	354.373
Atkinson, W.H.	Pte	Ply5.304
Baker, W.T.	Sto	161.949
Ball, J.	AB	121.869
Baptiste, H.	Seedie	
Barracka.	Seedie	
Barry, W.	Ord	196.167
Begg, A.	Sto	282.446
Bennett, N.C.	L/Sto	144.376
Bird, W.	Sto	154.957
Bowyer, T.	AB	182.076
Brahmin, W.E.	Seedie	
Bridge, J.J.	L/Sto	174.219
* Brown, A.	Engr	
Brown, F.E.	AB	191.618
Brown, S.	L/Sto	152.101
Burton, C.	Sh/Cook	144.983
Cadou, E.E.	Act/Lieut	
Cammice.	Seedie	
Cavill, G.	Pte	Ply5.092
Chapman, W.	Pte	Ply5.559
Chown, W.G.	L/Sto	139.688
Chubb, W.H.	Dom	86.780
Clarke, J.	PO1	130.689
Clifford, W.J.	PO1	163.811
Cole, W.	Sto	286.172
Counter, S.	Sto	156.133
Curtis, J.	Sto	284.171
Cussack, M.	Sto	177.013
Dalby, F.G.	Sto	288.625
Daly, J.	Sto	282.503
Darch, A.	Pte	Ply6.965
Davies, G.	Sto	166.661
De Souza, C.A.	Dom	153.388
De Souza, S.	Dom	115.972
Deacon, J.	Act/Ch/Sto	144.752
Deas, A.	Lieut	
Deem, A.J.	AB	192.514
Donovan, J.	Sto	282.653
Doody, G.	Pte	Ply1.446
Dunn, R.H.	Blksmth	120.361
Edwards, B.C.	ERA	269.049
Edwards, F.	Sto	280.376
Eussof, S.	Seedie	
Feroze, A.	Seedie	
Fiddes, R.	Sto	288.219
Foley, J.	Carp/Mte	92.203
Forse, W.G.	Sto	276.192
Franklin, D.	PO2	146.663
Gardener, G.	Pte	Ply7.724
Gardiner, J.W.	Pte	Ply7.961
Garry, A.F.	ERA	268.538
Godfrey, C.P.	Plmbr/Mte	342.039
Haynes, E.C.	Dom	103.057

Hayward, B.	Sto	286.053
Helmore, A.C.	Ch/Sto	130.749
Henry, J.S.	Lieut	
Henry, W.	Pte	Ply7.777
Hensch, F.	AB	185.396
Hill, F.G.	Q/Sig	174.709
Hobson, R.G.	Lieut	
Horrell, A.H.	L/S	149.402
Horswell, W.	ERA	149.161
* Hughes, A.B.	Lieut	
Hughes, W.E.	L/Sto	163.097
Jenkins, J.V.	ERA	268.778
Juma.	Seedie	
Karnise.	Seedie	
* Keate, R.H.	Lieut	
King, J.	AB	108.521
Kumsin.	Seedie	
Legge, C.J.	Sh/Std	136.720
Lineham, T.	Sto	288.736
Littler, F.C.	AB	181.997
Lloyd, T.G.	Sto	170.633
McKenna, J.	2/Cooper	341.479
Manley, H.T.	AB	190.991
Maxim, J.	Seedie	
Miall, G.	Payr	
Mills, J.	Pte	Ply5.811
Monkey.	Seedie	
Moore, A.	Pntr	340.671
Morley, W.	Carp/Mte	155.470
Neale, W.G.	L/Shpwrt	158.961
Norris, E.G.	Sto	169.654
Norris, H.	Sto	278.337
O'Kelly, J.	Sto	288.442
O'Neill, D.	L/Sto	150.721
O'Toole, T.	Sto	283.306
Ollson, J.	AB	187.742
Organ, W.E.	Bugler	Ply8.385
Othman.	Seedie	
Oxenbury, A.E.C.	L/Sto	144.397
Paltridge, H.	ERA	269.244
Parker, J.	Pte	Ply7.826
Parnell, J.	Sto	159.494
Pearce, W.T.	Ch/Sto	137.532
Platt, R.	ERA	269.232
* Pollard, P.	Asst/Engr	
* Polyblank, E.J.	Carp	
Powell, T.J.	Cpl	Ply4.664
Pulleyblank, J.E.	Carp/Crew	183.506
* Pym, W.H.J.	Payr	
Richards, J.	L/Sto	161.187
Robearn.	Seedie	
Rogers, F.G.	L/S	176.170
Rowlands, W.J.	Sh/Std/Asst	341.485
Salter, F.C.	Sto	288.896
Sarson, H.	Sto	175.900
Screech, J.	Ch/PO	43.669
Scutt, A.	Pte	Po9.781
Seaward, T.	L/Sto	148.854
Shepherd, A.J.T.	Q/Sig	144.265
Shew, F.G.H.	Sto	289.926
Short, H.W.	L/Sto	113.273
Sime, J.	ERA	268.678
Simmons, J.	L/Sto	148.172
Skinner, G.	L/Sto	168.727
Smart, Jack.	Kroo	
Smith, R.S.	Act/Payr	
Soper, F.A.	Sto	286.150
* Sparks, E.F.	Ch/Engr	
Spurr, C.T.	Sto	288.905
Squance, E.	Dom	353.287
Stalt, D.J.	Dom	145.989
Stammers, W.H.	AB	134.768
Sullivan, J.	L/Sto	165.694
Taylor, F.J.	Dom	353.249
Taylor, J.	Ch/ERA	112.383
Thompson, G.	Sto	283.248
Tonkyn, C.	Dom	356.605
Toto.	Seedie	
Trebilcock, E.J.	Ch/Sto	139.177
Underhill, G.	Sto	284.332
Warner, W.	Ord	171.756
Whitby, H.J.	Sto	119.911
White, J.	Pte	Ply7.526
Williams, T.H.	Sto	166.759
Willis, A.P.	Sto	285.637
Wills, C.H.	Pte	Ply6.593
Woodley, C.	Sh/Cpl	122.381

Duplicate medals:

Ball, J.	AB	121.869
Barry, W.	Ord	196.167
Brown, F.E.	AB	191.618
Cussack, M.	Sto	177.013
Gardener, G.	Pte	Ply7.724
Hughes, A.B.	Lieut	
Monkey.	Seedie	
O'Kelly, J.	Sto	288.442
Robearn.	Seedie	

Returned medals:

Abdullah (No. 2).	Seedie	
Bartlett, G.	L/Sto	125.845
Cairns, A.	Sto	277.134
Cullinane, J.	AB	134.642
Frier, E.H.	Pte	Ply7.055
Johanna.	Seedie	
Kearns, J.	Sto	276.885
King, H.J.	Sto	277.689
Lewis, J.L.	Sto	154.941
Long, T.	Sto	287.241
McColm, A.	2/SBStd	145.850
Mackay, A.	Sto	287.595
Murphy, T.	Sto	176.676
Nahoda.	Seedie	
Parfitt, W.C.	Sh/Std/Asst	
Slater, F.	Sto	286.877
Stalt, W.R.	Dom	356.609
Uledi.	Seedie	
White, H.	Sto	151.250

EXTENDED PERIOD
No Bar Medals

Abelwhite, G.	Ord	206.730
Adams, F.L.	Sig	205.202
Browning, A.	Ch/ERA	127.189
Cote A.J. de la	Boy	206.910
Holloway, W.C.	Sig/Boy	208.009
Petheram, G.	Boy	206.887

Returned medals:

Dark, J.	Kroo	
December, J.	Kroo	
Four O'Clock.	Kroo	
Kirby, F.H.	Ord	190.292
Lewis, B.	Kroo	
Peter, Tom.	Kroo	
Salt, T.	Kroo	
Savage, J.	Kroo	
Seaman, J.	Kroo	
Turner, H.J.	Sig/Boy	208.040

H.M.S. POWERFUL

Period for which entitled:
14th October 1899 to 27th March 1900

Bars	Total	Returned	Entitled
8	2	0	2
7	17	1	16
6	2	0	2
5	19	0	19
4	28	0	28
3	5	0	5
2	15	2	13
1	316	8	308
0	494	79	415
	898	90	808

Notes:
* Medal presented on Ophir.
† Medal presented by H.M. The King.
[1] This medal and bars was sent to H.M.S. Barracouta to the recipient. The recipient is also on that medal roll as having received a no bar medal and later the clasps for Cape Colony and South Africa 1902.
[2] The recipient may be entitled to another clasp; the roll is unclear.
[3] The Marines number (Po8.547) is questioned on the roll.
[4] The original medal was returned to the Arsenal; This medal issued in 1920.
[5] Recipient's service number incomplete on roll.
[6] Also noted on roll as Wright.

Bars: Belmont, Modder River, Paardeberg, Driefontein, Johannesburg, Diamond Hill, Belfast, Relief of Kimberley

Franklin, G.	Pte	Po8.406
Mann, A.J.	Pte	Po8.422

Bars: Belmont, Modder River, Paardeberg, Driefontein, Johannesburg, Diamond Hill, Belfast

Chrystal, G.	Pte	Po8.373
Churchman, F.	Sergt	Po3.128
Conway, J.	Pte	Po6.105
Donaldson, J.	L/Cpl	Po7.152
* Game, J.	Pte	Ply6.451
Haggar, J.	Pte	Ch8.763
Holt, T.	Pte	Ply5.738
Lader, W.J.	Bugler	Po8.034
Lock, R.W.	Pte	Po8.423
Piper, C.T.	Pte	Po6.935
Priscott, E.J.	Pte	Po5.970
Silley, A.	Pte	Po5.304
* Tildesley, J.H.	Pte	Po7.134
* Tillman, W.T.	Pte	Po8.266
Watts, J.C.	Cpl	Po8.432
Wheeler, F.G.	Pte	Po8.414

Returned medal:

Hanstead, T.J.	Gunr	RMA5.536

Bars: Belmont, Modder River, Paardeberg, Driefontein, Johannesburg, Diamond Hill

Honour, F.J.	Pte	Po8.366
Huckin, F.	Pte	Ply4.406

Bars: Belmont, Modder River, Paardeberg, Driefontein, Johannesburg

Robins, T.	Pte	Ply7.183

Bars: Belmont, Modder River, Paardeberg, Driefontein, Relief of Kimberley

Abberley, F.W.	Ord	186.766
Armstrong, J.C.	Midn	
Bayne, S.H.	PO2	136.137
Branton, J.H.	AB	178.059
Chase, C.T.	PO2	157.583
Coombes, W.J.	AB	181.923
Davies, E.	AB	186.752
Day, A.E.	AB	186.229
Gregory, F.J.	AB	174.161
Ingersoll, A.E.	AB	186.088
Mason, W.	L/S	133.388
Roxburgh, S.	AB	181.974
Saunders, A.C.	AB	186.116
Smith, C.A.	L/S	155.564
Smith, J.M.	AB	149.626
Sullivan, T.	Sto	159.992

Bars: Belmont, Modder River, Paardeberg, Driefontein, Relief of Kimberley *continued*

Tubb, C.W.	AB	166.384
Whitehead, W.	AB	187.290

Duplicate medals:

Bayne, S.H.	PO2	136.137
Chase, C.T.	PO2	157.583

Bars: Belmont, Modder River, Paardeberg, Driefontein

Ashdown, E.	Sto	277.042
[1] Beadnell, C.M.	St/Surgn	
Bulbeck, A.E.	Gunr	RMA5.516
Butt, C.	Pte	Po5.255
Cassey, G.	Pte	Po8.401
Clark, W.	Pte	Po8.490
Cull, J.	Pte	Ply9.487
Davey, R.	Pte	Po8.525
Fudge, H.S.	Sto	144.777
Hammond, A.	Pte	Ply6.477
Laming, G.T.	Sto	146.802
Lewin, G.E.	Midn	
McCoy, T.	Pte	Po4.049
Peaks, C.H.	AB	141.771
Ranner, L.G.	Bugler	Po8.058
Roades, J.A.	Pte	Po8.523
Rogers, J.	Arm	143.244
Saunders, F.J.	Lieut(RMLI)	
Scutchings, R.	Gunr	RMA5.520
Shipton, J.	Dom	355.730
Shute, H.C.W.	Pte	Po11.529
Wakely, G.	Cpl	Ply5.202
Warren, C.	Pte	Po8.035
West, G.	Sto	174.407
White, F.B.	L/Cpl	Po4.726
White, R.F.	Lieut	
Winchester, R.	2/SBStd	350.211

Bars: Belmont, Modder River, Paardeberg, Relief of Kimberley

Skinner, W.E.	Sergt	Ply4.097

Bars: Belmont, Modder River, Paardeberg

Rawlings, C.R.	Pte	Ply6.450

Bars: Belmont, Modder River, Orange Free State

Goldring, T.A.	Sergt	Ply6.243

Bars: Paardeberg, Driefontein, Cape Colony

Carpenter, J.R.	Cpl	Po8.327
Urmston, A.G.B.	Major(RMLI)	
Whittle, P.G.	Sh/Std/Asst	341.410

Duplicate medal:

Carpenter, J.R.	Cpl	Po8.327

Bars: Belmont, Modder River

Ayerst, S.D.	Pte	Po4.949
Barnes, J.J.C.	AB	166.916
Davis, W.H.	Sto	281.134
Dean, J.	AB	142.730
Gould, W.	Pte	Ply6.452
Harwood, A.	Pte	Po8.409
Lampard, A.E.	Pte	Po8.516
[2] Stewart, J.	AB	179.172
Taylor, H.J.	Pte	Po6.476
Whale, A.E.	Pte	Po8.309

Returned medals:

Harvey, H.	Pte	Po7.772
Perkins, C.	Gunr	RMA2.506

Bars: Tugela Heights, Relief of Ladysmith

Connor, M.	PO1	161.886
Cripps, H.	L/Sto	131.807
Prickett, C.B.	Midn	

Bar: Belmont

Barnes, W.H.	Pte	Po8.371
Bartlett, G.A.	Pte	Po8.527
* Bath, E.	Gunr	RMA5.509
Beesley, S.R.	Gunr	RMA5.518
Brown, A.J.	Pte	Po6.258
Butt, A.H.	L/Carp/Crew	140.390
Caplen, A.	Pte	Po6.679
Cartwright, H.T.	Pte	Po7.461
Coldrick, J.E.	Pte	Ply6.426
Dentry, J.	Pte	Ply6.475
Dowland, S.	Pte	Po8.384
* Elmes, H.J.M.	L/Cpl	Po5.719
Ethelston, A.P.	Comdr	
Gasson, W.	Sergt	Ply4.001
Goat, A.	Pte	Po6.813
Greagsby, H.	L/Cpl	Po6.960
Hall, A.H.	Pte	Po8.417
Holland, W.C.	Act/Sergt	Po6.481
Hughes, T.J.	Pte	Ply6.379
Isern, H.R.	Pte	Ch6.359
Kelleher, J.	Gunr	RMA5.527
Lewis, F.C.	L/Cpl	Po6.371
* Livingstone, J.	Pte	Ply3.396
Mabbett, F.	Pte	Po7.273
Martin, H.W.	Pte	Po6.913
Metcalfe, J.H.	Pte	Po8.439
Miller, J.	Pte	Ch7.086
Mole, C.	Gunr	RMA5.047
Peacock, H.	Pte	Ply4.811
[3] Percival, J.R.	Pte	Po8.547
Weingaerton, B.	Gunr	RMA5.506

Duplicate medals:

x Hughes, T.J.	Pte	Ply6.379

x Two duplicate medals issued.

Bar: Cape Colony

Edge, F.P.	PO2	153.932
Holbrow, H.	Pte	Ch6.598

Bar: Defence of Ladysmith

	Abram, E.W.	AB	167.361
	Adames, A.H.	Arm/Crew	341.309
	Adams, R.	Sto	281.121
	Allen, F.	Sto	144.770
	Annett, J.F.	AB	186.778
	Archer, E.A.	Ord	187.369
	Arscott, C.H.	Ord	186.322
	Ashley, J.	Ord	180.278
	Atlee, R.	L/Sig	151.599
	Baker, C.S.	AB	156.189
	Barham, C.	AB	136.135
	Barnaby, W.	AB	188.182
	Bartlett, A.C.	AB	162.386
	Beaumont, H.N.	PO1	122.351
	Bennett, A.R.	PO1	100.979
	Bennett, W.A.	Pte	Po8.433
	Benson, A.	PO1	118.547
	Benton, A.W.	AB	175.256
	Beves, H.	AB	151.739
	Bignell, H.G.	AB	158.527
	Bishop, W.	AB	187.117
	Blaber, H.	AB	187.154
	Blake, J.C.	Sto	283.367
	Blumson, B.	AB	161.843
	Bly, W.B.	PO1	125.702
	Bone, R.S.	AB	186.793
	Boorman, S.W.	AB	186.823
	Botting, H.H.	AB	163.797
	Bowen, R.	Sto	283.955
	Bowman, H.J.	Sto	281.096
	Boyce, C.	AB	151.746
	Bradford, J.	AB	126.651
	Bradley, A.C.	2/Yeo/Sig	184.286
	Branford, J.R.	L/Sig	156.999
	Brien, P.	AB	123.786
	Brien, W.J.	AB	133.845
	Brine, W.	AB	179.974
	Brook, A.C.	AB	156.625
	Brown, A.	AB	154.020
	Brown, G.E.	AB	151.529
	Buckland, W.H.	AB	166.362
	Buckly, J.W.	AB	156.646
	Burchell, C.	Sto	192.332
	Burton, G.W.	Sto	159.031
	Burwood, W.J.	PO2	129.975
	Buxton, F.E.	AB	187.094
	Caldwell, A.	Ord	175.748
	Capron, F.G.	AB	185.864
†	Carnegie, Hon. I.L.A.	Midn	
	Chapman, W.A.	AB	183.312
	Cheesman, E.	AB	156.267
*	Chichester, E.G.	Midn	
	Christmas, A.H.	PO1	131.366
	Clapp, A.	Sto	153.771
*	Clark, C.L.	Ord	166.379
	Cobby, J.H.	L/S	167.867
	Cole, J.	Sto	283.162
	Comden, S.G.	SBStd	132.041
	Connell, J.	AB	157.046
	Connor, V.	PO1	124.959
	Coombs, C.	Sto	282.660
	Couzens, W.J.	Act/2/Sh/Cook	340.014
	Cowling, C.J.	Ord	187.085
	Crawley, J.	Sto	174.377
	Creese, C.H.	AB	167.407
	Dallas, A.E.	Sto	129.739
	Dancy, W.H.	Sto	176.594
	Davies, T.	Sto	276.497
	Dear, T.	AB	187.213
	Denny, A.E.	Sto	282.956
	Dixon, W.	Q/Sig	188.731
	Doel, J.	Sto	122.786
	Dunn, E.F.	AB	169.637
	Durrant, G.C.	AB	160.993
	Dyer, G.H.	AB	148.403
	Egan, J.	L/S	148.889
	Egerton, F.G.	Lieut	
†	Ellis, E.H.	Engr	
	Ellis, G.	Sto	282.545
	Emly, J.	AB	159.638
	Evans, S.L.	AB	167.411
	Field, A.H.	Ord	179.433
	Finnimore, A.	PO1	156.160
	Flake, W.J.	AB	184.721
	Foley, E.E.	AB	173.512
	Ford, W.J.	L/S	149.587
	Fotheringham, A.	Ord	187.026
	Fowler, J.G.	Surgn	
	French, T.	Sto	283.932
*	Fuggle, W.J.	PO2	139.794
	Gardner, H.W.G.	Sto	282.698
	Gatehouse, W.E.	Sto	283.450
	Gaulter, E.J.	L/S	147.596
	Gerhold, P.C.C.	PO1	114.734
	Glading, G.W.	Ord	186.665
	Gladman, G.	L/S	132.067
	Gosling, C.	L/S	132.630
	Gover, W.E.	AB	185.426
	Gritt, B.	AB	171.112
	Groves, G.H.	PO1	124.261
	Gundry, J.C.	PO2	145.202
	Haggar, W.E.	Sto	282.688
	Halsey, L.	Lieut	
	Hamilton, R.C.	Midn	
	Hand, R.T.	PO2	138.846
	Hannifin, T.	PO1	148.100
	Hardy, H.J.	L/S	143.411
	Hardy, S.	PO2	151.050
	Harmer, L.	AB	173.178
	Harriss, W.E.	Sto	282.672
	Hatch, G.	Ch/ERA	122.691
	Hayes, H.T.	Midn	
	Hemmings, S.E.	PO2	126.309
	Henderson, W.H.	Act/2/Sh/Cook	340.267
	Heneage, A.W.	Lieut	
	Heppel, F.W.	AB	175.566
	Hickman, A.A.	PO2	142.785
	Higgs, G.H.	AB	144.207
	Higgs, P.	PO2	146.036
	Hipperson, H.T.	Sto	158.054

Bar: Defence of Ladysmith *continued*

	Hitchcock, J.H.P.	Pntr	132.429
	Hodges, M.H.	Lieut	
	Hone, H.J.	Ord	186.791
	Humphreys, F.	AB	165.588
	Humphreys, F.	AB	186.783
	Isaacs, H.J.	Sto	154.551
	Jacobs, G.A.	AB	175.555
	James, W.	Sto	175.914
	Jardine, J.	AB	180.947
	Jarvis, E.H.	AB	181.924
	John, G.	AB	181.755
	Johnson, F.	Arm/Crew	340.131
	Johnson, W.S.	Sto	281.253
*	Johncox, E.A.	Ord	190.774
	Jones, T.S.	AB	183.311
	Kay, W.H.F.	Fl/Payr	
	Keen, W.	AB	151.890
	Kierl, H.J.	AB	136.180
	Kilminster, T.	Q/Sig	142.184
	King, F.	Blksmth/Mte	175.916
	Kinsman, F.J.	AB	160.897
	Knight, A.S.	Yeo/Sig	104.560
	Knott, G.	PO2	145.624
	Lacey, F.	PO1	133.652
†	Lambton, Hon. H.	Capt	
*	Land, C.E.	AB	167.357
	Lawrence, H.	AB	157.995
*	Le Quelenac, J.A.	Ord	172.057
	Leary, A.J.	AB	174.149
	Leather, J.	Sto	175.883
	Ledson, J.J.	PO2	135.215
	Lee, H.W.C.	Act/Ch/PO	128.225
	Lintern, A.J.	Sh/Cpl	350.104
	Lister, H.A.	AB	159.658
	Lockhart, W.H.	Carp/Mte	131.742
	Lovesey, T.S.	AB	180.475
	Ludlow, C.W.	Sto	175.358
	McCarthy, E.M.	AB	186.012
	McCarthy, P.	PO2	161.769
	McLoughlin, J.	AB	176.819
	McMeehan, J.	AB	156.319
	McNichol, R.	Ord	186.895
	McNulty, J.	AB	131.345
	Martin, F.	Pte	Po7.118
	Masters, W.G.	Ord	181.926
	Maxwell, R.	AB	144.463
	Middleton, J.R.	Midn	
	Mills, G.H.	AB	175.568
	Minshaw, C.E.	Ord	182.623
	Moore, A.	Sto	279.325
	Moran, P.	AB	162.528
	Morris, A.	L/S	137.924
	Mott, J.	Sto	282.134
	Murphy, W.	AB	167.251
	Murray, J.	AB	147.469
	Musgrove, A.	AB	166.323
	Nail, J.F.	Ord	172.445
	Newell, B.	AB	168.097
	Newling, W.	Sto	282.232
	Newman, H.	Pte	Ch6.207
	Norris, W.J.	AB	176.081
	Notton, R.	Sto	167.204
	Oldfield, W.	AB	175.249
	Ousley, T.	AB	188.168
	Pannifer, H.W.	Ord	186.287
	Parrisey, A.W.	Sto	282.980
	Passmore, H.	AB	181.688
	Paton, D.H.	Sto	282.960
	Payne, A.G.	AB	146.993
	Pealtie, G.	Ord	181.120
	Pearce, A.J.	AB	186.315
	Pepper, E.	AB	132.073
	Pettit, J.E.	AB	165.456
	Philpott, J.R.	AB	173.135
	Pilgrim, C.W.	Sto	282.955
	Pilkington, J.	Sto	175.896
	Pitman, W.	AB	125.745
	Pomeroy, G.	AB	144.279
	Pratt, A.C.	L/S	156.154
	Ramsay, D.H.	Sto	281.935
*	Read, W.C.C.	Ord	162.263
	Richards, C.F.	Ord	192.235
	Richardson, A.H.	AB	122.642
	Rogers, J.	AB	146.507
	Rolls, A.P.	Sto	282.713
	Ross, F.	L/S	149.347
	Sadler, S.T.	Carp/Mte	148.053
	Saunders, A.	PO2	152.255
	Saunders, T.H.	L/S	183.817
	Scott, T.J.	Sto	284.358
	Scott, W.G.	Carp/Mte	131.753
	Seares, G.O.	Sto	279.770
	Segrott, H.	AB	160.263
	Semmens, W.J.	AB	176.565
	Shakespeare, W.	AB	121.826
	Sheen, C.C.	Engr	
	Shefford, R.R.	AB	187.178
	Shevlin, J.	Sto	278.297
	Sisk, P.T.	PO1	106.766
	Slade, E.D.	Ord	187.100
	Smees, E.W.	L/S	145.614
*	Smith, A.E.	Sto	282.946
	Smith, L.	AB	180.083
	Spence, J.	AB	187.027
	Stace, A.H.	AB	191.154
	Stearman, W.S.	AB	168.109
	Stenning, H.W.	AB	165.625
	Stenton, M.	Sto	280.798
	Stewart, R.	Ord	186.884
	Stokes, A.	Midn	
	Sullivan, J.	AB	139.280
	Sullivan, W.F.	AB	188.134
	Sweetingham, F.W.	L/S	173.527
	Taylor, T.W.	AB	183.541
	Thompson, G.	PO2	136.970
	Thurgood, J.E.	AB	180.071
	Thurston, H.	AB	151.910
	Timlin, J.	AB	174.952
	Trevett, H.	Ord	175.300
	Tribe, W.	L/S	169.393
	Triggs, F.C.	PO1	143.439

Troke, J.A.	Sto	283.896
Truesdale, W.W.	PO1	147.740
Turner, E.	AB	145.028
Tynedale-Biscoe, E.C.	Lieut	
Wakeham, A.J.	AB	182.108
Ward, A.E.	AB	172.753
Waters, W.G.	Sto	282.241
Wells, M.	AB	163.366
Wheeler, A.	Sto	154.739
Wheeler, D.J.	Ord	170.909
Wheeler, H.	AB	190.766
White, C.	AB	177.241
White, H.J.	PO2	139.216
White, J.S.	Act/Arm/Mte	340.450
White, R.	PO1	85.732
White, S.G.	PO1	147.690
White, S.O.	L/S	152.299
Whiting, J.	AB	165.547
Whyte, R.	Sto	283.157
Wilkins, H.E.	AB	144.292
Wilkinson, J.	AB	136.800
Williams, G.G.	AB	175.257
Williams, L.	Ch/ERA	153.586
Williams, R.R.	AB	175.253
Wills, J.	Sto	160.756
Wilson, F.C.	AB	162.997
Winchester, C.	Sto	169.301
Wise, E.	AB	145.287
Withecombe, J.	PO2	144.549
Withers, A.G.	PO1	133.878
Wittcomb, J.	Sh/Std/Asst	341.088
Wolfe, W.A.	PO2	148.136
Wykes, E.	Sto	281.118
Wynn, R.	AB	145.837

Duplicate medals:

Couzens, W.J.	Act/2/Sh/Cook	340.014
Crawley, J.	Sto	174.377
Fotheringham, A.	Ord	187.026
Gosling, C.	L/S	132.630
Higgs, P.	PO2	146.036
Thurgood, J.E.	AB	180.071

Returned medals:

Blake, H.E.	AB	186.745
Broomfield, C.W.	AB	181.958
Dexter, E.E.	Sig	181.844
Harris, R.	AB	160.850
Rhodes, J.H.	Ord	180.964
Sims, W.	Lieut	
Smith, J.	Ord	187.490
Stabb, E.	Lieut	

No Bar Medals

Ablett, D.	AB	113.312
Ablett, F.W.	Sail/Crew	134.172
Adams, A.	L/Sto	154.559
Adams, J.	PO1	42.765
Addicott, J.E.	AB	180.883
Ahern, J.	Sto	171.931
Aling.	Dom	
Allardyce, W.	Sto	282.167
Allen, A.	Ord	187.099
Attridge, A.J.	AB	167.870
Avery, A.	PO1	118.151
Avery, H.	PO1	106.938
Bailey, C.	L/S	103.701
Bailey, W.J.	PO1	103.517
Baker, F.S.	L/Sto	146.087
Barney, C.T.	Sto	184.666
Barrett, J.T.	Ch/ERA	133.022
Barrow, H.	Blksmth/Mte	156.672
Bartlett, G.	Sto	131.626
Bates, A.T.	Ch/Sto	114.092
Bates, G.E.	L/Shpwrt	142.419
Beal, J.	Blksmth	157.086
Beale, D.D.	L/Sto	114.462
Beck, S.	Sto	156.691
Beddard, H.	Sto	282.984
Bell, J.S.	Ord	185.539
Bennett, J.	Ch/Sto	110.788
Billinghurst, G.	L/Sto	149.828
Bishop, H.	AB	149.620
Blackmore, G.	Ord	173.930
Blair, J.	AB	186.898
Bland, F.	PO1	125.562
Blewett, E.	Sto	149.854
Bolton, E.B.	AB	169.374
Bond, W.	Sto	146.829
* Bowes, J.	Sto	153.881
Broadhurst, E.	Sto	278.709
Broadrick, J.G.	Sto	282.164
Brothers, C.	Sto	156.142
Brown, A.E.	AB	186.770
Brown, C.C.	AB	155.936
Brown, F.W.	Gunr	RMA5.504
Brown, J.	Act/ERA	165.995
Browning, J.	Blksmth/Mte	176.580
Buckle, H.P.	Lieut	
Buncombe, A.E.	Sto	277.857
Bunter, H.	L/Sto	131.859
Burgis, A.G.	Pte	Ply7.434
Burton, J.T.	AB	175.310
Bustin, G.A.	Sto	282.907
Butler, F.H.	Act/MAA	150.087
Button, R.J.	ERA	154.701
Cahill, T.	Sto	282.967
Cain, F.J.	Sto	283.931
Callaway, A.	AB	100.603
Cannon, J.	Sto	283.457
* Carpenter, A.A.	Ord	187.102
Casey, J.E.	AB	176.955
Catlin, T.	Band	356.005
* Chant, F.G.	Ord	193.151
Charlton, F.J.	Engr	
Chegwidden, C.	AB	169.851
Ching, Ah.	Dom	
Chung, Ching.	Dom	
Clarke, G.	AB	175.020
Clarke, H.E.	Ch/Cook	131.017
Clarke, J.H.	Sto	176.579
Clarke, T.F.	ERA	156.491

No Bar Medals *continued*

	Claw, S.T.	Ord	186.777
*	Claxton, A.A.	L/Carp/Crew	145.559
	Claxton, J.	Sto	119.766
	Coaffee, G.E.	AB	182.942
*	Coate, J.J.	Sto	183.468
	Cockerill, W.F.	Sto	276.416
	Coker, A.	Ch/Sto	127.478
	Cole, G.	Sto	129.717
	Collinson, B.	Sto	277.937
	Compton, W.	Carp/Mte	142.933
	Compton, W.B.	Lieut	
	Connett, T.W.	Arm	110.720
	Cook, E.W.	Q/Sig	165.544
	Cooper, C.	Pte	Po2.137
	Cooper, E.	Sto	282.268
	Cooper, S.	Ord	177.837
	Craig, R.	Sto	277.338
	Croft, P.	Sto	281.206
	Cull, Rev. E.C.	Chaplain	
	Davidson, F.	Sto	143.083
	Davies, J.	Sto	154.537
	Davies, R.T.	L/S	130.267
	Davis, J.	AB	166.085
	Davis, W.	Sto	281.872
	Dawson, J.L.	Sto	281.342
	Dear, S.	Sto	282.279
	Dearing, C.	Band	155.097
	Dearling, J.	Sto	187.357
	Delaney, J.	Sto	156.318
	Deluchy, J.	Sto	283.359
	Dench, W.	PO2	117.273
*	Dilton, W.J.	Sto	165.933
	Diplock, G.	Sto	282.973
	Dominy, J.C.G.	L/Sto	144.526
	Done, R.J.	Q/Sig	
	Dow, J.C.	Fl/Surgn	
	Dow, J.G.	Ord	186.792
*	Dowden, F.	Ord	175.472
	Dowling, H.E.	Asst/Engr	
	Draper, J.R.	Sto	353.530
	Duggan, D.	L/Sto	152.573
	Duke, A.H.	L/Sto	159.027
	Duncan, J.	Boy	196.883
	Eagling, G.T.	Sto	154.564
	Earwalker, R.	Sto	162.099
	Eason, W.	Ord	187.187
	Edwards, R.W.	Fl/Engr	
	Ellison, A.E.	AB	186.168
	Emmerson, D.	AB	127.094
	Everett, G.F.	Sto	283.276
	Fairbrass, E.J.	SBStd	150.253
	Fairweather, W.J.	AB	181.857
	Farrell, W.	Band	177.820
	Ferris, S.P.C.	ERA	268.241
	Field, C.H.	Cpl	
	Fielder, J.J.E.	Sto	277.984
	Finemore, S.A.	Sh/Std	121.505
	Fleming, H.	PO1	106.250
	Flynn, J.	PO1	145.833
	Foo, Ah.	Dom	
	Foo, Ah (2).	Dom	
	Forster, J.	PO1	99.790
	Forward, J.T.	Sto	280.810
	Foster, S.T.	Plmbr	340.007
	Gain, C.	Sto	282.971
	Gardiner, W.	Sto	172.431
	Gardner, H.	AB	169.394
	Gauntlett, H.R.	Art/Engr	
	Giles, J.R.	AB	187.101
	Gillam, J.H.	L/Sto	144.437
	Gillard, A.	Dom	
	Glew, A.	Sto	148.334
	Going, J.P.	MAA	55.120
	Gomes, H.	Sto	125.412
*	Gooch, J.A.	Ord	159.697
	Gowen, J.J.	L/Sig	167.945
	Grace, J.	Sto	159.047
	Graham, A.G.	2/Wrtr	161.204
	Grant, J.W.	Sto	281.089
	Greet, B.	Sh/Std	126.453
*	Gregson, J.	Sto	278.345
	Grierson, J.	L/Sto	161.660
	Grieve, T.	Sto	282.714
	Griffen, C.	L/Sto	151.945
	Grimes, F.	Sto	127.396
	Gulberry, W.	Sto	174.334
	Gurden, A.W.	AB	171.590
*	Guyatt, F.	Pte	Po7.816
	Hall, T.H.	AB	151.074
	Hallett, D.	AB	171.177
	Harding, C.A.	Engr	
	Harfield, O.C.	Carp/Mte	131.750
	Harn, A.G.	PO1	105.878
	Harris, J.	Dom	152.480
	Harris, J.	AB	181.280
	Harris, W.	Band	177.235
	Hart, A.	Sto	283.388
*	Hart, H.	Sto	284.386
	Hart, W.J.	Sto	282.669
*	Harvey, E.	Gunr	RMA5.641
	Harvey, E.G.	Sto	280.750
	Harvey, W.A.	AB	155.519
	Harwood, S.D.	PO1	145.859
	Hawken, J.	Sto	276.911
	Heap, A.	Sto	277.343
	Heath, H.L.	Comdr	
	Hewitt, C.	Sto	154.696
	Hibbert, A.C.	AB	181.887
	Hicks, R.L.	SBStd	129.915
	Hill, H.	AB	173.927
	Hitchings, W.H.	PO2	155.338
	Hogg, R.R.	Carp/Crew	340.625
	Hoills, F.W.	Sto	282.709
	Hollingdale, J.	Sto	281.221
	Homer, W.G.	Sto	282.937
	Hopkins, J.	Sto	145.450
	Horn, G.	AB	151.728
	Horton, W.	Sh/Cpl	166.480
	Howley, D.	PO1	135.466
	Huband, W.	PO1	119.178
	Hudson, R.	Sto	283.773

Hunt, A.G.	L/Sto	145.343	Mills, C.T.	Sto	173.559
Ingles, J.A.	Lieut		Mills, E.	AB	160.619
Innes, T.	PO2	83.297	Mitchell, J.	Sto	282.272
Ives, H.	Sto	166.960	Moore, T.	Sto	168.873
* Jacobs, W.	Ord	180.568	Mootoo, Tamby.	Dom	70.550
Jacobs, W.J.	Sto	146.316	Morbey, G.H.E.	AB	180.990
Jackson, F.	L/Sto	154.554	Morgan, M.J.	PO1	109.521
Jackson, V.	Sto	278.752	Moss, G.N.	Sto	165.952
Johns, P.S.	ERA	142.627	Murray, G.W.	Engr	
Johns, R.	PO1	106.661	Musgrave, W.	Sig	186.642
Johnson, E.W.	Sto	156.531	Myers, A.H.	PO1	59.019
Johnston, W.J.C.	Asst/Payr		Nash, A.	L/Sto	126.539
Jones, J.	AB	136.447	Nash, H.	Sto	175.893
Jones, J.H.	Sto	282.954	Nash, W.	Sto	277.093
Kearns, P.	PO1	144.414	Nay, E.	L/Sto	142.602
Kennard, J.	Sto	280.689	Needham, J.	Sto	281.148
Kennedy, G.	PO2	109.408	Newell, F.	Sto	282.905
Kilgour, A.D.	ERA	167.880	Newman, R.M.	ERA	154.303
* Killan, T.	Sto	284.177	Nicholas, J.	Lieut	
Kimpton, A.	Pte	Po5.602	Nicholls, C.R.	Carp/Crew	340.439
Kippens, G.	Ord	182.143	Nicholson, G.	L/S	126.020
Kive, E.G.	AB	181.965	Nicol, W.J.	Sto	171.245
Knee, A.L.	ERA	149.535	Nightingale, A.	Sto	282.274
Knight, J.W.	Sto	156.544	North, H.	PO1	164.158
Knight, S.J.	AB	186.713	Notton, W.H.	AB	182.722
Kung, Ah.	Dom		Nugent, E.W.	Band	340.543
Lawder, T.W.	AB	135.623	O'Brien, J.	L/Sto	154.482
Langton, J.F.	Sto	284.495	Oldbury, A.	Ch/Arm	127.669
Lashman, R.G.	PO1	129.895	On, Ah.	Dom	
Lawrence, G.	Cooper	109.606	Paddon, W.	Sto	278.756
Leatherby, D.	Sto	283.358	Palmer, E.C.	Pte	Po5.471
Leverton, G.	Pte	Po8.528	Pankhurst, T.W.	Act/Ch/Sto	149.527
Lewer, J.	Pntr	341.440	Peachey, J.	Sto	277.079
Leyburn, W.	SBStd	135.456	Pearce, R.W.	AB	155.869
Leythorn, W.H.	Sto	123.482	Perry, A.	Sto	152.611
Little, A.J.	AB	130.403	Perry, G.F.	L/Sto	143.259
Lodge, H.G.	Sh/Std/Asst	341.128	Pidwell, C.J.	L/Shpwrt	340.922
Long, J.G.	Ch/Sto	126.541	Pitt, C.G.	L/Sto	142.938
Loung, Wung.	Dom		Pooley, D.	Ch/Sto	110.746
Lovejoy, A.E.	AB	172.068	Potham, H.	Sto	152.114
Lovell, A.	Ch/PO	108.631	Pow, Ah.	Dom	
Lucas, W.	L/Sto	87.575	Powell, A.	L/Sto	146.808
McBrearty, J.	Ch/Sto	124.875	Price, W.H.	Sto	121.360
McHenry, J.	AB	111.237	Purvor, F.W.	Pte	Po5.815
McNeill, J.	Ord	186.836	Redgrave, G.	Sto	152.455
Madge, H.A.	Clerk		Reed, J.W.	L/Sto	157.701
Madgwick, J.T.	Sh/Cpl	143.263	Reid, R.H.	L/Sto	144.857
Maguire, J.	AB	176.036	Renn, W.H.	Ch/Carp	
Maidlow, H.	Band	129.422	Rice, W.	Sto	282.261
Maidment, F.	Bosn		Richards, E.	ERA	268.320
Marks, A.W.	Ord	186.302	Richards, T.	Sto	162.134
Marshall, A.R.	Sto	283.390	Ridley, C.J.	AB	176.294
Marshall, H.	Sto	153.867	Roberts, G.H.	Bosn	
Martin, W.H.	Q/Sig	187.137	Robinson, G.F.	Sto	146.611
Matthews, T.S.	Bosn		Rogers, J.	Sto	152.684
Maynard, H.	Sto	169.279	Rogers, T.	Sto	153.208
Meredith, H.	PO2	126.319	Rosam, G.	Sto	279.729
Milbourn, E.H.	Sto	280.846	Rosevear, T.	L/Sto	145.500
Millen, F.W.	Ch/Sto	125.410	Russell, H.G.	Sto	127.459
Miller, H.	Ord	187.157	Sageman, G.W.	Sto	154.504
Miller, R.	Sto	281.193	Salmon, W.J.	Sto	280.019

No Bar Medals *continued*

	Sam, Yong.	Dom	
	Sampson, J.	ERA	174.390
	Satcher, W.	PO2	128.701
	Savage, W.F.	Sto	176.595
	Sawyer, P.E.	Sto	158.072
	Schofield, E.	Band	132.754
	Scorey, G.	Act/Band/Cpl	155.582
	Seagrove, J.	Sto	150.949
	Sednell, F.C.	AB	150.982
	Seeley, G.H.	AB	140.331
	Sharpe, H.	2/Wrtr	138.821
	Shaw, J.	Sto	283.724
	Shearer, W.H.	Ord	181.434
	Shearsby, H.	Sto	176.583
	Shepherd, H.	Sto	276.167
	Shepherd, J.	Sail	99.960
	Sheriff, H.P.	AB	176.296
	Shirvell, J.J.	Asst/Engr	
	Shoesmith, T.	Sto	276.373
	Simms, W.C.A.	L/Sto	158.712
	Sinclair, J.W.	PO1	119.455
	Sing, Ah (1).	Dom	
	Skelton, H.	L/Sto	159.022
5	Small, P.	Pte	7.863
	Smith, G.W.	Sto	283.836
	Snudden, T.J.	Sto	159.966
	Soo, Ah.	Dom	
	Southam, J.H.	Ch/Sto	143.097
	Sparrow, J.	Ch/Sto	131.854
*	Spencer, E.	Sto	158.713
	Stannard, W.P.	Ord	173.522
	Stansfield, L.S.	Comdr	
	Stewart, E.F.	Sto	281.149
	Stickley, A.	Ch/Sto	131.808
	Stoneman, W.	Sto	153.094
	Street, C.W.	L/Sto	116.083
	Stupple, W.H.	Sto	131.930
	Swan, J.	L/Sto	152.690
	Swan, M.A.	Dom	148.984
	Swanton, M.	PO1	126.431
	Tanner, C.	Sto	279.726
	Taylor, P.H.	Sto	277.567
	Terry, A.	Ord	183.844
	Terry, W.H.	Ch/Sto	126.969
	Tew, C.	Sto	283.155
	Thomas, E.J.	AB	159.574
	Thompson, L.M.	Ord	186.802
	Thorp, E.H.	L/Sto	129.407
	Timms, A.H.	Sto	280.775
	Tipton, J.	Sto	280.801
	Titley, F.	Band	164.628
	Toms, A.S.	AB	180.582
	Toogood, G.H.	PO1	129.785
	Truscott, R.J.	Ch/ERA	148.864
	Tucker, W.	AB	187.078
	Tumber, F.C.	Pte	Po4.065
	Turner, A.	AB	143.510
	Turner, A.	Sto	283.166
	Turner, F.H.	L/Carp/Crew	340.257
	Turner, H.C.	Ch/PO	102.134

	Turner, H.W.	Sto	174.269
	Turner, W.	Sto	282.687
	Tyrrell, R.W.	Sto	282.667
	Twine, H.	Sto	281.276
	Urie, S.	Sto	280.736
	Vickery, H.	Sto	283.887
	Wall, L.	Engr	
	Walton, F.	Act/2/Sh/Cook	175.730
	Ward, C.	Sto	282.959
	Warner, G.E.	Gunr	RMA5.812
	Warrell, E.	PO1	130.204
	Washbourne, W.H.	L/Sig	157.665
	Watkins, F.C.	Band	180.120
	Watson, C.	Sto	279.788
	Watson, F.C.J.D.	Pte	Po8.412
	Watson, J.G.	Sto	154.672
	Watts, W.E.	Band	135.579
	Watts, W.J.	Act/Ch/Sto	147.843
	Webber, W.	Pte	Ply6.412
	Welch, J.E.E.	Act/2/Sh/Cook	340.266
	Went, G.	Sto	283.811
	West, E.	Sto	176.584
	Weston, C.F.	AB	187.173
	White, H.	Sto	282.975
	Whittaker, J.	Ch/ERA	133.302
	Wild, E.	Ch/ERA	130.811
	Williams, G.	Sto	283.254
	Williams, J.	Sto	284.966
	Williams, W.	AB	109.746
	Williams, W.H.	Sto	281.122
	Williamson, A.J.	AB	164.161
	Wilson, J.	Cooper/Crew	279.804
	Winch, R.	Sto	279.539
	Wisdom, W.	Sto	280.546
	Wolton, S.	Ord	181.110
	Wood, G.	Ord	186.822
	Wood, J.H.	Sto	277.604
	Woodhouse, F.	Sto	169.315
	Wright, E.B.	Ch/PO	85.945
	Wright, W.	Sto	90.001
	Wyckaert, J.E.	Sto	280.822
	York, L.	L/Sto	152.666
	Young, A.	Sto	282.273
	Young, G.W.	Sto	282.952

Duplicate medals:

	Brothers, C.	Sto	156.142
	Claw, S.T.	Ord	186.777
	Croft, P.	Sto	281.206
	Davidson, F.	Sto	143.083
	Ellison, A.E.	AB	186.168
	Fielder, J.J.E.	Sto	277.984
	Foo, Ah.	Dom	
	Heap, A.	Sto	277.343
	Hunt, A.G.	L/Sto	145.343
	Johnston, W.J.C.	Asst/Payr	
	Marks, A.W.	Ord	186.302
	Meredith, H.	PO2	126.319
	Miller, H.	Ord	187.157
x	Newell, F.	Sto	282.905
	Price, W.H.	Sto	121.360

Sharpe, H.	2/Wrtr	138.821
Walton, F.	Act/2/Sh/Cook	175.730
Watson, J.G.	Sto	154.672

x Two duplicate medals issued.

Returned medals:

Aldridge, T.J.	AB	130.681
Allistone, T.H.	Pte	
Austin, P.J.	Boy	198.659
Beney, J.F.	Sto	281.268
Bennett, H.C.	Sto	154.513
Bolton, J.	Pte	
Boylan, J.	Sto	278.068
Bridges, H.C.	Sub Lieut	
Brown, A.	Pte	
Brown, A.	Pte	
Burt, F.H.	Dom	173.726
Carmichael, J.R.	Pte	
Chanings, W.	Sto	
Clark, A.E.	Plmbr/Mte	
Clarke, F.	Ord	161.855
Codd, G.R.	AB	155.101
Coombes, F.N.	Ord	
Cooper, A.	Bugler	Ch10.416
Coward, G.J.	Pte	
Doe, Jim.	Kroo	
Dover, W.C.	Boy	197.597
Farrant, A.	Ord	
Fleming, J.	Sto	148.555
Fouk, Ah.	Dom	
Glavin, J.	AB	
Goff, W.E.	Sto	175.843
Goodings, E.A.	Pte	
Gray, G.	Sto	159.984
Hay, W.W.	Sto	279.018
Heard, W.	Pte	
Horder, G.H.	Ord	
Hughes, E.J.	Pte	Po5.907
Hughes, T.J.	Sto	282.976
Hynes, T.	Sto	176.700
Jeffery, J.	Sergt	
Kent, W.H.	Ord	186.666
Killpatrick, T.L.	Ch/ERA	123.266
Knibbs, R.	AB	134.286
Lee, C.J.	Ord	
Locke, H.R.	PO1	132.587
Loveridge, J.H.	Band	155.648
McKay, N.	Shpwrt	340.897
McKenna, F.	Sto	277.929
Mack, H.	Sto	
Magee, W.	Sto	282.711
Mallin, T.	AB	
Morbey, G.H.G.	AB	
Morgan, W.H.	Dom	
Mortimer, E.W.	Sto	154.681
Mortimer, W.	AB	187.489
New, L.G.H.	Ord	188.499
Night, G.	Sto	
O'Connor, M.	Sto	
Organ, G.L.	AB	
Osborn, C.H.	Sto	
Park, W.T.	Sto	
Parsons, W.	L/Sto	
Peters, T.H.	Pte	
Phillips, T.	AB	134.162
Powis, A.B.	AB	186.785
Read, J.R.	Pte	
Richardson, C.D.	Act/Sub Lieut	
Riley, W.	Sto	284.043
Saundercock, W.J.	PO1	
Saunderson, R.	Sig	
Silvester, T.G.	Gunr	
Sloane, D.	Sto	284.315
Spendelow, H.	AB	159.352
Stangroom, G.	AB	124.794
Stanton, R.A.	AB	
Stopford, J.	Pte	Ch8.693
Stout, C.	Q/Sig	145.292
Sutton, R.	AB	
Thwaites, B.W.	Ord	189.800
West, F.W.	Gunr	
Whatley, J.W.	Sto	156.487
White, A.	PO2	
[6] White, W.J.N.	Ord	186.885
Yow, Ah.	Dom	

H.M.S. RACOON

Period for which entitled:
13th January 1900 to 15th July 1900.

Bars	Total	Returned	Entitled
1	3	1	2
0	205	29	176
	208	30	178

Notes:
[1] This officer received this medal for service in H.M.S. Doris; the medal for H.M.S. Doris was returned (See medal roll)
[2] The original was lost and then found. It was then returned to the Mint, as a duplicate medal had been issued.

Bar: Natal

Davison, J.	AB	182.940
Green, C.H.	AB	189.274

Returned medal:

Sumner, R.W.	Supply Lieut	

No Bar Medals

Adams, W.	Sto	288.874
Alexander, W.	AB	185.231
Andrews, C.	Sto	277.997
Atter, G.W.	Pte	Po8.561
Attwood, C.	Pte	Ch8.513
Bailey, F.J.B.	AB	188.938
Baker, J.P.	AB	189.517
Ballard, E.E.	Sto	276.454
Balls, G.H.	AB	177.829
Bardell, A.	AB	183.226
Barnes, F.W.	AB	125.663
Barrett, S.C.W.	AB	189.250
Beal, A.R.G.	Payr	
Bear, J.H.	PO2	119.092
Beardmore, H.	Sto	276.130
Beavis, H.V.	Sto	279.200
Bennett, H.D.	Pte	Ch9.319
Beresford, W.H.	L/Sto	148.668
Best, C.J.	ERA	159.085
Boothroyd, S.W. alias Moorhouse	Sh/Cpl	106.306
Bradbury, R.	Ch/Arm	117.723
Brazill, W.J.	Pte	Ch8.522
Brown, G.	L/Sig	147.895
Brown, R.O.G.	AB	180.598
Burt, A.	Pte	Ch8.454
Buxton, H.	AB	183.188
Callen, A.J.	AB	183.230
Campbell, J.R.R.	AB	182.622
Capoutrie, B.	Shpwrt	83.929
Chadwick, E.J.	AB	164.699
Clark, H.J.T.	AB	184.113
Cobley, C.	Plmbr/Mte	341.205
Collins, E.	Sto	284.240
Conneely, T.	Sto	287.147
Cornthwaite, T.W.	Pte	Ch2.562
Crisfield, C.F.	ERA	154.302
Davis, S.J.	Pte	Ch7.462
Devereux, E.H.	AB	193.093
Duma.	Seedie	
Dunt, W.C.	AB	182.308
Faint, J.	Sto	284.626
Fido, A.	AB	180.796
Finch, G.	Ch/PO	125.162
Fisher, A.C.	Sto	277.360
Fremblin, J.W.J.	AB	167.513
Froud, G.	Sto	154.052
Fullwood, C.A.	AB	164.781
Furham, A.	Seedie	
Furoze, S.	Seedie	
Gage, A.	Pte	Ch5.130
Gibbons, A.	AB	187.685
Gibson, H.	Gunr	
Gibson, J.W.	L/S	175.100
Gillham, W.	2/Yeo/Sig	137.151
Glanville, J.T.	AB	168.017
Gomez, J.	Dom	107.459
Goodman, W.C.	Pte	Po6.881
Goodsell, A.J.	L/Sto	177.435
Goodwin, E.	Sto	279.048
Graham, S.J.	Arm/Crew	341.196
Grant, A.E.A.	Comdr	
[1] Grant, F.N.	Lieut	
Greenfield, B.L.H.	Lieut	
Guy, A.C.J.	AB	181.667
Hackert, E.C.	AB	180.713
Hall, E.	PO1	148.462
Hanshaw, H.	2/SBStd	136.331
Hare, H.J.	Sto	290.198
Harman, E.G.	Sto	290.197
Harvey, F.C.	Sh/Std	141.520
Hewett, G.H.	Capt.	
Hewlett-Cooper, C.T.	Lieut	
Holmes, E.W.	2/Wrtr	165.812
Ibbotson, T.	AB	166.745
Ingham, R.	Pte	Ch8.324
Jeffries, H.J.	AB	188.870

Johns, H.	L/Shpwrt	139.870
Jones, A.H.	L/S	173.994
King, C.E.	AB	180.965
Know, R.	Sto	280.305
Lawson, J.	AB	176.757
Leaney, T.	Sto	126.073
Leblond, G.	Ch/Sto	144.803
Lee, R.C.	AB	187.159
Leedham, C.H.	AB	189.134
Love, G.F.	Sto	279.701
Ludgate, G.T.	AB	186.981
McAsey, G.	PO1	115.779
McCubbine, G.	Ord	189.153
MacGuire, T.	AB	184.267
McLennan, J.F.	Sto	277.025
Makin, G.	Pte	Ch8.459
Malby, C.H.	AB	155.739
Mancer, F.W.	PO2	155.639
Marbrook, H.	Seedie	
Marshall, F.J.	AB	173.114
Mascarinhas, D.J.	Dom	357.914
Mathers, T.	Pte	Ply5.087
Matthew, A.F.	AB	178.525
Montague, H.B.	Lieut	
Moore, R.H.	PO1	136.641
Murfitt, A.A.	Pte	Ch6.768
Naylor, E.	AB	189.136
Nepean, E.St.M.	St/Surgn	
Oughton, G.	PO1	147.896
Patterson, D.	Sto	279.076
Peel, A.E.	AB	159.225
Peel, R.G.	L/S	177.661
Percival, T.H.	AB	154.000
Pereira, J.A.J.	Dom	357.174
Pettit, A.J.S.	AB	183.721
Philp, W.	Carp/Crew	340.714
Pinto, A.R.	Dom	356.996
Pool, W.	Ch/Carp/Mte	110.715
Pound, J.	PO1	95.265
Price, H.T.	Sh/Std/Asst	341.338
Prickett, J.	Sto	158.738
Primmer, W.G.	Sto	172.820
Puddle, C.C.M.	L/Cpl	Ch5.070
Quinn, J.	AB	181.944
Read, R.	AB	189.164
Reddy, J.	AB	175.988
Rennie, H.	Sto	277.047
Ritchie, W.	AB	127.064
Robinson, A.B.	AB	180.987
Robinson, G.	AB	174.555
Rolph, F.	L/Sto	276.386
Runham, W.	Pte	Po8.229
Russell, G.	Dom	
Saunders, G.P.	AB	168.328
Sealey, C.	Sto	277.087
Sears, H.	Pte	Po6.385
Shoebrooks, F.L.	Arm/Mte	340.461
Shorter, C.E.	Act/Ch/Sto	149.697
Sinclair, C.J.	ERA	268.221
Skeene, T.	PO2	168.790
Smith, A.J.	AB	185.028
Smith, G.W.	Sergt	Ch4.869
Souza, J.C.D'.	Dom	164.586
Souza, V. de	Dom	122.779
Steell, H.R.	PO1	129.070
Stewart, C.J.	PO2	152.893
Stewart, J.J.	AB	181.668
Stocker, P.	Engr	
Stokes, A.H.	Cpl	Ch8.662
Stone, G.G.	Pte	Ch5.367
Stratford, A.	Sto	290.154
Sulleyman, J.	Seedie	
Swan, C.	Sto	278.415
Terry, F.	Sto	283.136
Thatcher, A.W.	Pte	Ch7.224
Thomsett, F.D.	Ch/Engr	
Tiddy, J.	Blksmth	341.206
Townsend, G.J.	AB	183.004
Turner, F.J.	Sto	284.619
Wakerell, R.T.	AB	158.503
Wallis, R.H.	Sto	278.410
Walton, D.Y.	L/S	173.848
Warn, G.T.	Pte	Ch8.127
Waterfield, H.A.	AB	166.536
Welch, W.J.	AB	189.158
Whitai, A.	Seedie	
Whitaker, R.	Sto	284.611
White, A.E.	AB	183.918
Wilkes, A.J.	AB	121.456
Willburn, T.	AB	164.710
Willder, G.F.	Sto	284.632
Williams, J.H.R.	Sto	148.652
Williams, W.	Sto	290.196
Willis, R.G.	L/Sto	148.413
Wood, A.	Ch/Sto	135.919
Woodruff, W.G.	AB	189.263
Wright, J.	Ch/ERA	132.385
Yapp, A.C.	L/Sto	153.640
Young, D.	AB	167.471
Young, L.H.	ERA	268.871

Duplicate medals:

[2] Campbell, G.	Q/Sig	150.644
Crisfield, C.F.	ERA	154.302
Davis, S.J.	Pte	Ch7.462
Dunt, W.C.	AB	182.308
Gibson, H.	Gunr	
Hare, H.J.	Sto	290.198
King, C.E.	AB	180.965
Price, H.T.	Sh/Std/Asst	341.338
Saunders, G.P.	AB	168.328
Sinclair, C.J.	ERA	268.221
Sulleyman, J.	Seedie	
Turner, F.J.	Sto	284.619
Whitai, A.	Seedie	

Returned medals:

Abderso.	Seedie	
Abdullah, S.	Seedie	
Azis, Y.A.	Seedie	
[2] Campbell, G.	Q/Sig	150.644
Chaney, H.	AB	178.182

No Bar Medals *Returned medals, continued*

Coles, J.	AB	189.137
Connolly, J.	Sto	285.690
Davis, E.	Sto	282.994
Dews, H.A.	AB	162.220
Egan, J.	Sto	285.340
Farrow, H.	Pte	Po7.798
Field, S.J.	AB	
Hammett, G.G.	Pte	Po8.119
Hasson, F.	Seedie	
Hill, W.	Sto	286.408
Jaffer, M.	Seedie	
Johns, H.	AB	
Kamna, A.	Seedie	
Leitas, B.	Musn (Native)	
M'zee.	Dom	
Mahomed, S.	Seedie	
Mereicka, E.	Blksmth (Maltese)	
Moth, T.L.	Sub Lieut	
Penn, W.	Ord	188.833
Ratcliff, F.	Ord	189.139
Saad, A.	Seedie	
Songor, B.	Seedie	
Spilsbury, W.	Sto	280.725
Tean.	Seedie	

H.M.S. RAMBLER

Period for which entitled:
5th November 1899 to 26th June 1900

Bars	Total	Returned	Entitled
0	145	35	110
	145	35	110

No Bar Medals

Adams, R.	Sto	287.773
Allen, G.F.	AB	156.923
Bennett, J.L.	Pntr	341.055
Bertram, W.J.	AB	180.988
Bowdon, W.W.G.	Ord	180.089
Brindle, J.	L/Sto	159.973
Buchanan, J.H.	AB	159.118
Buckett, G.	PO1	97.999
Bull II, J.	Kroo	
Casemore, G.H.J.	Pte	Ch5.521
Cassing, J.W.	Ord	188.509
Clarke, G.L.	Payr	
Codd, G.R.	AB	155.101
Cook, C.	Bosn	
Curtis, W.	Kroo	
Cust, H.E.P.	Comdr	
Cuthbertson, T.A.	ERA	268.599
Davis, J.	Ord	187.123
Day, E.A.	Lieut	
Dew, C.W.	L/Sto	131.636
Dibben, R.	PO1	156.957
Eaton, G.A.	AB	157.979
Ellen, G.	AB	181.884
Fitter, G.	AB	182.195
Fity, P.	Carp/Crew	341.691
Friend, T.	AB	181.781
Frost, W.E.T.	Sto	162.143
Fuller, W.	Ord	187.155
Gamblin, G.	Dom	108.767
Garraway, J.G.	Pte	Ch4.792
Gay, W.	Ch/Carp/Mte	149.500
George, J.H.	L/Shpwrt	143.607
Gibson, A.	AB	149.373
Giles, G.E.	Pte	Ch8.548
Harrad, G.H.	Sto	279.079
Harris, J.J.	PO2	150.788
Hatchard, J.	Pte	Ch8.530
Hearn, A.P.	AB	159.294
Hendy, H.C.	Ch/PO	109.927
Higham, W.	PO1	97.350
Hodgetts, J.W.	Ord	190.233
Holcroft, B.	Ord	202.961
Horn, M.	L/Sto	155.208
Horne, R.	Lieut	
Howard, T.H.	AB	164.344
Huntlea, J.	Ord	187.687
Janman, J.	AB	146.506
Jones, T.P.	Ch/ERA	127.767
Kemp. J.F.	Cpl	Ch5.971
Knock, A.	Sto	165.552
Land, W.H.S.	Sh/Cook	152.532
Lang, J.	Ord	197.095
Lavelle, P.	Sto	285.333
Lawrence, H.J.G.	Lieut	
Letton, S.D.	Dom	168.491
Levett, J.	AB	179.156
Linington, C.	PO1	99.308
Lovett, A.	Sto	143.306
Lukes, T.F.	PO2	126.878
McKoy, A.	Dom	355.794
McLeod, W.G.	Ord	184.505
McTear, A.H.	Art/Engr	
Marescaux, A.E.H.	Lieut	
Martell, A.E.G.	AB	159.252
Martin, E.S.	Arm/Mte	263.461
Martyn, F.C.	3/Wrtr	340.563
Mitchell, J.W.	Pte	Ch8.371
Monro, C.E.	Lieut	
Morgan, W.H.	Dom	154.734
Nelson, T.	Cooper	340.890
Nicolson, G.C.	Engr	
Page, J.S.	AB	162.212
Pate, S.G.	PO1	101.649
Payne, C.A.	AB	97.917
Penfold, L.D.	Lieut	
Phillips, M.D.	Ord	198.932
Pinn, T.	Sto	139.864
Price, F.	Sto	172.136
Ralph, T.	AB	165.053
Roe, T.	Sto	187.285
Rose, J.R.	Pte	Ch3.638
Rowland, A.G.	L/S	152.887
Rumsby, H.	AB	155.790
Sainsbury, C.W.	Shpwrt	342.674
Scott, J.	AB	150.837
Seeber, C.H.	Sh/Std	133.475
Sexton, W.	Sh/Cpl	350.039
Sharp, T.P.	Ord	193.593
Sinden, C.E.	ERA	268.278
Skinner, G.W.J.	L/Sig	179.093
Smith, W.J.	Sto	284.859
Spendelow, H.	AB	159.352
Storkey, W.G.	AB	182.054
Strangroom, G.	AB	124.794

No Bar Medals *continued*

Taylor, J.	Sto	286.456
Thornbarrow, S.J.	AB	188.515
Tilley, F.	Pte	Ch6.257
Tomlinson, H.E.	Surgn	
Wagner, A.	Ord	190.662
Wall, A.J.	Ord	191.744
Walter, G.J.	Ch/PO	103.584
Warner, C.	L/Sto	160.510
Waterston, J.G.	ERA	268.049
Webb, J.	L/Sto	154.776
Whomsley, T.	Blksmth	144.554
Widger, W.	PO1	147.039
Wildman, W.	Pte	Ch8.951
Woodward, E.	AB	182.196
Wright, G.	Pte	Po9.097
Young, C.L.L.	Sub Lieut	

Duplicate medals:

Dibben, R.	PO1	156.957
Ellen, G.	AB	181.884
Knock, A.	Sto	165.552
Rumsby, H.	AB	155.790
Spendelow, H.	AB	159.352
Young, C.L.L.	Sub Lieut	

Returned medals:

Bannerman, H.	Ord	178.582
Bull I, J.	Kroo	
Dandy, Peter.	Kroo	
Doe, Jim.	Kroo	
Edmonds, F.J.S.	Q/Sig	191.008
George I, Jim.	Kroo	
George II, Jim.	Dom	
Hay, W.W.	Sto	279.018
Holloway, H.C.	SB/Attn	350.432
Holme, G.	Sail/Mte	115.645
Ide, C.G.	AB	162.867
McTaggart, A.	Ord	190.566
Matthews, W.H.	L/S	162.312
Medhurst, J.F.C.	SB/Attn	151.279
Munn, G.A.	Shpwrt	340.648
Murray, T.E.	PO2	163.909
New, L.G.H.	Ord	188.499
Norris, R.E.	PO2	156.062
O'Brien, J.	PO2	146.037
Pearce, R.W.	AB	155.869
Peberdy, T.	AB	158.193
Royal, Tom.	Kroo	
Ryder, G.	L/S	131.374
Seymour, Tom.	Kroo	
Simpson, J.M.	PO1	122.358
Starkey, H.G.	Sto	154.761
Stokoe, S.R.	L/Sig	152.829
Taylor, W.	Dom	354.706
Trewolla, J.	L/Carp/Crew	340.307
Turner, A.	AB	143.510
Turner, J.H.	Pte	Ch6.810
Warren, George.	Kroo	
Westall, C.W.	Pte	Po8.677
Woods, B.	Ord	190.450
Worrall, P.H.	Pte	Ch10.406

H.M.S. RATTLER

Period for which entitled:

Extended period only:
19th September 1901 to 31st May 1902.

Bars	*Total*	*Returned*	*Entitled*
0	86	10	76
	86	10	76

No Bar Medals

Alderson, J.	Pte	Ply9.147
Ashman, J.	PO1	125.624
Audy, R.S.	AB	187.523
Aylmer, H.E.F.	Lieut	
Bannister, P.H.	Surgn	
Barnett, W.A.	Cpl	Ply3.478
Beal, W.	Dom	357.558
Beasley, G.	L/Sto	172.771
Best, H.M.	AB	163.851
Brampton, W.R.	AB	178.060
Brewer, W.J.	Sto	284.777
Bridgland, R.C.	SB/Attn	350.580
Bright, H.A.	AB	172.716
Browning, P.G.	L/S	176.137
Carr, E.	Pte	Ply6.207
Cheater, J.	Act/Ch/Sto	150.958
Chesney, J.	Carp/Crew	343.721
Clarke, R.	Dom	165.315
Colbourne, B.L.	Boy	210.055
Coningsby, C.W.	AB	186.102
Corbyn, W.	L/Sig	175.771
Cross, C.	L/Sto	147.017
Crow, Tom.	Kroo	
Curtis, A.W.	Dom	358.820
Curtis, E.A.	AB	181.071
Davenport, E.	Dom	163.454
Davis, R.	Sto	353.887
Dingain, G.F.	PO1	166.808
Ford, G.E.	Gunr	
Forrest, P.	Ch/Sto	139.629
Foulger, P.	PO1	156.759
Fuller, A.	AB	200.628
Gardiner, J.D.	Art/Engr	
Gary, A.J.	Pte	Ply10.714
Good, J.A.	Pte	Ply9.300
Goodman, W.J.	Pte	Ply6.562
Hall, W.R.	Arm/Mte	340.465
Harling, W.J.	L/Sig	143.377
Harris, T.W.	AB	187.599
Heath, A.J.	Ord	205.750
Hogg, O.W.	AB	173.902
Hopcroft, A.E.	L/Sto	165.955
Hopper, R.S.	Ch/Sto	140.943
Howard, F.C.	AB	179.826
James, T.	ERA	269.077
Kelly, B.J.	Ord	204.675
McCollum, P.	Sto	141.048
Marchant, J.H.	Sto	283.070
Marcon, R.E.	Lieut	
Martin, G.E.	ERA	159.087
Mason, W.	AB	178.020
Mills, W.G.	1/Wrtr	167.640
Mundy, C.A.	AB	186.118
Murray, W.H.	Sto	172.106
O'Hare, P.L.	AB	205.521
Phillips, H.T.	AB	182.412
Rendle, F.A.	Sh/Std	340.110
Rhead, J.A.	Pte	Ply8.866
Roberts, Bob.	Kroo	
Sadd, G.A.	L/S	172.730
Sadler, E.E.G.	Ord	206.394
Saville, T.	Sto	284.405
Smith, G.H.	PO1	130.595
Starck, E.	AB	206.717
Stevenson, J.	PO2	167.929
Strange, T.G.	Cook/Mte	146.736
Street, H.L.	Sub Lieut	
Thorne, A.J.	AB	156.917
Tibbets, G.	Lieut	
Tremble, R.	PO2	167.400
Vincent, C.	ERA	268.458
Wakefield, H.F.H.	Lieut	
Webb, H.G.	Pte	Ply8.991
Williams, W.J.R.	Sto	159.932
Wilson, J.	PO1	187.440
Wright, J.E.	Carp/Mte	169.208

Duplicate medal:

Crow, Tom.	Kroo	

Returned medals:

Brook, C.	Pte	Ply10.405
Coaster, J.G.	Pte	Ply9.188
Coleman, P.	Ord	193.212
Conqueror, W. the	Dom	359.346
Johnson, B.	Kroo	
Mark, S.	Kroo	
Onley, H.	AB	166.318
Smith, J.H.	Sig	193.775
Upsidedown, J.	Kroo	
Willies, A.R.	Ord	206.762

H.M.S. REDBREAST

Period for which entitled:
12th February 1901 to 8th March 1901.

Extended period:
9th March 1901 to 1st April 1901.

Bars	*Total*	*Returned*	*Entitled*
0	87	4	83
	87	4	83

No Bar Medals

Abdullah.	Tindal	
Allen, A.	Ch/Sto	129.259
Aubrey, A.	Sto	291.711
Baird, T.B.	Ch/ERA	127.191
Bassett, J.	Ord	197.201
Beavis, R.H.	AB	184.513
Bentley, A.H.	SB/Attn	353.363
Bradford, H.G.	AB	194.496
Brewer, F.H.	L/Sto	133.793
Brewer, W.	AB	196.284
Brookman, F.J.	AB	184.757
Bull, A.W.	Sh/Cook	152.535
Burton, H.	Pte	Ply6.128
Carson, R.	AB	181.255
Childs, H.J.	Sh/Std	170.046
Cole, F.J.	AB	185.268
Conlan, R.	Sto	290.045
Conroy, T.	Ord	199.802
Crews, C.F.	Sto	291.296
Cummins, A.	AB	157.331
Dart, S.L.	AB	203.020
Dias, N.C. de R.	Dom	358.005
Dickson, R.T.	Lieut	
Docking, A.	Sto	278.280
Faye, W.	PO1	145.652
Forster, J.	L/Sergt	Ply3.233
Gonsalves, A.C.	Dom	358.396
Gracious, M.	Dom	83.697
Gregory, W.G.	ERA	269.392
Habib.	Seedie	
Habib, Melik.	Seedie	
Halliday, S.D.T.	Surgn	
Herron, D.	Ord	199.514
Hicks, W.T.	AB	189.088
Hill, M.R.	Lieut Comdr	
Hoare, W.	AB	193.926
Hocking, J.M.	Ch/Sto	140.996
Holbrook, E.T.	L/S	161.910
Holder, R.J.	PO1	131.525
Howard, W.J.	Sto	292.162
Hudson, H.J.	Pte	Ply7.950
Johard, Hasib.	Seedie/Sto	
Kerr, R.	Pte	Ply7.670
Kierman, M.E.	AB	200.146
Langmead, A.	AB	180.473
Lazzarischi, H.	Ch/Sto	120.139
Lindsay, P.	AB	181.014
Locke, G.T.	Ord	199.513
Luckham, J.F.	Arm/Mte	340.377
McArthur, R.	L/Sig	159.171
Mangan, P.	AB	186.668
Marles, J.	L/Sto	123.806
May, A.W.	L/S	125.927
Mockett, W.J.	AB	198.928
Moran, J.	Pte	Ply8.858
Murray, J.	Sto	279.558
Neale, W.G.	Ch/Wrtr	89.775
O'Brien, B.	L/Carp/Crew	342.829
Parrott, G.C.	Gunr	
Paul, H.C.	PO2	161.933
Pepperell, W.F.	Art/Engr	
Perry, F.W.	PO1	162.775
Powell, T.	ERA	268.745
Ramage, J.	Pte	Ply6.272
Redmond, J.	AB	199.676
Roe, A.	L/Cpl	Ply8.055
Said.	Seedie	
Smith, A.	Pte	Ply7.296
Smith, H.	PO2	123.029
Snagge, A.L.	Lieut	
Souza, F.X. de	Dom	353.100
Stewart, J.P.	L/Sto	149.219
Stratford, A.	AB	174.041
Thomas, G.	Sto	279.856
Tilley, H.W.	PO1	135.749
Tucker, W.J.	Sto	292.720
Wallis, J.E.	AB	193.643
Watson, E.	Pte	Ply7.726
Westacott, W.J.	AB	200.566
Whitewash alias Fredge.	Tindal	
Wilkinson, F.	AB	178.379
Williams, J.	AB	199.668

Duplicate medals:

x Carson, R.	AB	181.255
Childs, H.J.	Sh/Std	170.046
Faye, W.	PO1	145.652

Kerr, R.	Pte	Ply7.670

x Two duplicate medals issued.

Returned medals:

Cruse, W.	Q/Sig	191.926
Ferag, Ali.	Seedie	
Ferooz.	Seedie	
Ferro, J.	Dom	146.486

EXTENDED PERIOD

No Bar Medal

Gage, J.W.	Sto	290.857

H.M.S. SAPPHO

Period for which entitled:
23rd February 1901 to 8th March 1901.

Extended period:
9th March 1901 to 27th July 1901.

Bars	*Total*	*Returned*	*Entitled*
2	1	0	1
1	0	0	0
0	273	19	254
	274	19	255

Note:
[1] Also noted on roll as Ronayne.

Bars: Cape Colony, South Africa 1901

Longridge, T.	Act/Carp	

No Bar Medals

Adams, H.	Sto	293.436
Andrew, W.	Carp/Mte	135.187
Andrews, C.	2/Yeo/Sig	160.243
Appleby, J.E.	Pte	Ch7.929
Apps, R.A.	Ch/Sto	145.523
Archibald, J.	Ord	202.409
Ashlee, G.T.	Ch/Sto	139.898
Ashton, E.	Sto	293.514
Ayre, F.J.	L/Sto	170.458
Baker, J.G.	Ord	197.936
Barry, J.	St/Surgn	
Bean, S.J.	AB	177.884
Black, R.P.	Sto	293.775
Blackmore, J.	Ch/Sto	140.129
Bland, J.T.	Sto	292.671
Bolitho, F.J.	AB	167.341
Bonney, W.E.	ERA	269.062
Box, W.	Plmbr/Mte	343.450
Bremner, E.A.	Payr	
Bridge, G.H.	Sto	284.953
Britton, P.H.	Sto	285.542
Brocklebank, J.	ERA	160.542
Broomham, W.	AB	172.555
Brown, H.J.	Arm/Crew	342.823
Brown, S.	Sto	285.492
Burney, C.	Capt	
Carter, A.G.	Ord	194.703
Charman, J.P.	AB	194.784
Cheal, W.J.	AB	178.273
Chennell, E.	Sto	291.447
Chitty, T.H.	Sto	292.992
Clarke, A.	Ord	203.162
Clarke, S.	PO1	124.600
Clarkson, H.A.	Ord	203.010
Cockerell, W.J.	Pte	Ch9.465
Cockle, F.E.	Pte	Po9.458
Cooke, F.J.	AB	179.718
Cooke, J.W.	Pte	Ch1.912
Cotter, C.	PO1	135.947
Coughlin, D.	Sto	284.916
Crewe, J.	Sto	289.396
Croxon, J.W.	AB	181.869
Damant, W.S.	Asst/Engr	
Darley, H.C.	ERA	268.556
Dart, W.E.	Sto	152.442
Darts, W.	AB	181.228
Davis, C.	Sto	290.545
Davis, P.	L/Sto	279.947
Dent, G.	Sto	287.564
Dimond, F.	Q/Sig	188.852
Dodson, H.	Pte	Ch10.166
Donovan, D.	PO1	151.826
Ducker, G.	AB	193.959
Durney, J.	AB	168.903
Dyke, T.S.	Pntr	341.762
Eccles, R.	Sh/Cook	123.954
Eliner, J.H.	L/S	168.002
Elkin, W.J.	AB	174.504
Elliott, W.W.	2/SBStd	353.040
Ellis, W.H.	Ord	203.403
Fisher, L.D.	Lieut	
Foster, J.	Sto	290.541
French, W.C.	Sto	276.040
Fuchler, P.L.J.	Sh/Cpl	350.128
Gardner, S.H.	Sto	292.215
Gascoigne, G.	Dom	
Gaul, W.D.	Pte	Ch5.198
George, S.W.	Sto	288.807
Gibson, H.	AB	188.606
Girven, W.A.	AB	170.304
Goodhew, F.W.	Sto	290.727
Graham, J.	Sto	291.523
Grant, T.J.D.	L/Sig	175.269
Green, A.R.	Sto	291.200
Green, D.	Ord	197.328
Greer, J.	Cook/Mte	354.471

Gribben, M.	L/S	183.447	May, F.D.	PO1	144.235
Grimster, E.	AB	194.771	Maywood, G.E.	Ord	194.707
Guy, C.E.	AB	180.819	Menghim, F.P.	Dom	357.140
Hallam, F.G.	Sto	283.508	Minshull, C.F.	Cooper	341.044
Hammond, F.J.	Pte	Ch9.906	Moore, A.	AB	174.115
Hand, C.J.	Pte	Ch8.997	Moran, J.	AB	174.553
Harrington, W.N.	Sto	285.228	Mullarky, J.	L/Sto	167.792
Hart, W.H.	Blksmth	342.627	Murphy, J.	L/Sto	171.276
Healey, J.	AB	182.528	Neale, J.H.	Carp/Crew	295.322
Hearn, A.E.	Sto	285.750	Needham, L.	ERA	268.368
Hendy, F.	Sto	293.431	Neeve, B.	Ord	203.214
Hendy, R.J.	Ch/ERA	117.973	Nicholson, J.B.	Asst/Engr	
Hewitt, C.T.	Boy	202.381	O'Neill, C.	L/Sig	130.434
Hill, H.H.	Arm/Mte	340.503	Page, F.	Sto	288.392
Hill, M.F.	PO1	147.148	Palmer, C.	Sto	293.451
Hillman, G.E.	L/S	166.121	Palmer, R.	Sto	288.796
Hillman, H.	Sto	292.966	Parsons, A.W.	Sto	131.937
Hodgson, W.	Boy	202.950	Parsons, J.	ERA	159.459
Hogg, W.A.	Ord	195.282	Parsons, O.L.	Clerk	
Holbrook, H.W.	AB	174.179	Pawley, G.F.	Sto	283.822
Holland, A.P.	AB	194.045	Pearce, G.W.	AB	169.852
Holland, W.T.	Boy	202.742	Peet, J.	AB	174.805
Holly, T.	Ord	197.402	Pepperell, G.E.	Sto	170.124
Hook, J.T.	PO1	122.939	Perey, M.	Dom	84.199
Houghton, R.N.	Dom	359.117	Pleming, J.W.	St/Engr	
Howard, A.W.	AB	194.699	Pope, E.	AB	202.412
Howard, F.R.	L/Sto	158.104	Porter, G.H.	AB	169.078
Hubbard, C.	AB	128.268	Price, C.S.	Q/Sig	147.637
Humphries, J.	AB	197.811	Proctor, H.	L/S	155.365
Huntley, H.R.	Ord	204.368	Proctor, O.G.	Sto	287.036
Hutchinson, M.R.	AB	180.932	Proctor, W.	Pte	Ch5.032
Hyland, C.	Sto	285.494	Pye, W.	PO1	152.914
Jackson, A.C.	Ord	202.418	Quilter, W.	Sto	170.213
Jennings, R.F.	Ord	202.419	Rae, A.T.	Sto	293.995
Johnstone, A.L.	PO2	172.932	Redfern, W.	Boy	203.380
Johnstone, G.A.	Sto	293.876	Reed, A.	Sto	285.778
Jordan, P.	Yeo/Sig	151.841	Reed, F.J.	Dom	357.064
Keen, S.W.	PO2	162.860	Reed, R.	Ord	202.735
King, A.	Sto	293.208	Reeve, H.R.	Pte	Ch9.752
King, W.S.	Dom		Richards, F.	Ch/Sto	141.096
Kinnon, W.	Sto	285.805	Roades, T.R.	Sto	293.464
Lardy, P.	Dom	358.797	Roberts, S.A.	L/Shpwrt	168.220
Lee, E.F.	L/Sto	157.713	Roberts, T.M.	Shpwrt	340.280
Lewis, P.L.G.	AB	178.272	Robinson, J.	Ord	202.953
Littlewood, E.	Dom		Robinson, J.W.	Sto	281.436
Loftie, J.H.	Lieut		Roblett, J.	Pte	Ch5.592
Lowe, C.	L/Sto	161.997	Roch, W.R.	Sh/Std	159.472
Lowne, W.G.	L/S	168.095	Rose, R.	Pte	Ch4.644
McDonnell, J.	Ord	197.691	Rosoman, R.R.	Sub Lieut	
Machin, J.G.	Pte	Ch7.366	Rowberry, A.C.	Sto	293.134
Machin, J.W.	Sto	287.020	Roynane, P.	Sto	285.315
McKoy, W.	Pte	Ch6.225	Ryder, H.	AB	158.627
McLoughlin, J.	AB	190.294	Saunders, A.N.	Ord	203.345
Main, J.	Sto	284.242	Saunders, P.E.	Sto	284.224
Malcolm, H.E.	Ord	185.782	Saunders, W.	Sto	152.327
Mansfield, G.	Ch/Arm	135.920	Saunders, W.J.T.	Lieut	
Mant, F.	Ord	192.491	Sawyers, C.	Sto	284.930
Markham, T.E.	Sto	292.546	Scott, G.	L/Sto	152.627
Marsh, E.F.	Ord	195.116	Scott, T.	PO2	122.297
Marsh, H.A.	Ord	203.263	Scougall, A.	Sergt	Ch5.970
Martin, G.	AB	177.270	Seddon, J.	AB	175.798

No Bar Medals *continued*

Sellen, J.	Ch/Sto	121.789
Shannon, W.	Pte	Ch10.458
Simpson, F.E.	L/Sergt	Ch7.371
Simpson, J.E.	L/Sto	131.780
Sinclair, A.K.R.	Sig	190.877
Sisk, W.	PO1	130.375
Slight, L.	Gunr	
Smith, R.	AB	144.612
Smith, W.F.	Pte	Ch8.981
Smythe, C.	Sh/Std/Asst	341.403
Spiller, H.	AB	167.512
Struthers, J.	AB	182.334
Summerfield, V.	PO2	155.394
Taylor, F.	Sto	171.088
Taylor, F.C.	3/Wrtr	341.411
Taylor, W.	AB	155.810
Terry, H.	Sail/Mte	158.515
Thomas, H.	Sto	151.445
Thomas, J.	L/Sto	145.431
Topple, G.S.	Ord	202.218
Tregidge, W.	AB	176.798
Troll, H.R.	AB	162.778
Trueman, G.	Sto	292.872
Varndell, W.	Pte	Ch10.079
Venns, W.T.	PO2	181.289
Viles, J.H.	Sto	291.848
Vincent, J.H.	Sto	285.816
Vore, J.W.	Pte	Ch10.841
Wallace, W.H.	Ord	201.451
Watson, F.	Pte	Ch10.348
Watson, P.S.	Lieut	
Weekes, A.	Gunr	
Weeks, J.H.	Sto	168.848
Weller, E.	Ch/Sto	143.190
Weston, A.A.	Carp/Crew	342.778
Weston, A.E.J.	Sto	287.499
Wheatley, A.	Sto	293.453
Wheelan, R.	PO1	132.008
White, C.B.	AB	189.425
White, E.G.	MAA	117.562
Whitehouse, J.H.	L/Sto	146.162
Wiggs, E.C.	Ord	
Wilkins, G.E.	L/Carp/Crew	151.190
Wilkinson, G.	AB	174.045
Williams, P.	Gunr	
Wilson, P.J.	ERA	269.363
Wiltshire, F.	AB	175.267
Winn, A.	Ch/ERA	154.300
Winter, J.W.T.	AB	203.417
Wood, E.	Q/Sig	182.521
Wright, R.W.	Sto	284.026
Wyatt, J.	AB	183.558
Yates, H.W.	PO2	128.133

Duplicate medals:

Ayre, F.J.	L/Sto	170.458
x Black, R.P.	Sto	293.775
Bremner, E.A.	Payr	
Foster, J.	Sto	290.541
Goodhew, F.W.	Sto	290.727
Grant, T.J.D.	L/Sig	175.269
Harrington, W.N.	Sto	285.228
Hendy, F.	Sto	293.431
Hyland, C.	Sto	285.494
McLoughlin, J.	AB	190.294
Marsh, E.F.	Ord	195.116
Neale, J.H.	Carp/Crew	295.322
Parsons, O.L.	Clerk	
Rose, R.	Pte	Ch4.644
Rosoman, R.R.	Sub Lieut	
Terry, H.	Sail/Mte	158.515
Thomas, J.	L/Sto	145.431
Weston, A.A.	Carp/Crew	342.778

Returned medals.

Barnes, J.E.	Sto	282.799
Doyle, T.	Dom	358.168
Goodhead, G.	Sto	285.229
Hamley, F.	Sto	284.797
Hartley, J.	Pte	Ch10.834
Hewitt, T.	Sto	292.405
Isitt, R.	Carp	
Johnstone, F.	ERA	269.588
Jordan, A.	AB	182.437
Keeble, G.H.	Pte	Ch9.032
Kirtwood, J.	Sto	291.276
Mackie, A.	Pte	Ch9.991
Marston, J.L.	Pte	Ch7.639
Peters, T.	Sto	
Pook, R.	Dom	102.492
Smissen, F.J.	Dom	
Vigor, A.	Ord	197.127
Wallace, J.	Boy	203.086

EXTENDED PERIOD
No Bar Medals

Parsons, J.	Carp	
Read, M.	Pte	Ch9.646
Strachan, A.	Bugler	Po9.927

Returned medal:

Limpo, J.	Kroo	

H.M.S. SYBILLE

Period for which entitled:
2nd January 1901 to 25th February 1901.

Bars	Total	Returned	Entitled
2	6	1	5
1	88	8	80
0	218	31	187
	312	40	272

Notes:
Attached to the medal roll to this ship is a list of the "Officers and men landed at Lamberts Bay from H.M.S. Sybille." This gives the dates of landing and return to the ship, and these have been recorded against the recipients names where appropriate.

Bars: Cape Colony, South Africa 1901

Gale, H.E.	2/SBStd	150.432	9 Jan–18 Feb 1901
Howell, H.	Boy	204.314	
Winder, G.H.	PO2	167.254	10 Jan–18 Feb 1901
Wright, J.	Pte	Po9.746	9 Jan–18 Feb 1901
Returned medal:			
Murphy, P.	Sto	284.268	19 Jan–18 Feb 1901

Bars: Cape Colony, South Africa 1902

Whiting A.E.	Boy	202.770	

Bar: Cape Colony

Adaway, G.	Boy	204.025	
Anderson, J.	Pte	Po5.486	9 Jan–18 Feb 1901
Andrews, A.W.	Pte	Po9.653	9 Jan–18 Feb 1901
Barry, D.	AB	194.171	9 Jan–18 Feb 1901
Batchelor, E.	Sergt	Po4.365	9 Jan–18 Feb 1901
Bere, A.C.	Asst/Payr		9 Jan–20 Feb 1901
Bird, G. J.	AB	156.793	26 Jan–18 Feb 1901
Biscoe, T.W.	Pte	Po5.005	9 Jan–18 Feb 1901
Brewer, H.A.	Boy	203.774	9 Jan–18 Feb 1901
Brewer, W.	Pte	Po4.684	17 Jan–18 Feb 1901
Brown, E.R.	AB	168.359	10 Jan–18 Feb 1901
Burt, E.	Cpl	Po8.911	17 Jan–18 Feb 1901
Cannon, W.	Ord	194.199	10 Jan–12 Jan 1901
Charge, W.H.	Boy	203.788	10 Jan–25 Jan 1901
Christopher, C.	Pte	Po9.660	17 Jan–18 Jan, 21 Jan, 23 Jan–29 Jan 1901
Clark, G.T.	AB	184.921	10 Jan–18 Feb 1901
Cooper, A.W.	Pte	Po9.657	17 Jan–18 Feb 1901
Cooper, E.	AB	157.819	9 Jan–23 Jan 1901
Crow, E.J.	Ord	204.320	19 Jan–18 Feb 1901
Dabbs, H.	L/S	173.852	9 Jan–18 Feb 1901
Davitt, J.	PO1	112.930	9 Jan–18 Feb 1901
Deasey, A.R.	PO1	133.660	9 Jan–18 Feb 1901
Doyland, W.	L/S	172.022	9 Jan–18 Feb 1901
Drain, A.	AB	183.217	9 Jan–29 Jan 1901
Driver, W.	Sto	295.045	9 Jan–18 Feb 1901
Durrant, J.	Pte	Po9.699	9 Jan–18 Feb 1901
Elliott, G.	Pte	Po9.721	9 Jan–18 Feb 1901

Bar: Cape Colony *continued*

Elvy, C.F.	AB	192.307	9 Jan–18 Feb 1901
Etherington, F.R.	Sto	284.689	10 Jan–8 Feb 1901
Gee, W.J.	L/Cpl	Po9.980	10 Jan–18 Feb 1901
Grainger, A.	L/S	156.967	19 Jan–18 Feb 1901
Gregory, J.H.	PO1	118.854	9 Jan–18 Feb 1901
Grinter, B.C.	Sh/Std/Boy	342.292	9 Jan–18 Feb 1901
Hallard, F.	AB	179.035	10 Jan–25 Jan 1901
Harding, W.S.L.	Pte	Po9.383	9 Jan–18 Feb 1901
Hardy, C.	L/Sto	142.959	10 Jan–18 Feb 1901
Harries, R.	Ord	191.482	9 Jan–18 Feb 1901
Heath, F.C.	AB	171.524	9 Jan–18 Feb 1901
Herbert, F.	PO1	125.043	19 Jan–26 Jan 1901
Hibberd, T.	L/Sto	142.121	19 Jan–18 Feb 1901
Hickman, F.G.	Pte	Po9.595	9 Jan–18 Feb 1901
Hoggett, H.	Act/Gunr		13 Jan–18 Feb 1901
Jennings, A.	Sig	195.780	19 Jan–18 Feb 1901
Joyce, E.	AB	160.823	9 Jan–18 Feb 1901
Lee, C.J.	Boy	203.755	9 Jan–18 Feb 1901
Lord, C.	AB	160.602	10 Jan–14 Jan 1901
Lovegrove, J.	Ord	186.095	9 Jan–18 Feb 1901
Lunnen, E.J.	Pte	Po9.379	9 Jan–18 Feb 1901
McColl, A.	AB	195.517	26 Jan–18 Feb 1901
McEvely, T.	L/Sig	165.449	9 Jan–18 Feb 1901
Maddy, R.	AB	170.337	26 Jan–18 Feb 1901
Maitland, P.E.	St/Surgn		20 Jan–20 Feb 1901
Marsh, T.J.	AB	187.383	19 Jan–18 Feb 1901
Morris, F.W.	Pte	Po7.226	11 Jan–18 Feb 1901
Newman, W.T.J.	Pte	Po9.496	17 Jan–18 Feb 1901
Noble, H.S.	AB	184.933	9 Jan–18 Feb 1901
Oldbury, F.	Arm	340.552	
Padfield, W.	Arm/Crew	343.711	9 Jan–18 Feb 1901
Parkes, W.S.	Ord	200.202	9 Jan–18 Feb 1901
Pawsey, G.	AB	174.166	10 Jan–18 Feb 1901
Perring, A.E.	AB	172.734	9 Jan–12 Jan, 19 Jan, 26 Jan–18 Feb 1901
Perry, F.	AB	179.613	26 Jan–18 Feb 1901
Peters, C.J.	Sto	284.461	19 Jan–18 Feb 1901
Pigou, G.C.	Lieut		9 Jan–18 Feb 1901
Reynolds, T.	Cook/Mte	356.045	2 Feb–18 Feb 1901
Rouse, C.	PO2	147.683	9 Jan–18 Feb 1901
Sarel, A.F.M.	Lieut		9 Jan–3 Feb, 9 Feb–18 Feb 1901
Smith, G.E.	Ord	203.789	9 Jan–18 Feb 1901
Smith, W.	Pte	Po5.284	9 Jan–11 Jan, 17 Jan–18 Jan, 21 Jan–29 Jan, ? Jan–18 Feb 1901
Snowden, T.	Sail/Mte	160.152	24 Jan–25 Jan 1901
Stroud, A.	Pte	Po9.480	17 Jan–11 Feb 1901
Sugden, W.R.	Sto	283.381	19 Jan–18 Feb 1901
Tapper, C.H.	Sto	284.704	19 Jan–18 Feb 1901
Terry, H.E.	Boy	204.328	
Trotter, T.	Sto	283.801	9 Jan–18 Feb 1901
Turner, C.	AB	180.007	9 Jan–18 Feb 1901
Ward, A.	Pte	Po6.782	17 Jan–18 Jan, 21 Jan–18 Feb 1901
White, J.	Sto	293.750	9 Jan–18 Feb 1901
Williams, H.P.	Capt		9 Jan–20 Feb 1901
Wynn, R.F.J.	Pte	Po7.909	17 Jan–18 Feb 1901

Duplicate medals:

Elliott, G.	Pte	Po9.721	9 Jan–18 Feb 1901
Grainger, A.	L/S	156.967	19 Jan–18 Feb 1901
Harries, R.	Ord	191.482	9 Jan–18 Feb 1901
Maddy, R.	AB	170.337	26 Jan–18 Feb 1901

Marsh, T.J.	AB	187.383	19 Jan–18 Feb 1901
White, J.	Sto	293.750	9 Jan–18 Feb 1901

Returned medals:

Athey, W.	Pte	Po10.311	17 Jan–18 Feb 1901
Curtis, W.	Pte	Po9.684	17 Jan–18 Feb 1901
Fryer, W.C.	Sto	291.010	19 Jan–18 Feb 1901
Gaffney, T.	Pte	Po9.519	9 Jan–18 Feb 1901
Long, T.J.	Ord	195.256	10 Jan–18 Jan 1901
Stout, C.E.	Q/Sig	145.292	9 Jan–18 Feb 1901
Tiller, W.	Sto	284.548	9 Feb–18 Feb 1901
Weaver, F.W.	AB	173.122	26 Jan–18 Feb 1901

The following men are also indicated as having landed at Lamberts Bay from H.M.S. Sybille, but are not shown on the medal roll for H.M.S. Sybille

Furness, A.	Pte	Po6.384	17 Jan–18 Feb 1901
Knott, G.	Dom	354.675	19 Jan–23 Jan, 31 Jan 1901
Longridge, T.	Act/Carp		9 Jan–18 Feb 1901
Marsh, W.C.	AB	193.062	26 Jan–18 Feb 1901

No Bar Medals

Andrews I, Jack.	Kroo	
Andrews II, Jack.	Kroo	
Arthur, S.	Sto	294.654
Atwell, J.	Carp/Crew	342.509
Ayling, W.	ERA	153.897
Bailey, H.	Sto	284.399
Ballard, R.J.	Dom	358.885
Balmain, J.	Sto	280.496
Barker, W.	AB	189.163
Barnes, H.	PO1	123.286
Benham, A.W.	L/Sto	85.725
Bennett, F.C.	L/Sto	119.753
Bestman, J.	Kroo	
Bowley, J.W.	Sh/Std	158.558
Boy, Tim.	Kroo	
Bradbury, T.	Sto	293.639
Brading, C.A.E.	Sh/Cpl	133.903
Bradshaw, C.	AB	143.604
Bramley, G.	Sto	284.744
Brooks, A.	AB	184.312
Burch, E.	Pte	Ply7.040
Callen, A.A.	Sto	284.668
Carroll, J.	Sto	284.276
Carter, A.J.	Ord	195.458
Cass, F.	L/Sto	167.136
Castellano, A.E.	Bugler	Po9.351
Cave, J.H.	Boy	203.747
Cayley, H.	Lieut	
Chapman, C.	AB	169.201
Chapman, W.P.	Ch/Engr	
Cheetham, T.	PO2	154.352
Churchill, W.H.	L/Sto	146.255
Clarkson, H.	AB	192.356
Coffee, Ben.	Kroo	
Cole, C.	Ch/Sto	123.113
Cole, F.	Ord	198.991
Conaghan, H.	Sto	284.720
Constantine, H.	Payr	
Cooke, G.	Ch/Sto	142.967
Cooper, G.	L/Shpwrt	167.101
Croucher, A.	ERA	269.163
Cuff, E.W.	Boy	204.116
Curtis, H.W.	AB	165.479
Daniels, W.	PO2	153.979
Davidge, C.J.	Boy	203.848
Davies, C.	Sto	283.959
Davies, J.	Sto	295.159
Dawson, W.	Asst/Engr	
Deasey, M.	AB	188.881
Dellbridge, A.C.	Ch/ERA	145.592
Dicker, G.	Dom	137.045
Dimmick, A.	Sto	293.617
Dobbie, W.A.	ERA	269.503
Doddrell, F.	Sto	294.093
Duffey, G.A.	L/Sto	162.136
Earl, A.	AB	157.970
Eckersley, E.W.	ERA	268.685
Endall, W.	Boy	203.728
Farley, T.	Sto	161.329
Fitzsimons, J.	Sto	284.716
Fletcher, E.	L/Sto	167.137
Flewin, H.	Sto	174.594
Flux, F.	Sto	284.669
Frampton, A.	Sto	294.658
Frankham, H.	L/Sto	156.534
French, W.C.	PO1	126.705
Friday, Jack.	Kroo	
Garrett, F.	Dom	358.884
Gavin, F.	Sto	284.970
George, W.	Carp/Mte	132.218
Glasson, G.	Blksmth/Crew	152.115
Glenny, J.J.	PO1	161.142
Goodall, C.	Sto	164.076
Goodson, F.C.	AB	178.610
Gore, J.	Ch/Sto	141.133
Gregory, A.H.	PO1	139.116
Hackley, A.A.	Yeo/Sig	139.121
Hamon, W.W.	Carp/Crew	343.013

No Bar Medals *continued*

Harrison, J.	Sto	174.606
Harvey, J.	Carp/Crew	343.010
Hodge, W.R.	Sto	294.097
Hodgson, W.H.	2/Cooper	165.953
Hodnett, J.	Sto	285.341
Holden, J.R.	Sto	163.676
Holland, H.H.	Lieut	
Holt, F.	Dom	353.898
Howell, O.	ERA	152.597
Hudson, E.B.	PO1	156.077
Hughes, T.E.	Asst/Engr	
Johnson, James.	Kroo	
Johnson, T.	Sto	175.453
Jones, W.J.	Sto	283.904
Jowett, W.R.	Gunr	
Kemp, F.	Sto	284.540
King, A.	AB	185.490
Knight, A.	Dom	358.883
Lewinton, C.	L/Sto	141.275
Long, E.H.	Dom	156.606
Long, W.	Sig	198.821
Lovell, G.T.	AB	175.193
McCluskey, J.	Ord	91.959
McWilliams, J.	ERA	140.426
Manners, S.J.	AB	187.368
Mardlin, H.	Boy	203.794
May, P.T.	Boy	203.749
Maynard, F.	Boy	204.306
Meggs, G.	L/Sto	165.001
Miller, W.A.	Arm/Crew	143.367
Mills, W.	Boy	203.469
Mirams, A.C.	Pntr	343.080
Mitchell, J.	Ch/Gunr	
Mortley, W.H.	Q/Sig	170.314
Newman, J.	AB	135.255
Nicholl, C.T.	AB	167.073
Nolan, J.	Pte	Ply4.033
O'Keefe, B.	AB	189.362
Palk, T.F.	Act/Ch/Arm	148.256
Parr, J.H.	Sto	161.326
Pattinson, A.	PO1	130.597
Payne, R.	Plmbr/Mte	166.254
Pearce, W.J.	ERA	268.168
Pedder, A.	Ch/Sto	141.139
Penson, W.	Sto	143.374
Perrin, A.A.	Boy	204.443
Perry, J.W.	L/Sto	141.323
Peter I, Tom.	Kroo	
Phelps, A.	Ord	186.091
Pibworth, H.J.T.	Ord	194.680
Pibworth, W.	Carp	
Potter, E.H.	PO1	133.756
Povey, G.	Sto	284.344
Powell, W.P.	Sto	293.572
Prangnell, F.W.	Sto	284.738
Pullinger, W.	Sto	283.892
Raywood, R.	Sto	176.060
Read, W.T.	L/Sto	145.567
Rees, T.	Sto	284.659
Richards, G.	Arm/Crew	138.084
Riddles, F.	AB	187.878
Roach, F.	AB	179.632
Robson, J.	AB	131.556
Roe, F.E.M.	Lieut	
Rowe, J.	L/S	133.214
Shea, F.A.	Sto	284.582
Short, W.H.	ERA	268.139
Sloper, W.	Sto	284.674
Smith, F.G.	AB	169.488
Smith, John.	Kroo	
Smith, W.	Sto	284.971
Sorrell, E.J.	Sh/Cook	135.199
Sparks, H.A.	Ch/Sto	122.881
Stanhope, G.	Sto	284.683
Street, A.G.A.	Sub Lieut	
Stroud, A.	Ord	195.178
Sweeney, M.	Sto	284.254
Tapper, J.J.	Gunr	
Taylor, J.	Boy	204.081
Thomas, G.	AB	175.034
Toby, Tom.	Kroo	
Todd, S.H.	PO2	148.412
Totman, W.	L/S	155.670
Treleaven, A.	L/Sto	152.593
Tuitt, A.	L/Sig	180.068
Turrall, C.W.	Boy	204.563
Turton, W.	AB	178.143
Warburton, J.E.	Ch/Sto	131.131
Wareham, A.E.	Boy	204.118
Watkins, C.D.	Ch/ERA	129.335
Watts, F.	Sto	284.685
Watts, J.A.	Sto	175.449
Webb, E.A.	2/Wrtr	340.080
Wells, W.H.	Ch/ERA	158.346
White, G.	Sto	284.743
White, G.E.	Boy	203.769
Whitfield, F.	Boy	204.119
Wightman, W.	MAA	125.762
Wilkie, A.T.	PO1	123.346
Willcox, A.E.	Sto	294.462
Williams, W.C.	Ch/ERA	153.822
Willis, F.	Sto	294.663
Wills, G.	AB	177.861
Wilson, Andrew	Kroo	
Wilson, T.R.	Sto	284.393
Woodford, G.	AB	169.371
Would, J.C.	Sto	283.812
Wride, O.	Dom	358.520
Wright, W.C.	Boy	204.333

Duplicate medals:

Arthur, S.	Sto	294.654
Johnson, James.	Kroo	
Lewinton, C.	L/Sto	141.275
Whitfield, F.	Boy	204.119
Willcox, A.E.	Sto	294.462
x Wills, G.	AB	177.861
Woodford, G.	AB	169.371

x Two duplicate medals issued.

Returned medals:			Lewis, Tom.	Kroo	
Brown, J.	Sto	290.582	McHugh, J.	Sto	284.990
Catmore, T.J.	Boy	203.781	Mitchell, W.J.	Pte	Ply5.988
Dawkins, S.	AB	187.828	Neverfear, J.	Kroo	
Deeble, A.	Dom	358.588	Parson, Jack.	Kroo	
Doran, T.L.	Boy	204.325	Peter II, Tom.	Kroo	
Egan, P.	Ord	183.530	Pierpoint, V.	Boy	203.702
Finn, J.	Sto	294.502	Preston, T.	Sto	284.388
Ford, G.J.	Dom	357.383	Seabreeze, Tom.	Kroo	
Fox, W.F.	Sto	290.774	Stevenson, G.	Sto	284.485
Frampton, J.	Sto	294.620	Talley, F.	Sto	291.031
Furlong, F.G.	Sto	284.658	Varney, F.J.	Pte	Ply8.874
Glasgow, John.	Kroo		Wade, L.E.	Dom	355.574
Harris, W.H.	Sto	291.025	Walker, Tom.	Kroo	
Hooker, G.	Sto	284.725	Wills, W.E.	Sto	295.039
Jones, W.	Ord	192.147	Wisbey, F.J.	Ord	178.301

H.M.S. TARTAR

Period for which entitled:
11th October 1899 to 2nd October 1900.
11th January 1901 to 8th March 1901.

Extended period:
9th March 1901 to 29th July 1901.

Bars	*Total*	*Returned*	*Entitled*
6	1	0	1
5	18	0	18
4	1	0	1
3	4	0	4
2	9	0	9
1	64	5	59
0	140	37	103
	237	42	195

Notes:
† Medal presented by H.M. The King.
* Medals presented on Ophir.

Bars: Belfast, Cape Colony, Orange Free State, Tugela Heights, Relief of Ladysmith, Laing's Nek

† Lees, E.	Act/Comdr	

Bars: Orange Free State, Transvaal, Tugela Heights, Relief of Ladysmith, Laing's Nek

Baldwin, G.B.	AB	156.289
Chadwick, F.	AB	171.880
Cheeseman, E.	AB	137.157
Crawford, W.	AB	163.957
Edwards, J.	AB	163.409
Edwards, W.G.	AB	179.161
Epsley, G.W.	PO2	158.931
Field, J.	AB	176.127
Hart, O.A.	Arm/Mte	340.171
McDonald, J.	AB	180.418
McKinnell, D.	AB	187.720
Maddick, H.T.	Q/Sig	189.024
Munro, A.L.	Ch/PO	110.602
Restall, J.	Ch/Arm	135.646
Sawyer, J.F.	AB	153.493
Smith, D.	AB	165.714
Taylor, C.E.	AB	177.061
* Wright, H.	AB	179.875

Bars: Cape Colony, Orange Free State, Transvaal, Laing's Nek

Hughes, J.D.	St/Surgn	

Bars: Diamond Hill, Belfast, Natal

Connor, C.	AB	142.561
Moog, G.	AB	138.019
Read, E.J.	AB	187.682
Thompson, W.	AB	160.621

Duplicate medal:

Connor, C.	AB	142.561

Bars: Cape Colony, Relief of Ladysmith

Cornish, J.W.	Ch/PO	118.778

Bars: Cape Colony, South Africa 1901

Ghent, F.	AB	162.776

Bars: Tugela Heights, Relief of Ladysmith

Bird, F.W.	L/S	161.259
Hart, W.	AB	162.841
Haylett, J.W.	AB	170.005
James, H.W.	Snr/Lieut	
Moors, J.	AB	162.450
* Walker, F.S.	AB	186.955
Winter, E.H.	L/S	160.197

Bar: Cape Colony

Alden, J.R.	AB	168.786
August, R.	Sto	286.359
Baldwin, C.	AB	184.969
Ballard, C.B.	Lieut	
Bourne, J.	AB	167.477
Carter, P.	L/Sig	188.053
Dale, R.J.C.	Ch/Wrtr	84.409
Dunn, J.W.	AB	188.933
Eades, T.G.	AB	138.731
Eastwood, H.E.	Pte	Ch10.417
Forsyth, J.	AB	106.931
Garrod, G.A.	AB	155.076
Gilkinson, W.	AB	176.821
Grigg, W.J.S.	Pte	Ch6.397
Gudge, L.	AB	178.925

Halliwell, H.C.	AB	187.717
Hamilton, W.	AB	184.265
Hammond, J.	AB	160.151
Hollis, J.A.	AB	170.681
Keenan, J.	AB	189.949
Knight, T.	PO2	165.128
Lamming, J.D.	Sto	176.006
Linkin, J.	AB	187.509
Londesborough, H.	AB	191.295
McDonald, A.	AB	166.504
Moy, F.J.	AB	190.360
Myburgh, R.W.	Lieut	
Phillips, W.S.	Sh/Std/Boy	341.340
Reed, A.	Pte	Po8.995
Richmond, J.T.	AB	178.724
Saunders, W.M.	Sergt	Ch3.731
Sheridan, A.	L/S	181.931
Siggins, A.	AB	163.800
Simpson, T.E.	Cpl	Po5.023
Smith, J.	Pte	Ch9.380
Smithson, C.	Pte	Ch9.377
Sweatman, G.W.	PO1	139.200
Taylor, J.W.	AB	198.950
Townsend, J.W.E.	Lieut	
Travers, R.	Comdr	
Veitch, G.	PO1	168.511
White, A.	L/Sto	154.253
Wilkie, G.	AB	189.996

Duplicate medals:

Bourne, J.	AB	167.477
Richmond, J.T.	AB	178.724

Returned medals

Belcher, M.	Ord	201.654
Head, G.A.	AB	171.576
Kelf, A.R.	AB	187.286
Stanley, E.	AB	190.634
Stoat, W.	Sto	159.079

Bar: Relief of Ladysmith

Nicholls, C.G.	L/S	155.085
White, R.	AB	179.368

Bar: Natal

Ash, F.T.	Pte	Ch5.744
Brown, R.W.	Pte	Ch4.623
Bushill, A.E.	Pte	Ch5.155
Drake, A.	Pte	Ch5.352
Fagan, W.	Pte	Ch8.275
Hymas, E.	Pte	Ch5.574
Inglis, C.S.	Payr	
Johnson, F.	Pte	Ch9.379
McRae, J.	PO1	125.007
Mason, W.	Gunr	
Morgan, F.R.W.	Comdr	
Shave, C.E.	Act/Arm/Mte	167.595
Symes, F.	Pte	Ch8.205
White, R.	L/Shpwrt	146.910

No Bar Medals

Andrews, A.	Sh/Std	172.827
Ansell, A.	ERA	268.405
Ashton, J.	Sto	277.295
Bacon-Habell, C.R.	Lieut	
Baker, C.J.	Sto	286.308
Beckett, W.J.	Sto	285.946
Bennett, R.E.	PO1	121.778
Blackwell, W.J.	Sto	281.281
Bowdery, W.	Sto	279.053
Brazier, W.	Sto	285.897
Brennan, M.	PO1	107.702
Broughton, A.	Ch/ERA	141.150
Brown, T.	Kroo	
Burrlock, A.	Sto	278.405
Burrows, J.G.	Sh/Cpl	350.009
Capon, T.G.	Sto	277.383
Chambers, E.C.	Sto	285.541
Charlton, M.	Carp/Crew	343.623
Chilvers, H.	AB	178.351
Coakes, G.F.	Ch/Sto	123.649
Coleman, W.	Blksmth	151.685
Collins, F.	Sto	149.464
Crump, W.	Sto	286.352
Cruz, A. de.	Dom	122.516
Davis, J.	Kroo	
Dahomey.	Interpreter	
Denford, G.W.	Pntr	177.957
Dewberry, A.	Ord	184.289
Downs, P.G.	AB	178.894
Dredge, H.	MAA	126.243
Edisbury, A.	L/Sto	169.213
Edwards, W.E.	ERA	268.513
Epton, W.H.	SBStd	150.272
Fagg, J.	L/Sto	154.790
Falkner, M.W.	Surgn	
Fernandez, A.	Dom	164.870
Gerald, L.	Pte	Ch4.751
Glasgow, T.	Kroo	
Gould, J.	Carp/Crew	164.209
Grainger, W.E.	PO1	170.740
Grant, W.	Shpwrt	343.336
Guthrie, W.	ERA	173.004
Hall, W.F.	Sto	278.491
Halley, P.	Ch/Carp/Mte	137.033
Hardy, W.	Sto	277.378
Hayman, R.	PO2	161.568
Jarman, C.	Pte	Ch9.369
Jarrett, D.	Sto	151.229
Jessup, A.	Sto	285.413
Kane, J.T.	L/Cpl	Ch4.761
Killpartrick, T.E.	Ch/ERA	123.266
Kingsland, E.	Sto	174.460
Mair, W.	Sto	277.045
Mann, C.	Sto	276.467
Martin, C.G.	Shpwrt	342.075
Mason, R.G.W.	Sub Lieut	
Medhurst, W.	L/Sto	154.121
Norris, G.W.	Dom	355.233
Norris, H.W.	PO2	162.260

No Bar Medals *continued*

Parker, A.	Sto	276.451
Pavis, W.	Dom	356.964
Petty, A.	Sh/Cook	144.988
Ringer, W.	Ch/Sto	153.601
Robinson, J.	AB	189.461
Robinson, W.	L/Sto	135.649
Rolph, W.E.	Pntr	341.121
Sampson, C.J.	Sto	176.622
Sampson, J.	Kroo	
Sanderson, R.	Ord	203.604
Sawyer, J.	Sto	285.895
Searle, F.	Plmbr/Mte	341.208
Shelley, G.	AB	182.151
Simpkin, H.	Sto	286.107
Smart, J.	Kroo	
Spring, J.	Dom	112.470
Staples, W.F.	Ch/Cook	144.519
Stephens, E.G.	Sh/Std	159.473
Sullivan, W.	Sto	285.341
Symonds, A.	Sto	172.777
Thomas, A.	Ord	182.101
Thompson, G.	AB	184.213
Tilley, W.	2/Yeo/Sig	157.659
Toby, T.	Kroo	
Treneman, J.	AB	198.531
Triggs, A.	L/Sto	279.077
Tronson, H.	Lieut	
Tucker, J.	ERA	145.522
Turinam, A.H.	PO2	173.137
Turner, E.	AB	129.221
Vicary, C.J.	L/Sto	155.706
Wallis, C.	L/Sto	282.789
Warden, J.	Sto	160.503
Watkins, B.J.	Ch/Engr	
Watson, J.	AB	188.830
Whewell, F.W.	AB	190.386
Wilson, G.M.	AB	188.591
Wilson, J.	Kroo	
Wingate, W.	Ch/Sto	105.367
Winch, J.D.	Sto	285.947
Wright, A.	Sto	129.020
Young, E.C.	Art/Engr	

Duplicate medals:

Baker, C.J.	Sto	286.308
Sanderson, R.	Ord	203.604
Tucker, J.	ERA	145.522

Returned medals:

Ansell, S.	Sto	277.384
Blackwhale, J.	Kroo	
Bottle, B.	Kroo	
Breeze, S.	Kroo	
Crow, J.	Kroo	
Curacoa, J.	Kroo	
Cusack, J.M.L.	Clerk	
Delanga, J.	Dom	
Dooner, J.K.	Lieut	
Doughty, J.C.T.	Boy	197.283
Dunk, J.	Blksmth	340.390
George, T.	Kroo	
Gilbert, H.	Q/Sig	190.549
Goldring, H.	Pte	Ch8.748
Gording, G.	Dom	359.372
Howe, R.C.	L/Sig	164.388
Johnson, B.	Kroo	
Johnson, L.	Kroo	
Jones, A.	L/Sto	155.490
Limbroy, T.	Kroo	
Love, J.	Sto	149.742
Monrovia, T.	Kroo	
Morrison, J.	AB	189.037
Peter, T.	Kroo	
Punch, T.	Kroo	
Purser, J.	Kroo	
Shergold, G.	Q/Sig	
Souza, St. Anna de	Dom	355.672
Spencer, B.	Q/Sig	135.930
Stephens, J.G.	Sub Lieut	
Toby, Tom.	Kroo	
Wesley, J.	Kroo	
Worsley, W.G.	AB	196.122
Wroxall, C.	Band	121.574

EXTENDED PERIOD

No Bar Medals

Eames, W.	Sto	141.263
Halley, P.W.	Ch/Carp/Mte	137.033

Returned medals:

Martin, J.	Pte	Ply9.135
Vincent, J.	Pte	Ply9.539
Vinnicombe, J.V.	Bosn	

H.M.S. TERPSICHORE

Period for which entitled:

Extended Period only:
29th March 1901 to 6th April 1901.
29th July 1901 to 15th March 1902.

Bars	*Total*	*Returned*	*Entitled*
2	150	13	137
1	0	0	0
0	163	27	136
	313	40	273

Notes:
[1] Bars entered on roll in pencil.
[2] Recipient's Service No. also shown as 161610.
[3] Original medal returned to Mint in Feb. 1922; medal roll states, "new medal issued to Party 29/12/33."
[4] Also noted on roll as Moffatt.
[5] Service No. also noted on roll as 143.501.

Bars: Cape Colony, South Africa 1901

	Ackerman, G.A.	Sto	277.355
	Adams, H.W.	Pte	Ply6.422
	Akehurst, G.	AB	182.295
	Alton, W.W.	Payr	
	Amy, P.C.	AB	183.536
	Andrews, C.T.	PO1	146.590
	Andrews, G.	Sto	285.755
	Ball, S.B.	AB	180.053
	Barker, F.J.	AB	198.542
	Barnley, H.	PO2	184.347
	Barter, W.	Pte	Ply5.050
	Batchelor, W.S.	Sto	293.951
	Beck, S.	Ord	197.895
	Beehan, J.	Sto	170.232
	Blackman, G.W.	Gunr	
	Blackwell, J.H.	Pte	Ply4.958
	Booth, W.E.	AB	200.839
	Boxhall, E.F.	Ord	198.128
1	Brewer, P.G.	AB	184.914
	Brown, E.H.	Plmbr/Mte	343.933
	Buglear, W.	L/S	177.376
	Challis, F.D.	AB	183.204
	Chilton, G.A.	AB	159.218
	Chivers, H.T.	Ord	203.246
	Coates, J.J.	Pte	Ply10.171
	Cobb, F.N.	Q/Sig	188.202
	Coke, C.H.	Capt	
	Cook, J.R.	Pte	Ply9.270
	Cox, W.A.	PO1	181.160
	Crees, W.C.	Pte	Ply9.149
	Croydon, W.J.	Boy	206.150
	Dale, C.J.	L/Carp/Crew	341.841
	Davey, C.H.	Lieut	
	Davis, A.O.	AB	189.243
	Davis, J.	AB	189.152
	Dawe, J.	Cpl	Ply5.215
	Denning, G.	Ord	204.612
	Eamey, R.C.	Ch/Arm	142.942
	Edgcomb, C.	Pte	Ply3.683
	Elder, J.	AB	200.846
	Ellis, G.H.	Ch/Sto	146.859
	Errington, J.T.	Ord	200.981
	Etherton, E.H.	AB	198.901
	Evans, A.E.	Carp/Mte	145.320
	Facey, F.J.	Bugler	Ply9.434
	Farmes, H.E.	Ord	206.241
	Fiddick, G.A.	Shpwrt	340.105
	Finlayson, H.W.	Surgn	
	Firth, G.	Ch/Sto	125.245
	Fletcher, R.	Carp/Crew	294.875
	Flynn, F.C.	AB	207.894
	Flynn, J.	Pte	Ply7.807
	Ford, W.	Blksmth	341.886
	Forder, W.	Yeo/Sig	171.618
	Freeman, J.S.	Dom	358.055
	Garfield, W.H.	2/Yeo/Sig	162.839
	Gibson, W.	PO1	134.171
	Grimwood, W.	Sto	295.117
	Grover, F.C.	Lieut	
	Guy, E.	AB	183.343
	Hackett, E.	AB	160.809
	Hambly, J.R.	Act/Gunr	
	Haw, W.C.	Q/Sig	147.860
2	Holmes, J.H.	PO1	161.602
	Horner, G.R.	Cpl	Ply4.161
	Horsnell, C.L.	Sto	284.783
	Hovell, J.	AB	151.963
	Hulse, H.	AB	178.163
	James, C.	L/Sig	187.297
	James, T.	Pte	Ply9.107
	Johnson, W.	Ord	206.499
	Jolly, A.C.	Sto	285.761

Bars: Cape Colony, South Africa 1901 *continued*

Kennedy, B.J.	AB	185.704
Kimble, H.	Pte	Ply4.498
Lambert, S.G.	PO1	187.454
Lawrie, A.E.	Sto	285.532
[3] Lawton, M.	Sto	154.170
Lee, T.	Pte	Ply9.953
Lewis, W.	AB	189.097
Leyshon, E.G.	Clerk	
Mace, M.A.	PO2	174.740
Mann, E.G.	PO1	146.365
Marjoram, J.W.	AB	191.735
Martin, M.	Sto	294.891
[4] Moffett, W.J.	Sto	294.043
Molyneux, R.H.	Sig	193.541
Murby, W.H.	AB	196.470
Newhouse, E.	Pte	Ply5.203
Northover, J.	PO1	118.105
O'Connor, J.	L/Sto	173.894
O'Neill, S.W.	Sto	295.131
Pankhurst, J.	Sto	294.961
Parry, G.	L/Sto	172.795
Patrickson, T.H.	MAA	350.016
Pelham, H.	Ord	191.672
Phillips, A.	Ord	202.399
Phillips, A.H.	Sto	294.735
Prior, E.F.	AB	177.612
Punter, J.	PO2	176.863
Reed, W.H.	Carp	
Reeve, F.C.	AB	204.618
Rhodes, W.	Sto	285.535
Richmond, J.	AB	168.543
Roberts, E.W.	Asst/Engr	
Rogers, P.	PO1	155.323
Saxby, H.S.	2/Cooper	340.651
Scoates, W.	PO2	177.851
Seager, E.	Sto	277.361
Smale, W.H.	AB	136.726
Smith, B.T.	PO1	180.894
[5] Smith, F.	AB	143.561
Smith, H.P.	AB	183.565
Smith, R.	AB	183.601
Smith, T.C.	PO1	143.731
Sturley, W.T.	L/Sto	284.638
Styants, W.J.	AB	168.386
Thomas, R.J.	AB	181.934
Tice, R.	AB	177.915
Tregoning, P.B.	Ord	204.951
Turnbull, C.H.	Pte	Ply9.249
Turnbull, W.S.	AB	178.719
Tweddell, T.C.	AB	196.196
Walker, J.J.	AB	158.431
Ward, H.A.	Sergt	Ply4.477
Wardley, J.W.	AB	174.025
Waters, T.R.	Arm/Mte	341.363
Watson, T.	L/S	181.433
Weeks, T.	L/S	186.133
Wenn, A.J.	Ord	192.254
West, J.	Sh/Cook	132.018
Wheatley, F.	Ord	205.848
Whitcher, B.G.	AB	188.138
Wicks, T.H.	AB	188.999
Williams, E.A.	Ord	204.316
Wright, A.	AB	182.258
York, G.S.	AB	185.658
Young, W.G.	L/S	176.801

Duplicate medals:

Batchelor, W.S.	Sto	293.951
x Chivers, H.T.	Ord	203.246
Molyneux, R.H.	Sig	193.541
Wheatley, F.	Ord	205.848

x Three duplicate medals issued.

Returned medals:

Bradley, J.	Sto	281.734
Falconer, C.	Sto	288.802
Furlong, H.E.	AB	180.871
Gill, J.	Ord	195.272
Hinkley, H.T.	Sto	155.190
Keeble, D.A.	Boy	205.133
[3] Lawton, M.	Sto	154.170
McLeod, G.	Pte	Ply6.787
Marygold, W.E.	Boy	205.731
O'Brien, D.E.	Sail/Mte	156.910
Richardson, S.	Sig	202.330
Sewell, A.W.	Sto	293.213
Shoulders, G.E.	Boy	205.581

No Bar Medals

Allen, A.H.	Pte	Ply10.243
Allen, C.A.	Ord	204.866
Baddley, J.	Sto	134.811
Banks, T.	Sto	278.462
Barber, C.	Dom	127.334
Barber, C.	Arm/Crew	341.702
Bartlett, J.F.	L/Sto	130.027
Batchelder, J.A.	Cook/Mte	341.792
Beadle, J.W.	ERA	151.223
Beckett, W.J.	Sto	164.128
Bennett, T.	Sto	163.934
Berrey, J.H.	Sto	276.107
Bissett, C.	Lieut	
Blake, N.G.	Ord	215.181
Brackwell, G.H.	Ord	206.720
Bradburn, A.E.	AB	173.539
Brickles, I.	Boy	206.159
Brown, F.W.	Sto	294.413
Bush, F.C.	Sto	285.772
Butcher, J.W.	Sto	175.939
Canton, W.	Sto	285.569
Champs, S.	L/Sto	163.578
Chappell, J.T.	AB	188.152
Charndler, G.S.	L/Sto	278.509
Churchill, W.J.	Ch/ERA	128.242
Clapperton, W.J.	Pte	Ply9.537
Clark, J.W.	Sto	293.926
Cogdale, H.	Pte	Ply9.102
Cole, H.	Pte	Ply9.776
Cole, P.	Kroo	

Cole, W.	Sto	285.566
Cooper, F.	Sto	291.599
Craven, F.J.	2/SBStd	350.444
Cripps, J.J.	Sto	285.549
Cross, A.	Sto	295.125
Cross, W.E.	Sto	293.215
Croyne, T.	Sto	169.285
Cudby, C.	Ch/Sto	129.028
Darlow, H.	Pte	Ply9.757
Davenport, G.H.	Sh/Std	149.791
Dean, W.	Sto	285.476
Drew, G.	Sto	172.307
Dudley, W.J.	Sto	296.865
Dunbar, W.C.	ERA	269.224
Ellis, F.J.	AB	179.572
Emms, G.H.	Act/Pntr	199.639
Fitch, W.H.	Sto	172.083
Flewers, F.J.	L/Sto	154.814
Foster, J.	Boy	214.692
Fraser, A.	Sh/Cpl	150.125
Garland, S.T.	Pte	Ply8.195
Goodship, W.	AB	177.348
Gorman, J.	Boy	215.309
Grenyer, A.G.	AB	201.051
Griffiths, W.J.	Q/Sig	183.551
Haddock, S.G.	St/Engr	
Haimes, H.	L/Sto	163.700
Hall, J.A.	Sto	294.042
Hamilton, D.M.	Lieut	
Harris, J.T.	Sto	294.979
Hatton, T.	Sto	297.074
Hayes, F.	2/SBStd	350.263
Hodgson, W.D.	Sto	296.790
Hogg, J.F.	Sto	285.559
Inkpen, R.S.	Ch/ERA	120.739
Isaac, H.	Sto	296.777
Joyce, W.J.	ERA	269.151
Kelly, M.T.	Boy	215.159
Kelly, R.	Pte	Ply9.805
Kitt, J.H.	Sto	285.635
Lambert, G.	Dom	122.865
Lambert, J.	L/Sto	276.241
Larkin, T.A.	L/Sto	172.888
Lee, T.S.	Ch/Sto	140.174
Leith, G.P.	Lieut	
Lennard, H.E.	Pntr	343.588
Liddy, W.	Sto	297.075
Lucock, G.L.	Sto	280.173
McCarthy, M.	Sto	285.338
McNerney, J.	Boy	210.062
Mankelow, H.	Dom	359.655
Martin, S.	Kroo	
Mather, M.	ERA	270.115
Mitchell, T.	Gunr	
Mockett, A.	L/Sto	163.654
Morcom, F.	L/Sto	147.246
Morgan, J.	Sto	285.576
Morley, A.C.	Sto	295.520
Morris, M.	Sto	294.939
Morrison, H.	ERA	268.714
Norman, H.	Pte	Ply9.745
Overall, G.J.	Sto	287.074
Owens, E.	Boy	215.137
Pengelly, J.	Ord	205.236
Penrose, F.D.	ERA	269.608
Peters, T.	Kroo	
Price, F.J.	Sh/Std/Asst	343.137
Reeve, T.H.T.	Dom	360.088
Richards, J.T.	L/Sto	147.508
Roberts, John.	Kroo	
Roberts, W.H.	Sto	294.436
Roche, W.J.	Boy	214.714
Russell, A.J.	3/Wrtr	342.051
Sanders, F.	Carp/Mte	116.731
Sanders, J.	Sto	280.393
Saunders, G.J.	PO2	141.488
Scallon, E.	Sto	284.912
Scott, A.	Pte	Ply7.497
Sinclair, D.A.	ERA	268.690
Skinner, S.H.	AB	171.744
Smith, H.T.	Sto	293.943
Smith, J.	Sto	295.145
Smith, J.	Dom	358.506
Smith, W.H.	Sto	292.066
Snashall, G.W.	Sto	294.047
Spayne, W.J.	Ord	201.622
Spiller, S.A.	Ord	196.035
Sprake, H.J.	Ord	204.919
Stapleton, R.	Ch/Sto	147.222
Start, A.	Sto	276.514
Stephens, F.	PO2	179.143
Stroud, E.P.W.	Act/Sub Lieut	
Swinden, R.E.	Pte	Ply6.707
Taylor, H.W.	Ch/ERA	145.531
Taylor, J.	Kroo	
Tongue, T.A.	AB	178.183
Tucker, J.	Kroo	
Twyman, A.F.	Carp/Crew	343.447
Wallace, C.J.M.	Engr	
Webb, J.	Boy	210.040
Weir, A.L.	Act/ERA	269.784
White, F.J.	Ord	191.558
White, G.L.	Sto	285.168
Williams, T.	Sto	297.320
Wilson, J.	ERA	269.220
Wood, J.H.	Sto	153.464

Duplicate medals:

Allen, A.H.	Pte	Ply10.243
Beckett, W.J.	Sto	164.128
Haddock, S.G.	St/Engr	
Leith, G.P.	Lieut	
McCarthy, M.	Sto	285.338
Sinclair, D.A.	ERA	268.690
Start, A.	Sto	276.514
Williams, T.	Sto	297.320
Wood, J.H.	Sto	153.464

Returned medals:

Ali bin Saidi.	Dom	359.486
Anson, J.	Kroo	
Baxter, C.	Sto	293.813

No Bar Medals *Returned medals, continued*

Blackey, T.	Kroo	
Brickell, T.	Pte	Ply6.177
Fitzsimmons, W.J.	Pte	Ply9.208
Flight, T.H.	ERA	141.825
Fowler, S.H.	Dom	357.126
Goddard, A.E.	Ord	193.493
Godwin, C.F.	Sto	295.333
Hawkins, F.R.	Pte	Ply9.175
Joyce, T.	Sto	153.120
Lifebuoy.	Kroo	
Magin, R.	Sto	294.305
Mello, R. de	Dom	103.085
Moore, S.	Ch/Sto	128.612
Peterson, P.	Kroo	
Reilly, E.E.	Dom	357.120
Robinson, R.	Pte	Ch3.383
Rowlands, W.	Sto	295.088
Rowley, J.E.	Dom	148.514
Sartain, P.	Ord	205.613
Simons, W.J.	Sto	162.167
Simple, J.	Kroo	
Small Boy.	Kroo	
Turner, W.	Dom	359.009
Tyler, J.O.	Dom	359.223

H.M.S. TERRIBLE

Period for which entitled:
14th October 1899 to 27th March 1900.

Bars	*Total*	*Returned*	*Entitled*
5	1	0	1
4	0	0	0
3	13	0	13
2	265	4	261
1	289	16	273
0	579	41	538
	1147	61	1086

Notes:
* Two ratings are shown on the roll; the lower of the two is shown here.
[1] Also noted on the roll as M.W. Hallwright.
[2] Medal presented by H.M. The King.
[3] The original medal was returned to Arsenal; a duplicate medal was issued later.
[4] Also noted on the roll as C.H. Hughes-Onslow.
[5] The medal roll indicates that these two medals are both to the same recipient.
[6] Similar to Note 5, these medals are to the same recipient.
[7] The medal roll states, "Pte KRR Army man, RET'D TO ARSENAL."
[8] Medal roll states, "Medal found & Retd. from Jupiter 21.10.05. Papers under Dup 671." Roll is also endorsed RET'D TO Mint Feb 22.

Bars: Orange Free State, Transvaal, Tugela Heights, Relief of Ladysmith, Laing's Nek

	Stephens, B.R.	Ch/PO	115.781

Bars: Cape Colony, Tugela Heights, Relief of Ladysmith

	Annetts, J.	Pte	Po8.750
	England, G.P.	Lieut	
	Gulliver, C.	Pte	Po8.694
	Jones, W.J.	ERA	268.790
	Mills, J.E.	Pte	Po8.675
	Murray, A.E.J.	Asst/Engr	
	Nowell, H.A.	Pte	Po8.684
*	Ogilvy, F.C.A.	Lieut	
	Porteous, J.	Pte	Po9.144
	Roper, E.	Sergt	Po4.952
	Skerrin, A.	Midn	
	Stubbington, W.	Pte	Po8.683
	Whitlock, C.H.	Arm	340.928

Bars: Tugela Heights, Relief of Ladysmith

	Acland, A.E.	Midn	
	Adams, H.	Carp/Crew	341.559
	Aldworth, J.	Sto	285.254
*	Alexander, A.	Ord	183.212
	Alexander, W.	Ord	195.525
*	Allison, C.	Ord	195.542
	Alsbury, J.	Ord	187.203
	Altree, W.S.	SB/Attn	350.407
	Arnell, W.G.	Sto	287.824
	Arnold, J.N.	Yeo/Sig	146.983
	Arthur, J.F.	Engr	
	Ashton, F.	AB	161.127
	Aughton, J.	Sto	172.418
	Austin, F.	Sto	280.719
	Bailey, F.	Sto	166.246
	Baldwin, T.	Ch/PO	102.545
	Ball, G.H.	Ord	185.588
	Bate, W.S.T.	Ch/PO	127.128
	Beaty, J.A.	L/S	167.835
	Belsey, W.J.	Sto	288.518
	Bird, C.E.	Ord	189.960
	Bishop, W.J.	Sto	161.281
	Bobbett, J.J.	AB	183.495
	Bonnick, F.	Ord	197.124
	Bradbury, G.W.	AB	169.803
	Brennan, F.W.	Ord	190.529
	Brimble, C.	PO1	110.048
	Brown, H.V.	L/Sig	154.374
	Brown, W.	Carp/Mte	341.022
	Bryant, J.H.	AB	183.979
	Burnett, D.	Blksmth	341.388
	Burnham, G.	AB	169.568
	Burns, H.	Sto	175.441
	Campling, W.F.	PO1	177.327
	Carey, W.G.	PO1	121.805
	Carpenter, W.J.	Ord	182.085
	Caws, H.	AB	167.423
	Challinor, C.	PO2	170.293
	Channon, S.	Ord	180.380
	Clarke, F.	L/Sto	175.923
	Clifton, R.	Sto	157.065
	Cole, E.T.	Gunr	
	Cole, W.J.	AB	175.469
	Cook, W.	Ord	184.127

Bars: Tugela Heights, Relief of Ladysmith *continued*

*	Cooke, H.	Ord	176.138
	Cooper, H.	Sto	286.455
*	Cotcher, W.J.	Ord	190.225
	Cotton, J.	Ord	196.434
*	Courtney, T.W.	Ord	184.658
	Couzens, A.G.	Cook/Mte	341.872
	Cox, P.J.	Ord	185.056
	Cox, T.F.	Sto	167.140
	Crowe, G.	MAA	112.100
	Curtis, E.D.	AB	176.076
	Davies, R.	Ord	190.177
	Dear, T.	PO1	138.435
	Dennis, J.W.	AB	160.938
	Dennis, W.F.	Ord	190.208
	Dews, H.A.E.	AB	162.220
	Dibdin, H.E.	AB	171.133
	Dooner, J.K.P.	Lieut	
	Down, R.S.	Midn	
	Drummond, J.E.	Lieut	
	Dunstall, W.	Sto	279.955
	Dyer, G.	Ord	195.537
	Eames, P.	Sto	281.927
	Edney, A.W.	Ord	197.957
	Elliott, W.J.	Ord	169.392
	Ellis, H.C.	Arm	155.654
	Elms, W.G.	Ord	192.613
	Evans, R.C.	Sto	282.344
	Evans, W.	AB	161.370
	Fazackerley, A.	Pte	Po5.301
*	Fegan, J.	Ord	187.651
	Fisher, F.J.	Ord	177.206
	Fitzgerald, M.	PO2	145.835
	Foord, A.	Sto	285.453
	Ford, F.M.	Ord	189.531
	Ford, J.A.	Arm/Mte	340.379
	French, C.J.	Sto	284.710
	Frood, C.F.O.	Ord	189.006
*	Funnell, H.	Ord	195.539
	Gardiner, T.R.H.	L/S	156.072
	Gardner, C.A.	Ord	196.628
	Goldsmith, W.	Sto	284.544
	Gouge, S.W.	Sto	164.088
	Gould, G.L.	AB	176.069
	Grady, J.	AB	164.960
	Grounds, W.	L/S	180.374
	Gurney, A.F.J.	Ord	190.335
	Gurr, E.	Ord	190.383
	Haberfield, G.	Sto	289.801
1	Hallwright, W.M.	Midn	
	Harris, G.	Ord	185.125
	Harris, W.	Ord	189.000
	Harvey, E.A.J.	L/Shpwrt	161.650
	Harwood, H.	Ord	183.985
	Hayles, F.	Ord	195.506
	Helman, H.	Ord	186.172
	Hicks, E.L.	AB	167.979
	Hodson, G.L.	Midn	
	Honnibal, H.	PO1	128.018
	Hooker, F.J.	Sto	168.847
	House, H.E.	AB	157.391

	Howard, S.	Sto	282.594
	Howe, F.H.	Ord	189.687
	Hughes, H.	Ord	190.327
	Hunt, C.	L/S	155.585
	Hurl, F.W.	Ord	186.562
	Hutchinson, R.B.C.	Midn	
	Jeffery, J.	PO1	151.372
	Johnstone, J.	Sto	277.758
*	Jones, H.	Ord	195.491
	Jones, W.	AB	180.379
	Judd, G.H.	Ord	196.225
	Kenyon, H.	Ord	181.308
	Kewell, G.	AB	171.125
	Kimber, R.	Ord	192.721
	King, H.	Sto	282.609
	Kirby, A.G.	Ord	192.679
	Knight, J.	Sto	286.222
*	Knight, W.J.	Ord	185.617
	Lane, H.T.	Sto	176.585
	Large, A.	L/Sig	173.079
	Laver, J.G.	AB	180.252
	Legg, B.T.	Ord	189.247
	Lenihan, W.H.	AB	138.108
	Lessey, R.	Pte	Po4.250
	Limpus, A.H.	Comdr	
	Lindridge, H.	AB	171.713
	Lintern, W.H.	AB	182.999
*	Lock, L.	Ord	195.536
	Lomas, E.C.	Surgn	
	Long, F.	Ord	188.719
	Lovelady, H.	AB	161.383
	Lovell, F.	Pte	Po8.149
	McGuire, P.	Sto	279.968
	McLeod, A.	AB	158.848
	McLeod, A.	Shpwrt	341.869
	Macmillan, C.C.	Surgn	
	Majoram, C.	Ord	189.641
	Marsh, W.H.	Ord	182.922
	Metcalfe, J.J.	PO2	166.883
	Milbourne, W.	AB	161.869
	Miles, G.T.	Sto	284.727
	Mitchell, H.G.	PO1	120.111
	Mitchell, R.	PO1	124.007
	Moloney, J.	AB	147.347
	Morgan, E.	Sto	175.444
	Morris, J.	Sto	285.994
	Moyce, T.J.	Ord	201.872
	Mullis, J.	PO1	137.195
	Murphy, J.	AB	175.548
	Murray, J.	Sto	282.240
	Murray, M.P.	Arm/Crew	176.743
	Murray, T.	AB	158.619
	Newcome, S.	Sub Lieut	
	Newstead, W.	Ord	192.850
	Nightingale, J.	AB	157.375
	Orr, W.G.	AB	172.765
	Osborne, E.A.	AB	176.567
	Ousley, J.	AB	176.409
	Palmer, A.	AB	189.976
	Parham, H.	L/Sto	154.742
	Patten, C.W.B.	Boy	193.782

	Pearce, P.G.	AB	185.415
	Peckett, J.H.	PO2	136.844
	Pellett, H.	Ord	192.931
	Perkis, H.R.	AB	167.827
	Phillips, E.W.	Ord	183.344
	Pledge, W.J.	AB	155.047
	Plummer, F.	Ord	193.804
	Pope, E.	Ord	196.251
	Powell, E.G.	AB	174.017
	Prince, G.	PO1	145.605
	Randall, F.C.	AB	160.926
	Ratcliffe, S.	Ord	189.570
	Reading, A.E.	Ord	196.257
	Rees, W.J.	AB	161.857
	Reid, A.	AB	179.991
	Richards, S.R.S.	Lieut	
	Riddle, E.C.	Sto	283.609
	Robertson, L.H.	Ord	189.945
	Roman, W.	AB	173.878
	Rood, S.A.	AB	181.095
	Ross, J.	Sto	282.239
	Rovery, L.	Ord	189.141
	Rowe, J.	AB	162.400
	Russell, T.B.	AB	151.600
	Ryall, F.W.	AB	167.799
	Sales, J.H.	Ord	194.564
	Salter, M.	Ord	201.281
	Sandry, H.A.	AB	169.531
	Sawyers, C.G.	AB	186.205
	Sears, G.F.	Sto	283.496
	Sheldon, F.	Sto	158.149
	Shepherd, D.	AB	115.218
*	Shepherd, E.C.	Ord	187.485
	Shergold, E.	Ord	197.214
	Shoulder, E.	AB	190.333
	Silver, C.W.	Ord	193.857
	Simmons, T.E.	Ord	183.026
	Skeene, W.	Sto	283.251
	Skinner, G.M.	Midn	
	Smith, F.G.	AB	174.665
	Smith, W.T.	Ord	193.084
	Smithen, J.	AB	166.339
	Stansmore, A.	Ord	193.169
	Starling, F.J.	AB	155.791
	Stephens, H.	Ord	177.844
	Sterck, R.	Sto	280.535
	Stevens, F.	Sto	286.453
	Stevenson, H.	Sto	152.775
	Stewart, J.	SBStd	121.651
	Stone, A.E.	Sto	281.344
	Stones, A.E.	AB	192.314
	Strudwick, F.J.	PO2	158.180
	Sweeney, E.	Sto	282.583
	Symes, A.E.	AB	156.916
	Symons, H.	PO1	146.687
	Talbot, C.H.	AB	187.322
	Taylor, F.	Sto	284.896
	Terry, A.E.	Ord	195.489
	Thomas, E.P.	Sh/Std/Asst	168.422
*	Thomas, L.A.F.	Ord	187.923
	Thomas, W.	AB	168.900

	Toms, J.	AB	176.693
	Towers, A.	AB	129.226
	Treharne, P.	AB	141.551
2	Troup, J.A.	Midn	
	Tuck, F.	Ord	190.544
	Tucker, H.W.	AB	176.941
	Tuttle, G.	AB	185.988
	Varnham, A.B.	AB	162.297
	Venness, J.F.	PO1	128.560
	Vickers, H.	Sto	276.635
	Vosper, F.J.W.	AB	179.700
	Ward, G.W.	L/S	156.637
	Warren, S.J.	AB	166.226
	Webb, H.	AB	189.621
	Webster, T.M.	AB	189.466
	Weippert, C.N.	AB	159.620
	Weir, J.McC.	Sto	276.631
	White, A.H.	L/S	125.048
	White, S.	AB	144.620
	White, W.	L/Sto	161.316
	Whyte, H.E.W.C.	Midn	
	Wilde, J.S.	Lieut	
	Wilkins, A.E.	Sto	287.819
	Willey, W.H.	Sto	282.806
	Williams, E.	Act/Gunr	
	Williams, W.C.	Ord	186.774
	Willoughby, P.F.	Midn	
	Wilson, H.	Ord	181.351
	Wiltshire, W.H.	AB	175.149
	Woodward, E.	Ord	193.969
	Woolley, G.A.	Sto	287.898
2	Wright, J.	Gunr	
	Wright, J.E.	PO2	128.197
	Yeomans, A.	Sto	149.864
	Duplicate medals:		
	Bradbury, G.W.	AB	169.803
	Couzens, A.G.	Cook/Mte	341.782
3	Curtis, C.A.	Sto	285.448
	Drummond, J.E.	Lieut	
	Elms, W.G.	Ord	192.613
*	Fegan, J.	Ord	187.651
x	Gardner, C.A.	Ord	196.628
	Hicks, E.L.	AB	167.979
	Hodson, G.L.	Midn	
	Hughes, H.	Ord	190.327
	Kenyon, H.	Ord	181.308
	McLeod, A.	AB	158.848
	Marsh, W.H.	Ord	182.922
	Palmer, A.	AB	189.976
x	Patten, C.W.B.	Boy	193.782
	Randall, F.C.	AB	160.926
	Silver, C.W.	Ord	193.857
	Wilson, H.	Ord	181.351

x Two duplicate medals issued.

	Returned medals:		
	Allen, F.	PO1	128.140
	Cripps, H.	L/Sto	134.807
3	Curtis, C.A.	Sto	285.448
	Livermore, P.	Ord	193.646

Bars: Orange Free State, Natal

Holland, A.J.	AB	184.098

Bar: Cape Colony

Ashley, W.	Pte	Po8.785
Blake, J.	Pte	Po2.015
* Brogan, T.	Ord	193.610
Case, H.T.	Pte	Po8.774
Cashman, W.	L/Sto	145.455
Crees, E.J.	L/Carp/Crew	341.595
Dellow, H.	Pte	Po8.700
Faulkner, E.	AB	187.236
Ford, E.	Sto	280.281
Ford, R.	Bosn	
Hanagan, J.	AB	186.213
Harris, H.E.	Pte	Po8.681
Hopkins, G.	Pte	Po8.701
Kemp, H.	Ord	201.873
Mace, R.J.	AB	187.477
Manwaring, M.	Sto	281.345
Mather, W.B.	Gunr	
Mears, G.	L/Shpwrt	168.217
Mitchell, C.	Carp/Mte	117.757
Mullins, G.J.H.	Capt (RMLI)	
Nunn, F.J.	PO2	169.385
O'Mara, T.H.	Pte	Po7.890
Onslow, G.T.	Lieut Col	
Pashley, T.J.	Sto	278.379
Paterson, H.J.	Lieut	
Penn, W.	Pte	Po7.962
Prime, A.E.	Pte	Po7.878
Tomkins, A.H.	Pte	Po7.789
Wanstall, T.W.	AB	175.765
Werndley, F.	Pte	Po8.150
Williams, J.	L/Carp/Crew	342.057
Worthington, J.G.	AB	187.788

Duplicate medals:

Crees, E.J.	L/Carp/Crew	341.595
Williams, J.	L/Carp/Crew	342.057

Returned medals:

Blake, T.W.	2/SBStd	150.291
Forsyth, A.	Sto	174.112
Houghton, H.	Pte	Po7.381

Bar: Defence of Ladysmith

Sharp, C.R.	Midn	

Bar: Relief of Ladysmith

Barrett, J.	AB	144.271
Boldero, H.S.W.	Midn	
Codd, F.C.	PO2	150.851
Hamon, G.	Ord	186.724
Haynes, R.J.	Ord	189.514
Horner, E.B.	PO2	183.747
Hunter, F.	AB	170.566
Leach, J.	Ord	193.075
McNeill, J.	Sto	284.505
Maloney, D.	Ord	196.245
Nethercoat, E.	Ord	197.579
Skinner, H.D.	PO2	140.623
Summer, C.S.C.	Midn	
Taylor, T.	PO1	127.142
Thomas, G.	AB	183.228
Thomas, T.R.	Ord	196.258
Wheater, P.	Engr	
White, E.C.	Ord	191.331

Bar: Natal

Abraham, F.J.	Pte	Po8.708
Abraham, N.J.	L/S	157.432
Andrews, A.G.	St/Surgn	
Armitage, T.W.	Bugler	Po7.989
Aylesbury, E.	Ord	185.628
Baker, S.	AB	175.064
Barnard, F.R.	L/Cpl	Po8.007
Barnett, R.	Ord	183.983
Bartlett, G.	L/Sto	125.845
Beard, T.B.	PO2	116.400
* Benn, J.	Ord	190.096
Best, F.	AB	196.786
Bicker, H.P.	PO1	158.671
Blanchflower, E.C.	Asst/Clerk	
Blewdon, H.	Ord	201.875
Bogle, R.H.	Lieut	
Boland, W.H.	AB	170.915
Bolt, H.W.	Ord	190.541
Boyes, E.J.	Pte	Po8.679
Brady, H.	AB	188.620
Briggs, J.	Pte	Po5.084
Bright, A.S.	AB	179.884
Brown, J.S.	Sail	195.968
Brown, R.J.	Pte	Po9.583
Buckett, A.	Ord	196.213
Bull, E.L.	Sto	286.447
Burt, S.	Pte	Po4.208
* Bush, G.H.	Ord	195.543
Butler, A.W.	Ord	189.527
Butler, J.	Pte	Po8.249
Carter, H.	Bugler	Po8.394
Chalmers, G.	Pte	Po8.020
Chapman, G.A.	PO1	147.290
Childs, C.R.	AB	179.912
Clarke, W.	Pte	Po7.082
Clemens, G.	Sto	281.769
Collins, J.	ERA	168.187
Collins, J.	Pte	Po5.285
Cooper, F.	Sto	286.005
Cooper, J.A.	Pte	Po8.775
Cooper, W.	Sto	290.251
Copplestone, J.A.	Sto	286.003
Cousins, J.W.	AB	176.413
Cox, W.	Pte	Po5.596
Creese, A.E.	Ord	191.064
Cuell, A.J.	Pte	Po7.574
Cullinane, W.F.	Asst/Payr	
Curtis, W.	Carp/Crew	342.140
Daniells, C.J.	AB	160.778

Daniels, W.	L/Sto	152.590
Dark, H.C.	Sto	278.615
Dean, J.	Ord	190.199
Dedman, F.J.	Pte	Po9.335
Deed, J.C.	Sto	283.151
Denham, A.	L/Sto	131.115
Denny, H.	Pte	Po7.921
Dighton, G.	Pte	Po9.278
Donovan, A.E.	L/S	138.255
Dugdale, A.E.	AB	164.966
Dyer, C.H.	AB	156.418
Easson, R.	Ord	186.115
Eaton, A.W.	AB	181.811
Eden, J.H.	AB	172.649
Edwards, W.	Pte	Po8.005
Elliott, W.E.	Ch/Wrtr	121.173
Ellis, C.H.	Pte	Po4.049
Ellis, G.	Pte	Po5.097
Elton, J.	AB	196.240
Endean, H.	Ord	181.129
England, F.H.	Ord	189.470
Everett, C.G.	Blksmth/Mte	166.975
Fairman, J.	Sto	283.145
Farley, E.	Pte	Po5.968
Fisher, H.A.	Ord	181.592
Fitch, F.	Sto	283.626
Foley, W.J.	L/Sto	173.632
Foote, G.	Pte	Po6.339
Franklin, F.W.	AB	170.567
Gardner, W.S.	Sto	281.102
Giles, T.	AB	181.677
Goff, A.	Sto	282.617
Goodwin, F.R.	Asst/Engr	
Goodwin, L.H.	Ord	187.254
Goulter, J.G.	AB	166.685
Gowan, H.G.	L/Sig	165.308
Goyns, F.J.	3/Wrtr	168.933
Grant, A.	Sto	281.098
Griggs, G.A.	Ord	190.174
Grubb, W.	AB	178.782
Haddrell, P.J.	Pte	Po6.798
Harding, A.	Sto	287.813
Harrison, W.	Pte	Po6.455
Hart, E.	Sto	280.274
Harvey, A.E.	AB	155.353
Hawkins, H.	AB	152.138
Hayes, J.	Pte	Po9.557
Hayson, F.W.	Pte	Po8.702
Hayward, F.	Cook/Mte	340.938
Hefferman, T.	L/S	158.031
Heyburn, H.	AB	181.082
Holland, F.J.	Ord	179.145
Holman, C.	Sto	284.372
Hook, R.W.	Pte	Po7.591
Hopkins, J.	Sh/Std	101.910
Hopkins, J.	Sig	189.755
Horsley, H.	Pte	Po8.641
Hovell, R.	Sto	149.747
Howard, C.	Pte	Po6.267
Hutchence, A.H.	L/S	136.861
James, F.G.	AB	154.396

Jenkins, W.J.	L/S	163.269
Jeremy, A.H.	Surgn	
Johns, J.	Carp	
Johnson J.	AB	165.792
Jones, A.G.	Pte	Po2.466
Jones, H.M.	Pte	Po6.718
Jones, J.	Pte	Po2.458
Kent, G.	PO1	120.490
Keohane, C.	Ord	190.426
Kirby, E.R.W.	Midn	
Knight, W.B.	AB	159.700
† Laker, W.	Pte	Po8.773
Laurie, F.B.A.	Lieut (RMLI)	
Lawes, J.	Pte	Po8.613
Lawrence, F.	Q/Sig	179.212
Legg, W.J.	Pte	Po8.678
Lester, G.F.W.	Cpl	Po7.513
Lewis, C.	Ord	186.228
Lidstone, H.W.	Pte	Po8.761
Lockett, T.W.	AB	177.224
Luckham, G.H.	Ord	201.616
McDonald, J.	Ord	176.515
McKenzie, G.	Ord	190.405
Major, E.W.	Ord	193.469
Marsh, F.	Q/Sig	180.550
Martin, J.	Sto	286.410
Moorse, W.E.	Sto	287.740
Murray, T.	Sto	280.222
Nash, J.	Arm/Crew	154.168
Neil, W.	PO1	119.309
Newland, G.E.	Sto	282.176
Newman, J.W.	Q/Sig	160.203
Nicholson, S.	Pte	Po9.382
Novis, H.A.	AB	156.064
* Onslow, H.C.	Lieut	
Osborne, S.W.	Pte	Po6.402
Palmer, C.	Sto	168.207
Parker, A.W.	Pte	Po8.680
Parrott, W.	AB	189.405
Partridge, A.F.	AB	138.418
Peck, H.	Sergt	Po2.704
Pellatt, A.	Carp/Mte	135.885
Pinkerton, S.	PO2	160.654
Plumbe, A.G.	Sto	282.341
* Pollard, H.	Ord	189.966
Porch, F.	PO1	107.694
Randall, C.	Ord	196.243
Rayner, J.W.	Pte	Po5.847
Reilly, F.J.	Pte	Po8.857
Relf, C.	Pte	Po8.777
Riley, J.L.	Pte	Po9.400
Ritchie, W.H.	AB	156.952
Robertson, G.	Asst/Engr	
Roper, R.	Cook/Mte	340.873
Roper, W.A.	Pte	Po4.392
Rose, G.	Pte	Po7.455
Roskruge, F.J.	Asst/Engr	
Royce, W.	AB	185.498
Rudgley, W.C.	Pte	Po8.684
Rushworth, J.	Sto	283.149
* Scarlett, J.	Ord	188.626

Bar: Natal *continued*

Scott, P.M.	Capt	
Scriven, B.J.	Pte	Po8.668
Sears, W.H.	Ord	189.442
Sennett, E.N.	AB	91.742
Shaw, H.	L/Sto	152.328
Sheldrick, E.W.	3/Wrtr	193.794
Shepherd, G.	3/Wrtr	340.612
Shepherd, R.H.	Sto	280.545
Sherwin, H.A.	AB	173.855
Shorrock, W.J.	Ord	188.174
Silvers, B.	L/Cpl	Po6.330
Simmonds, W.A.	Cook/Mte	341.108
Skinner, W.	Sto	276.024
Slater, G.	Ord	189.439
Sleeman, W.	AB	181.233
Smith, C.	Sto	289.480
Smith, C.W.	Sto	152.689
Smith, J.	Sto	153.587
Smith, R.J.	Pte	Po8.783
Southard, A.	Pte	Po8.065
Sparkes, A.E.	PO1	129.206
Stanbridge, A.	L/Sergt	Po4.073
Stilges, W.H.	Sh/Std/Boy	341.601
Strickland, H.	Ord	195.472
Sullivan, T.	Sto	288.535
Swift, G.	Ord	189.460
Syson, J.L.	Asst/Clerk	
Thomson, G.	Pte	Po6.567
Timblin, J.	AB	182.863
Tovey, A.C.	Pte	Po8.704
Trim, H.P.	Ord	195.495
Trivett, F.	Ord	190.105
Turberfield, H.	Pte	Po8.768
* Underwood, F.	Ord	189.143
Vail, F.	Ord	183.656
Walker, D.McC.	Pte	Po8.695
Warburton, C.L.O.	ERA	166.256
Watt, S.T.	Pte	Po8.758
Webster, H.O.	Ord	189.798
Wedmore, A.J.	AB	172.073
Welling, A.	Ord	190.133
White, J.J.	Pte	Po7.070
Whitter, W.	Pte	Po6.934
Whyte, W.H.	AB	164.728
Wood, E.W.	Ord	190.160
Wood, W.	PO1	132.982
Woolcombe, A.	Surgn	
Wright, P.	Pte	Po4.950
Wright, W.H.	Sto	167.116
Yeomans, P.E.A.	Pte	Po4.336
York, T.	Sergt	Po4.718

Duplicate medals:

Barnard, F.R.	L/Cpl	Po8.007
x Bartlett, G.	L/Sto	125.845
Deed, J.C.	Sto	283.151
Eaton, A.W.	AB	181.811
Fairman, J.	Sto	283.145
Harvey, A.E.	AB	155.353
Horsley, H.	Pte	Po8.641
+ Laker, W.	Pte	Po8.773
Marsh, F.	Q/Sig	180.550
Southard, A.	Pte	Po8.065

x Two duplicate medals issued.
+ Three duplicate medals issued.

Returned medals:

Bourke, E.	Ord	198.069
Connor, M.	PO1	161.886
Dodd, W.	Ord	183.715
Foster, W.	Pte	Po6.920
Gates, F.	AB	162.287
Holmes, H.	Sh/Cpl	116.214
Jacques, S.J.	PO1	148.353
Laycock, R.A.	Clerk	
Neaves, J.H.	AB	178.772
Pasker, W.J.	Pte	Po6.205
Rigby, W.	AB	177.962
Saunders, J.	Ord	194.709
Wroxall, C.	Band	121.574

No Bar Medals

Abrams, G.	Dom	356.356
Aburrow, E.	Sto	148.346
Ackfield, T.	Sto	149.902
Akehurst, C.E.	Ord	188.640
Alford, J.	L/Sto	149.877
Alway, F.G.	Ord	198.659
Ames, J.H.	Band	340.385
Anderson, W.A.	L/S	136.281
Andrews, H.A.	Sto	114.603
Arthur, W.	Pntr	122.173
Ash, H.W.	Ord	196.054
Ashwell, W.	Boy	197.908
Atkins, T.	Act/Ch/Sto	148.646
Austin, P.J.	Boy	198.659
Bailey, H.	L/Sto	138.360
Baker, A.	L/Sto	161.688
Baker, B.G.	Dom	357.686
Baker, J.H.	Boy	198.657
Baker, W.A.	Sto	284.728
Baker, W.T.	Sto	285.272
Baldwin, A.	Sto	287.642
Baldwin, H.	Boy	197.484
Balls, J.S.	Ord	176.243
Banbury, R.	Boy	196.380
Barnes, A.	Boy	199.040
Barrett, J.H.	Boy	197.753
Barritt, R.S.	Pte	Po7.048
Barter, H.R.	Boy	197.746
Bartlett, E.E.	Asst/Engr	
Baskerville, H.S.	Fl/Payr	
Bates, H.	ERA	269.362
Bates, J.	Sto	289.961
Bell, J.	Sto	283.394
Belsworth, F.W.	Boy	198.313
Bendell, A.E.	Sh/Std/Asst	341.994
Bennett, F.J.	Sto	288.521
Bennett, T.R.	Sto	284.703

Berry, H.	Boy	197.904	Coggins, W.J.	PO1	86.042
Bevis, C.	2/Wrtr	161.203	Colbourne, J.A.	L/Sto	158.734
Bewers, W.J.E.	Sto	280.241	Coleman, W.	Sto	285.885
Black, A.	Sto	281.950	Collenso, J.G.	Ord	189.928
Blackwell, J.	Sto	276.677	Collier, H.B.	Sto	284.117
Blake, F.	Ord	150.224	Collins, W.A.	Sto	285.273
Bland, A.	Ord	190.112	Conlon, M.	Sto	283.530
Bourne, J.H.	Ord	188.443	Cook, T.J.	Sto	284.950
Bowbyes, H.	2/Yeo/Sig	135.887	Cook, W.	Sto	282.607
Bowden, T.	Boy	196.080	Cook, W.A.	Sto	176.609
Bowring, R.	Boy	197.870	Cooper, A.E.	PO1	142.526
Boyd, J.	Sto	276.052	Cooper, S.	Sto	167.124
Bradford, J.	Band	166.667	Cooplestone, W.	Sto	269.212
Bray, J.	Ord	201.640	Corfield, F.	Sto	289.742
Brenan, M.	Ch/Sto	121.124	Cosham, J.	Sto	287.820
Brewer, H.E.	Ord	195.495	Coulston, T.	L/Sto	159.951
Brickell, S.E.	Ord	197.282	Crawford, G.	Ch/Cook	100.002
Brindle, E.	Ord	189.680	Creedon, J.	Sto	285.447
Brock, A.A.	Boy	193.324	Cripp, W.G.	L/Sto	142.417
* Brock, G.F.	Ord	190.418	Crispin, A.		
Brown, C.	Sto	276.425	alias S. Martin	Sto	289.822
Brown, H.J.	Sto	142.435	Cuell, J.A.	Ord	195.551
Bullock, E.F.	Ord	200.196	Cullinane, J.	Ch/Sto	142.114
Bunday, J.	PO1	110.829	Cummings, A.J.	Sto	287.814
Bunday, J.	Sto	280.855	Cunningham, E.	Ord	201.938
Burke, A.E.	Ch/Arm	133.927	Cushion, J.	Sto	350.479
Burn, G.E.	Sto	276.407	Cutler, W.	Ord	201.605
Burridge, P.	Sto	284.983	Daly, W.T.	Boy	197.915
Burridge, R.	Sto	289.789	Daniels, E.	Ch/Sto	136.534
Burtenshaw, G.	L/S	122.618	Dart, J.	Boy	194.750
Burton, W.	Sto	167.786	Davie, A.	ERA	153.706
Bush, W.J.	Ord	196.047	Davies, A.	AB	147.859
Butler, H.	L/Sto	130.745	Davies, R.	Boy	194.749
Byron, W.	Sto	289.795	Davies, W.	Boy	197.394
Cable, G.W.	Ord	193.685	Davis, G.	Sto	290.010
Caldicott, W.	Sto	119.738	Davis, I.S.	Sto	282.004
Calloway, A.B.	Sh/Std/Boy	341.828	Dawson, H.	Carp/Crew	287.857
Campbell, J.R.	Sto	278.033	Day, H.	Sto	284.357
Campbell, R.	Sto	278.706	Deacon, D.	Sto	151.156
Carr, H.	Sto	278.396	Delea, E.	Boy	197.699
Carr, W.	Ch/ERA	141.652	Denham, H.T.	ERA	269.018
Carress, W.	Sto	281.943	Deuzy, R.	Sto	286.518
Carter, C.	Sto	286.002	Dillon, A.J.	Sto	284.698
Carver, W.	Sto	280.835	Dobson, G.	Sto	157.068
Casey, P.	Sto	283.319	Dodd, C.R.	Sh/Std/Boy	341.830
Cassell, F.	L/Sto	144.869	Dolphin, W.J.	Dom	144.070
Cassell, F.W.	Ch/Sto	140.413	Donnon, J.	Boy	197.522
Chambers, W.	L/Sto	152.711	Dorling, H.T.	Midn	
Chandler, F.R.	Ord	184.023	* Downer, E.J.	Ord	186.134
Chapman, F.	Sto	283.131	Downton, W.J.	ERA	133.008
Chase, J.E.	Fl/Engr		Doyle, M.J.	Sto	286.197
Chisholm, B.	ERA	268.927	Draper, W.	PO2	157.590
Chittendem, G.	Sto	280.552	Draper, W.	Dom	355.534
Christmas, J.	Sto	280.534	Driver, W.	Ord	197.941
Churchman, A.	Sh/Cpl	117.542	Dumbleton, C.	Pte	Po6.915
Clark, A.E.	Pntr	341.724	Dummer, H.	AB	177.944
Clarke, G.H.	Dom	153.529	Dunnert, J.	Boy	197.715
Clarke, W.O.	L/S	170.363	Dye, H.E.	Ord	194.778
Cleaves, S.	Ch/Sto	129.513	Dyer, F.J.	Dom	173.488
Clements, R.	Sto	283.327	Dyer, T.	ERA	269.017
Clifton, J.	Ord	190.114	Eames, J.H.	Sto	166.929

No Bar Medals *continued*

Earwaker, T.	Sto	284.741
Eaton, A.G.	Ord	189.457
Edwards, G.	Ord	190.090
Edwards, J.	L/Sto	136.524
Edwards, J.D.	Ord	196.222
Ellis, J.W.	Dom	356.209
Everard, W.A.	Pte	Po4.373
Farmer, D.	Sto	282.232
Fernandez, R.W.	L/Sto	141.392
Ferns, H.J.	Ord	196.242
Fidgett, T.	Boy	197.424
Fielder, H.	Ord	193.722
Finch, A.	Band	180.234
Flaherty, D.	Ord	188.880
Flury, W.R.	AB	187.174
Flyde, F.	Sto	290.017
Foord, A.	Cook/Mte	340.630
Foote, G.	Sto	284.682
Forbes, A.	Sto	282.382
Forward, B.	Boy	197.826
Foster, A.	Sto	285.094
Foster, J.	PO2	117.626
Foster, R.	L/Sto	130.099
Fowler, W.	Sto	173.808
Foyle, R.J.	Ord	196.259
Fraser, J.	Boy	197.563
Frost, R.J.	Boy	197.805
Gardiner, G.	Ord	193.025
Garland, R.	Ord	190.110
Garraway, W.B.	Ord	194.901
Gayford, A.	L/Sto	153.582
Geary, A.	AB	151.939
Genting, W.	Sto	283.708
Gibb, W.	Sto	276.693
Gibbons, T.	Ch/ERA	142.023
Gilbert, J.	Sto	282.231
Goff, W.E.	Sto	175.843
Goff, W.V.	Sto	148.679
Goodwin, E.	Ch/Sto	130.321
Gordon, J.	Sto	169.344
Gore, J.	Boy	198.954
Gosling, J.	Sto	283.755
Gough, E.F.	Cook/Mte	342.112
Gough, W.S.	Boy	
Grady, J.	AB	182.459
Grant, H.	Sto	148.298
Gray, A.	AB	277.614
Gray, G.	Sto	159.984
Green, G.	Sto	287.735
Green, J.	Sto	167.197
Green, L.	Sto	285.998
Greening, A.C.	Ord	189.178
Greenwood, C.	Sto	282.782
Gregory, H.	Sto	284.214
Grierson, R.	Sto	282.818
Griffiths, A.	Boy	197.494
Griffiths, F.J.	Plmbr	159.976
Griffiths, J.	Ch/Sto	120.749
Hall, C.	Sto	172.841
Hall, J.T.	Sto	287.899
Hall, R.	Ord	190.172
Hallifax, C.	L/Sto	164.151
Halligan, J.	Boy	197.706
Ham, H.	Boy	196.070
Harber, W.J.	Boy	197.768
Harding, C.	Sto	283.033
Hardy, W.	Sto	285.866
Harris, E.D.	Sto	282.793
Harvey, A.	Ord	195.473
Harwood, G.	Sto	276.877
Hatherley, W.C.	Ord	196.082
Hatt, E.	Band	340.211
Hayes, C.	Sto	282.801
Hayler, C.	ERA	269.054
Hayter, E.	Sto	280.715
Hayward, L.	L/Sto	151.716
Heath, W.S.	Ord	195.108
Hendley, L.	Sto	285.452
Henson, G.N.	Midn	
Herriott, T.A.	L/S	176.477
Hewitt, W.	Ch/Sto	119.940
Hide, C.E.	Arm/Crew	341.975
Hill, E.	Ord	198.998
Hillman, A.	Sto	284.994
Hirst, S.	PO1	131.398
Hoar, G.	AB	195.470
Hoare, R.	Ord	201.604
Hockin, C.J.	Boy	197.772
Holdway, C.	Sto	285.449
Hollinsworth, C.	Ch/ERA	128.230
Hookway, H.	2/Cooper	341.345
Hoptrough, C.	Sto	146.531
Horne, S.F.	Ord	192.840
Hubbard, C.	Sto	288.530
Huckle, F.A.	Sh/Cpl	124.122
* Hurst, A.	Boy	197.980
Hussey, H.	Boy	197.818
Hutchinson, H.	Act/Lieut	
Inger, W.B.	ERA	153.143
Ireland, J.	Ord	199.555
Jannen, H.	Sto	276.639
Jeames, W.G.	Carp/Crew	342.690
Jenkins, W.	Boy	197.259
Jerred, W.N.	Ord	196.211
Johnston, A.R.	Boy	197.644
Johnstone, A.	Ord	199.044
Johnstone, J.	L/Sto	158.807
Jones, C.H.	Sto	285.879
Jones, E.B.	Sto	284.719
Jones, J.	Sto	289.465
Jones, J.C.	Sto	282.767
Jones, R.	L/S	126.225
Joy, W.A.	Sto	286.194
Jupp, F.	Sto	287.771
Kaye, H.	Sto	284.742
Kealy, W.	Ord	197.853
Keefe, T.	Sto	285.352
Keeping, C.	Sto	161.295
Kemp, T.W.	Sto	286.414
Kennedy, G.	Sto	276.046
Kerr, D.	Cooper	174.490

Kersley, A.	Band	340.183
Kierman, E.	Boy	197.683
Kimber, W.H.	Sto	285.001
Knight, C.S.	Ord	196.264
Knight, H.E.	Boy	197.832
Knight, W.	Sto	282.342
Ladd, W.H.	Band	122.226
Lake, F.	Sto	281.947
Lambert, C.E.	Sto	286.421
Lane, W.H.	Sh/Std/Boy	341.835
Langdown, G.W.	Sto	285.443
Layton, J.	L/Sto	140.895
Leadingham, A.	Sto	282.313
Lee, C.	Ord	190.167
Lee, H.	Boy	197.748
Lee, P.	Ord	197.690
Lee, W.J.	Ord	193.808
Lees, A.E.J.C.	Boy	196.016
Light, P.A.	Sh/Std/Asst	341.215
Lillie, F.H.	Sto	284.925
Linton, H.	L/Sto	109.321
Long, A.T.	Sh/Cpl	350.084
Long, J.	Sto	288.522
Lovell, G.	Sto	113.937
McCormick, T.J.	Sto	289.982
McCracken, J.S.	Ord	197.888
McGrane, E.	Ord	196.180
McGrath, W.	Ch/Sto	140.920
McMillan, J.	Boy	198.022
McNeill, W.	Boy	197.600
Macey, G.R.	Arm/Crew	341.902
Major, C.G.	Sto	284.724
Maple, F.W.	Sig	190.263
Masters, H.S.	Boy	197.968
Matthews, F.B.	Ord	202.213
Matthews, P.	Boy	197.621
Mayhew, S.H.	Sto	287.640
Mead, F.	ERA	268.938
Mepstead, W.J.	Cook/Mte	353.486
Meredith, O.	Dom	171.454
Mihell, J.	Dom	97.654
Miller, E.A.	Ord	195.845
Miller, E.J.	Ord	195.292
Mitchell, T.	Ch/Sto	116.737
Moore, A.J.	Sto	115.776
Moore, C.	Sto	127.571
Mordaunt, C.	Boy	196.886
Morgan, E.F.	Sto	159.961
Morling, H.W.	Ord	193.202
Morrison, D.	Sto	287.942
Munn, W.C.	Ord	196.375
Murch, A.	Ord	201.606
Murdock, R.	Ch/Sto	119.900
Murphy, J.	Ord	188.879
Murphy, J.	Sto	288.644
Murray, J.L.	Boy	197.905
Neal, A.	PO1	152.273
Neal, J.	Sto	282.807
Neiass, T.J.	Ord	194.824
Neil, A.	Ord	180.616
Neville, O.	Ord	186.015
New, G.W.	AB	179.975
Newman, H.	Sto	145.783
Newton, J.J.	Boy	197.802
Nolan, H.		
alias H. Noble.	Sto	161.644
Norman, W.J.	Sto	282.379
O'Connell, D.J.	Dom	355.206
O'Flaherty, J.J.	Sto	165.222
O'Norley, T.	Sto	282.767
Ogden, J.	Sig	190.654
Oldbury, C.	L/S	109.701
Oliver, J.	Ord	193.784
Oram, J.	Boy	197.828
Osborne, H.	Sto	281.589
Otty, T.	Sto	279.961
Owens, M.	Sto	285.085
Pacey, R.	Sto	289.823
Pagett, J.	Sto	288.497
Paice, W.J.	Ord	183.357
Painter, H.A.	Boy	197.817
Painter, I.	AB	166.537
Palmer, G.	Boy	197.816
Pameley, A.	ERA	268.601
Park, S.	Ord	193.787
Parkhurst, J.H.	Sto	282.217
Parkhurst, T.J.	L/S	145.639
Parnell, E.J.	Boy	195.302
Parsons, G.	Sto	173.786
Parsons, H.	Sto	285.270
Payne, S.J.	Sto	282.006
Payne, W.	Act/Ch/Sto	136.568
Pead, D.	ERA	268.596
Pearson, W.	Sto	283.496
Peat, J.	AB	186.998
Perkins, A.	Sto	282.798
Peterson, A.	Ord	197.645
Phillips, C.	Boy	196.847
Phillips, E.W.	Boy	197.502
Phillips, M.	Ord	201.878
Pidgeon, A.	Ch/ERA	134.471
Pilcher, A.S.	Sto	283.130
Pillar, J.G.	Ord	196.017
Plomer, H.	Sto	283.705
Pocock, W.	Sto	284.706
Pollock, J.	Ord	174.516
Pomeroy, A.	Boy	195.300
Porteons, G.	Boy	197.609
Porter, J.G.	Sto	281.291
Porter, W.	Sto	152.581
Pratt, H.C.	Pte	Po4.004
Pratt, H.J.	PO1	125.768
Price, J.	Shpwrt	341.650
Prior, W.B.	Ord	189.673
Purchase, G.	AB	195.504
Ray. H.T.	Ord	197.281
Reader, G.	Boy	197.640
Redman, F.G.	AB	145.606
Reed, G.G.	Sto	284.989
Reed, W.	AB	166.139
Reed, W.S.	Dom	357.351
Reinold, B.E.	Midn	

No Bar Medals *continued*

Rice, W.L.	AB	182.530		Treadaway, E.	Boy	198.872
Richards, A.	Sto	284.711		Trengrove, J.	PO1	113.844
Richens, C.	PO1	110.151		Tubb, H.	Dom	67.427
Rider, R.T.	Art/Engr			Tucker, W.G.	Ord	198.315
Rinder, G.S.	Ord	190.359		Tuffley, H.J.	PO1	113.692
Rogers, W.E.	Sto	165.929		Tullis, T.	PO1	110.802
Rowe, A.	Sto	284.709		Turner, A.	Act/ERA	269.203
Rundall, J.	L/Sto	140.265		Turrell, A.	Cook/Mte	161.695
Runnalls, W.J.	Cook/Mte	166.120		Twidale, D.	Sto	289.352
Sack, F.C.	Sto	165.931		Tyler, G.H.	Pte	Po4.988
Sandercock, W.J.	PO1	112.140		Utton, W.	Ord	194.028
Sanderson, R.	Sto	154.756		Vare, G.	Sto	285.884
Schooley, D.J.	Ord	177.824		Venness, T.	Sto	276.031
Scott, A.	Carp/Mte	151.478		Ventham, J.	Band	146.517
Scott, G.L.	ERA	269.310		Vick, H.	ERA	128.918
Self, G.L.	Ord	193.634		Vincent, A.	Ord	192.829
Seymour, W.	Sto	279.761		Vine, C.A.	Sto	284.691
Shanahan, J.	Blksmth/Mte	340.535		Voar, A.J.	Sto	285.274
Shannahan, H.	Sto	285.996		Wagg, A.C.	Sto	177.189
Shannon, J.	Sto	162.609		Walker, W.	AB	162.563
Sharp, J.T.	Boy	198.138		Wallis, J.	Sh/Std/Boy	341.757
Sheridan, M.	Ord	197.705		Walsh, R.	Cooper	134.452
Sheridan, P.	Sto	276.686		Walters, H.A.	Pte	Po8.699
Shirley, E.	Sig	187.399		Warn, R.T.	PO1	119.154
Silvester, F.A.	Sto	284.205		Warne, L.J.	Sto	286.452
Simmons, W.	Ord	196.064		Waterman, F.C.	Boy	198.320
Skene, C.H.	Boy	197.570		Waters, H.	Sto	165.207
Sliney, J.	Boy	196.665		Watson, D.	Ch/Sto	141.136
Smith, F.	Sto	282.795		Watson, R.	ERA	268.908
Smith, H.G.	Ord	192.680		Webb, H.	Boy	197.425
Smith, R.	Ord	197.903		Weekes, B.	Sto	288.546
Smith, R.H.	Boy	197.750		Weekes, W.R.	ERA	268.974
Smith, T.F.A.	Sto	165.232		Welch, H.	Boy	197.575
Spooner, H.	Ord	192.573	*	Weldon, E.F.	Ord	197.180
Spurgeon, S.T.	Sto	156.535		Wells, A.	Sto	285.071
Squire, J.H.	Band	340.489		West, G.	Sto	144.775
Stallard, T.	L/Sto	119.744		West, H.	Boy	197.482
Stanbury, E.	Cook/Mte	340.949		Whatley, C.L.	Chaplain	
Standen, A.	Sto	285.277		Wheatley, H.J.	Ord	189.438
Starck, F.	AB	155.992		Wheeler, A.	Ord	197.604
Starling, E.	ERA	268.914		Wheeler, T.	Ord	187.062
Steele, A.E.	Sto	285.271		Wherley, R.	Boy	197.652
Stevens, A.	Ord	190.224		Whincup, B.	Ord	189.550
Stewart, C.	Ord	195.035		White, A.E.	Sto	281.161
Street, A.	Sto	281.106		White, W.	Ord	190.071
Strickland, W.	AB	141.233		Whitehead, H.	Sto	283.499
Sullivan, J.	Boy	196.821		Whittaker, J.	Boy	197.553
Sullivan, P.	Sto	288.520		Whyte, D.S.	Ord	189.944
Swaffield, C.	Sto	284.723		Wicks, W.	Ch/Sto	118.656
Tame, H.	Ord	191.736		Wilkins, W.	Sto	151.462
Taylor, D.	Boy	197.716		Willcox, C.	Boy	197.831
Taylor, H.	Ord	201.639		Willey, H.	Boy	196.226
Thickett, T.	Boy	197.650		Williams, D.	Sto	288.519
Thomas, A.	ERA	268.017		Williams, G.E.	L/Sto	159.945
Thomas, J.	AB	156.596		Williams, H.	L/Sto	156.953
Thompson, J.	Ord	195.039		Williams, H.T.	L/Sto	151.931
Thompson, T.	AB	187.274		Williams, J.	Sto	284.984
Thornhill, H.	Sto	288.543		Williams, J.J.	ERA	268.990
Titheridge, W.	Sto	168.871		Williams, R.H.	Sh/Std/Boy	342.023
Tolson, E.	Boy	197.201		Wilton, C.	Sto	284.733
				Winnett, A.S.	Ord	190.101

Withers, J.	L/Sto	153.799
Witty, J.T.	Sto	280.355
Wood, H.	Ord	197.651
Wood, J.M.	Boy	197.564
Wood, R.	L/Sto	172.810
Woodgate, W.	Sto	285.092
Woolf, T.A.	Asst/Clerk	
Woolgar, G.T.	Sto	282.756
Wright, B.	PO2	148.262
Wright, E.	Ord	198.997
Wright, J.E.	Ord	189.969
Wright, W.D.	Boy	198.740
Wyman, W.J.	Sh/Cpl	350.038
Yarham, W.	L/Carp/Crew	341.944
Young, C.T.	Dom	357.352
Young, W.	Boy	197.517
Young, W.J.	PO1	147.673

Duplicate medals:

Ashwell, W.	Boy	197.908
Bell, J.	Sto	283.394
Brickell, S.E.	Ord	197.282
[8] Bridger, W.J.	Sto	153.637
Collier, H.B.	Sto	284.117
Copplestone, W.	ERA	269.212
Doyle, M.J.	Sto	286.197
Dyer, T.	ERA	269.017
Grady, J.	AB	182.459
x Grierson, R.	Sto	282.818
Harding, C.	Sto	283.033
Hockin, C.J.	Boy	197.772
Hubbard, C.	Sto	288.530
Maple, F.W.	Sig	190.263
Masters, H.S.	Boy	197.968
Mayhew, S.H.	Sto	287.640
Neal, J.	Sto	282.807
Pillar, J.G.	Ord	196.017
Sheridan, P.	Sto	276.686
Shirley, E.	Sig	187.399
Smith, F.	Sto	282.795
Thomas, A.	ERA	268.017
Tucker, W.G.	Ord	198.315
Welch, H.	Boy	197.575
Wheeler, T.	Ord	187.062
Wherley, R.	Boy	197.652
Williams, R.H.	Sh/Std/Boy	342.023

x Two duplicate medals issued.

Returned medals:

Bone, W.	Sto	153.865
Bourke, J.	Ord	181.943
[8] Bridger, W.J.	Sto	153.637
Carr, A.	Boy	197.624
Clarke, W.	Sto	285.302
Connell, R.J.	Band	163.330
Cooke, A.R.	L/Shpwrt	342.332
[5] Coombes, S.	Dom	356.436
[5] Coombes, S.H.	Dom	356.436
Cowell, C.F.	Boy	195.225
Fildes, V.	Q/Sig	183.797
[6] Fleming, S.	Dom	357.604
[6] Fleming, S.G.	Dom	357.604
Fugler, R.J.	PO2	155.812
Gillman, J.	Sto	173.792
Gradden, F.	L/Sto	125.537
Green, H.	Ord	195.493
Halliwell, H.C.	Ord	187.717
Hawthorne, A.	Sto	289.337
Hetheway, A.	AB	167.961
Hodson, W.E.	Ord	187.660
Holbrow, H.	Pte	Ch6.598
Hughes, E.J.	Pte	Po5.907
Hurst, H.	Sto	288.052
Joy, A.	Ord	204.313
McCoyd, W.	Boy	197.525
Marriott, F.C.	Band	340.570
Nye, H.W.	AB	187.378
Pailes, H.	Band	340.352
Pike, W.	Boy	197.318
Robbins, W.	Band	340.147
Saunders, W.	Sto	144.501
Scorey, G.H.	Ord	196.265
Smith, H.	Sto	151.943
Trout, F.	Sh/Std/Boy	341.754
Turner, E.	AB	192.221
Underwood, W.	Sto	284.985
Vaughan, C.W.	Dom	355.503
Veitch, G.	PO1	168.511
Walker, C.	Boy	197.633
[7] Wise, G.	Pte (KRRC)	

H.M.S. THETIS

Period for which entitled:
5th November 1899 to 8th March 1901.

Extended period:
9th March 1901 to 28th April 1901.

Bars	*Total*	*Returned*	*Entitled*
2	1	0	1
1	104	3	101
0	192	9	183*
	297	12	285

* The above figure includes one Bronze No Bar Medal.

Notes:
[1] Roll states, "Medal only ret'd in damaged condition." A duplicate medal was issued.
[2] The *duplicate medal* was returned to the Mint in Feb 1922.
[3] This is the only bronze medal on the Naval rolls. The medal was sent to the recipient on 10th March 1902.

Bars: Cape Colony, South Africa 1901

Bennett, E.M.	Sub Lieut	

Bar: Natal

Acteson, T.H.	Pte	Ch7.858
Ault, W.S.	PO2	167.372
Baum, A.H.L.	AB	181.657
Beckett, W.J.	Pte	Ch7.514
Blackburn, C.L.	AB	188.497
Bloxham, G.	AB	189.518
Borgeest, A.	AB	175.733
Brown, H.	Pte	Ch9.021
Buckland, W.C.	PO2	179.332
Burton, T.C.	PO1	159.828
Cavanagh, J.M.	AB	170.039
Chapman, B.	AB	180.347
Chorlton, J.	Pte	Po5.697
Cook, W.H.	AB	176.257
Coole, F.	Sto	284.893
Coolican, J.P.J.	St/Surgn	
Cormack, G.M.	AB	176.330
Coul, H.G.	AB	192.470
Crimmins, B.J.	AB	189.022
Davidson, A.P.	Snr/Lieut	
Deighton, W.	Pte	Ch10.142
Dickson, J.S.	AB	185.733
Dixon, A.G.	L/Sergt	Po8.725
Doe, C.	Arm/Mte	340.519
Drewett, G.F.	Pte	Ch9.628
Duncan, J.B.	L/S	168.768
Eddey, J.T.	Carp/Mte	153.355
Ellis, J.	Pte	Ch7.092
Evans, G.B.	L/Sig	171.904
Fildes, V.	Q/Sig	183.797
Fitch, H.	Sto	279.149
Flynn, E.	L/Cpl	Ch2.218
Franklin, W.J.	AB	190.462
Fry, W.H.	AB	167.747
Fuller, A.H.	AB	173.437
Gainen, T.	AB	182.719
Glover, J.H.T.	AB	181.831
Graham, J.G.	Q/Sig	186.427
Graham, W.C.	AB	168.754
Harrison, G.A.H.	Gunr	
Haslam, W.	Pte	Ch7.715
Henry, D.	L/S	165.838
Hill, C.	AB	181.224
Holmes, J.	AB	178.591
Jackman, R.A.	Sto	277.964
Kemish, W.J.	Ord	191.067
Kemp, W.H.	PO1	120.344
Landale, J.S.	Pte	Po5.710
Lavender, A.J.	Ch/Arm	128.260
Lawson, H.W.	AB	188.478
Leale, P.	AB	191.289
Lynch, J.	AB	178.177
MacKenzie, R.	L/Carp/Crew	340.650
Martin, R.W.	PO2	160.452
Maybank, H.	Pte	Ch8.569
Mayhew, G.	AB	183.442
Maxwell, C.	L/S	158.853
Miller, L.	AB	172.493
Mitchell, H.J.	Pte	Ch8.597
Moir, W.M.	Lieut	
Moore, D.T.	Sergt	Ch3.655
Morrison, J.	AB	189.037
Murphy, J.	Sto	285.342
Newton, P.J.	AB	191.279
Norman, E.S.	Gunr	
Nugent, G.F.E.	Lieut	
Oliver, C.H.	AB	190.897
Ossenton, C.H.	AB	179.210
Parham, A.	Act/PO1	172.446

Pedder, R.	L/S	166.159
Perry, A.F.	L/Shpwrt	166.495
Phillips, E.	AB	188.849
Phippen, C.R.	Pte	Ply4.482
Powell, G.	L/Sto	159.456
Quill, J.	PO2	127.206
Robinson, R.J.	AB	163.004
Rodgers, M.	Arm/Crew	341.452
Rudman, J.N.	2/Yeo/Sig	161.500
Sands, E.S.	AB	177.272
Sayer, J.P.	AB	176.967
Selwood, G.W.	AB	172.175
Snell, C.E.	Yeo/Sig	139.773
Snelling, H.	Pte	Ch8.500
' Spendelow, F.T.	AB	175.053
Stewart, C.J.	AB	189.029
Stretch, F.W.	AB	177.254
Sullivan, F.	AB	186.385
Wakeford, R.H.	PO1	127.230
Walker, A.J.	AB	177.842
Walker, H.	Pte	Ch8.412
Wallace, C.	PO1	121.941
Wand, J.T.	AB	184.990
Warner, C.R.	Pte	Ch5.160
Watson, H.J.	Sto	284.894
Watts, J.A.	Pte	Ch6.631
Webb, C.	Sto	279.517
Webster, T.S.	AB	185.894
Whatley, H.J.	AB	182.552
Whitlock, E.W.	Pte	Ch10.148
Woodward, J.A.	Act/MAA	123.848
Wright, W.	Pte	Ch6.913

Duplicate medals:

Buckland, W.C.	PO2	179.332
Doe, C.	Arm/Mte	340.519
Fuller, A.H.	AB	173.437
Selwood, G.W.	AB	.172.175
' Spendelow, F.T.	AB	175.053
Whatley, H.J.	AB	182.552

Returned medals:

Mehigán, J.	Sto	285.336
Sawyer, A.	Sto	285.972
Weston, W.	AB	182.597

No Bar Medals

Abbott, T.	Sto	172.236
Abella, S.	Sto	195.693
Agins, C.	Ch/Sto	123.077
Ahilalah.	Seedie	
Alcock, E.G.	AB	193.367
Amering, A.	Sto	289.724
Aquilina, A.	Dom	350.037
Bakara.	Seedie	
Bakari.	Seedie	
Baker, C.J.	Sto	280.581
Baldry, G.W.	Sail/Mte	131.385
Bale, E.C.	AB	194.464
Banbury, T.	Sto	147.210
Barnard, J.	Sto	154.063
Barratt, A.	Sto	290.530
Bidgood, J.	Sto	286.607
Bishop, W.N.	AB	190.493
Blake, C.N.	Shpwrt	342.192
Bonno.	Seedie	
Bryett, H.S.	Sto	284.897
Buckingham, W.W.G.	Ch/ERA	131.444
Callus, A.	Dom	357.605
Carroll, M.	Sto	276.802
Catchpole, G.J.	L/Sto	159.450
Cilia, C.	Dom	173.729
Clark, A.R.	PO1	122.977
Clark, R.J.	Sto	279.552
Clements, T.H.	Ord	194.970
Cleveland, H.	St/Payr	
Clohessey, M.	Sto	287.272
Cole, F.E.	Pte	Ch5.124
Coleiro, J.	Dom	355.213
Cooper, F.	L/Sto	153.318
Darmanin, J.	Dom	356.016
Davidson, A.	Sto	278.574
Davies, J.S.	Cook/Mte	340.936
Davis.	Seedie	
Day, F.J.	Bugler	Ch4.903
Daysh, H.J.	Dom	167.700
Denley, W.J.	AB	191.560
Denny, H.M.	Lieut	
Dixon, J.	PO1	126.764
Doherty, E.	Sto	281.577
Eddey.	Seedie	
Ede, H.W.	Ord	193.379
Elkington, G.	Ch/Cook	137.561
Ellul, C.	Dom	357.717
Elvin, W.	L/Sto	154.837
Evans, E.	Sto	284.921
Everest, W.H.	Pte	Ch9.587
Faraizie.	2/Tindal	
Farlowe, J.T.	Sto	151.938
Flaherty, T.	Ch/ERA	141.634
Foster, G.	Sto	289.496
Friend, W.H.	Sh/Std/Asst	341.417
Fryer, A.	Sto	175.763
Fuller, A.D.	Pte	Ch8.583
Gamble, G.	Ord	196.670
Gatt, P.	Dom	356.252
Gibbons, T.	AB	194.204
Gilford, J.	Sto	289.163
Goodwin, W.E.	L/Sto	161.058
Grant, P.	Ord	196.669
Gray, R.F.	Pntr	168.729
Green, H.E.	Carp/Crew	341.787
Hall, W.	L/Sto	155.261
Hammond, C.	ERA	268.265
Handford, W.C.	2/SBStd	350.256
Hardy, E.	L/Sto	159.406
Harrington, E.C.	2/Wrtr	169.591
Harris, E.A.	AB	191.891
Hocking, E.	Plmbr/Mte	341.210
Hoddle, E.	Sto	284.954
Hodge, J.	Sto	154.653

No Bar Medals *continued*

Hopkins, C.	AB	151.565
Horrocks, H.	AB	193.544
Hunt, F.	AB	191.546
Hunter, F.M.	Sto	154.608
Hutchings, P.	AB	187.272
James, W.G.	Sto	279.704
Jardine, H.	Sto	284.922
Joad, G.T.	Q/Sig	188.897
Juma No. 1.	Seedie	
Juma No. 2.	Seedie	
Jurd, J.	Ord	193.377
King, C.	Sto	284.903
Kitchingham, S.	Sto	277.080
Laitt, J.	Boy	194.347
Lake, E.	L/Sto	158.813
Lawson, W.	Sto	290.533
Lewis, H.	AB	198.644
Lilley, F.	Sto	280.923
Lucy, S.	L/Sto	165.983
McDevitt, P.	Sto	149.765
MacKenzie, J.	Carp/Crew	341.773
McKenzie, W.G.	Ord	193.629
MacKsodi.	Tindal	
McNally, H.	Sto	284.515
Mabrook, Ali.	Seedie	
Madden, P.	Sto	285.328
Mahomet.	Seedie	
Mallet, W.H.	Sto	284.895
Mallia, S.	Dom	94.822
Marriage, A.	AB	194.339
Martin, C.	Sto	290.164
Martin, T.	Sto	276.336
Martin, W.R.	PO1	128.628
May, E.	Sto	286.613
Miller, W.J.	Sto	174.432
Monaghan, J.H.	Sto	284.892
Morrison, F.	Asst/Engr	
Murray, W.S.	Ch/ERA	118.646
Muscat.	Seedie	
Muscatt, C.	Cooper	141.795
Mutter, A.R.	Sh/Std	138.992
Nash, P.	AB	192.567
Natali, P.V.	AB	193.312
Neale, W.	Carp	
Norcott, W.	Sto	281.492
Ockleford, R.G.	AB	191.876
Osborne, E.	PO1	109.338
Osborne, J.W.	Act/Ch/Sto	154.089
Osmer, H.	Ch/Sto	145.391
Palmer, W.H.	AB	142.386
Patmore, A.	Sto	284.459
Perkins, G.L.R.	St/Engr	
Perkins, M.	Sto	289.732
Phillips, F.D.	AB	191.582
Pine, W.J.	MAA	113.573
Poppy, H.	AB	188.428
Posener, S.	PO2	167.763
Powell, A.E.	L/Sto	159.491
Ramadan.	Seedie	
Rawlins, H.P.	AB	194.466

Renwick, G.	ERA	268.054
Riley, C.	Sto	284.906
Ripley, C.	ERA	268.201
Roberts, C.K.	Act/Lieut	
Robson, J.	ERA	268.346
Rodo, J.	Dom	356.793
Rogers, W.A.	Ch/Sto	138.553
Sadi.	Seedie	
Sainsbury, H.C.	AB	147.387
Saunders, A.	Engr	
Saunders, T.C.	PO1	163.299
Sedgman, R.	Sto	286.610
Sefton, G.E.	Sto	284.901
Setterfield, W.	Act/Sh/Cpl	151.634
Seymour, H.J.	AB	191.477
Simpson, J.	Pte	Ch8.336
Smith, A.	Sh/Std/Asst	185.037
Smith, R.G.	Sto	284.891
Snipp, E.	Sto	280.313
Soliman.	Seedie	
Spiller, W.	Bosn	
Stafford, J.	Pte	Ch8.781
Stephens, T.	PO2	114.718
Stewart, J.R.	AB	122.110
Stokes, P.	PO1	124.599
Stokes-Rees, W.	Capt	
Strong, C.G.	AB	194.230
Trainer, F.	L/Sto	153.798
Tredwell, J.T.	Sto	176.605
Thompson, C.W.	Ord	193.473
Thompson, W.J.	Sto	284.957
Trickey, F.J.W.	Ch/Sto	151.140
Troughton, F.	L/Sto	154.100
Tyler, F.J.	L/Sto	144.144
Vassallo, L.	Musn (Maltese)	356.796
Vassalo, E.	Dom	151.319
Walsh, M.	Ch/Sto	115.275
Waters, D.	Blksmth	342.002
Watts, H.H.	Q/Sig	188.014
Weekes, H.	ERA	268.560
Wilkins, H.	ERA	152.465
Willson, H.A.	Sto	289.723
Wilson, J.W.	Sto	278.018
Windust, P.G.	Sto	284.512
Woladi.	Seedie	
Woodley, F.G.	AB	193.459
York, J.	Ord	193.314
Young, W.	Ord	190.272

Duplicate medals:

	Abella, S.	Sto	195.693
	Baker, C.J.	Sto	280.581
	Fuller, A.D.	Pte	Ch8.583
x	Goodwin, W.E.	L/Sto	161.058
	Horrocks, H.	AB	193.544
	Lucy, S.	L/Sto	165.983
	Marriage, A.	AB	194.339
	Ockleford, R.G.	AB	191.876
2	Rawlins, H.P.	AB	194.466
	Rodo, J.	Dom	356.793
	Seymour, H.J.	AB	191.477

Vassalo, E.	Dom	151.319

x Two duplicate medals issued.

Returned medals:

Alee, H.	Seedie	
Combo, A.	Seedie	
Lavin, M.	Sto	277.055
Leach, S.	Sto	285.927
Luck, T.	Sto	281.478
Penn, W.	Ord	188.833
Rees, T.V.	Sto	173.601
Revill, W.	Sto	284.908
Sadallah.	Seedie	

BRONZE No Bar Medal

[3] Lunge, H.J.	Interpreter.	

H.M.S. THRUSH

Period for which entitled:
11th January 1900 to 4th September 1900.

Extended period:
23rd March 1901 to 1st January 1902.
1st May 1902 to 31st May 1902.

Bars	*Total*	*Returned*	*Entitled*
2	15	0	15
1	2	2	0
0	99	34	65
	116	36	80

Bars: Cape Colony, South Africa 1901

Binsted, F.	Arm/Mte	340.927
Hogan, P.	L/Sig	125.471
Lobb, F.F.	Surgn	
McCullock, S.A.	Gunr	
Mitchell, A.	AB	170.967
Perry, H.J.	PO1	128.043
Raveney, A.	Pte	Ch6.335
Richardson, A.	PO1	171.617
Steer, S.J.	Pte	Ch8.810
Stephenson, J.H.	Pte	Ch3.548
Vanstone, J.	Sh/Std	168.537
Webb, G.J.	Q/Sig	174.632
Wilson, W.E.	AB	171.482

Bar: Cape Colony

Returned medal:

Morris, R.	Pte	Ch10.413

Bar: Natal

Returned medal:

Brady, J.J.	AB	119.153

No Bar Medals

Amber Feroze.	Seedie	
Beddard, W. alias Johnson.	Ord	196.751
Biss, F.	PO1	115.085
Bolton, F.W.	AB	162.746
Brock, W.	L/Sto	135.006
Broderick, W.J.	AB	167.377
Brown, F.H.	Sto	155.210
Brown, H.	AB	167.221
Brownhill, J.R.	Ord	196.833
Clarke, R.	Ch/Sto	149.745
Combo.	Seedie	
D'Oyly, W.H.	Lieut Comdr	
Dale, J.A.	PO2	161.096
Davison, G.A.	AB	175.175
Down, A.J.	Ord	198.143
Druig, J.	AB	158.352
Drummond, D.	ERA	268.772
Forsdike, W.H.	Pte	Ch7.554
Gardner, C.	Sto	276.134
Gilbert, J.E.	Ord	187.590
Gillard, H.H.	Ord	197.223
Grossmith, F.	AB	171.024
Hanson, F.J.	Cpl	Ch7.683
Hardy, H.	Sto	288.647
Hingston, R.W.	Art/Engr	
Homer, R.H.	PO2	160.808
Hopwood, A.H.	L/S	127.914
Jones, L.T.L.	Lieut	
Kent, R.	Pte	Po9.191
Loveland, W.	L/Sto	152.774
Manton, R.	AB	171.781
Marchington, W.	Pte	Ch10.404
Marsden, L.W.	Ch/ERA	134.411
Melson, A.G.V.	AB	167.759
Millican, F.L.	2/Sh/Cook	159.801
Molina, Jose.	Dom	167.014
Ovenstone, W.	Sto	170.196
Peattie, W.D.	Ord	196.578
Penfold, F.	Pte	Ch5.622
Penfound, E.J.	AB	166.702
Pickett, W.E.	SB/Attn	350.465
Rayner, W.	Ord	187.588
Read, F.	AB	172.675
Resaise.	Seedie	
Richardson, H.	ERA	268.439
Simpson, M.	PO1	123.763
Scully, C.	Sto	170.176
Sparks, F.G.	Ch/Wrtr	155.667
Steele, J.	Sto	161.987
Threadgold, W.	Ch/Sto	140.915
Turner, A.W.	Carp/Mte	149.499
Turner, G.W.	L/Sto	276.092
Ward, W.	Ch/Sto	133.504
Way, W.G.M.	Sub Lieut	
Webb, H.O.	Sto	284.634
Wilson, D.P.	Carp/Crew	343.088

Duplicate medals:

Beddard, W. alias Johnson.	Ord	196.751
Kent, R.	Pte	Po9.191
Manton, R.	AB	171.781

Returned medals:

Abery, F.	Dom	357.897
Ali, Bil.	Seedie	
Bowie, J.R.	Ord	196.890
Cross, J.	PO1	162.412
Daish, A.J.	Pte	Ply8.667
Denning, C.G.	PO1	137.747
Dunbar, J.	Ord	196.343
Freeman, T.	Kroo	
Harris, A.C.	AB	176.453
Hopkins, C.	AB	151.565
Johnson, W.	Dom	
Leahy, W.	AB	154.179
Manning, Jim.	Kroo	
Manny, Jim.	Kroo	
Mendes, J.M.	Dom	170.959
Newman, T.W.	Dom	104.379
Pierira, N.	Dom	358.219
Pointer, G.R.	L/S	161.640
Quinnell, H.	Pte	Po8.830
Reed, A.	Pte	Po8.995
Robey, J.	AB	177.936
Smith, H.	Pte	Ch9.859
Songoro.	Seedie	
Tim, W.	Dom	152.986

EXTENDED PERIOD

Bars: Cape Colony, South Africa 1901

Moir, D.F.	Sub Lieut	
Stares, T.H.	Ord	202.884

Duplicate medal:

Stares, T.H.	Ord	202.884

No Bar Medals

Copus, H.G.	Ord	206.754
Everyday, J.	Kroo	
Garlick, A.H.	Boy	206.751
George, J.	Kroo	
Hobbs, E.E.	Sig	208.053
Hopwood, J.W.	Ord	206.790
Pepple, H.	Dom	360.165
Stapleton, J.	Ch/Wrtr	133.069
Whitfield, C.A.	Pte	Ply9.678

Returned medals:

Blackman, T.	Kroo	
Cole, J.	Kroo	
Cooper, J.	Kroo	
Mascariuhas, F.	Dom	359.760
Mendes, B.	Dom	359.761
Miles, W.	Dom	358.325
Pinto, C.	Dom	353.470
Powell, C.	Ord	206.783
Toby, T.	Kroo	
Two Pound Ten.	Kroo	

H.M.S. WIDGEON

Period for which entitled:
11th October 1899 to 8th March 1901.

Extended period:
9th March 1901 to 5th June 1901.

Bars	*Total*	*Returned*	*Entitled*
1	81	9	72
0	31	12	19
	112	21	91

Note:
[1] Roll states, "Medal and clasp sent to Vernon 19 Dec 03." There is no clasp number indicated in the appropriate column.

Bar: Natal

Adams, W.V.	AB	187.222
Arathoon, H.C.	Surgn	
Barrett, A.C.	AB	182.937
Basting, T.	Cpl	Ply3.979
Blackhall, J.	Ord	185.754
Brown, F.W.	AB	188.236
Buckler, A.J.	Pte	Po7.588
Bunday, S.	PO1	118.037
Burgess, G.	AB	188.397
Colyer, A.J.	Q/Sig	186.278
Couch, A.G.J.	Carp/Crew	340.291
Davis, H.G.	Sto	152.331
Davis, J.	Kroo	
Davison, W.	Act/ERA	269.719
Daw, J.	Kroo	
Dawson, H.F.	Lieut	
Doe, J.	Kroo	
Drewitt, J.J.	L/Sto	154.808
Edhouse, J.	Pte	Ch2.524
Fairhead, J.	L/Sto	173.013
Gifford, R.S.	AB	168.279
Gilbert, O.F.S.	AB	196.361
Gillespie, J.	L/Sig	177.810
Greensmith, O.	Pte	Ply8.200
Greensmith, R.	AB	188.081
Gurney, A.F.	Lieut	
Hanscomb, H.W.	AB	182.102
Hards, F.	AB	184.241
Harfield, J.H.	Ch/ERA	120.406
Harper, W.	AB	172.585
Harris, C.E.	L/Sig	186.240
Harvey, R.T.	Ch/Sto	126.400
Hatchley, G.H.	PO1	122.728
Hickford, F.H.	Pte	Ch8.519
Hill, C.	Ch/Sto	130.773
Hobbs, J.	PO2	173.404
Hurd, W.	L/S	165.790
Ives, J.	AB	185.893
Jarvis, E.	ERA	268.436
Jones, A.E.	AB	184.422
Jones, G.W.	PO1	157.945
Lawrence, W.G.	Engr	
Lecky, H.S.	Sub Lieut	
Lewis, J.	Kroo	
Lynch, J.	Sto	276.440
McAdam, J.	AB	145.229
Marks, R.	Ord	196.518
Marks, R.J.	PO2	170.825
Middleton, H.	Gunr	
Millard, W.H.	AB	166.149
Murphy, J.P.	AB	182.447
Nicholson, F.P.	L/S	173.665
Paterson, A.	Sto	278.236
Porter, G.	Pte	Ply8.175
Rambridge,	Carp/Crew	283.089
Ratcliffe, H.	2/Wrtr	161.220
Richards, L.	Dom	355.000
Rickwood, A.R.	2/SBStd	354.146
Slater, E.J.	Ch/Sto	120.210
Slaughter, H.	AB	170.715
Smart, A.T.	Sh/Std	162.696
Smith, G.P.	Dom	356.000
Stevens, J.	Sto	290.047
Styles, W.	AB	179.208
Thurston, A.E.	L/Sto	276.442
Toby, T.	Kroo	
Tomlinson, J.A.	AB	196.692
Truscott, C.	Sh/Cook	147.965
Turner, J.	AB	160.862
Watts, F.E.	AB	188.210
Williams, J.	Dom	
Woolley, G.F.	Pte	Ch7.925

Duplicate medals:

	Adams, W.V.	AB	187.222
	Burgess, G.	AB	188.397
	Colyer, A.J.	Q/Sig	186.278
	Hanscomb, H.W.	AB	182.102
	Lynch, J.	Sto	276.440
	McAdam, J.	AB	145.229
x	Stevens, J.	Sto	290.047

Tomlinson, J.A.	AB	196.692
Watts, F.E.	AB	188.210

x Two duplicate medals issued.

Returned medals:

Crosscombe, E.	AB	125.101
Donnison, G.W.	Sto	286.970
Dough, J.	Kroo	
Lamont, D.	Arm/Mte	340.513
Norman, E.S.	Gunr	
Peter, T.	Kroo	
Peters, T.	Kroo	
Taylor, H.	Sto	280.622
Williams, J.	Kroo	

No Bar Medals

Barrett, T.	Sto	168.726
Beale, D.	AB	183.179
Beament, J.W.	Ch/Sto	143.959
Bennett, C.W.	Pte	Ch4.780
Brown, H.	Sto	148.319
Clark, P.	Sto	283.922
Forbes, W.	Lieut	
[1] Hampton, T.	PO1	131.324
Jackson, H.	ERA	268.279
M'zee.	Dom	
Outred, P.S.	Pte	Ch6.337
Petts, W.R.	Ch/Sto	114.386
Powell, G.W.	Q/Sig	168.151
Spilsbury, W.	Sto	280.725
Stephens, S.T.	Lieut	
Urquhart, A.	Pntr	165.102
Whitehead, H.E.	Carp/Mte	100.574
Wildman, W.R.	AB	186.126
Woods, H.	PO1	143.404

Returned medals:

Baser, F.	Sto	354.264
Burton, J.W.	Pte	Po8.990
Davis, G.T.	Sto	166.661
Deane, A.	AB	192.514
Edwards, J.	AB	163.409
Edwards, W.G.	AB	179.161
Faint, J.	Sto	284.626
Jacques, S.J.	PO1	148.353
Mendes, J.M.	Dom	170.959
Murphy, T.	Sto	
Radley,	Cpl	Ply6.521
Souza, I. de.	Dom	168.743

H.M.S. JUNO, OPHIR & ST. GEORGE

The following names are taken from Public Record Office File reference WO.100.232. The men listed will be found on the appropriate Roll for the ship indicated, with the exception of Midn G.L. Saurin and Act/Ch/Yeo/Sig A.H. Farnley. These two medals are not included in the analysis of medals on pages 147 and 148.

Notes:
H.M.S. Ophir
[1] "This man's medal was not presented as he was discharged to the shore for misconduct on the 16th March /01."
[2] This man is on the medal roll of H.M.S. Tartar.

H.M.S. JUNO

Barwell, W.	Pte	Po9.471	Monarch
Bowes, J.	L/Sto	153.881	Powerful
Chant, F.G.	Ord	193.151	Powerful
Dowden, F.	Ord	175.472	Powerful
Gooch, J.A.	Ord	159.697	Powerful
Le Quellenec, J.A.	Ord	172.057	Powerful
Spicer, J.G.	Yeo/Sig	125.137	Philomel

H.M.S. OPHIR

Amos, J.E.	Gunr	RMA4.197	Monarch
Banbury, W.	Carp		Niobe
Bath, E.	Gunr	RMA5.509	Powerful
Blackler, E.R.	PO1	138.978	Niobe
[1] Brooks, A.J.	Dom	355.853	Niobe
Bryer, S.M.G.	Engr		Niobe
Coak, G.	PO1	114.036	Niobe
Collins, A.D.	Shpwrt	341.209	Partridge
Crichton-Maitland, C.M.	Lieut		Niobe
Dingle, A.	AB	182.842	Fearless
Dilton, W.	Sto	165.933	Powerful
Elmes, H.J.M.	Pte	Ch11.359	Powerful
Farnley, A.H.	Act/Ch/ Yeo/Sig	147.391	Diadem
Fraser, R.	Gunr	RMA5.265	Monarch
Fuggle, W.J.	PO1	139.794	Powerful
Game, J.	Pte	Ply6.451	Powerful & Doris.
Gosling, J.S.	L/S	158.692	Niobe
Gregson, J.	Sto	278.345	Powerful
Guyatt, F.	Pte	Po7.816	Powerful
Harvey, E.	Gunr	RMA5.641	Powerful
Herring, C.R.	Gunr	RMA4.540	Monarch
Hogan, A.J.	L/S	180.318	Niobe
Holdway, W.	L/Sto	151.709	Fearless
Hutchings, F.	Pte	Ply5.808	Niobe
Killan, T.	Sto	284.177	Powerful
Knight, D.J.	Act/Ch/PO	130.376	Niobe
Land, C.E.	AB	167.357	Powerful
Lee, W.R.	AB	183.137	Fearless
Livingstone, J.	Pte	Ply3.396	Powerful
McCormack, C.	MAA	109.665	Niobe
Martin, J.F.	Sto	142.963	Fearless
Millington, J.	Pte	Ply6.742	Niobe

Musk, W.	2/Yeo/Sig	161.890	Niobe
Norris, J.	Gunr	RMA4.367	Monarch
Raikes, G.L.	Lieut (RMA)		Monarch
Read, W.G.	AB	182.574	Monarch
Ridgway, F.	Act/Cpl	RMA4.260	Monarch
Saurin, G.L.	Midn		Diadem
Smith, A.E.	Sto	282.946	Powerful
Spencer, E.	Sto	158.713	Powerful
Stockley, H.H.F.	Lieut (RMLI)		Niobe
Stone, R.J.	PO1	124.598	Niobe
Stumbles, G.E.	PO2	163.303	Niobe
Taylor, E.	L/Sto	153.866	Fearless
Tildesley, J.H.	Pte	Po7.134	Powerful
Tillman, W.T.	Pte	Po8.266	Powerful
Toms, E.	PO1	133.659	Niobe
Tye, A.C.	Pte	Ch4.569	Monarch
Walker, F.S.	AB	186.955	Tartar
Wemyss, R.E.	Comdr		Niobe
Winsloe, A.L.	Capt		Niobe
Wreford, F.A.	PO1	112.186	Niobe
[2] Wright, H.	AB	179.875	Monarch

H.M.S. ST. GEORGE

Bunker, S.	AB	174.718	Niobe
Carpenter, A.	Ord	187.102	Powerful
Chichester, E.G.	Midn		Powerful
Clarke, C.L.	Ord	166.379	Powerful
Claxton, A.A.	L/Carp/Crew	145.559	Powerful
Coate, J.J.	Sto	183.468	Powerful
Jacobs, W.	Ord	180.568	Powerful
Johncox, E.A.	Ord	190.774	Powerful
Read, W.C.C.	Ord	162.263	Powerful
Stannard, W.P.	Ord	173.522	Powerful
Terry, F.G.	Midn		Niobe
Walker, B.C.	Midn		Niobe

CAPE & TRANSPORT STAFF

Bars	*Total*	*Returned*	*Entitled*
3	1	0	1
2	1	0	1
1	10	0	10
0	35	0	35
	47	0	47

Notes:
[1] The entitlement to the Cape Colony clasp has been queried on the roll. Unlike the other bars sent to the recipients there is no date showing when the bar was despatched.
[2] Reference WO 100/231.

CAPE HOSPITAL
Bar: Cape Colony

Davidson, W.E.	Storekeeper & Cashier
Hill, Rev. A.P.	Chaplain
James, C.	FL/Surgn
Penny, H.L.	Surgn
Richardson, H.A.W.	Fl/Surgn

CAPE VICTUALLING YARD
Bars: Cape Colony, South Africa 1901

Hickman, J.B.	Victualling Staff Officer

Bar: Cape Colony

Edwards, W	Storehouseman
Ford, G.H.	Storehouseman
Lane, C.R.B.	Asst/Vict/St/Off.
Lubbock, J.W.	Storehouseman
Renny, F.t.	Cooper

No Bar Medals

[1] Arnold, H.G.	Dep/Vict/St/Off
Redclift, A.	L/Man of Stores

DOCK YARD & CAPE HOSPITAL
No Bar Medal

Rice, A.C.H.	Chaplain

HARBOUR BOARD OFFICIALS
No Bar Medals

Cape Town

Brown, W.	Tug Capt
Christensen, C.M.	Pilot
Giese, F.	Pilot
Haakensen, B.J.	Berth/Master
Harvey, W.E.	Ch/Sig
Hinman, D.	Pilot
Johnson, A.P.	Tug Capt
Leigh, R.A.	Asst/Port/Capt
Mullins, T.	Tug Capt
Rickson, G.W.	Asst/Sig
Slattery, J.	Tug Capt
Steel, R.D.	Tug Capt
Stephen, W.	Port Capt
Swan, M.	Tug Capt
Wheeler, F.	Sig
White, J.	Asst/Berth/Master

Durban

Barnes, A.	Jnr/Pilot

East London

Barrie, E.C.	Asst/Pilot
Boardman, H.J.	Berth/Master
Jones, J.T.	Head/Pilot
Morison, J.C.	Lighter/Supt

Port Elizabeth

Clift, W.E.	Marine/Supt
Harding, A.C.	Asst/Marine/Supt
Perrott, R.R.	Shore/Supt
Steed, W.	Jetty/Foreman

MISCELLANEOUS
No Bar Medal

Partridge, S.	Sergt	Ply2.908

TRANSPORT STAFF (Not borne on Ship's Books.)
No Bar Medals

Bourchier, H.E.	Comdr
Callwell, W.H.	Lieut
Day, G.	Snr/Wrtr
Hill, J.N.	Comdr
Law, H.D.	Comdr
Pitt, F.J.	Naval/Asst

[2] **Bars: Cape Colony, South Africa 1901**

Hickman, J, Blair.	Sup/V.S.O.

Hickman, J.B.

Roll says, "Specially awarded by the Admiralty as his name did not appear on any roll. The medal was obtained direct from the Mint." This officer's name does in fact appear on the Navy Medal Roll for Cape Victualling Yard.

[2] Bars: Cape Colony, South Africa 1901, South Africa 1902

Price, T.S.	Lieut (RNR)

Roll states, "Attached to Dock Comd at Cape Town."

MARINES LENT TO ARMY, NOT BORNE ON SHIP'S BOOKS

Bars	*Total*	*Returned*	*Entitled*
4	3	0	3
3	9	0	9
2	3	0	3
1	8	0	8
0	9	0	9
	32	0	32

Notes:
(K) These men are also on the medal roll for the King's South Africa Medal.
* Medal presented by H.M. The King.
[1] Reference WO100/231.

Bars: Wittebergen, Cape Colony, Orange Free State, Natal

Wingell, R.	Pte	Ch9.839

Bars: Cape Colony, Orange Free State, Transvaal, Rhodesia

[1] Collard, C.E.	Capt(RMLI)	
Paris, A.	Major	

Bars: Wittebergen, Cape Colony, Transvaal

(K) Hutchison, A.R.H.	Capt	
(K) Simmons, J.J.	Pte	Po4.062

Bars: Cape Colony, Orange Free State, Transvaal

(K) Barnes, G.E.	Capt	
(K) Howard, H.M.	Capt	
(K) Landen, C.H.	Pte	Ch6.906

Bars: Orange Free State, Transvaal, Natal

(K) Clark, J.A.M.A.	Capt	
Higgins, A.E.	Pte	Po3.548
Hurst, F.G.	Pte	Ply4.582
(K) Nelson, F.A.	Lieut	

Bars: Wittebergen, Cape Colony

Aston, G.G.	Major	
(K) Lovett, W.	Pte	Po6.278
(K) White, F.	Major	

Bar: Wittebergen

Cushion, H.	Gunr	RMA4.713

Bar: Cape Colony

* Adair, W.T.	Lieut Col	
Holmes, M.	Pte	Ch9.743
Leefe, J.B.	Lieut Col	
Money, H.C.	Lieut Col	
O'Connor, C.	Pte	Po2.674
Skinner, J.J.	Pte	Ch4.875
Timmins, J.L.	Pte	Ch4.514

Duplicate medal:

O'Connor, C.	Pte	Po2.674

No Bar Medals

Burbidge, G.E.	Gunr	RMA6.611
Cottingham, E.R.	Capt	
Ellis, A.H.	Pte	
Evans, T.J.P.	Lieut Col	
Hood, C.H.	Lieut	
Robertson, C.W.	Capt	
(K) Tanner, H.	Gunr	RMA2.657
Turner, G.	Gunr	RMA2.266
Ward, H.	Pte	Po8.936

ROYAL INDIAN MARINE

Bars	Total	Returned	Entitled
1	8	0	8
0	34	0	34
	42	0	42

Notes:
[1] Commander Holland was Marine Transport Officer (Durban) Indian Contingent from 2/10/99 to 20/10/00 and Divisional Naval Transport Officer (Durban) from October 1900 to April 1901. Three times mentioned in despatches.
[2] Lieut Rowland was Assist. Marine Transport Officer Natal Transport Staff (Indian Contingent) from 2/10/99 to June 1900. He was then transfered to China where he was mentioned in despatches.
[3] These men were the crew of the steam launch.
+ Reference WO100/231.

+ Bar: Natal

[1]	Holland, G.E.	Comdr
[2]	Rowland, A.	Lieut
[3]	Sheikh Jainoo Bawaodeen	2/Syrang
[3]	Sheikh Aboo	1/Lascar
[3]	Sheikh Alli Baba	1/Lascar
[3]	Sheikh Ebrahim	2/Engine Driver
[3]	Mahomed Essoo Mahomed Kassim	1/Sto
[3]	Tajoodeen Dhurmoodeen	1/Sto

No Bar Medals

Goodridge, W.S.	Capt

R.I.M.S. Canning

Acheson-Grey, R.	Lieut
Barnes, J.C.	Gunr
Goldsmith, O.	Lieut
Hamilton, A.H.J.	Sub Lieut
Hutchinson, F.J.B.	Lieut
Jones, B.H.	Lieut
Perrett, C.	3/Clerk
Piffard, A.J.G.	Comdr
Rodriguez, T.	1/Clerk
Thyne, W.K.	Lieut
Wakefield, T.R.	Engr
Walker, R.	Ch/Engr
Wheatley, W.	Asst/Engr
Wilson, C.B.	Asst/Engr
Wood, G.E.	Engr
Yates, J.G.	Engr

R.I.M.S. Clive

Azavedo, P.	1/Clerk
Baugh, G.J.	Comdr
Belton, R.W.	Gunr
Blunt, C.C.	Carp
Bowden, A.St.C.	Lieut
Brumby, W.H.K.	Asst/Surgn
Ellis, J.F.	Engr
Guppy, E.	Asst/Engr
Harold, A.E.	Lieut
Lamb, F.S.	Ch/Engr
Moilliet, H.M.K.	Sub Lieut
Nutter, J.H.	Engr
Reynolds, T.C.	Asst/Engr
Siqueira, A.J.	3/Clerk
Stocken, E.	Lieut
Vibart, J.F.	Sub Lieut
Walker, T.J.	Lieut

NATAL NAVAL VOLUNTEERS

Bars	*Total*	*Returned*	*Entitled*
5	25	0	25
4	2	0	2
3	7	1	6
2	28	3	25
1	73	5	68
0	0	0	0
	135	9	126

Notes:
Medal Rolls to the Natal Naval Volunteers are found both in ADM171.53 and WO100.261. In some instances the entitlement to bars is unclear.
[1] The recipient received a medal for service with the Natal Nl. Med. Corps. This medal was returned to the War Office 26 Jan 1912 with the Defence of Ladysmith clasp only.
[2] Roll states, "Dismissed the force for misconduct.

Bars: Cape Colony, Orange Free State, Transvaal, Defence of Ladysmith, Laing's Nek

[1]	Jordan, R.	Gunr

Bars: Orange Free State, Transvaal, Tugela Heights, Relief of Ladysmith, Laing's Nek

Abbott, J.	Gunr
Ambler, G.	Gunr
Anderton, J.E.	Lieut
Anthony, W.	L/Gunr
Bargate, W.	Gunr
Chisholm, W.	Gunr
Currie, T.	Gunr
Dickens, R.	Gunr
Druce, T.	Gunr
Durno, J.C.	Gunr
Harford, S.	Gunr
Higgins, G.	Gunr
Holt, M.T.	Gunr
Hulme, F.H.	Gunr
James, E.	Gunr
Jewitt, C.	Ch/PO
Johnstone, J.F.	Gunr
Middlebrook, H.	Gunr
Prideaux, T.H.	Gunr
Pye-Smith, F.	L/Gunr
Tamplin, E.H.	Gunr
Trim, A.	L/Gunr
Whitehouse, W.	Gunr
Wilson, H.G.	Gunr

Bars: Orange Free State, Transvaal, Defence of Ladysmith, Laing's Nek

Barrett, N.	Lieut
Thompson, W.	Gunr

Bars: Orange Free State, Transvaal, Laing's Nek

Lucien, R.	Gunr

Bars: Transvaal, Defence of Ladysmith, Laing's Nek

Kenny, D.C.	Sig.
Phoenix, T.	Sig.

Returned medal:

[1]	Fernandez, H.E.	St/Surgn

Bars: Tugela Heights, Relief of Ladysmith, Laing's Nek

Brown, W.	Gunr
Campbell, W.	Gunr
Dowling, E.H.	Gunr

Bars: Tugela Heights, Relief of Ladysmith

Adams, A.S.	Gunr
Appleton, H.	Gunr
Benson, G.V.	Gunr
Bruce, R.G.	PO2
Burford, H.	Gunr
Champion,	Gunr
Chiazzari, N.W.	Lieut
Duke, F.J.	Gunr
Farrell, J.L.	L/Gunr
Fawcett, J.	PO1
Goble, G.D.	Gunr
Hanson, A.	Gunr
Hoyle, J.B.	Gunr
Riddle, D.	Gunr
Roadknight, W.G.	PO2
Robertson, J.	Gunr
Ross, P.	Gunr
Salter, H.J.	L/Gunr
Smith, C.	Gunr
Stafford, A.	Gunr
Stafford, E.	PO2
Steele, J.	Gunr
Wade, J.	L/Gunr
Watkin, J.F.	Gunr
Williams, D.	Gunr

Duplicate medal:

Wade, J.	L/Gunr

Returned medals:

Doyle, R.	Gunr
Hewett, W.	Gunr
Imrie, W.	Gunr

Bar: Defence of Ladysmith

* Adrain, A.	PO2/Bugler
Ballantyne, W.	Carp
Bartlett, J.F.	QM/Sergt
Beaumont, C.L.	PO2
* Bellengere, C.J.	Orderly/Secretary
Bennett, J.	Gunr
Bennett, J.S.	Gunr
Burnett, J.	Gunr
Cairns, T.	Gunr
Clegg, H.C.	Gunr
Cunningham, J.	Gunr
* Deeves, D.	PO2/Sig
Dumaresq, H.N.	Gunr
Duncan, A.	L/Gunr
Dunning, C.R.	Gunr
Ellis-Brown, R.	Gunr
Elston, G.	Gunr
Franklin, G.P.	Musketry/Instructor
Frost, A.	Gunr
Godwin, T.E.	Sig
Gordon, A.	Gunr
Hall, C.	Master/Gunr
Hamilton, J.R.	Gunr
Harmer, G.T.	Gunr
Hatch, W.A.	Gunr
Higgins, M.	Gunr
Hoare, F.	Lieut
Hutcheon, J.	Gunr
Jones, J.	Gunr
Kirsh, H.L.	PO2
Kirsh, R.D.	Gunr
Lawrey, M.	Gunr
Lord, F.	PO1
McDermott, M.B.	Gunr
Marillier, C.K.	Gunr
Oliver, E.P.	Gunr
Pattison, W.	Gunr
Pigg, N.V.	Gunr
Plowright, W.G.	Gunr
Poole, H.	Gunr
Rickerby, J.	Gunr
Rowse, H.B.	Gunr
Russell, J.	L/Gunr
Shearer, W.J.	Gunr
Sivil, F.M.	Gunr
Smith, J.W.	Gunr
Sparnon, E.	Gunr
Strachan, C.	PO2
Strachan, G.	Gunr
Sutherland, A.H.	Gunr
Tatum, G.E.	Comdr
Toppin, R.M.	Gunr
Trim, W.	Gunr
Turner, C.R.	Gunr
Turnley, V.S.F.	Gunr
Velkoop, H.	Gunr
Venner, W.H.T.	Gunr
Wark, W.	Gunr
Winton, D.G.	Gunr

Returned medals:

Flarcus, C.	Gunr
Hamilton, C.G.	Gunr
Kirby, J.	Gunr
Stehn, A.	Gunr

Bar: Relief of Ladysmith

Coleman, W.	Gunr

Bar: Natal

Adcock, C.	Gunr
Francis, E.M.	PO1
Goulding, A.G.	L/Sig
Mackenzie, W.	Gunr
Pike, J.	Gunr
Rainsbury, E.C.	Payr (Hon Capt)
Sinclair, G.D.	Gunr
Wykesmith, A.	PO1

Returned medal:

[2] Powell, J.	Gunr

KING'S SOUTH AFRICA MEDAL

Bars	*Total*	*Returned*	*Entitled*
2	33	0*	33
1	0	0	0
0	0	0	0
	33	0	33

* See Note 1 below.

Notes:
[1] The medal roll states, "Run 9.10.03." unlike the other entries on the roll there is no indication that the medal was ever delivered, so this medal may have been returned to the Mint.
D These recipients are on the Q.S.A. medal roll of H.M.S. Doris.

Bars: South Africa 1901, South Africa 1902

Transport Staff

	Andrews, H.P.	Ch/Wrtr	90.598
D	Barnes, G.H.	Pte	Ch5.072
D	Beresford-Whyte, W.	St/Payr & Secretary	
D	Edge, R.H.	Ch/Wrtr	105.513
D[1]	Gilbert, H.W.	Q/Sig	190.549
D	Hadley, T.	Comdr	
D	Hebbes, W.	Art/Engr	
D	Lacey, S.J.	Ch/Carp	
D	Luscombe, F.St.L.	Capt	
D	Martin, J.	Capt	
D	Perry -Aspenough, S.A.	Comdr	
D	Reypert, C.G.	Bosn	
D	Richardson, J.	Ch/Engr	
D	Shergold, G.	Q/Sig	182.015
	Slater, J.R.	Dom	360.611
	Smith, T.	Sto	165.431
D	Tambling, W.	L/Sto	172.113
D	Thomas, W.J.	1/Wrtr	158.888

Marines serving with the Army

Barnes, G.E.	Capt	
Clark, J.A.M.A.	Capt	
Dunkinson, W.	Pte	Po11.970
Howard, H.M.	Capt	
Hutchison, A.R.H.	Capt	
Landen, C.H.	Pte	Po6.906
Lovett, W.	Pte	Po6.278
Nelson, F.A.	Capt	
Simmons, J.J.	Pte	Po4.062
Tanner, H.J.	Gunr	RMA2.651
White, F.	Lieut Col	

The following men have also been noted as being awarded the K.S.A. Medal on their respective ship's medal rolls:

H.M.S. Doris

Allen, T.	AB	182.639
Lingham, A.	Lieut	
Slater, J.R.	Pte	Ch7.485

H.M.S. Magicienne

Luke, F.R.	Payr	

NAVAL CASUALTIES OF THE BOER WAR

This casualty roll is derived from the following sources:

ADM 171.54 Nominal rolls of men and officers served in South Africa 1899–1900.
WO 100.231
The South African War Casualty Roll 1899–1902, published by J.B. Hayward & Son.

KILLED IN ACTION/DIED OF WOUNDS

	Archer, E.A.	Ord	187.369	Powerful	Ladysmith	13/12/99
	Austin, S.	Ord	187.211	Monarch	Graspan	25/11/99
	Barnes, W.H.	Pte	Po8.371	Powerful	Graspan	25/11/99
	Bennett, A.	Gunr	RMA4.408	Monarch	Graspan	25/11/99
	Boyle, J.	Pte	Ply8.034	Doris	Graspan	25/11/99
	Brown, A.J.	Pte	Po6.258	Powerful	Graspan	25/11/99
	Cartwright, H.T.	Pte	Po7.461	Powerful	Graspan	26/11/99
	Doran, F.	Pte	Ply6.820	Doris	Graspan	28/11/99
	Doyle, F.	AB	184.651	Monarch	Paardeberg	26/02/00
	Egerton, F.G.	Comdr		Powerful	Ladysmith	03/11/99
	Ethelstone, A.P.	Comdr		Powerful	Graspan	25/11/99
	Greagsby, H.	L/Cpl	Po6.960	Powerful	Graspan	25/11/99
	Huddart, C.A.E.	Midn		Doris	Graspan	25/11/99
	Hurst, H.T.	AB	188.362	Monarch	Graspan	25/11/99
	John, G.	AB	181.755	Powerful	Ladysmith	19/01/00
	Leather, J.	Sto	175.883	Powerful	Ladysmith	09/01/00
	Martin, H.W.	Pte	Po6.913	Powerful	Graspan	25/11/99
	Metcalfe, J.H.	Pte	Po8.439	Powerful	Graspan	25/11/99
	Parkinson, J.	AB	171.640	Philomel	Elandslaagte	09/04/00
	Payne, A.G.	AB	146.993	Powerful	Ladysmith	22/01/00
	Plumbe, J.H.	Major (RMLI)		Doris	Graspan	25/11/99
	Radford, F.H.	Pte	Ply7.470	Monarch	Graspan	25/11/99
*	Robertson, C.W.	Capt (RM)		With Army	Kosk's River	21/07/00
	Senior, G.	Capt (RMA)		Monarch	Graspan	25/11/99
†	West, C.W.	PO1	115.157	Forte	Natal	26/04/00
	Wheeler, D.J.	Ord	170.909	Powerful	Ladysmith	23/01/00
	Wilkes, F.	AB	166.872	Philomel	Elandslaagte	09/04/00

† This man died by committing suicide.
* This officer was a Marine serving with the Army and not on a ship's books.

DIED OF DISEASE

Arscott, C.H.	Ord	186.322	Powerful	Ladysmith	05/02/00
Belcher, R.	AB	143.810	Philomel	Modderspruit	21/05/00
Benton, A.W.	AB	175.256	Powerful	Ladysmith	03/02/00
Blake, H.E.	AB	186.745	Powerful	Ladysmith	16/01/00
Blumson, B.	AB	161.843	Powerful	Ladysmith	22/12/99
Boyce, C.	AB	151.746	Powerful	Mooi River	09/04/00
Brock, W.J.	PO1	124.780	Philomel	Poplar Grove	06/03/00
Brodest, G.	AB	134.273	Forte	Durban	09/06/00
Caldwell, A.	Ord	175.748	Powerful	Ladysmith	14/12/99
Coleman, F.A.	AB	131.500	Doris	Simonstown	18/04/00
Dacey, J.	AB	139.228	Monarch	Chieveley	09/05/00
Daniels, W.	Pte	Po9.139	Monarch	Bloemfontein	09/04/00
Dews, H.C.A.	AB	162.220	Terrible	Chieveley	14/04/00

Died of Disease *continued*

Dexter, E.E.	Sig	181.844	Powerful	Ladysmith	20/12/99
Donaldson, J.	L/Cpl	Po7.152	Powerful	Johannesberg	15/06/00
Dunn, E.F.	AB	169.637	Powerful	Ladysmith	13/02/00
Fido, T.	AB	143.807	Monarch	Bloemfontein	17/05/00
Finnimore, A.	PO1	156.160	Powerful	Ladysmith	26/11/99
Fugler, R.J.	PO2	155.812	Terrible	Durban	04/05/00
Gardner, H.W.G.	Sto	282.698	Powerful	Ladysmith	01/03/00
Gould, G.L.	AB	176.069	Terrible	At sea	02/05/00
Hannifin, T.	PO2	148.100	Powerful	Ladysmith	03/03/00
Harris, R.	AB	160.850	Powerful	Ladysmith	07/01/0
Haylett, J.W.	AB	170.005	Tartar	Natal	25/02/00
Hill, J.	AB	185.614	Barrosa	Kimberley	14/03/00
Holloway, W.	Gunr	RMA4.520	Monarch	Bloemfontein	08/05/00
Hook, J.E.	Ord	190.966	Doris	Bloemfontein	10/05/00
Hopkins, J.	Sig	189.755	Terrible	Durban	25/02/00
Horner, E.B.	PO2	183.747	Terrible	Frere	05/02/00
Hughes, W.H.	Gunr	RMA6.512	Monarch	Kimberley	28/03/00
Izzard, H.	Pte	Ch9.084	Monarch	Bloemfontein	19/05/00
Johnson, F.	Arm/Crew	340.131	Powerful	Intombi	19/03/00
Kay, W.H.F.	Fl/Payr		Powerful	At sea	26/03/00
Knott, G.	PO2	145.624	Powerful	Ladysmith	26/02/00
Lister, H.A.	AB	159.658	Powerful	Ladysmith	02/02/00
Lloyd, L.R.E.	Midn		Doris	Kimberley	27/04/00
Lockett, W.	Sto	172.988	Doris	Bloemfontein	25/04/00
Menzies, J.	Midn		Doris	Bloemfontein	18/05/00
Minshaw, C.E.	Ord	182.623	Powerful	Ladysmith	25/02/00
Moat, E.T.	AB	169.955	Monarch	Orange River	20/03/00
Musgrove, A.	AB	166.323	Powerful	Ladysmith	12/03/00
Newell, B.	AB	168.097	Powerful	Ladysmith	17/12/99
Newman, H.	Pte	Ch6.207	Powerful	Ladysmith	05/02/00
O'D'Grainey, P.	AB	165.513	Philomel	Durban	20/11/99
Pannifer, H.W.	Ord	186.287	Powerful	Ladysmith	10/03/00
Paton, D.H.	Sto	282.960	Powerful	Ladysmith	05/03/00
Payne, W.	PO1	113.108	Philomel	At sea	25/04/00
Perkis, H.R.	AB	167.827	Terrible	Mooi River	22/04/00
Phillips, W.J.T.	2/SBStd	156.715	Doris	Simonstown	19/03/00
Robertson, S.	Midn		Doris	Modder River	25/02/00
Roche, F.C.	AB	156.220	Monarch	Modder River	04/03/00
Rolls, A.P.	Sto	282.713	Powerful	Chieveley	07/04/00
Seares, G.	Sto	279.770	Powerful	Ladysmith	24/12/99
Siggins, A.	AB	163.800	Tartar	Estcourt	15/04/00
Smith, F.G.	AB	174.665	Terrible	Durban	31/03/00
Stabb, E.	Lieut		Powerful	Ladysmith	15/01/00
Stewart, J.	AB	179.172	Powerful	Simonstown	12/04/00
Thomas, G.	AB	183.228	Terrible	Estcourt	04/01/00
Trevett, H.	Ord	175.300	Powerful	Ladysmith	06/01/00
Tribe, W.	L/S	169.393	Powerful	Ladysmith	26/12/99
Triggs, F.C.	PO1	143.439	Powerful	Ladysmith	21/02/00
Truesdell, W.W.	PO1	147.740	Powerful	Ladysmith	19/01/00
Wells, L.	Dom	357.083	Doris	Bloemfontein	23/04/00
White, J.S.	Act/Arm/Mte	340.450	Powerful	Ladysmith	15/01/00
Whitehead, J.	Sto	281.040	Monarch	Bloemfontein	05/05/00
Winning, F.	Gunr	RMA7.171	Monarch	Bloemfontein	29/03/00
Wise, M.W.	AB	152.069	Doris	Pretoria	04/07/00
Wolfe, W.A.	PO2	148.136	Powerful	Chieveley	08/04/00

TAKEN PRISONER

Connor, C.	AB	142.561	Tartar	Frere	15/11/99
Hickin, F.	Pte	Ply4.406	Powerful	Roodeval	07/06/00

Holt, T.	Pte	Ply5.738	Powerful	Roodeval	07/06/00
Moog, G.	AB	138.019	Tartar	Frere	15/11/99
Reed, E.J.	AB	187.682	Tartar	Frere	15/11/99
Thompson, W.	AB	160.621	Tartar	Frere	15/11/99

WOUNDED IN ACTION

Adams, A.	Pte	Po7.232	Monarch	Graspan	25/11/99
Allchin, G.	Gunr	RMA3.736	Monarch	Graspan	25/11/99
Amos, F.	Pte	Ply7.429	Doris	Graspan	25/11/99
Ashard, E.G.	Gunr	RMA5.666	Monarch	Graspan	25/11/99
Bartlett, G.A.	Pte	Po8.527	Powerful	Graspan	25/11/99
Bath, E.	Gunr	RMA5.509	Powerful	Graspan	25/11/99
Beesley, S.R.	Gunr	RMA5.518	Powerful	Graspan	25/11/99
Blades, W.B.	AB	184.295	Monarch	Graspan	25/11/99
Braco, C.D.	Pte	Ply7.997	Doris	Graspan	25/11/99
Brinklehurst, E.	Pte	Ch8.623	Monarch	Graspan	25/11/99
Brown, C.F.	Gunr	RMA5.052	Monarch	Graspan	25/11/99
Brown, W.J.	Gunr	RMA3.283	Monarch	Graspan	25/11/99
Bull, W.	Pte	Ch10.083	Monarch	Graspan	25/11/99
Burroughs, E.	L/Sergt	RMA4.281	Monarch	Graspan	25/11/99
Bussey, R.	Pte	Ch8.313	Monarch	Graspan	25/11/99
Caplen, A.	Pte	Po6.679	Powerful	Graspan	25/11/99
Clark, W.	Gunr	RMA4.068	Monarch	Graspan	25/11/99
Cokayne, F.G.	Pte	Ply7.695	Doris	Graspan	25/11/99
Colderick, J.E.	Pte	Ply6.426	Powerful	Graspan	25/11/99
Coles, A.	Pte	Ply6.349	Doris	Graspan	25/11/99
Collicott, J.	Pte	Ply4.116	Doris	Graspan	25/11/99
Collinson, C.H.	Pte	Po7.793	Doris	Graspan	25/11/99
Cotton, H.	Pte	Po6.872	Monarch	Graspan	25/11/99
Creasey, W.J.	Pte	Ply7.959	Doris	Graspan	25/11/99
Cunnington, G.R.	Gunr	RMA3.444	Monarch	Graspan	25/11/99
Davis, A.	Pte	Ply8.058	Doris	Graspan	25/11/99
DeHorsey, S.V.Y.	Comdr		Monarch	Pretoria	04/06/00
Dentry, J.	Pte	Ply6.475	Powerful	Graspan	25/11/99
Dowland, S.	Pte	Po8.384	Powerful	Graspan	25/11/99
Dyson, G.H.	Col/Sergt	RMA1.478	Monarch	Graspan	25/11/99
Edgson, W.H.	Sergt	Ch2.774	Monarch	Graspan	25/11/99
Elmes, H.J.M.	L/Cpl	Po5.719	Powerful	Graspan	25/11/99
				& Roodeval	07/06/00
Emly, J.	AB	159.638	Powerful	Ladysmith	30/10/99
Ford, W.J.	L/S	149.587	Powerful	Ladysmith	30/10/99
Foster, A.	Gunr	RMA5.942	Monarch	Graspan	25/11/99
Freeman, H.	Pte	Ch8.588	Monarch	Graspan	25/11/99
Gasson, W.	Sergt	Ply4.001	Powerful	Graspan	25/11/99
Gill, G.	Sergt	RMA4.335	Monarch	Graspan	25/11/99
Goat, A.	Pte	Po6.813	Powerful	Graspan	25/11/99
Gosling, A.E.C.	Gunr	RMA4.948	Monarch	Graspan	25/11/99
Greenfield, J.H.	Col/Sergt	Ply2.901	Doris	Graspan	25/11/99
Hall, A.H.	Pte	Po8.417	Powerful	Graspan	25/11/99
Hayden, T.	AB	187.911	Monarch	Graspan	25/11/99
Hinton, F.J.	L/S	176.876	Doris	Graspan	25/11/99
Holland, W.C.	Act/Sergt	Po6.481	Powerful	Graspan	25/11/99
Hughes, T.J.	Pte	Ply6.379	Powerful	Graspan	25/11/99
Isern, H.R.	Pte	Ch6.359	Powerful	Graspan	25/11/99
Johnson, W.G.	Pte	Po8.884	Monarch	Graspan	25/11/99
Jones, H.	AB	140.282	Doris	Graspan	25/11/99
Jones, T.	Pte	Po7.004	Doris	Graspan	25/11/99
Jones, W.T.C.	Capt (RMLI)		Doris	Graspan	25/11/99
Kelleher, J.	Gunr	RMA5.527	Powerful	Graspan	25/11/99

Wounded in Action *continued*

Kemp, E.	Pte	Ch4.981	Monarch	Graspan	25/11/99
Knox, D.	Gunr	RMA4.339	Monarch	Graspan	25/11/99
Leach, D.	Sergt	Ch4.216	Monarch	Graspan	25/11/99
Lewis, F.C.	L/Cpl	Po6.371	Powerful	Graspan	25/11/99
Livingstone, J.	Pte	Ply3.396	Powerful	Graspan	25/11/99
Mabbett, F.	Pte	Po7.273	Powerful	Graspan	25/11/99
McShane, G.	AB	167.019	Monarch	Graspan	25/11/99
Martin, E.	Gunr	RMA6.111	Monarch	Graspan	25/11/99
Miller, J.E.	Pte	Ch7.086	Powerful	Graspan	25/11/99
Mole, C.	Gunr	RMA5.047	Powerful	Graspan	25/11/99
Moon, F.	Ch/PO	100.623	Doris	Graspan	25/11/99
Morcambe, W.	Gunr	RMA5.335	Monarch	Graspan	25/11/99
Murphy, J.P.	AB	191.090	Doris	Graspan	25/11/99
Nail, J.F.	Ord	172.445	Powerful	Ladysmith	30/10/99
Norris, J.	Gunr	RMA4.367	Monarch	Graspan	25/11/99
O'Brian, W.	Bugler	Ply8.458	Doris	Graspan	25/11/99
				& Paardeberg	24/02/00
Pape, B.H.	Gunr	RMA3.889	Monarch	Graspan	25/11/99
Parritt, E.	PO1	153.971	Doris	Graspan	25/11/99
Peacock, H.	Pte	Ply4.811	Powerful	Graspan	25/11/99
Percival, J.R.	Pte	Po8.547	Powerful	Graspan	25/11/99
Perkins, C.	Gunr	RMA2.506	Powerful	Graspan	25/11/99
Piper, C.T.	Pte	Po6.935	Powerful	Graspan	25/11/99
Pitters, E.A.	Pte	Po8.385	Doris	Graspan	25/11/99
Prothero, R.C.	Capt		Doris	Graspan	25/11/99
Rawlings, C.	Pte	Ply6.450	Powerful	Graspan	25/11/99
Rigsby, F.T.	Pte	Ply5.157	Monarch	Graspan	25/11/99
Sheen, C.C.	Engr		Powerful	Ladysmith	06/01/00
Simons, J.	Pte	Ch9.995	Monarch	Graspan	25/11/99
Spencer, W.F.	Gunr	RMA5.866	Monarch	Graspan	25/11/99
Steele, J.T.	Pte	Po8.886	Monarch	Graspan	25/11/99
Stockman, G.C.	AB	189.408	Doris	Graspan	25/11/99
Stubbs, H.C.	Gunr	RMA5.329	Monarch	Graspan	25/11/99
Thompson, B.	Ord	188.486	Monarch	Graspan	25/11/99
Tilley, T.J.	AB	188.352	Doris	Graspan	25/11/99
Tillman, W.T.	Pte	Po8.266	Powerful	Graspan	25/11/99
Tribbeck, W.C.	Pte	Ply7.958	Doris	Graspan	25/11/99
Vass, A.	Pte	Ch8.303	Monarch	Graspan	25/11/99
Waghorn, W.	Pte	Ch9.153	Doris	Graspan	25/11/99
Weingaerton, B.	Gunr	RMA5.506	Powerful	Graspan	25/11/99
Wilson, L.O.	Lieut (RMLI)		Monarch	Belfast	27/08/00

Table 1. Summary of Q.S.A. medals.

Ship/Unit	Number of Bars										Total	Returned	Entitled
	0	1	2	3	4	5	6	7	8	Unknown			
Barracouta	262	1	36	19							339	21	318
Barrosa	102	31	1	7	17						194	36	158
Beagle	110	0	17								139	12	127
Blanche	155	5	13								216	43	173
Doris	346	183	28	31	67	16	9	33	5		804	86	718
Dwarf	176										286	110	176
Fearless	145										151	6	145
Forte	415	122	9	1	4	23					683	109	574
Gibraltar	617	4									673	52	621
Magicienne	230	6									256	20	236
Magpie	75	13	1								95	6	89
Monarch	812	58	37	31	18	18	50	39	17	11	1262	171	1091
Naiad	133	0	117								274	24	250
Niobe	530	129	1								755	95	660
Partridge	150	8	3								174	13	161
Pearl	189	0	14								230	27	203
Pelorus	215	13	1								249	20	229
Philomel	152	30	17	3	3	24	1				269	39	230
Powerful	415	308	13	5	28	19	2	16	2		898	90	808
Racoon	176	2									208	30	178
Rambler	110										145	35	110
Rattler	76										86	10	76
Redbreast	83										87	4	83
Sappho	254	0	1								274	19	255
Sybille	187	80	5								312	40	272
Tartar	103	59	9	4	1	18	1				237	42	195
Terpsichore	136	0	137								313	40	273
Terrible	538	273	261	13	0	1					1147	61	1086
Thetis	183	101	1								297	12	285
Thrush	65	0	15								116	36	80
Widgeon	19	72									112	21	91
Cape & Transport Staff	35	10	1	1							47	0	47
Marines serving with Army	9	8	3	9	3						32	0	32
Royal Indian Marine	34	8									42	0	42
Natal Naval Volunteers	0	68	25	6	2	25					135	9	126
TOTAL	7237	1592	766	130	143	144	63	88	24	11	11537	1339	10198

Table 2. Summary of Q.S.A bars.

Ship/Unit	Belmont	Modder River	Paardeberg	Driefontein	Johannesburg	Diamond Hill	Belfast	Wittebergen	Relief of Kimberley	Cape Colony	Orange Free State	Transvaal	Rhodesia	Tugela Heights	Defence of Ladysmith	Relief of Ladysmith	Laing's Nek	Natal	South Africa 1901	South Africa 1902	TOTAL
Barracouta										55									25	50	130
Barrosa			25	24						56		17									122
Beagle										17									17		34
Blanche										18									13		31
Doris	129	109	152	149	44	54	50		13	222	13	46		1		1	1	14	6	1	1005
Dwarf																					0
Fearless																					0
Forte										2	25	28		32		37	28	120		2	274
Gibraltar										4											4
Magicienne										3								3			6
Magpie										14									1		15
Monarch	116	100	170	168	120	118	107	1	27	146	8	1		5		5	1	1	1	1	1096
Naiad										117									117		234
Niobe										129			1							1	131
Partridge										6			5						3		14
Pearl										14										14	28
Pelorus										1								13	1		15
Philomel			2	1	2	2	2			2	27	30		41		41	30	30	1		211
Powerful	110	79	71	69	21	20	18		21	5	1			3	275	3					696
Racoon																		2			2
Rambler																					0
Rattler																					0
Redbreast																					0
Sappho										1									1		2
Sybille										85									4	1	90
Tartar						4	5			47	20	19		26		29	20	18	1		189
Terpsichore										137									137		274
Terrible										45	2	1		274	1	292	1	223			839
Thetis										1								101	1		103
Thrush										15									15		30
Widgeon																		72			72
Cape & Transport Staff										12									2	1	15
Marines serving with Army								7		18	10	11	2					5			53
Royal Indian Marine																		8			8
Natal Naval Volunteers										1	28	30		52	64	53	33	8			269
TOTAL	355	288	420	411	187	198	182	8	61	1173	134	183	8	434	340	461	114	618	346	71	5992

Flowers for a Girl

Plant Medicine and Sexual Trauma

by

Amanda Dilday

For Steven

Thank you for (still) loving me.

[with gratitude]

We were not meant to walk alone.

Along the way, our companions may not be quite who we expect they will be or want them to be, but in the end, they are always who we need them to be. This is true. Yet, on my path, I have not been disappointed. My companions have far exceeded all my expectations. They have been gentle, wise, kind, and full of compassion. I have been blessed, and desire to return the blessing.

Here, I offer this small beginning . . .

My hand rests over my heart, and I bow in humble thanks to the teachers and healers and friends who have walked with me, and at times, carried me along the way.

To each of you: may God abundantly bless you, cause His face to shine upon you, and give you peace both now and evermore. Amen.

Kyung Lee, Teresa Boardwine,
Matthew Wood, Katie Higson, Carey Chapman,
Deb Vail, Renee Dann, Amy Bowling,
and precious Steven.

[introductions]

Teresa Boardwine (www.greencomfortherbschool.com)
Washington, Virginia

My first and dearest teacher, Teresa introduced me to the plants, and she introduced me to Matthew. When I began to remember, Teresa was the one who was able to push into the memory. She was first the person I called and asked, *What do I do?* Teresa has ever and always shown me kindness, love, and compassion. Like no one else, she has both believed me and believed *in* me. Inside her magical yurt, she (unknowingly) gathered my healers, and inside her magical yurt, my healing began. In this book, it is she and her students who will drop tinctures on my wrists and whisper the names of plants to me.

Steven Dilday

My precious husband. How patient he has been. In these pages, he is the one who holds my hair, holds the phone, and holds sweet Ruby, our tiniest tiny. He has been my constant companion. Humanly speaking, I owe my life to him. He is my person.

Katie Higson
Cumberland, Maryland

A gentle healer trained in craniosacral therapy, Katie's touch and medicine defy definition. Throughout the book, it is Katie who asks me, *What do you see? What do you feel?*, and it is Katie who places her hands here and there, guiding me. I am forever grateful for the safe space she created and held for me. Without Katie, there is no book.

Matthew Wood (www.matthewwoodherbs.com)

Green Man, Gentle Bear, Matthew is a renowned and revered herbalist and author. *Does he need an introduction?* His spirit is kind and gentle, old and wise, deep and strong. It is said, *When the student is ready, the teacher comes*. And he did—just for me. I don't believe Matthew knows how significant his simple presence has been in my healing. He has held space, visited my dreams, taught me, encouraged me, accepted me, and most especially, been kind.

Deb Vail (www.sacredliving.net)
Zionville, North Carolina

A flower whisperer, Deb makes beautiful, gentle, powerful plant medicine. Held by the mountains, she offers holistic/ spiritual counseling. Matthew introduced me to Deb—who introduced me to Rue. It is Deb who wrote to me, saying, *Friend, you need a feather.* In Rue, Deb gave me a gift, and now, I give it to you.

FOREWORD

This is not a protocol or a prescription. Rather, it is something of a memoir, a healing memoir, an herbal memoir. A story.

It is the story of my pain, my path, my healing, and my medicine. Your pain, your path, your story, and your medicine will be different. But, I suspect, along the way, we will call to one another. I will stand at one edge of the night, and you will stand at the other. One of us will call, *Are you there? I am here.* And the other will respond, *I am here. Are you there?* With whispering echoes, we will make sure of one another.

And along the way, plants will call to us. I am sure of it.

Plants heal us. They ache to place their petals and leaves on our tender places. Yes, they soothe our scrapes and dissolve our bruises, but they also mend our very deepest wounds—the wounds which cannot be seen with human eyes, or touched with human hands. They touch our truest selves. They touch spirit. They touch soul. Healing is their purpose—and their pleasure.

The leaves of the tree are for the healing of the nations.

The healing of the people.

May you be healed—your heart comforted and loved. May your soul find all its pieces, and in their coming together, may you be made whole again—and anew. In dying, may you live. Along the way, may you never be alone, but always held by gentle hands and strong embraces. In the Dark, may you see Light. And may you find your way home.

This is my path. This is my story.
This is my medicine, and I offer it to you.

CONTENTS

Someone I loved once gave me a box full of darkness.
It took me years to understand that this, too, was a gift.

~ Mary Oliver ~

My hand is weary from writing . . .

O Lord, may it be your wisdom, not
my folly, which passes through my arm
and hand; may your words take shape
upon the page.

For when I am truly
faithful to your dictation,
my hand is firm and strong.

Let me never write words that are
callous or profane;
let your priceless
jewels shine upon these pages.

A Celtic Prayer, "The Scribe"

From the beginning, I knew I would tell.
I knew I would write myself into the light.

FLOWERS FOR A GIRL

BEFORE BEGINNING

Send forth your light and your truth;
let them be guides to me.

Psalm 43:3

My father sexually abused me.

And as strange as it may sound, for many, many years, I forgot. I didn't remember, couldn't remember, didn't want to remember—*that*.

But I did remember other things, like riding in the back of his blue Ford pick-up truck. The Eagles, BeeGees, and Bob Seger making music on the radio. Charred burgers, blue jean cut-offs, and a rusted, red grill. Heinz ketchup and American cheese.

I remember the cool, damp concrete porch of our little house on Broad Street, its gray paint, scratched and peeling, and the scruffy lawn littered with smoldering, discarded butts of Marlboro Lights, man-made fireflies sleeping among the plantain and white clover.

I remember a whitewashed cinderblock fence—my dad's summer seat of choice as he strummed his guitar, jotted down lyrics and chords on a yellow legal pad, and dreamed of making it big. (He did once—sort of. A Nashville radio station played one of his songs. The framed royalty receipt hung in the hallway by the bathroom door. Three dollars and seventy cents? Something like that.)

I remember him singing "You Are My Sunshine".

You are my sunshine,
my only sunshine.
You make me happy
when skies are gray.
You'll never know, dear,
how much I love you.
Please don't take
my sunshine away. . .

When I think of him, remember him, I see his bare feet, faded Levi's, yellowed smoker's fingers, bony knuckles, and a certain way he held his head when he laughed—and when he wondered. I smell cigarette smoke, incense, Old Spice, and Brut aftershave. I drink a root beer and suck on a Cert, strum a guitar and gaze at the stars.

That's what I did remember. But I didn't remember *it*.

I don't need to explain the forgetting—or the remembering. Other people, other books, do that. All I can say is this: you forget so you won't die. And you remember so you can finally live.

When I first began to remember, one of the images I saw of my father was from an old Polaroid shot. My father stands under a water tower on the top of a Tennessee mountain. He wears an old, brown, suede vest. The vest has mother-of-pearl buttons. The wind is blowing. (I can feel it.) It catches his hair. In true seventies style, his glasses are too big, too round, too brown, and too dark. But he smiles and seems happy. He is young, and it is autumn. Behind him, the trees are almost bare, and the brush is brown.

When I saw him, I loved him. I loved who he was before he did what he did. Chose what he chose. And I blessed him, thanking him for all the things he had given me: the wildflower meadows and dogwood mountains of Mendota, the autumn sun and summer creeks, pen and paper, words and spirit, a name and a song, and most especially (and unexpectedly), I thanked him for my Indian grandmother, the daughter of a Choctaw chief.

ai-nei-chi-hoyo
A woman to be preferred above all others.

I do not write what I remember to hurt him. Or to hurt others. I write what I remember so that I—and others—might heal.

I write so that we might live.

8

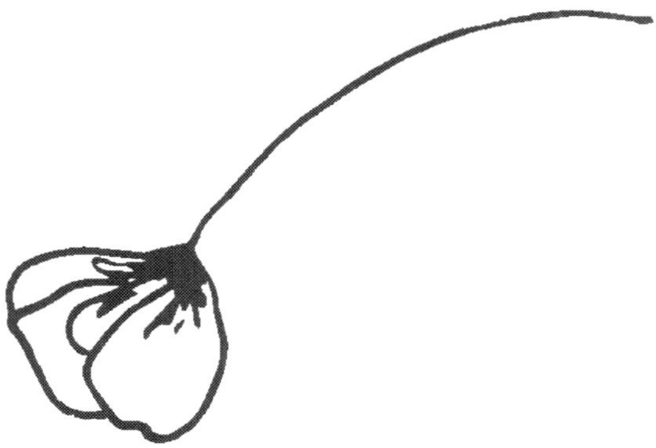

Once, I was small. I played on the playground and hung from the monkey bars. I made snow angels and clover crowns, climbed trees and jumped fences. A water baby swimming with the fishes, I spent every summer immersed in the pool. Playing in the mud, I baked in the sun until my skin was an ancestral brown.

I sipped honeysuckle nectar, drank from the hose, ran barefoot, and spit watermelon seeds. I read books and pretended to be . . .

On Saturday nights, I took a bath, and she rolled my hair. On Sunday mornings, my feet slipped into black patent leather shoes. I sung in the choir, knelt at the altar, gave the right hand of fellowship, passed the plate, and raised my hand for prayer.

Yes, sister, I see that hand.

I grew up, went to school, went to work, went to college. And in time, I graduated, fell in love, married, and became a mother.

And it was good. And I was blessed. I was fed, clothed, taught, and loved. I laughed. I played. I grew up.

I do want to say that it was good. What I remembered was good.

But what I didn't remember—what I chose to forget . . .

There are gaps—lost years and dark corners. There are rooms that, when I try to hold them in my mind, lose their shape. Their walls and corners simply fade.

In my mind, there is no bed in my bedroom. But there is carpet, coarse and frayed—its rough loops, black and dark blue. There are Raggedy Ann curtains sewn by my mother, thin attempts to block the beady, peering eyes of our neighbor, Mrs. R.

There are no toys, but there are books. Golden Books. Preciously kept in a small, plastic crate.

I can see my mother cooking, crying, vacuuming, sewing. But I rarely see him. He is only there—in the house—for a moment, smoking a cigarette, tickling my feet, waking from a nap, arguing with her.

Once, after I began remembering, I had a dream. In the dream, I walked every inch of the enormous, brick building that was my elementary school. Square inch by square inch, I turned every corner, climbed every stair, inspected every closet, twisted every knob, visited every classroom, walked every hall, looked out every window. I stepped on every green and brown tile. *Boys on brown; girls on green.*

(Who knew a building could breathe and live inside you? Oh, I write about it now and my heart aches for it.)

In my heart, I see the face of every teacher and every friend. Sadly, of the lost years, I see *only* the faces—nothing more. Miss M., my second grade teacher, has red hair and is warm, and always smiling. She always smiles and loves the color orange. Mrs. R., my third grade teacher, wears a black and white checkered skirt, full and flouncy to the floor. With porcelain skin and bobbed, black hair, she sits in a rocking chair and reads books

to us. Her son's name is Colin. That is all I have of those missing years. There are classrooms. I could take you to the doors, but I cannot walk inside them. There are no desks, no lessons, no fellow classmates. There are only these two, enduring images—impressions of the women who, I think, kept me alive.

Apologies

I see my dad.
He is sitting on my bed, and I am sitting on his lap.

There is nothing around us. No ceiling, no walls, no floor, no windows. We are suspended in space. Suspended in time.

He is crying. And I feel no sympathy, or compassion, or fear.
I feel nothing. Not even my heart.

He says, *I'm so sorry, Amanda. I'm so sorry.*
Do you forgive me?

His head is bowed, and he seems so sad.

And still, I feel nothing. Say nothing.
I do not love him. I am not angry with him.
I simply watch him.
I don't seem to know why he is sorry.

Do you love me? No matter what I do, will you always love me?,
he asks and pleads, tears streaming down his cheeks.

I do not move. I do not hug him. I do not take his hand or wipe his tears. I only slowly and silently shake my head, up and down, up and down.

Yes

Why is he asking me this? I am confused.

It is confusion, the preacher reads aloud.
Their nakedness thou shalt not uncover.
He is thy father.
The land is defiled.
It is confusion.

I listen closely. I've never heard a sermon on incest. Do preachers preach sermons on incest? Are sermons like this necessary? Does this need to be said? Need to be clarified?

It is confusion.

While vacuuming the carpet, an image flashes before me. I catch my breath. *Where did that come from?* Disgusted and disturbed, I shake my head, say a prayer, and try to clear my mind.

The next day, another image comes. And another. They are vulgar, and they make me feel ashamed. They occasion questions: *How would I know? Why would I see that? Is something wrong with me?*

I ask my husband to pray for me. I do not tell him what I am seeing.

I do not suspect my father. I think it is me. I need to change: read more Scripture, say more prayers, guard my heart, take thoughts captive.

Another image flashes.
It is confusion.

JOURNEYING WITH PLANTS

. . . every plant is a process, a story, an image . . .
Matthew Wood

Violet

That quiet place inside of her was getting louder and louder.
J. Hill

My eyes are closed. I am at ease, sitting in a comfy chair inside a warm, rustic yurt. The ladies, the wise herbalists, drop the tincture onto my wrist.

A perfectly round, lavender, light-filled ball forms at the base of my throat. I can't help it: a soft, gentle, joy-filled smile lifts the corners of my lips, softening my cheeks. I don't know which herb has been dropped and draped across my wrist, but I love how she makes me feel.

I love the ball of light she forms and places in the deep darkness at the base of my throat.

Violet. The herb was violet, they say. And without warning, a burst of child-like laughter rises from my heart, knocks open my lips, and tumbles with delight into the world.

Perfect!, I think. *Simply perfect!* Of course, small, simple violet would reveal her luminous self and her soothing ways by gathering her skirts in my throat. She loves this part of me.

And I love her: ball of lavender light, illuminating the darkness.

I am on our bed. The sheets are a tangled mess. I have twisted them in my frantic, fearful attempt to crawl away from whatever,

from whoever, is touching me.

Something's wrong. Something's wrong. Something's wrong. I say again and again. *Turn on the light! Turn on the light!*

My hands cover my eyes, and I am frozen in fear.

Are you okay?, he asks. *Are you all right? What's happening?*

I cannot answer.
I cannot breathe.
I cannot fill my lungs.
I suck the air into my mouth, direct it down and into my throat, but it will not fill my lungs.
It cannot reach them.
There is a line, an invisible line, and it has cut me in two.
There is only thick darkness where my lungs should be. They will not fill. Something is blocking them. Something has emptied them. Severed them.

I cannot breathe.

And then, I feel it. A small, hard pit sits at the base of my throat. A weighted pebble. It is choking me. A stopper, dense and black as ink, deflecting the air I am trying so desperately to give my lungs.

What is that? Why can't I swallow it? Why won't it go down?
Move!, I silently scream. *Move!*

And then, I remember her: Violet.
And in an urgent whisper, I say to my husband, *Violet. Get Violet!*
He rushes from our bedroom and into the hallway.

I don't understand what is happening to me. But I recognize her. I know her.

Wide-eyed and worried, my husband returns and kneels beside the bed, the violet-filled dropper in his hand. *How many drops?*, he asks. I have no breath with which to answer. So, I open my

mouth and lift my tongue.

He drops cool, sweet orbs of violet onto my lips. Into my mouth. My lips close. My eyes shut. And the pit slips away. Disappears.

My throat opens. Expands.
And life-giving air rushes into my lungs.

Shaken and afraid, yet full of wonder, my timid heart attempts to smile, remembering how Violet introduced herself so many months ago. She knew I would need her. She knew this was coming.

She touched my wrist, explored my heart, tapped my throat, and discovered a hidden something—something needing to be said. Something needing to escape.

Bless you, ball of lavender light, illuminating the darkness, showing the way up and out and into the world.

I vomit into the bucket.
Bile burns my throat and smears my lips.
My stomach lurches, viciously heaving in its determination to empty itself. Empty me.

I have been vomiting, the room has been spinning, for hours.

I cannot lift my head or open my eyes. I can barely speak. Barely breathe. There is hardly anything left of me. And yet, the pit remains. It sits at the back of my throat, having travelled from its starting place where I discovered it: cradled in the bones above my heart.

Why doesn't the vomiting give relief? Clear the way? What is holding it in place? What is *it?*

Hand shaking, I wipe my lips and spit into the bucket. My eyes ooze, and strands of sticky, damp hair smear my cheek. And suddenly, I know: *I have something to say.*

Steven? , I think (say?). *Steven*?

Get the phone. I have to call him.

I cannot see him, but I feel his hesitation. His disapproval. His fear. I am sick. It's a bad idea. I can't even hold the phone.

Get the phone, I say. *Hold it for me.*
I will say two sentences.
Then, hang up.

I spit into the bucket.

He dials the number. The phone rings.
Goes to voicemail.

Weakly, I take a breath and hope I can find my voice.

Hey. Leave a message.

Beep.

I remember.
I know what you did to me.

Click.

I collapse onto his shoulder, and he holds me.

My eyes are still shut. Paralyzed with fear.
I cannot lift my head. It lays heavy against his shoulder.
But in the darkness, I feel the corners of my lips lift—my heart attempting to smile.

The pit is gone.
I found my voice.

Rose

Eyes closed, I sit in the yurt. Slowly and deliberately, I breathe in the scents: bottled brandy, smoldering sage, drying herbs, and steeping tea. Having chosen their tincture, the ladies come and sit in the floor by my chair. We all become quiet, and my wrist waits for the drop.

But my heart doesn't.

Impatiently, she rises out of my chest and reaches for the bottle, gathering its healing into her arms. Soothed, she slips back into her place inside me, holding the soft comfort in her hands. With her—through her—I feel soothed, warm, and safe.

Rose, they say. *We offered you Rose.*
My heart sighs with longing.

Moments later, the world inside the yurt is crystal clear. Every edge is crisp and sharp. The lines are so clean, I can see their curves. Light sparkles. The room shimmers. It is a glistening globe of clarity. I've never seen so clearly. There's never been so much light.

On my way home, I buy myself roses. At home, unexpectedly, I begin to bleed. There was a baby. I hadn't known. *But Rose did.*

Drawing a bath, I sprinkle velvety, red petals over the surface of the water and slip into the warm, watery comfort. With a bottle of Rose in my hand, I fall asleep. My heart beats quietly.

A month later, the bleeding has stopped, and a veil begins to lift. I begin to see. To remember.

I once was blind but now . . .

When I tell him, he becomes angry. He hears only a few words before what is simmering inside boils over and spills onto the floor.

I try to take a deep breath. *Please don't let things escalate.* I don't want to hurt him, or lose him.

But as I answer his questions, my chest becomes tighter and tighter, clenching and protecting. *Oh my heart!* I find it harder and harder to breathe. *I know this feeling. I need her.*

There is a pause. Someone speaks into the empty space. For a moment, I am free. I rise from the couch and slip into the kitchen.

Where is she?

Knowing my time is short, my fingers skim the dusty, amber bottles crowding the countertop.

Vervain, agrimony, peach, dandelion, burdock . . . *Rose.*

With gratitude, I squeeze three drops under my tongue. *One. Two. Three.* So faithful, soft and sweet, she immediately soothes and comforts. I take a breath. My chest expands, and my body relaxes.

She lays herself over my heart—warming it, protecting me.

I slip back into the room and take my place on the couch.

He has another question.
I take a deep breath and answer it.

Black Cohosh

My mouth waters.
And the sores ache.

Inside my lip, under my tongue, along my gums,
there are white pockets of pain.

I cannot talk. I cannot eat.

The heat is rising, seeking its release.

A child, I sit at the dinner table. Bright yellow ears of corn sit steaming on our plates. We slather them with butter. Sprinkle them with salt. I cannot wait for the juicy kernels to melt on my tongue. But when I bring the golden cob to my mouth, I cannot take a bite. I cannot free the sweet kernels from their cozy cells. My two front teeth, grossly crooked, sit sideways, a railroad track in my mouth. My bottom teeth, also turned and twisted, sit equally useless.

Slowly, warm tears slide down my cheeks. I want to eat the corn.
I want to enjoy it. *Why am I broken? Crooked? Ugly?*
Why don't I work?

There is no compassion.
Get over it, she says. *Use a knife.*
A mocking smirk mixes with her ecstatically fluttering eyelids.
You don't know what you're missing.
She closes her eyes with buttery delight and licks her salty fingers.

An apparition, I hover above the crumbling stucco house. Its roof is filthy, gritty with years of dirt and debris, exposure and neglect. The day is bleak and overcast. Light-less. The sky is gray.

I hover and do not enter the house.
Why am I waiting? Why do I hesitate?

Where are you? she asks.
I am hovering above the house.
Let's not go inside today. Let's do something different.
Come into your body, she instructs.

I hear her words. But I remain above the house.
Where is my body? I cannot find it.

See your spine. Feel your spine, she directs.

I reach for it. Search for it. And find it. It is dull and lifeless, an empty bone resting deep within my darkness. I sink into my body and lay atop the hardened, knobby fossil.

It is dark, but I am here. I wait.

Do you feel it? she asks.
Do you feel that? There is excitement in her voice.
Your nervous system is coming alive, Amanda!
Greet it! Move with it!

I shift my focus, and I see . . .

A thousand—*a hundred thousand*—tiny points of light beginning to shine. Together, they penetrate the darkness. They are giddy with life. Their fresh awakening is contagious. Up and down. Over and around. I move and flow along my spine—which is becoming the bustling horizon of a waking, pulsing city.

A midnight rider, I shout, *Wake up! Wake up!*

There is a place where no light shines, and the darkness is so thick I can hold it. It takes the shape of a dense, tangled knot of dirt-speckled ghostly roots, and it sits at the base of my spine.

It is buried deep in my earth.

I tell her what I see, and she slides her hand beneath me, finding the gnarly knot.

Let's bring light into this place, she says.
Amanda, shine light into this place.

I try and I try—but I can't. My light is too dim; my beam too weak. The darkness is impenetrable, a fibrous tangle of dirt and earth and roots.

I don't want to sit in the dark! My heart races, and my mind begins to search. *A plant! I know a plant!*

And suddenly, she is there—suspended above me, a shimmering stalk, lined with glowing, white blossoms. *Black cohosh.*

I embrace her and draw her in.

Illuminating, undulating root of vitality.

I ache. I burn. A fever rages through me.

My eyes will not open. I cannot lay still. Turning from side to side, I rub my calves together and massage my inner thighs.

Tilting my chin up and back, I stretch my neck and struggle to relax my jaw. *Breathe, Amanda, breathe.*

My sheets are a tangled, messy nest of heat and sweat.

I open my hips, begging for relief from the ache that radiates down my back, through my hips, and into my legs.

Something black is moving through me. Memories of her hover above me, around me, in me. Looks. Words.

There is darkness in this fever and the hard work of a broken body—a broken spirit.

I am afraid.
I am afraid.

And then, I see her. Grandmother Spider. She sits, black and alert, atop the small of my back, on the tangled knot of my twisted spine. Her presence is powerful but peaceful. She sits, quiet and still.

Why is she here? Is there poison in my pain?

Please don't bite me.
Please don't bite.

Cleavers

His filthy face is nose-to-nose with mine. He is smiling at me, cooing. *He is good. He is kind. He is safe.*

But I know better.

Blinded by lies of his own making, his eyes see only a child's face. My face. A button nose sprinkled with freckles. A smooth brow—not yet creased with worry. Soft, rose-kissed cheeks. Brown doe eyes laced with lashes. Pink lips—quiet and closed. Perfect. He thinks I am compliant. He thinks I trust him—or desperately hopes I do.

Let him believe what he likes. But I am no fool, and with hawk eyes, I watch him—hiding my true face—true self. The eyes he sees are limp veils hung in empty sockets of bone. Recessed, my knowing eyes are hidden deep inside a cave. He cannot see them. He cannot see me. He cannot touch me—hurt me. Removed and safe, wise and aware, older than my tender years, I sit on a throne in my skull, watching him through the veiled windows to my soul.

I wear a mask. Gouged with intention and ceremony, it is ancient, mahogany red, and streaked with black. A knife shaped it, slashed it, dug deep gashes in it. It is the tribal mask of an angry god. A raging spirit. A blazing fire. And this mask is mine.

With a soul-penetrating gaze, I watch him. *Foolish man.* Behind my mask, inside my cave, I hide and dance my devilish dance—an ancient one—calling down curses on his filthy head. Curses on his lying, filthy face.

Her hand resting under my hip, she gently observes: *I feel rage.* Laying on the table, I breathe calmly. In and out, in and out.

Do you feel it, Amanda? Do you feel the rage?

Breathing deeply, I fill my lungs. They expand, and I am somewhere deep in my body. It takes great effort to come out—to speak.

No. No, I don't feel it. I whisper.
Let's try to feel it, she says. *Let's try to feel this rage.*

Willing, I direct my self to her hand—to my hip and what lies hidden there—what she has discovered. My breath catches. My heart is terrified! Clamping and clenching, it strangles.

Fear! I feel fear!

The panic rises, and I plead with her, *No! No! I can't! My heart will stop. It will stop! I can't feel the rage. The rage will kill me.*

My words are not exaggerations. They are a desperate plea for life. For deliverance and breath. I will die today—on this table—if what rests above her hand finds its way to my heart. Her voice calmly comes to me. She is not disappointed. She is not afraid.

You're okay. It's okay. Today, let's do something else. . .

Again, I rest on the table. Eyes closed. Safe. Breathing.

Do you feel it? Do you feel the rage?, she asks.

Lost in a dream, I slowly shake my head from side to side. *I feel no rage.* My body is relaxed. My mind is quiet. My head—cradled in her hands.
But I want to feel it. I know I must feel it, must find it, must

release it. *Where is it?*

And so, with her words prompting, I dive into my darkest deeps—searching.

Inky black rivulets trickle over my heart. *Is this Rage?* I move closer, narrow my eyes, and investigate. *Oh!* I see a hole in my precious heart. From it, black sludge oozes, seeping up from fathoms far below. The ominous, filthy muck spreads and simmers.

It does not belong here.

Suddenly, she is standing beside me. *Cleavers.* She lowers herself into the bubbling black tar. *I will remove what is stuck,* she promises.

Slipping away, she becomes infinite—an endless rope of clinging, grasping leaves. Tender chimney-sweep, she scrapes and seizes, purging and cleansing the river of blood—of memory. Brushing my heart, she gathers the filth and decay, placing it on her shoulders. Weighted by my hurts, she continuously rises from the bottomless, black pit of my hurting heart—and then, dives again.

When I see her intention—her cleansing work—I am in awe of her compassionate wisdom, of the depth and breadth of her generous healing, her tireless devotion. And so, I come alongside her.

I pull, too.

Yes! Let's do it. Let's pull and tug until the waters run clean—until they sparkle and flow. Pure and pristine.

We pull. And her leaves brush the walls of my wounded heart. I feel them—gently scraping, lifting, pulling. And then, it happens:

a spring bubbles from my heart. Sparkling water—clean and clear.

And without a word, Cleavers leaves me.

Blue Cohosh

I choose a place by the stream. Dropping my bag on the bank, I sink onto the warm, summer ground. Knees bent, my bare feet nestled in the cool grass, I close my eyes and turn my face to the summer sun. I breathe in its heat—soak up its life-giving light. Opening my eyes, I turn my head and spy a stream silently slipping over rocks and roots, winding its way around the bend and under the bridge.

Lulled by the green, my heart is quiet. I am ready—and so, I take the cardboard box from my bag and open it. My eyes scan the amber bottles nesting in the brown scraps of paper. So much medicine is here. I brush my hand over the bottles. Listening. Considering. Choosing. My fingers linger over a side-lying bottle. It hums. *This one.* I take hold. There is power in this medicine.

Without opening the bottle, I feel the medicine. It cannot—will not—be contained but surges up my arm, slips over my shoulder, and slides into my gut. There, it fills the space, and my core swells with a swirling ocean of strength and energy. If I do not breathe, it will overwhelm me—pull me down and in. And so, to keep above the waves, I strain for the surface and take in air, draw it in with strong, deep breaths. Expansive and powerful, the waves rise into my chest.

Keep breathing. Keep breathing.

Opening and expanding, I rise above, making space.

As the energy dissipates and the swells subsides, I breathe easier. No longer struggling to keep my head above the water, I am drawn to my feet—particularly the big toe on my left foot. Beginning there, I squeeze a drop of the essence on each toe. *Why not?* The drops slide over my skin and onto the blades of grass. Tears. These are tears—flowing down a cheek, dripping off a nose.

I think to myself: *Sad feet. Weary journey.*

The back of my neck aches for her. So, I lower my head, sweep my hair over my shoulder, and place a few, cool drops of liquid on the nape of my neck. She immediately dives deep and finds my gut. She swirls and splashes. She is home.

I tilt my head back, open my mouth, and let three drops fall under my tongue. I hold them there. Energy, strong and sweeping, gathers in my chest, pours into my gut, and rushes into the bowl of my pelvis, where it swirls and begins to overflow. Like a river, it courses down my legs and flows into my feet. The earth opens, and blue cohosh escapes through my soles, sinking deep into the earth.

Deep calling unto deep.

Grounding. Filling.
Downward flowing.
Swirling. Swelling.
Seeking source.
Rooting. Rooted.
Being earth.

There is power in this medicine.

A child, a little girl, sits on the bed. She is still and quiet—without expression. She looks straight ahead, seeing nothing. She is resigned. Absent.

I step closer. *Is she okay? Is she all right?*

I turn, and he is there—a threatening, imposing figure. He stands

across from us—watching her.

I turn and study her.
She has a head framed by long, soft, brown hair.
She has a chest, small and thin.
But below this, there is nothing—nothing but a perfectly round, black circle.
An abyss.
She has no gut. No root.
She is empty.
A black hole with legs.

I hear a voice.

Amanda, do you feel that?
Light is coming into your pelvis.
Into your hips. Do you feel it?
You're bringing your self, your soul, back into that space.
Someone told you it belonged to them,
and you're taking it back.

I don't feel the light. I don't see it. But I do begin to speak.
And so does the little girl.

We take turns. Her, then me. Me, then her.
It's mine! she yells.
And I echo, loud and strong, *It's mine! Mine!*
We pummel him with our words, defending ourselves with our protective, punctuated shouts of possession.

Mine! Mine! It's mine!

And I realize: she and I are not separate. We are one.
We are . . . me.
I step in front of her. Shield her.
And I yell, *It's hers! It's hers!*
And we merge, she and I.

Standing before him, my legs rooted and strong, I am tall.
I am grown. And I am towering over him—gaining inches with every shout.

I bellow, again and again, *It's mine! It's mine! It's mine!*

And then, I turn to her. This child. My self.
She is incomplete. She sits hollow, black, and empty.
I must pull her down. Down and into her self.
I grab the energy in her head and begin to pull. I tug and yank.
But it does not budge. It will not drop—
will not sink and stick.

What do I do? What do I need?

And then, she comes to me: blue cohosh. I look down, and her roots are in my hands.

I place the mass inside our lifeless gut, inside the hollow place.
And blue cohosh begins to swirl. She swirls and spins, creating a vortex of pulsing energy. A healing storm. A perfect storm.

The power of her dance engages the energy,
pulling it down and filling the void.
The darkness flees.
And nothing is left but warm, yellow light.
Nothing is left but the Sun.

She has a shape. A body. A belly.
Hips.
Roots.
She is whole.

Mugwort

Hurry! Hurry! Fast! Quick!
Frantically, Mugwort scurries across my body.

Rushing! Rushing!
Running! Running!
Here! There!
Not much time! There are so many!
Quick!
Hurry, hurry!

Leaving trails of otherworldly tingles, his bony fingers,
knobby and nimble,
adept and quick,
race across me,
skillfully tapping,
pricking, snatching,
pulling,
plucking.
Not on my skin. Not in my soul.
But somewhere between.
In a liminal space,
he hurries, scurries.
Plucking, pulling.
Busy, busy!
Rushing! Running!

I try to follow him. Hurry after him.
See what he is snatching.

What is he doing?

He will not show me. There is not time.
Frantically, he works.
Tirelessly.
Endlessly.

It is time! There is no time!
The time is now!

Pricking, pricking.
Plucking, plucking.
Hurry, hurry.
Rushing, running.

My eyes return to the beginning and read her words.

I am done. I am finished. Do not respond.

I pause. I must have misunderstood. I begin again.

I am done. I am finished. I have nothing more to say. Do not respond.

My eyes blur and do not see. My mind does not understand. But my heart—my heart knows. Has always known.

Her words plunge deep. A gutting dagger. Teeth clenched, she leans closer. Her breath is on my face, and she presses harder. She seethes and spits.

I am done. Finished. Do not respond.
You are never satisfied.
You are never happy.
Nothing is ever enough for you—
You. . .you. . .you.

It is confusion.

The wound opens and gapes.

Red and bleeding,
My soul is pierced.

I lay my hand over it—over the place that is no place—that my hand cannot touch but her words can pierce.

I am mortally wounded.
this hurts me more than it hurts you
Does it?

And then, I remember.
Rushing, running. Pulling, plucking.

I call her in—
direct her to the spirit-space bleeding inside me—
call her to the gaping hollow between my gut and my heart.

My wound needs tending, and her skillful hands slide the dagger from my soul.

It will take time, she says.
But you will be whole again.

The Bear, the Teacher, the Shoes, and the Path

His finger presses on the point at the base of my skull.
My breath catches. He presses harder and harder.
I whisper to myself, *Breathe. Just breathe. Relax into it.*
Fall into the pain.

He presses again, and I hear a voice. It is my body. I have never heard it speak, but I know its voice.

Why don't you release it?, my body asks. The voice is clear and calls from my deep. I struggle to release and relax into the point of pain pulsing under his hand.

I answer back, *I am. I'm trying.*

The voice, patient and purposed, presses. *Why don't you release it?*

I am bewildered and confused, searching and looking. I call out to the voice that is hiding:

Where are you? Who are you?
Release what?
What should I release?

There is no answer, and his finger slips from the point at the base of my skull.

Hello? Hello? No one answers.

After a moment, he says, *You can roll onto your stomach now.*

Only a moment has passed, and already, I have forgotten my body spoke to me. (Quite soon, I will learn: I am very good at forgetting.) Quieted and calmed by his strokes, I drift to the edge of sleep and linger there. It is then that I see him. The Bear. Across the meadow, at the edge of the forest, he stands before me, alert and upright. He is black. Burdock burs cling to his thick, oily fur. The light is dim. It is dusk. The Time Between. In the gloaming, he has come to me. Together, we stand silently, seeing one another.

Our eyes meet. And gently, we know. Quietly, we see.

Without a word, he slowly turns and lumbers away. Before I can wonder at his coming or his going—before I can miss him—he is behind me. Drawing closer, his oily, warm fur brushes my shoulder. His breath, hot and damp, falls on my cheek. My neck. I see his bony, curved, yellow claws.

I've never seen a bear before, I think to myself.

Without a sound, he places his paws are over my hands. Gently, his weight presses me down, and my head recedes into his hot open mouth. Sharp, yellowed teeth rest on my forehead. A jagged crown. A bony headdress.

I sink into him.
He slides into me,
And we meld together.
And are one.

I am held.
Tucked inside.
Covered and kept.
He has gifted me his pelt.
His mantle.
His hide.
I accept it—and whisper: *thank you*

I sit in a room where there is no lamp—no source for the dim, yellow light by which I see. Walls of rough wooden planks prickle with splinters. There are windows. Their glass strains under the weight of the pressing darkness. There is no view. No reflection. There is nothing outside of "here".

In this abandoned shack, I sit. My heart races, and my eyes dart. *Be alert. Watch. Stand guard!*

Still as a stone, I sit petrified in a ragged chair.

Something is coming. I can feel it. The air is ominous and thick, asking to be cut.

Something wicked this way comes.

A goose—a gander—stands before me. Angry, he purposes to peck me—to draw blood. Only able to move my right hand, I reach out and take hold of his face. He struggles to be free. But I tighten my grip, press into his beak, and wrestle him to the ground. If I let go, he will kill me. Choosing to live, I tighten my grip. Bested, the goose disappears. And my heart pulses with fear.

Another animal comes. And again, I stretch out my right arm, cover its face, muzzles its mouth, and wrestle it to the ground. Suffocate it.

This happens again and again. And each time, trembling with fear, I stretch out my hand and choose to live.

And then, he is there. The Bear.

I am not afraid. But still, I hesitate. *Am I sure he is safe?*

Better safe than sorry. I stretch out my arm and cover his face with my hand. But unlike the others, he does not struggle, does not fight back. He has no malice. He wishes me no ill. Through the muzzle of my gripping fingers, he calmly whispers, *I will not fight you. We are not meant to fight.*

Relieved but still unsure, my hand relaxes—but does not yet release. *At ease, soldier.* My taut arm slackens. My elbow bends. But I can't take my hand from his nose.

He is kind. *But is he safe?*

He is here, I say to her.
Who? Who is here? she asks.

I see his face. Eyes bright, he is smiling. His beard is streaked with gray, and his green hat, its rippled rim crinkled, sits perfectly atop his lovely head. He approaches me and greets me. He is happy to see me. He is happy *for* me.

He has never smiled at me like this. *Ever.*

In my dreams, he is always agitated with me. Frustrated. Ready to reprimand, chide, and argue. But not today. Not ever again. Today, he embraces me with his smile. The tension and distance, which had sat so thickly between us, is gone.

Matthew. Matthew is here, I say.
Expecting my father not my teacher, she is surprised.
Is he saying something? What is he doing? she asks.

I can't answer her. The moment is too beautiful. I only need to feel it.

Matthew and the Bear stand together. They are so very close—perhaps they are one.

They draw close to me, and I nuzzle my nose into Bear's oily, black fur. So soft, so deep. Matthew's hat brushes my forehead.

Together, they slip behind me and embrace me. Strong and able, they lift me up. Relaxing into their embrace, my toes brush the floor. Light is all around us, and the air pulses with something pure and lovely.

Held in their arms, I am met by crystalline water and pure light. They pour from above, rushing over my head. They baptize me. Anoint me. And angels do sing.

And then, they are gone—Matthew and the Bear. For a moment, I am sad. I didn't get to say good-bye. But then, I see they have left something. On my shoulders rests a mantle. The furry, black coat of a bear. My arms. My chest. Every part of me is covered. I am inside of it. *It is who I am.*

A sparkle catches my eye. A twinkle of light. I look down past the fur's edge, and I see them: glass slippers. *Lady's Slippers.* My toes wiggle inside them.

The coat of a bear. The shoes of a fairytale. What a sight I must be. *What a beautiful sight I must be.*

When I open my eyes, she gifts me a small brown bottle of Easter Lily tincture. Years ago, Matthew made it—gave it to her. Prompted, she brought it with her today, and now, she gives it to me. Matthew *was* here.

The Panther and the Deer

Catnip is calling, and I do not want to answer. He holds no appeal for me. I do not know him. But I do not ignore his call, his pressing presence. I have learned to listen to those who come calling. He is here to teach me something.

So, I reluctantly pour a cup of tea, sit with him, and wait.

Before my appointment, I take an early morning walk in the park. I am quiet, wondering what the day will bring, praying for strength and comfort for what may come—for what I may see . . .

Heart heavy with care, my eyes look down, watching my feet take one step and then another. As I round the bend and begin to cross the old, rusty bridge, my spirit cries, *Look up!* There is no choice but to do so. The command is urgent, and in a twinkling, I lift my head and my gaze. And there she is. The Deer. It is as if she has been there all morning—waiting.

Standing perfectly still, she is tall and elegant. Regal in her stance, she is poised and purposed. I cannot move, and I cannot look away. Her eyes lock with mine, and though her eyes are kind and gentle, they are gravely searching. A warning? A question? An invitation? *Are you ready?*

Slowly, she lowers her head, releasing me. She turns and walks away. It is moments before I move.

I lay on the table and sink deeper and deeper into myself.
I am afraid. What will I see? What will I feel? *What will he do?*

I know it is time to push through something—to go down and in. But I'm not ready.

She gently places her hands under the small of my back. And I see him: The Panther. His eyes are black, bottomless deeps. His ebony, smooth coat shimmers a midnight blue. His face is contoured, strong and powerful, and he, too, asks a question:
Are you ready? It is time.

My heart beats slowly. My breath comes in a steady rhythm. My spirit whispers, *Yes.* And I move to follow him.

He turns and begins to walk slowly and softly down a narrow, dirt path. Following, I see her. The Deer. She elegantly emerges from the tall grasses lining the path. With ease, she falls into step beside him.

The Lion and the Lamb.
The Panther and the Deer.

Old friends, they silently walk together, disappearing into a line of trees.

All is dark. I rest. I am at peace.

When the session ends, she is glowing. Turning to me, she says, *Did you feel that? Did you feel the rage?* Floating as if in a dream, I shake my head no.

She is surprised. *There was so much rage,* she says. *So much hurt. You did good work today. Good work.*

What did I do? I didn't do a thing. Deer and Panther went before me.

09

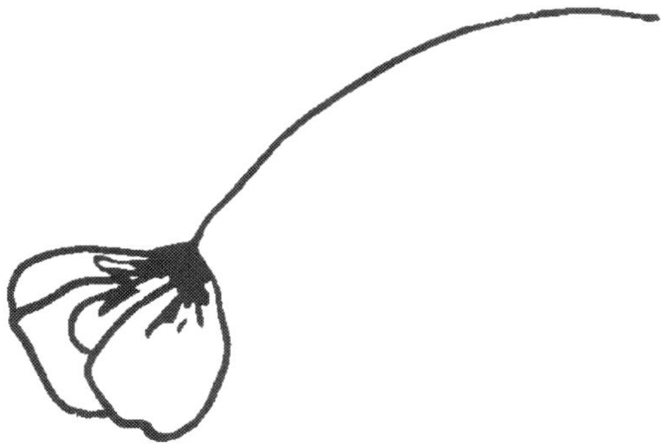

Dogwood

Day after day, year after year, I draw her. Four white petals, tipped with black, two green leaves.

She lines the margins of notebook pages, adorns the corners of homework papers, decorates the covers of three-ring binders.

Again, and again, and again. Year, after year, after year.

Four white petals,
tipped with black,
two green leaves.

I know her. She stands in the front yard, a sentinel posted in the weeds, rooted between the crumbling, concrete walk and the dusty gravel drive.

She makes the house less homely, somewhat pretty.
A flower in its tangled hair.

I am an awkward child.

Knobby knees,
Two left feet,
Gangly Grace.
Yes. *Grace.*
A nickname my father gave me.
Isn't it beautiful?
Elegant?

Way to go, Grace! he says,
shaking his head in dumbfounded disbelief.
I pick myself up off the sidewalk,
the scraped meat of my palms stinging,
bits of gravel and grass pressed into my raw, bleeding knees.
I try to brush away the dirt and shame.
He draws back his head, cocking it to one side, and stares:
baffled.

What is wrong with her? his eyes ask.

(*You don't know?* my buried spirit replies.)

Clumsy and exposed,
I wait for him to answer his question.

(After all, I am wondering, too.)

Glasses,
crooked teeth,
metal braces,
knobby knees.
No deer.
No gazelle.
Just me.

Bruised and scarred,
Name's Grace.
And yours?

Nothing fits me right.
Not even this skin.
Square peg, round hole
In this world I'm in.

Angles.
Corners.
Knobs and edges.
No rhythm. No poise.
Just a few questions.

Where should I put my hands?
Behind my back?
In front?
Over my chest?
That's better.
Wait, uh?

Yes, I see.
Over my face.
No deer.
No gazelle.
Just Grace.
Just me.

We are eating dinner together, sitting at a little table in a quiet restaurant.
I love him dearly. He has my attention.

I lean in to listen.
All ears.

Ah, yes, he says. *Dogwood. Deer medicine.*
Yes, that's you: awkwardly elegant.

Awkwardly elegant.

Taking another bite, he seems delighted at his observation.

I don't know how to respond—where to put my hands, my elbows, my self. Suddenly, I am ten years old again. Scraped and bleeding. Clumsy and exposed.

I smile at him.

Hi, name's Grace. And yours?

Zinnia

. . . at the heart of your play there is truth . . .
Frederick Buechner

My basket is full, brimming with glass bottles, pouches of tea, and brandy-preserved essences. Gifts for one who is dying. Gifts for one who is keeping vigil by the bed.

I turn to thank her for the generous offering, but before I can speak, she presses a small, unexpected gift into my hand.

And this is for you, she says. I glance down at the tiny treasure resting in my palm. ZINNIA, the label reads. *For the elf self*, she says. With a tender, knowing smile, she folds my fingers over the bottle and gives my hand a loving squeeze.

I thank her. And while she and her apprentices finish pouring and wrapping, I take a book from the shelf.

Zinnia, it says. *Helps one remember how to play.* Curious.

I slip the book back onto the shelf, offer a thank-you and good-bye, and grab my basket.

At home, not wanting to wake sleeping children, I cautiously open the side door, slip off my shoes, and lightly rest my basket of green gifts by the dish-filled sink.

I take the bottle of Zinnia in my hand and consider it.

Do I have an elf self? Can I play? Do I want to? Know how?

I hold her. And as I ponder, she leaps—without warning—from hand! Her glass house shatters, and she spills and spreads across the floor. A puddle of forfeited playfulness pools at my feet.

I am stunned. Her leap is unprecedented. (I've never broken a tincture bottle.) And it strikes me as a bit of elfin mischief. Or, perhaps, elfin wisdom.

There is still work to be done.

Maybe I'm not ready to play.

Come here. Come where my hand is, she says. *Come see what is here.*

I go to where her hand rests—under my hip.

In the darkness, I see her—little Amanda. She is rooted to the packed dirt floor. This cellar, her cell, smells of damp earth. Of roots and crawling things. Of puddles and shadows. The air is stale and cold—the light, dismal and brown. Long ago exiled and forgotten, she has rooted into the filthy floor of this self-made dungeon. Head down, chin tucked, she squeezes her knees to her chest. A dingy (but soft) cascade of long, brown hair hangs over her shoulders, falling across her face, hiding her. Protecting her. It is sprinkled with dirt, covered with cobwebs, and crawling with spiders.

Abandoned, she has sat, motionless, for years. She is frozen. A stone.

Doesn't she want to leave this prison?

I grab her shoulders and plead with her. Beg her. Shake her. But she will not come with me—will not even lift her head.

Salty tears streak my cheeks, weaving a salty web across my skin.

I'm frantic. Desperate. And I scream, *Don't give up! You can't give up! If you die, I die! Look at me! Look at me! Please! Don't you want to live?*

She doesn't move. Doesn't hear. (Or doesn't want to.)

She is angry, hurt, betrayed, abandoned. She is suspicious, hopeless, discarded—hardened. The transformation is nearly complete: what was once a little girl will soon be a lifeless stone. A statue in the witch's palace.

I begin to panic. I'm running out of time. We're running out of time!

And then, I understand: she needs to be loved. Not shaken. Not yelled at. Not compelled, or forced, or commanded. *But loved. She needs me to love her.*

Dropping to my knees, I wrap my arms around her tiny body. I squeeze her tightly and hold her close, nuzzling my nose into her soft, sweet, gritty, brown hair. And with a gentler, quieter, kinder voice, I plead with her again.

I love you. I love you so much. Do you hear me, Amanda? I love you.

It takes only a moment, only a few words, and her shoulders soften. I know her heart has done the same because she slowly turns to me. Her hair veils her face, but I can see her eyes, searching (hoping) in the darkness. *Who's here? Who loves me?*

She sees me. She knows me.

And then, we are standing side by side. Her hand in mine. Together, we walk out of my hip and into my heart. There, a red, comfy chair is waiting for her. A child, she eagerly scrambles into it, bounces a bit, kicks her scrawny legs, nestles into its center,

and looks up at me—*beaming*.

And this little chair was just right.

She is smiling. She is happy. Our eyes meet, and I announce (surprising myself): *I have a flower for you*.

In my hand is a zinnia.

Tulip Poplar

But, dear one, all those years of silence haven't allowed you to keep them.
You haven't kept them. On the contrary: they are keeping you.

When I tell them my dream, they look at one another with knowing, worried faces.

The three of us stand in a forest. Under a canopy of leaves, we are three. Between them, I exist. But I am not touched or seen. Their faces—eyes and attention—are turned elsewhere. Away from me. Away from one another.

She turns to leave. And so does he. No goodbyes are said. No reasons given. Under the trees, I am one.

The three of us stand at the edge of the ocean. Under a summer sun, we are three. Between them, I wait. Too small to be seen. No matter: they are not looking for me—or for each other.

She turns to leave. And so does he. I am forgotten. An afterthought. At the edge of the ocean, I am one.

The three of us stand in a bustling crowd. Surrounded by strangers, we are three. She turns to leave. And so does he. I am left alone. Small and still.

And in a circle of light,
I am one.

An impenetrable fortress. A bulwark of wood. These are the words my mind offers—or is given—to describe this old, towering tree. She is not yet ready to speak to me. Or, perhaps, I am not yet ready to hear.

Today, the young one, the one scarred and bleeding from the imbedded twists of rusted barbed wire, the one who has grown up timid and crooked because of his wound, sends me to the Old One. So, here I am.

Timidly, I ask if I may approach. Perhaps today she will speak—the air seems softer, more inviting. So, I step forward, carefully, and stand beside her tall, straight trunk. I am quiet. She is, too. Carefully, I lay my hand on her trunk. My fingers spread and press into her winding ridges and deep grooves. There is comfort in the rhythmic roughness of her bark. She is warm.

What should I say to her? What do I want? Why am I here?

We are standing by a stream which flows over cold, gray rocks, creating a hesitant, trickling waterfall. Tulip poplar keeps her feet cool, dipping them in the flowing water. The autumnal, afternoon sun is high in the sky, radiating its yellow warmth onto my face. It stretches and spreads its glowing fingers into my veins, my tissues, reaching and seeping deep into my bones. There is old warmth and light here. The settled certainty of fall.

I'm here, too. Look this way, I hear. I turn, and beside me is a second tulip poplar, tall and straight. How did I miss him? I greet him, thank him for his invitation, and then, cautiously, place my other hand on his trunk. Again, my fingers spread and find comfort. A pitiful Samson between two pillars, I stand—small and weak, having no strength, no anger, nothing to vindicate or prove.

I am blind.

Supported by the poplars, I close my eyes. And suddenly, they

soar above me, reaching for the sky, breaking through to a place far beyond its cerulean dome. They bend down their benevolent heads, creating a canopy above me. I feel their love, approval, delight, acceptance.

And then, I am a child, holding their hands. They lift me between them, playfully swinging me in the autumn breeze. We are laughing.

Yellow sunshine warms my face. Heat and light, pulsing red, enfolds me. I am full and vibrant. Alive and loved.

Together, they bend down their heads to me and say, *We will be your parents.* And then, gently, they place me on the ground—but do not let go—and are gone.

Together, we stand quietly again. Humble and awed, hands by my side, I rest between them. Loved. Moments pass. I am silent, as my heart absorbs their parental message. In gratitude, I bow my head, thanking them.

But whatever does it mean?

A month later, I begin to remember.

I am raw and stunned, wandering through my days, lost in a dream. *No. A nightmare.* I don't know who I am. Or have been. Or what is happening. Or what I should do. I don't understand what I'm feeling. Or seeing. I don't know what's real—what's true. *Someone help me.* I need help. But what kind? And from where? And from whom?

How do I start to walk out of this fog—out of this mist that lies thick and heavy over graves, holding skeletons and hiding secrets?

And then, I remember her book. Perhaps in such a book there is a section for me. A page that tells me what to do. How to heal. What is real. I go to the shelf, and my fingers find her writings, bound and waiting. Taking the book into my hands, I open to the Table of Contents. My eyes skim the page. *What would such a chapter even be called? Under what heading would help hide?* And then, I see it—quietly placed at the bottom of the page: *Trauma Down There*. Page 79.

Urgently, expectantly, I flip to the page. My eager eyes rest on the words, and I begin to read:

Grandmother and Grandfather Growth stand on either side of you. Their smiles curl the corners of their mouths; there is sadness in their eyes. They each take one of your hands. You feel like a small child as you walk with them. Sunlight slants through the trees in golden streams; there is the faint sound of a small waterfall. The ground rises up to meet your feet; it is yielding, soft, springy. Why are tears coursing down your cheeks?

"We cry with you." The words vibrate in your heart, and you wince. "It is hard to feel the joy of life when you have been hurt, especially by those who ought to care for you. But we do not cry for your injuries, precious one, grievous though they are. We cry because you cling to your pain. Dear grandchild, pain is inevitable. It is not your fault. It is part of life. You are not to blame. You did not call this upon yourself. There is no guilt in being abused. . .

I close the book. How could she know? Have they also held her hands?

I sit back. Stunned. Silent. My heart is overwhelmed, in awe of the wonder of the world and the rich, sufficient healing it holds.

They knew. They knew I needed them.

My heart hurts. I try to hold it, but it slips away from me.

I sit at tulip poplar's feet. I need her to speak to me. *She knows something*—something I don't.

So, I sit with her, and I beg her to speak.

Say something! Anything! Can't you feel my heart hurting? Don't you know I need you?

Her silence pulses, pregnant with knowing. She's holding out on me!

For the longest time, I sit. Waiting, pleading. Whispering, begging. But she does not bend down. She is tall and silent. And in the silence, she has given her answer: *No, not tonight. I will not talk tonight.*

I feel her green eyes taking me in. Full of pity. Asking me to trust her. To be patient. To understand.

But I don't.

Fine, I say. *Fine! You don't want to talk to me? Then, I'll leave. If that's how you're going to be, then I'll just leave!*

Stung and hurt—rejected, I stand and turn to go. And then, I feel them: her branches reaching for me. She calls to me, *Wait. Wait, small one. I'll tell you one thing. Just one thing.*

A chafing, needy child, I turn to her. *Fine. What?*

I wait.

Simply, quietly, she whispers, *I am for children who have no parents.*

My head falls to my chest. Sobs shake me. *How am I standing?*

Now, I understand: *I am not yet ready to hear all she has to say.*

It is not yet time.

For tonight, it is enough.

I am so drawn to her. She calls me. (Or do I call to her?) I don't know, and it doesn't matter. Somehow, our hearts are connected. Intertwined.

The sun is setting. The sky glows with the fading light of her diurnal descent. I gather my blanket and go to her. Go to tulip poplar.

Under a tent of stars, beneath a web of bare branches, I spread my blanket and make my bed. I lay my head on the cold, winter ground and make my confession. Releasing tears, I open my heart. And say to her (as always):

I am here. If you have something to say, something to teach, I am here. I will listen.

And (as always) she is silent.

Spent with tears (with her), I drift towards sleep. Lingering in the liminal space, the mist between, I see two images. They dance before me: a bear and a fox. Bear, I know. But, Fox?

The creatures disappear. All is black. My mind is quiet, emptied and spent.

And into the deep quiet, she speaks, *That is enough for one night.*

And gently, she dismisses me.

Gathering my things, I glance up at the star-speckled sky. Above me, Orion draws his bow. The crescent moon glows, a sliver of soft light.

Walking home, my heart—my self—announces:
You are releasing pain.

It has happened: what I feared. *She has left me.*

Only hours ago, I was a daughter. I had a mother. But now, tonight, I am orphaned. *Abandoned. Rejected. Discarded. Cut off.*

Her spewed words were sharp-edged swords.
She wielded them—spit them. Intending to wound and to lash.

And wound she did, piercing my skin, slicing my sinews, plunging into the very depths of me. I cannot name what she has pierced.

My soul? My self?
It is an ineffable space.
There is nothing to see or touch.
Only feel.

I cannot speak. I gasp for air. And when I find it, I hold it.
Do not exhale! Do not release! This is your last breath!
Your dying breath . . .
Hold it . . .

I rise from the couch. Or does someone lift me?. Finding the door, I turn the latch and stumble into the night air. A black sky

shelters me. A gibbous moon silently watches, witnessing.

And I go to *her*—to tulip poplar. I have questions. I need answers. (She has them; I know.) But when I come to her, she is as I have come to expect: tall, still, and silent.

She offers her presence. She speaks no words. But I feel her ache for me. With me. Tenderly, she places her green hand on my head. She strokes my hair, and then rests her hand on my shoulder. *There, there, dear one. There, there,* she whispers.

Desperately hollow and emptied, steps from dying, I whisper, *Can you heal the mother wound?* Her hand remains on my shoulder, she looks up and away, studying the darkness, seeing something in the distance. She answers so simply, *Yes.*

Get up! You're alive!, my spirit shouts.

There's a sun! A sky! Trees!
Get up! Go out!
You're alive!
You're free!

Animated by this glimpse (this realization) of freedom—the truth of it, I rush to the door, shove it open, and tumble into the wide, wide world.

I hurry to the meadow behind the barn. Something is calling me—beckoning me out and in. Standing in the open field, I breathe deeply, filling my lungs with the blue of the sky and the warmth of the sun.

And I want to run. Run because I can. *Because I'm free.* Certainly

not because I am strong. I am so weak. *But I am free.* In little spurts, my liberated heart is pounding. I dash a few feet here, and a few feet there. Exploring. Testing. *How does it feel to be free?*

What if I raised my arms, spread them wide?
What if I grow wings and fly?

Arms wide, I spread my scrawny wings and run. Run! A little feathered thing. Clumsy and weak. Learning the dance, learning to fly.

From the corner of my eye, I spy the grove. Maple, poplar, oak, sweet gum. They call me. Rustling their leaves, they motion me to them—gesturing, beckoning . . .

Come here; come this way. Come over; come in.

I tip and turn my wings, wandering nto the trees.

There is a hushed humming. All eyes are on me. They watch. Standing in their midst, I raise my hands to the sky. Lift my face to the sun.

And I hear the words of King David:
When you touch me, I am ten feet tall.

And there, surrounded by sweet gums and poplars, I grow by leaps and bounds. Roots down. Head up.

There is a murmur—a growing chant. I strain my ear to hear the rising challenge.

Run. Do it. Come on, Amanda. Do it! Run!

They hold out their leaves, green and waving, in ready reception.

You can do this. You can do it. Do it.

My heart skips at the possibility. *Maybe. Just maybe.* I attempt a little leap—a practice step. And then, I go for it. I take off running towards the trees. Arms high. Hands open. I slap their leaves. *High-five, my friends! High five!*

I jump! I leap!
Am I crazy?

Smiling and laughing, I run the circle, leaping high and slapping the leaves.

The trees on my right offer their leaves. The trees on my left watch and cheer. They motion me around and forward.

I run until I am dizzy.

My heart is no longer weak. It has found its rhythm. Something more than blood is making it beat.

Under the seeing Sun and the sheltering Sky, all of Creation claps her hands and lends her voice to my celebration.

The trees of the field will clap their hands, my heart sings.

I open my lips, and out pours a song.

They shall go out with joy,
and be led forth with peace.
The mountains and the hills will break forth before you.
There'll be shouts of joy,
And all the trees of the field
will clap, will clap their hands!

I leap. I laugh. I twirl. Singing, I spin around the circle, clapping my hands, keeping the beat, leading the trees in this victory song.

For a small eternity, we pour out our hearts in jubilant praise. In

triumphant life.

And then, it is time—time to be still.

I slow the rhythm, quiet my voice. My hands come together more gently. Together, we become quieter and quieter, until we whisper—until we stand together in satisfied peace.

Hand to my heart, I bow in gratitude, thanking the trees for lending their voices, for joining me in the song. In the dance.

What a gift I have been given.

Turning to leave, I raise my hand to the trees—in recognition, in thanksgiving, in communion. And I close my eyes, and—an image comes.

There is an empty cage. It is open and unguarded, and I stand outside of it. Free to leave. Free to go. Free to live.

He sets the captives free, my heart whispers.
He sets the captives free! my heart shouts.
And with those words—all the pieces come together.
My heart opens, and tulip poplar pours her heart into mine.

This time she holds nothing back. It is time. I am ready.

I am free.

Early Meadow Rue

Her harsh and unexpected response has made the darkness return.

I am finished, she decreed. *Finished.*

I cannot see. My eyes are sealed shut, and deep within, I am hiding. There are no lights. No signs of life.

Motionless and empty, collapsed on the cold, tile floor, I lean against the toilet. Too heavy to lift, my head hangs from my neck and rests on my chest.

I feel him touch me.
He places Ruby in my arms, turns her face toward me, and helps her latch. She begins to nurse.

Bursting, my heart swells with love for her, and in desperation, I cry out: *I want to see her! I want to see Ruby!*

Straining and stretching, I struggle to open my eyes.
Open! Open! I beg them. I plead with them.
I muster my will and demand: *Open!*

But they will not. There is danger. I cannot come out of hiding.

He sees my tears and promises, *You will see her again. Don't be afraid.*

Her little mouth suckles.
Bile bubbles into my throat.
My stomach spasms and heaves, and I lurch forward.
He grabs Ruby, and I empty my memories—my mother—into the toilet bowl.
I've had enough.
This has to stop.

I write to my friend.

What would you give a child who is afraid of the dark?

She answers, *I will write soon, friend.*

Days pass. I wait. And then, she writes.
Ya Rauf, my friend. Ya Rauf.
You need the love that is Ya Rauf.

It penetrates, quietly and gently,
Making its way to the deepest, most profound place in you--
Making its way to where you are human—
To your lovely soul.

Sweet soul, wounded from not having been seen,
Not having been accepted,
hear the words:
Ya Rauf.
May this peaceful calm be yours.
May you rest in God.

You are as steel—
tempered in the fire,
fashioned into a sword.

And so, remember:
To be calm, to be quiet is not to be passive--
But to be brave.
It is to face the foe with serenity.
It is to be at peace—
To emanate strength from a quiet center.

Be still.

Be quiet.
Rest in God—in God's love:
A love which has been from the beginning.

Ya Rauf.
May it soothe you,
reach to your very core.

You are not a failure, dear one—
though you feel shame at not having become
what others requested, required, wanted, expected,
There is no shame, dear one.

You are not a disappointment.

So you did not become what they wanted you to be—
So you did not meet their expectations—
But you have become what you were purposed to be.
What you were meant to be—
What Love made you to be.

(My child self begins to sing,
I am promise. I am a possibility.
I am a promise. With a capital 'P'.
I am a great big bundle of potentiality!
Yes, dear heart: *Sing! Sing!*)

You are not deficient.
Your soul is not lacking.
You are not less than.

Dear heart, sweet soul, you are all you were fashioned to be.
With His very hands, He shaped you.
Knit you. In the deepest, darkest places—the secret places,
He formed you.

You, dear one, are a precious, sparkling, hidden treasure.

He sings over you,
and looks at you with such tender affection,
such dreamy satisfaction—such ineffable delight.
It is good.
She is very good.
(And the morning and the evening were the sixth day.)

But, oh, I know: you are so tender.

They have wounded you here.
Right here—in your most tender part.
They have wounded you where you were most vulnerable--
where your homemade armor, your leaf of fig, failed to cover you.

And so: you fight, dear one.
You struggle to breathe,
To be,
To live.

It is time.
Lay down your weapons, weary warrior.
Lay down your weapons.

Rest your weary fists.
Find rest in the arms of God.

Fall into His arms, battered soldier.

The battle is not yours, but God's.
Stand still. And see the salvation of the Lord.

I know. I know.
No one saw what you were trying to do,
Heard what you were trying to say,
How you were hoping to heal them, help them, love them.
Mother. Father. Everyone.

And now, you feel a failure.

The pain is so deep. So devastating.
No one knows how to handle it—how to handle you.
How to touch it. How to heal it.
The wound is so raw. It bleeds and oozes.
You are so tender.
Even the gentlest touch causes pain.
Even the coolest ointment makes you recoil.

You have a tender wound in your sacred heart.

Delicate and deep.

You feel wounded by everything:
Your parents,
Your companions,
the human condition.

There is so much pain in the world. So much pain.
And you feel it—every slash, every cut.

This wound is deep. Unspeakably deep.

A salve will not do. An oil will not soothe.

This wound needs a feather rather than an ointment.

a feather, dear one.
a will-o'-the-wisp.

So, rest in quiet, unfailing love.
There is nothing to explain or defend.
There is only Light.
Only lovingkindness and gentleness.

*There is only **a feather**.*

It whispers to your wound;
It writes the answers to all your questions.

Panic. Fear. Terror.

Ya Rauf, dear one.
Ya Rauf.
God is here.

Emmanuel.
God with us—
with you,
dwelling among you,
dwelling inside you.

May this feather float through the layers,
brushing each one with a gentle calm,
whispering words of presence and peace,
as it sinks into the deepest part of you.

Ya Rauf.
A love that cannot be sought.
A love that must be discovered.

A gift of grace,
lying deep within,
Given at the beginning,
Waiting to be found.

May the gentle hand of compassion remind you
that you were never forsaken.
Never broken.
You have always been held.
You have always been whole.

The plant that whispers these words is Rue.

I write back: **Send me Rue**.

I take her from the box and hold her to my heart.
Closing my eyes, I whisper a prayer:
Bless her.
Let her heal me.

In the delicate, bone bowl between my collarbones, I place three, glistening drops of her essence.
One. Two. Three.
Immediately, my lungs expand and fill with air.
I take three deep breaths.
One. Two. Three.

Energy swirls down into my abdomen, gathering under my navel. It fills me and grows roots. And from these roots, it stretches up and into my chest. I breathe deeply and expand.

I open my mouth and squeeze five drops under my tongue. I can feel the very place where the drops rest. Above them, my tongue

will not be still. It moves, lifting and wiggling, shaking and shivering. It will not lay down—will not touch the Rue.

Why is it agitated? Excited? Trembling?

Though the windows are closed, I feel a cool, gentle breeze. It carries the soft, yellow sun.

Something is changing.

I am searching . . .

Breezes.
Open windows,
Painted eggs in the grass.
Fresh dirt.
A cool basement.

My lips tingle.

And without warning, my jaw releases—completely—and hangs on its hinges, open and loose. The release is remarkable. My mouth is open—slack and free.

A breeze passes through the open windows. A gentle wind blows through my head, brushing away the cobwebs, clearing away the mist.

Though I am smiling, I begin to cry.

Cradling Rue in my hands, I hold her over my heart.
And my soul whispers: *Your heart loves her.*
Taking its cue, my heart leans in and nuzzles her,
whispering, *Where have you been?*

A grandmother stands barefoot by the door, her feet planted solidly on the dirt floor. Under an open window, she works quietly and quickly with her hands, sorting green stems and leaves that are strewn across a table. A dancing breeze brushes the aged linen curtain that hangs loosely in the window.

The sun shines warm, further browning her skin.

A pot of green herbs sits by the door, at home in the sun and the dust.

The grandmother is brown and solid. Thick and stable. Quiet, serene, and strong. She is full of purpose, and watching her, I realize I belong to her. She is *my* grandmother.

Our spirits reach across time and space and know one another.

She is a healer.

I long to melt into her spirit. She knows this and does not withhold.

Today, I am sad.
So sad that I cannot write:
To write it, to record it, will make it true.

I'd rather leave it trembling in a whisper,
wavering in a thought.

My heart bows under the weight of the sadness and the fear.

I sit on my bed, holding the bottle of Rue.
She speaks to me. *Repeat after me*, she says.

I will not be afraid.
I will not be afraid.
I will not be afraid of this.
I will not be afraid of this.
This is not happening now. It is only a memory.
It is only a memory.
It happened then.
Then.
This is only a memory--
a memory.
from long, long ago.
long, long ago.
Then. Not now.
Then. Not now.

I have already survived.
I live—am alive.
My husband and children are here—in this very house,
talking and playing just outside the bedroom door.

There is a Sun.
A Sun.
A Sky.
A Sky.
Leaves and trees.
Trees.
It is fall.
And I am here.
Here.
No longer There.
No longer Then.
Here.
Here.
Now.
Now.

Fear wrestles me to the ground and pins me. Pressing my cheek against the hard, wooden floor, it wants to finish me. *But it will not finish me.*

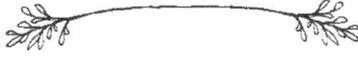

My heart rouses, and I say, *I am here. I am safe.*
I will keep moving.
I will keep living.

Today, I choose not to be afraid.
Today, Fear will not take hold of me.

I am here.

My stomach cramps and rumbles. My watery ear empties.
And Fear lets me go—
releases me.

Rue.

Her flower:
exquisite
dainty
feminine
beautiful

A dandelion seed
with gossamer wings and satin shoes.
A ballerina spinning on the wind,
delicately dancing through the ether.

You will be beautiful again, she whispers. I doubt her.

My hips fall open.

You can be open, Rue says.
Your heart can be open.
Your eyes can be open.

In the corner, I am crumpled in the chair. Blinded by tears, I look out the window.

I miss my mom.
I miss my dad.

How does this happen to someone?
How do you end up alone?
How were they always meant to leave me?
How would I always be right here,
crying,
in this chair?

I loved my parents, I tell him.
I know, he says.
Not just my mom, but my dad, too.
I know, he says.

I know the answer, but still, I ask, *Did something this awful really happen to me?*

His voice is sad, full with the weight of his answer:
Yes. Yes, it did.

In the dark, I sit on the couch. The house is quiet. Everyone is sleeping. Rue is with me. I drop her into my mouth.

She gently lays a blanket across my shoulders. Its soft weight and gentle warmth bring me comfort. Her presence is tender. With her, I am accepted and protected.

Around me, there is soft, white light. Pure and angelic. My stomach gurgles, and at my center, there is peace.

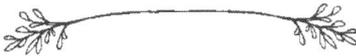

I am choosing to keep my eyes open, I say to myself.

Rue holds my hand tightly.
And today, I know:
She is going to help me finish this.

Perfect love casts out fear.
There is no fear in love.
Stand taller.
Walk with confidence.
You are not afraid.
There is no fear in love.
And you are loved.

My head is filling.
The room is spinning.

It's beginning.
I search for her.
Rue? Rue!

She whispers to me, *Today—today, you're going to be okay.*

I lay down on the bed, and in moments, my eyes are closed, and I sleep. When I awake, my head is clear, and I am renewed and refreshed. The whole room has crisp, sparkling edges.

And I realize: My eyes are open! I am not sick!

Full of gratitude, my heart leaps inside my chest.
She stopped the spinning!
She opened my eyes!

I stand in the shower, and praise pours from my lips. Water washes over my living, breathing, upright self.

But voices begin to whisper.

Tit for tat.
He's tit for tat.
He gave you this—
You'll give Him that.

Nothing is free.
Nothing is given.
No grace, no mercy.
Nothing's forgiven.

Tit for tat.
He's tit for tat.
He gave you this—
Now, He'll take that.

Her sweet face appears before my eyes.

And with everything in me, I shout *No!*
No! No! No! No!
He isn't like that.
God isn't like that!
If you ask for bread, He gives no stone.
If you ask for fish, He serves no serpent.

There is nothing to earn,
nothing to merit.
There is only grace and gifts.
Good and perfect gifts—
and if she is anything, she is that:
a good and perfect gift.

I shout, arguing and declaring into the midnight air—
The blood of Jesus! I claim the blood of Jesus!

All good, all wise,
All knowing.
And nothing—*nothing!*—can separate me from His love—
not height, nor depth—
nor any creature
can separate me from the love of God.

Ya Rauf, my soul.
Ya Rauf!

Water pours over my head, splashing down my back, and pools at my feet.

I am baptized in holy water—common water—shower water.

I plan to live
To look
To see
To be
Right here.
Right now.

I will not be afraid.
I am not afraid.

There is no fear.
There is only perfect love.
And perfect love casts out fear.

Let it be.
May it be.
And so it is.
Amen and amen.

One Last Thing

Know this: when you remember, when you begin to speak the Truth—they will not believe you.

They will say you are crazy.
They will say you are a liar.
They will say you are needy and craving attention.
They will say you are uncertain and unsure.
They will say you have a history of . . .
They will say you have always been . . .
They will say anything and everything—
except what you most need to hear.
They will say anything and everything—except what is true.

They will not say, *I believe you.*

They will not say it, dear one.

The Truth you remember, the Truth you speak, is so real and so weighty and so dark (and yet so full of light—so revealing) that they will want nothing to do with it. They will have ears to hear and eyes to see, but they will remain deaf and blind, choosing rather to stumble about in the filthy dark.

Your words make them squirm, cause them pain, shatter images, and up-end houses. Your words lead captives free, pulling skeletons from closets. Your words—because they are true, because they are light—shatter silences. *Shatter them.*

You will cry and scream, but they will not listen.
You will speak in a tired whisper,
You will plead with tears,
You will even speak bravely and with otherworldly calm,
And yet, they will not hear you.

Your tone of voice, your choice of words, your fervent expression,

your very self has no power to open their deaf ears. No power to open closed hearts.

Neither the zealous cracking of a whip nor the gentle healing of the lame will change this ancient truth: a prophet is hated in his own country. *Is not this the carpenter's son?* To them, you are common. To them, you are still a child and have no place to speak such words—such Truth. And so, they will endeavor to silence you, ignore you, discredit you. Wrestling you to the ground, they will cover your mouth with their hands and order you to *Stop Talking*.

But don't do it. Don't ever stop talking. Don't ever stop telling the Truth. Fight to stand up. Struggle to break free. And then open your mouth so the Truth can flow freely. Be a conduit of Truth, dear one.

The Truth will set you free.
The Truth will set them free.
The Light drives away the Darkness.
Be Light.
Be Truth.

Pray this: *Send forth thy light and truth; let them be guides to me.*

I am not naïve (and sadly, neither are you). Fighting back, breaking free, speaking the truth—and especially speaking it in love—will not be easy. You will be rejected, neglected, and abandoned all over again.

So, listen:
You must be brave.
You must stand in a strength that is not your own.
With a forehead of brass, you must speak the Truth.
And in courage, you must face your fears—and your foes.
And in doing so, you must lay down your worldly weapons,
for your weapons are not carnal but spiritual.

Swords beaten into ploughshares.

(Lay down your sword. Pick up a pen.)

And remember this:
You are no longer small. You are no longer young.
You are no longer a helpless child without a voice.
You have grown. You have survived.
And you are alive.

So, hear this, dear one: *Fear God rather than man.*

Open your mouth; speak the Truth.
Open your hands, and if they leave, tender heart,
if they let you go . . .
let them go.
Grieve, friend,
And let them go.

Do not be afraid.
You are not alone.
Perfect love will hold you.

THE PLANTS
Simple Introductions

The pages that follow hold basic introductions to the plant companions who have walked with me along the way. The words and descriptions are *by no means* exhaustive or authoritative, and not a single word has been approved by a single expert.
I am simply taking your hand and saying to you,
I'd like you to meet . . .

Should you choose to walk a little ways with any of these plants,
I recommend you do your own reading, your own researching,
your own listening.

In these pages, I offer no standard method of use or dosage.
After all, I am simply offering you my story. I cannot heal you.
Healing is found in your hands, your heart, your story.

But do not fear. You are not alone.

If you need it, seek counsel from a
qualified medical or spiritual adviser.

The help we need is always near us.

Cimicifuga racemosa

BLACK COHOSH

Actaea racemosa; Cimicifuga racemosa

Family: Ranunculaceae
Parts used: rhizome, root
Energetics: sweet, pungent, bitter, cool

Affinities
cerebrospinal fluid, circulatory system, female reproductive system, large intestine, liver, neck, nervous system, spine, spleen, stomach

Actions
anodyne, alterative, anti-inflammatory, anti-rheumatic, antispasmodic, emmenagogue, hypotensive, nervine, sedative

Constituents
phytoestrogens, salicylic acid, tannins, triterpene glycosides, volatile oils

Traditional Uses
childbirth, menstrual pains, neuralgia, rheumatism, spasms, tinnitus

Specific Indications
whiplash
symptoms better from onset of menses
in, or have been in abusive, possessive, or manipulative relationships
brooding, dark state of mind
meningitis

Safety
Contraindicated in early pregnancy

~ Light Piercing the Darkness ~

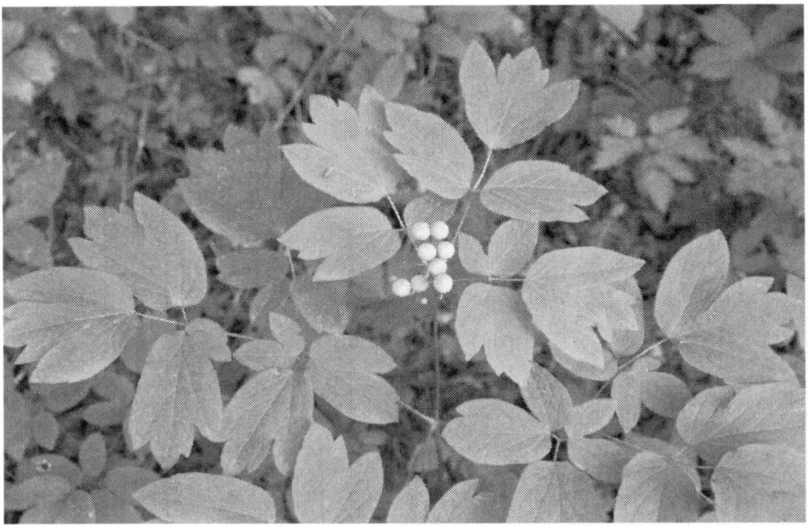

Caulophyllum thalictroides

BLUE COHOSH

Caulophyllum thalictroides

Family: Berberidaceae
Parts used: rhizome and root
Energetics: cool, dry, acrid

Affinities

cardiovascular system, digestive system, female reproductive system, nervous system, solar plexus

Actions

anthelmintic, antispasmodic, diuretic, emmenagogue, emetic, expectorant, laxative, uterine tonic

Constituents

alkaloids, steroidal saponins, tannins

Traditional Uses

childbirth, false labor pains, miscarriage, rheumatic pain, weakness or loss of uterine tone

Specific Indications

arthritis in small joints, fingers, and toes
pain or bleeding at ovulation
low estrogen, debilitated conditions
feeling of fullness with exhaustion

Safety

Contraindicated in early pregnancy
Mild heart stimulant

Swirl of pulsing light,
rushing down,
restoring what's been lost

Nepeta cataria

CATNIP

Nepeta cataria

Family: Lamiaceae
Parts used: flower, leaf
Energetics: pungent, moist, cool

Affinities
digestive system, nervous system, respiratory system, stomach

Actions
antispasmodic, astringent, carminative, decongestant, diaphoretic, nervine, sedative

Constituents
iridoids, tannins, volatile oils

Traditional Uses
colic, colds and flus, fevers, indigestion, respiratory infections, stomach upset

Specific Indications
trouble at home
tension held in the gut
quiet children who internalize things
hiatal hernia

Panther Medicine
~ the force is strong with this one ~

Galium aparine

CLEAVERS

Galium aparine

Family: Rubiaceae
Parts used: aerial parts (best used fresh)
Energetics: sweet, cool, moist

Affinities
breasts, heart, kidneys, lymphatics, nervous system, skin, urinary system, uterus

Actions
alterative, anti-inflammatory, astringent, diuretic, neoplastic, tonic

Constituents
citric acid, coumarins, flavonoids, glycosides, iridoids, saponins

Traditional Uses
cystitis, fluid retention, eczema and psoriasis, swollen glands under or behind ears

Specific Indications
mastitis
tonsillitis
mononucleosis
oversensitivity of nerve endings; tickly, itchy skin
fibrocystic breasts

Deer Medicine
~ Elegant, Green Chimney Sweep ~

Cornus florida

DOGWOOD

Cornus florida

Family: Cornaceae
Parts used: bark, flower
Energetics: bitter, acrid, cool, dry

Affinities

digestive system, kidneys, liver, nervous system, reproductive system, throat

Actions

analgesic, anodyne, anti-inflammatory, antiseptic, antispasmodic, astringent, bitter, febrifuge, stimulant, tonic

Constituents

cornin, tannins, resin

Traditional Uses

intermittent fever, biliousness, headaches, muscular tension, diarrhea

Specific Indications

digestive atonicity
feeble, relaxed tissues, exhausted from chills and fevers
general exhaustion
hardened, inflexible body due to abuse or trauma
awkward, clumsy

Elk Medicine
~ Way to Go, Grace. ~

Thalictrum dioicum

EARLY MEADOW RUE

Thalictrum dioicum

Family: Ranunculacea

"These plants were not used by the American Indians; at least there is no record of that fact. . . The standard works, such as the Dispensatories, Medical Dictionaries, Catalogues of American Medical Plants, etc., omit them. . . None of the American species of Thalictrum have been used by the Eclectic or the Botanic schools of medicine, nor have they ever been analyzed."
(Lloyd and Lloyd 1884-1887:
Drugs and Medicines of North America)

"Early Meadow Rue has no known medicinal properties. No literature exists describing its use by Native Americans, pioneers, or other early people for medical purposes."

Her story remains to be told.

As I was gathering her seeds,
I began to say,
~ Every part of you is precious. ~

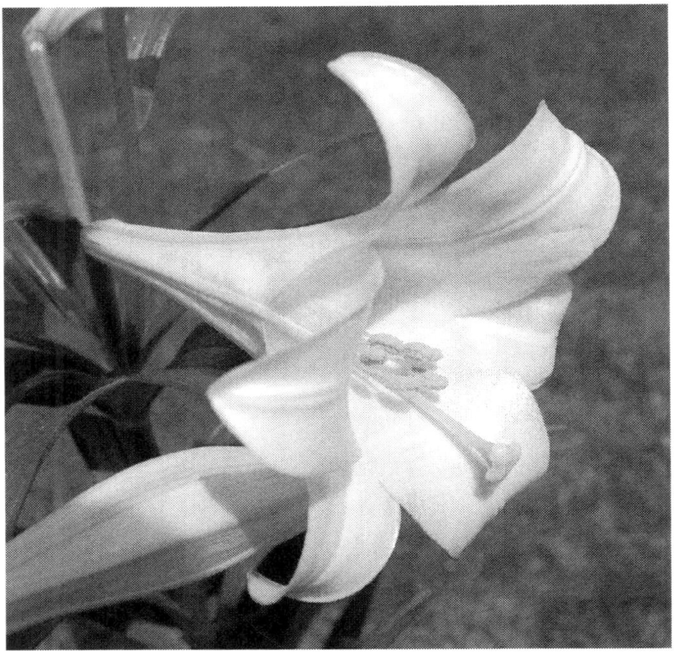

Lilium longiflorum

EASTER LILY

Lilium longiflorum

Family: Allium
Parts used: flowers, rhizome
Energetics: cool, moist

Affinities
breasts, female reproductive system, heart, respiratory system

Actions
expectorant, mucilage

Constituents
mucilage, quercetin glycosides, steroidal saponins

Traditional Uses
bronchitis, cysts, dry coughs,
infertility, irritability, PCOS, yin deficiency

Specific Indications
cysts in breasts, ovaries, and skin
infertility with mucus obstruction
brownish, stringy vaginal discharge or menstrual blood
conflicting thoughts about sexuality
androgen excess
yawning—unable to concentrate

With Water and Light, Made New

Artemisia vulgaris

MUGWORT

Artemisia vulgaris

Family: Compositae
Parts used: leaves
Energetics: bitter, pungent, dry

Affinities
digestive system, female reproductive system, gallbladder, liver, nervous system

Actions
antispasmodic, aromatic, bitter, cholagogue, diaphoretic, digestive tonic, nervine, uterine stimulant

Constituents
flavonoids, inulin, tannins, thujone, triterpenes, resin, volatile oils

Traditional Uses
dreaming, intermittent fever, menstrual cramps, tremors or epilepsy

Specific Indications
weak, sensitive women who have endured abuse and poverty
object of envy, especially from the mother
sensitivity to light
excessive androgenism

Diana the Huntress, Removing Arrows, Dressing Wounds, Restoring the Moon

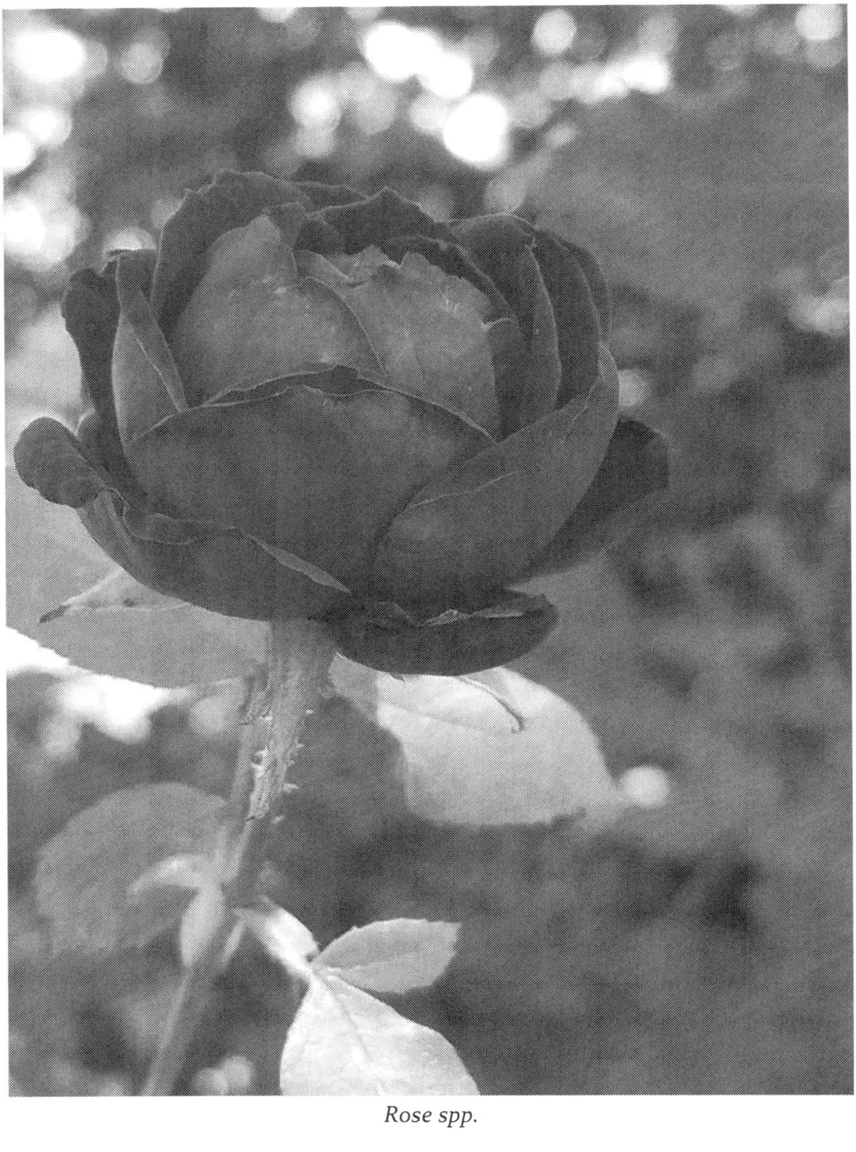

Rose spp.

ROSE

Rose spp.

Family: Rosaceae
Parts used: flowers, hips, leaves
Energetics: petals: sweet, bitter, warm, aromatic
hips: sour, sweet, cool, dry

Affinities
circulatory system, digestive system, eyes,
female reproductive system, heart, nervous system, skin

Actions
antidepressant, anti-inflammatory, aphrodisiac,
astringent, vulnerary

Constituents
hips: tannins, flavonoids, sugars, pectin, carotene
flowers: essential oils, volatile oils, anthocyanidins

Traditional Uses
clear toxins and heat, inflammation, irregular menstrual cycles,
re-establish digestive flora, strengthen vision

Specific Indications
anxiety, heartache, grief
shortness of breath
tightness in chest associated with anxiety
fascia surrounding the heart
delicate, sensitive children

~ The Heart Sees. ~

Liriodendron tulipifera

TULIP POPLAR

Liriodendron tulipifera

Family: Magnoliaceae
Parts used: inner bark, leaves
Energetics: acrid, aromatic, sweet

Affinities
digestive system, female reproductive system,
heart, nervous sytem

Actions
analgesic, anti-inflammatory, antioxidant, astringent, carminative,
diaphoretic, heart tonic, relaxant, tonic

Constituents
alkaloid tulipiferin, bitter resin, coumarin,
salicylates, steroids

Traditional Uses
arthritis, convalescence, headaches, lack of appetite,
intermittent chills and fevers,
heart tonic after heart attack or stroke,
toothaches

Specific Indications
restorative after heart attack
the back of the heart
blue blood
children without parents
imprisonment and captivity
for those who feel unforgivable or unlovable

Jesus Tree, Parent Tree
Setting Every Captive Free

Viola odorata

VIOLET

Viola odorata

Family: Violaceae
Parts used: flower, leaf
Energetics: sweet, salty, moist, cool

Affinities

breasts, female reproductive system, heart, lymphatics, respiratory system, throat, womb

Constituents

flavonoids, minerals, mucilage, phenolic glycosides, rutin, salicylates, saponins

Actions

alterative, anti-inflammatory, anti-neoplastic, demulcent, diuretic, emollient, expectorant, laxative, nutritive, vulnerary

Traditional Uses

asthma, bronchitis, chronic coughs, swollen glands, cysts and tumors, eczema, headaches, constipation

Specific Indications

anger that presents as sadness
grief
"plum pit", a lump in the throat
cancers and tumors of the throat, breast, ovaries, and womb
shyness
those who are overlooked or unnoticed
invisibility

Speak Your Truth

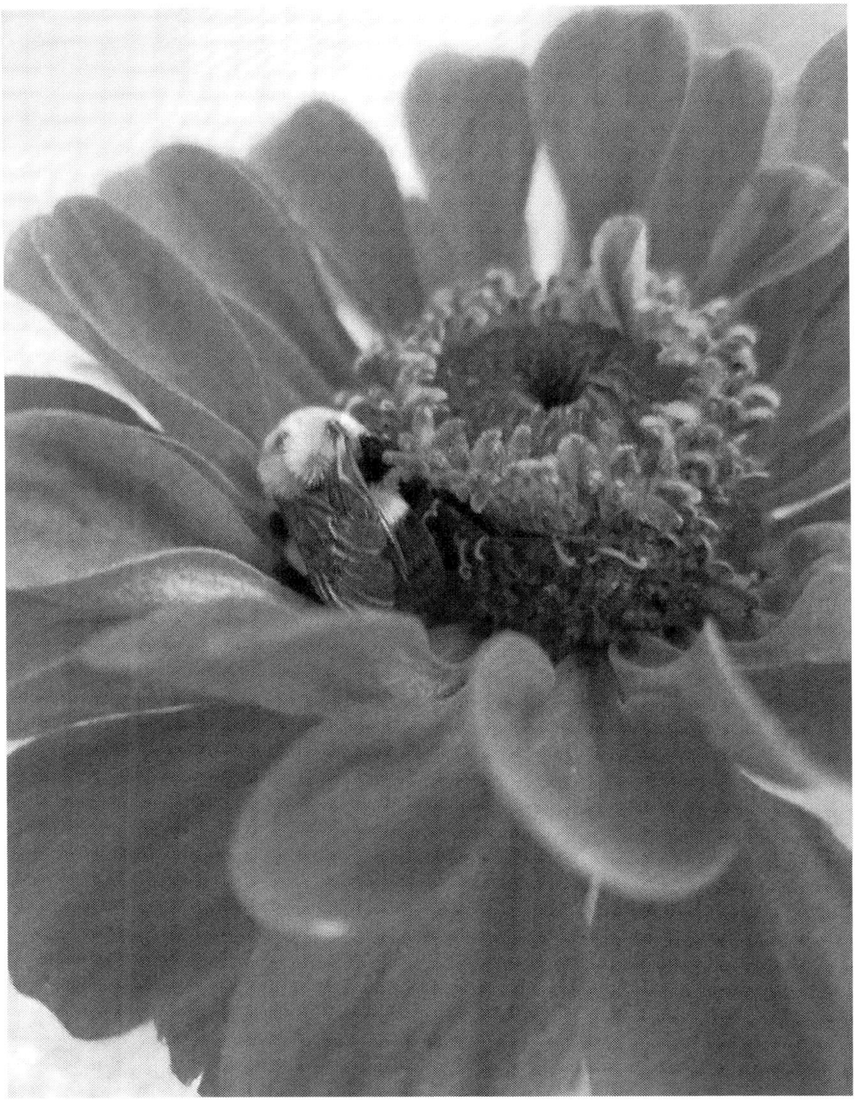

Zinnia elegans (and a sleeping bee)

ZINNIA

Zinnia elegans

Family: Asteraceae
Parts used: flower, leaves
Energetics: bitter, pungent, cool

Affinities
heart, kidneys, liver

Constituents
flavonoids, saponins

Actions
anti-inflammatory, antimicrobial, antioxidant, hepatoprotective

Common Uses
boils,
slow, painful urination

Specific Indications
forgotten how to play
lacking joy
no sense of adventure
childhood lost
too serious, too soon
rooted, steady, unwavering joy
the faith of a child

~ For the Elf Self ~

[resources]

Bennett, Robin Rose. *The Gift of Healing Herbs*. North Atlantic Books, 2014.

Hoffman, David. *The Herbal Handbook*. Healing Arts Press, 1998.

Kaminski and Katz. *Flower Essence Repertory*. Flower Essence Society, 1994.

McIntyre, Anne. *The Complete Woman's Herbal*. Holt Paperbacks, 1995.

Montgomery, Pam. *Plant Spirit Healing*. Bear & Company, 2008.

Rogers, Robert. *Herbal Allies*. North Atlantic Books, 2017.

Weed, Susun. *Down There*. Ash Tree Publishing, 2011.

Wood, Matthew. *Seven Herbs: Plants as Teachers*. North Atlantic Books, 1987.

Wood, Matthew. *The Book of Herbal Wisdom*. North Atlantic Books, 1997.

Wood, Matthew. *The Earthwise Herbal, Vol. 1 and 2*. North Atlantic Books, 2009.

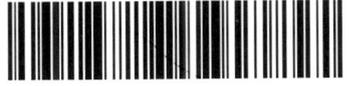

Printed in Great Britain
by Amazon

44083652R00092

Printed in the United Kingdom
by Lightning Source UK Ltd.
117678UKS00001B/235-237

9 781847 340986